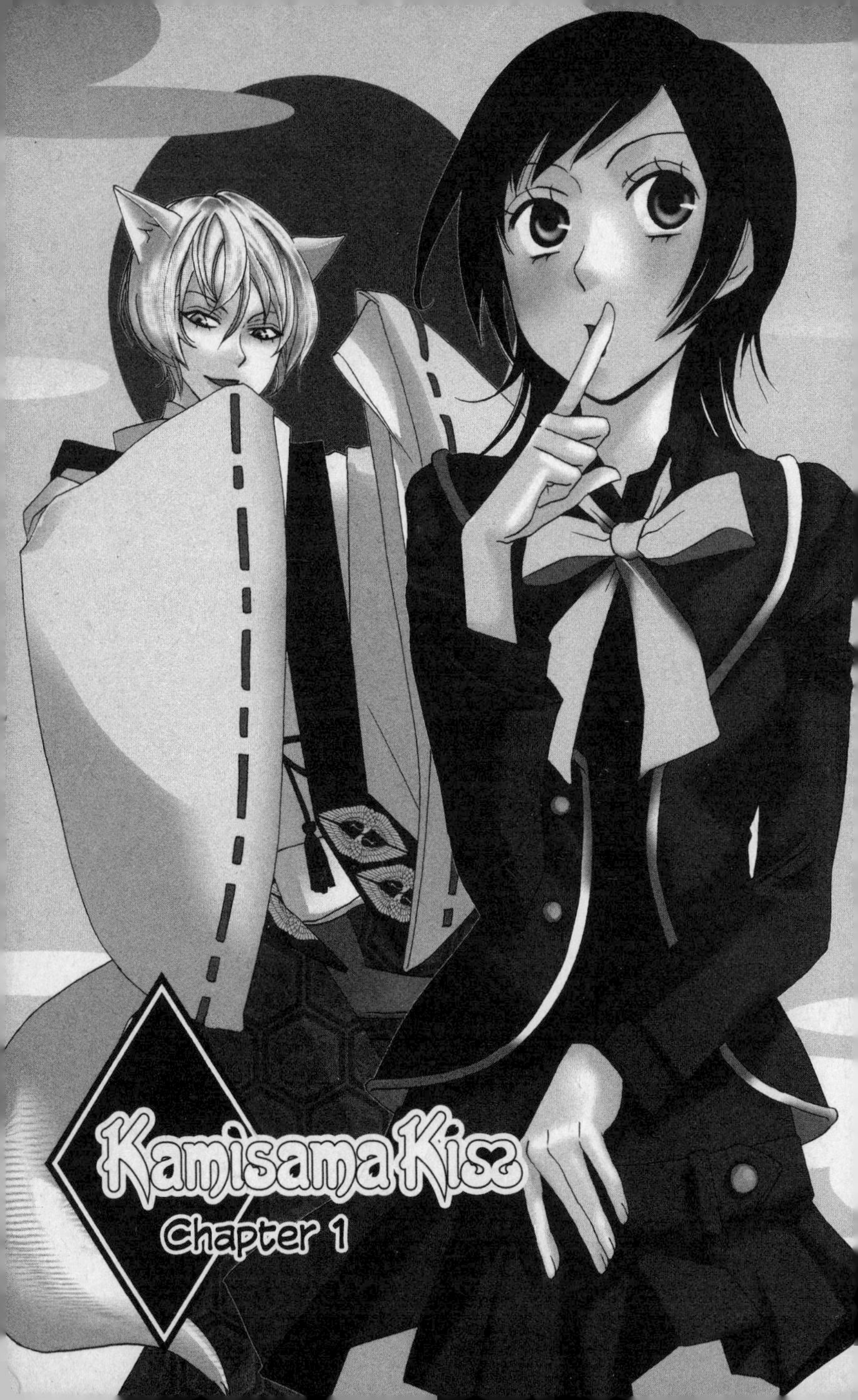
Kamisama Kiss
Chapter 1

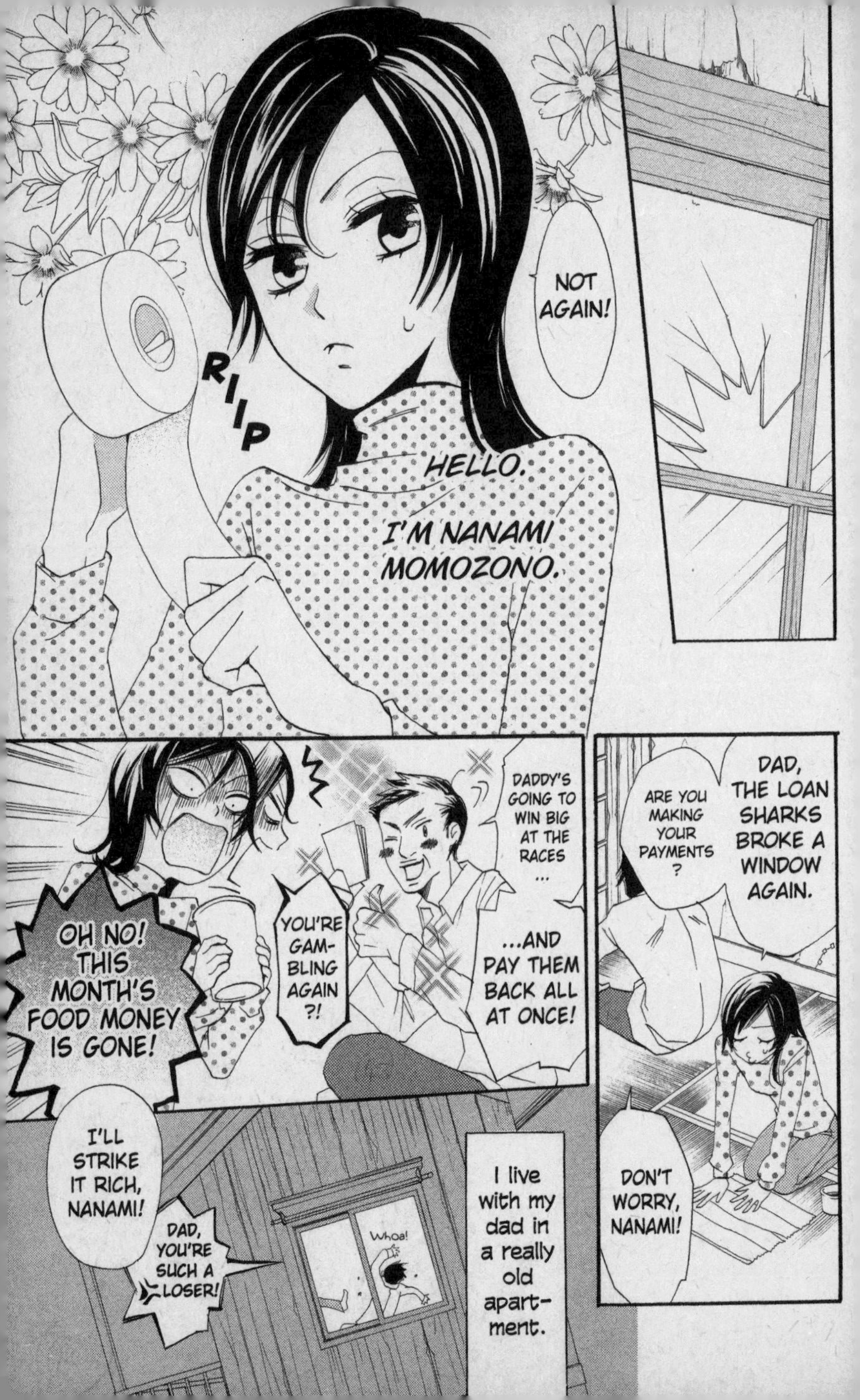
NOT AGAIN!
RIIP
HELLO.
I'M NANAMI MOMOZONO.
DAD, THE LOAN SHARKS BROKE A WINDOW AGAIN.
ARE YOU MAKING YOUR PAYMENTS?
DON'T WORRY, NANAMI!
DADDY'S GOING TO WIN BIG AT THE RACES...
...AND PAY THEM BACK ALL AT ONCE!
YOU'RE GAM-BLING AGAIN?!
OH NO! THIS MONTH'S FOOD MONEY IS GONE!
I live with my dad in a really old apart-ment.
I'LL STRIKE IT RICH, NANAMI!
Whoa!
DAD, YOU'RE SUCH A LOSER!

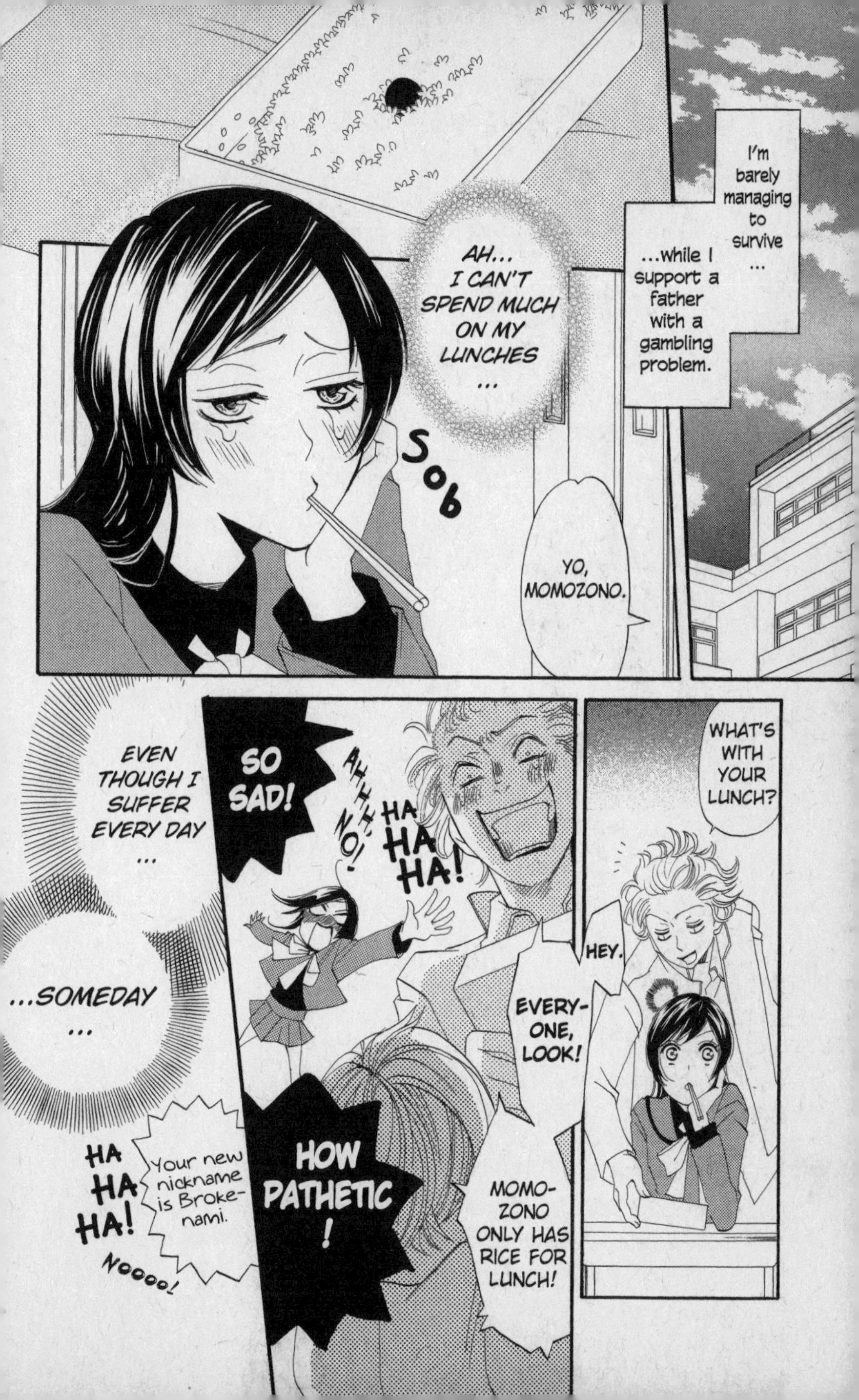
I'm barely managing to survive ...
...while I support a father with a gambling problem.
AH... I CAN'T SPEND MUCH ON MY LUNCHES ...
Sob
YO, MOMOZONO.
WHAT'S WITH YOUR LUNCH?
HEY.
EVERY-ONE, LOOK!
MOMO-ZONO ONLY HAS RICE FOR LUNCH!
HA HA HA!
AHHH, NO!
SO SAD!
HOW PATHETIC!
EVEN THOUGH I SUFFER EVERY DAY ...
...SOMEDAY ...
Your new nickname is Broke-nami.
HA HA HA!
Noooo!

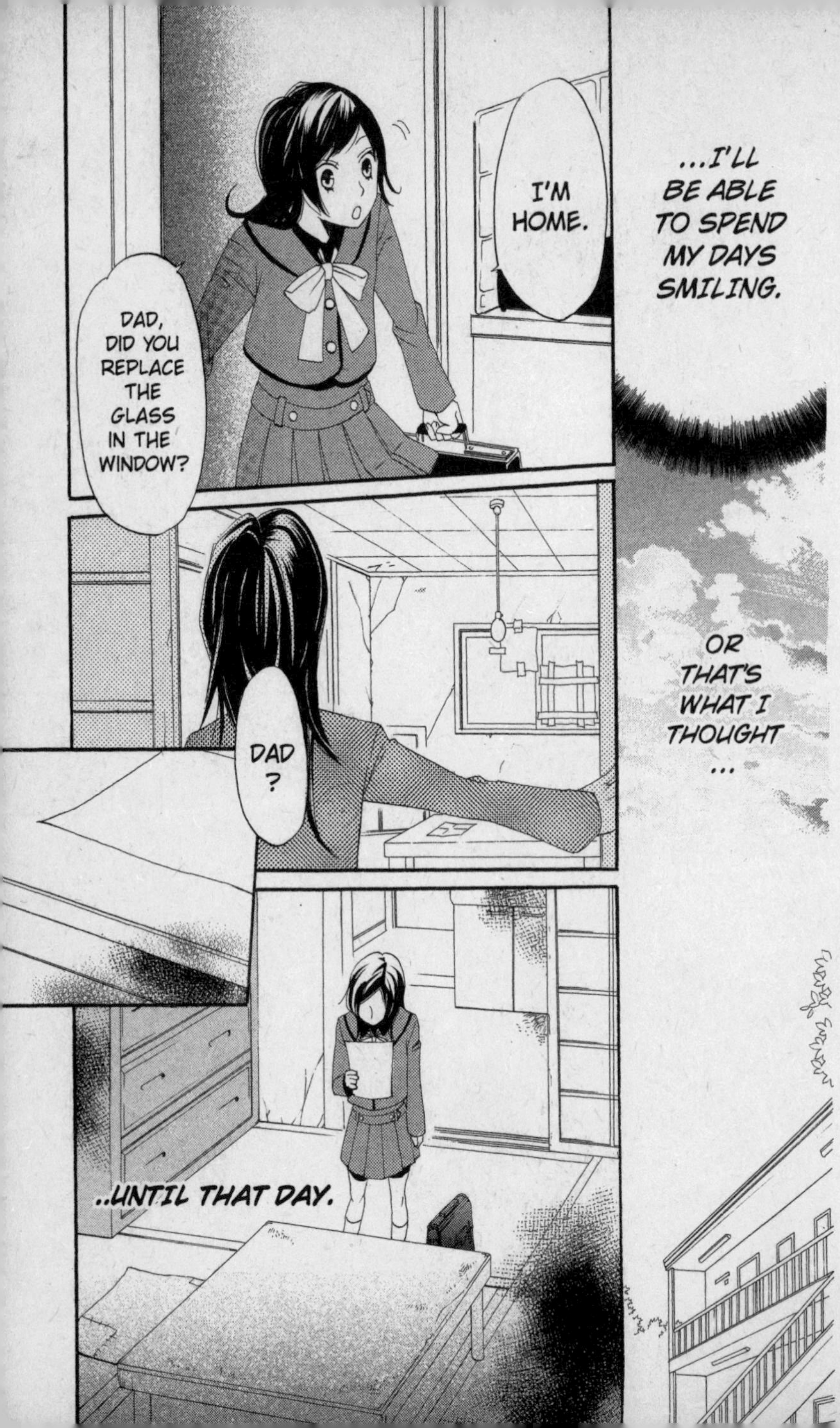
...I'LL BE ABLE TO SPEND MY DAYS SMILING.
OR THAT'S WHAT I THOUGHT ...
I'M HOME.
DAD, DID YOU REPLACE THE GLASS IN THE WINDOW?
DAD ?
..UNTIL THAT DAY.

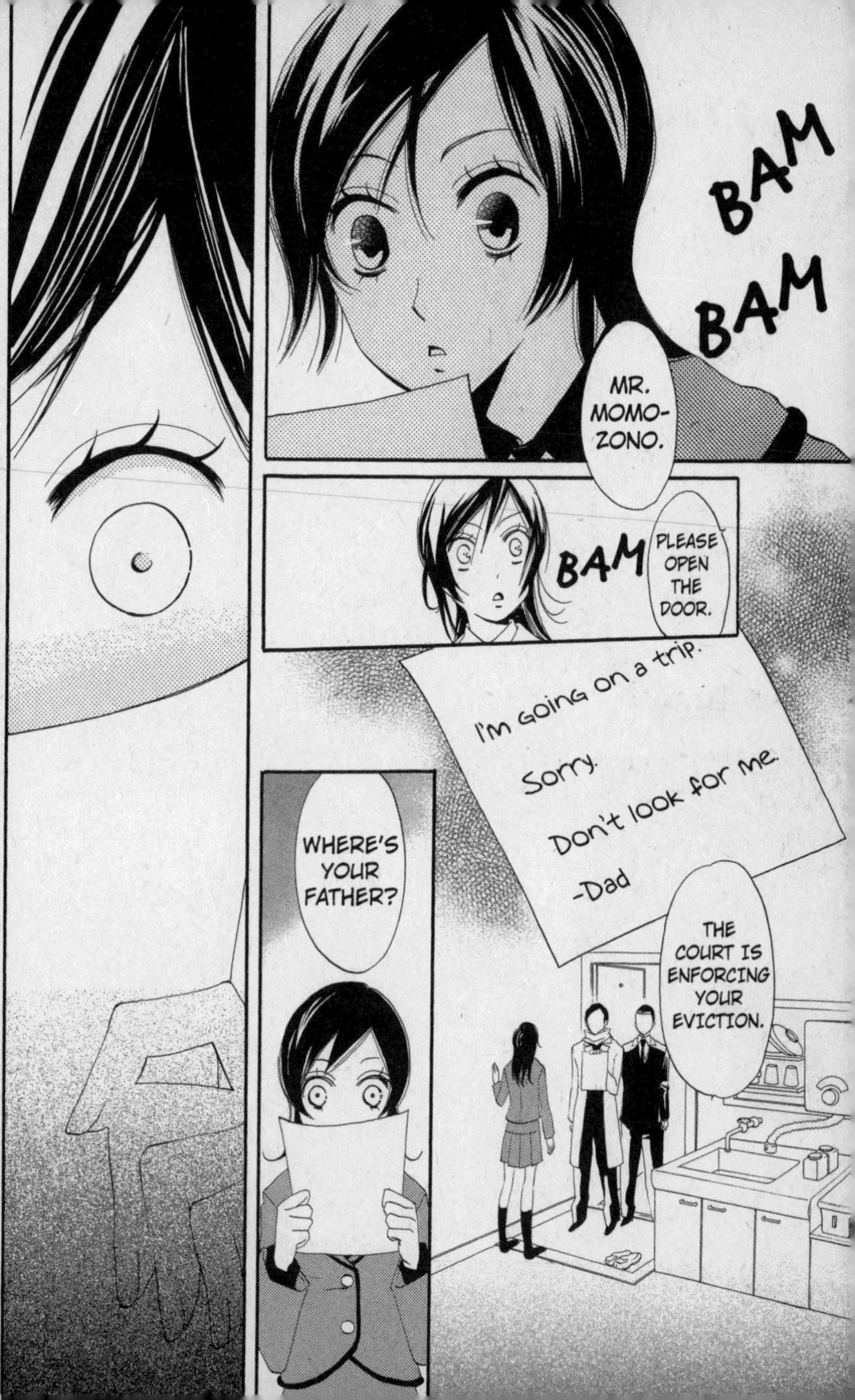
BAM BAM
MR. MOMO-ZONO.
BAM
PLEASE OPEN THE DOOR.
I'm going on a trip.
Sorry.
Don't look for me.
-Dad
THE COURT IS ENFORCING YOUR EVICTION.
WHERE'S YOUR FATHER?

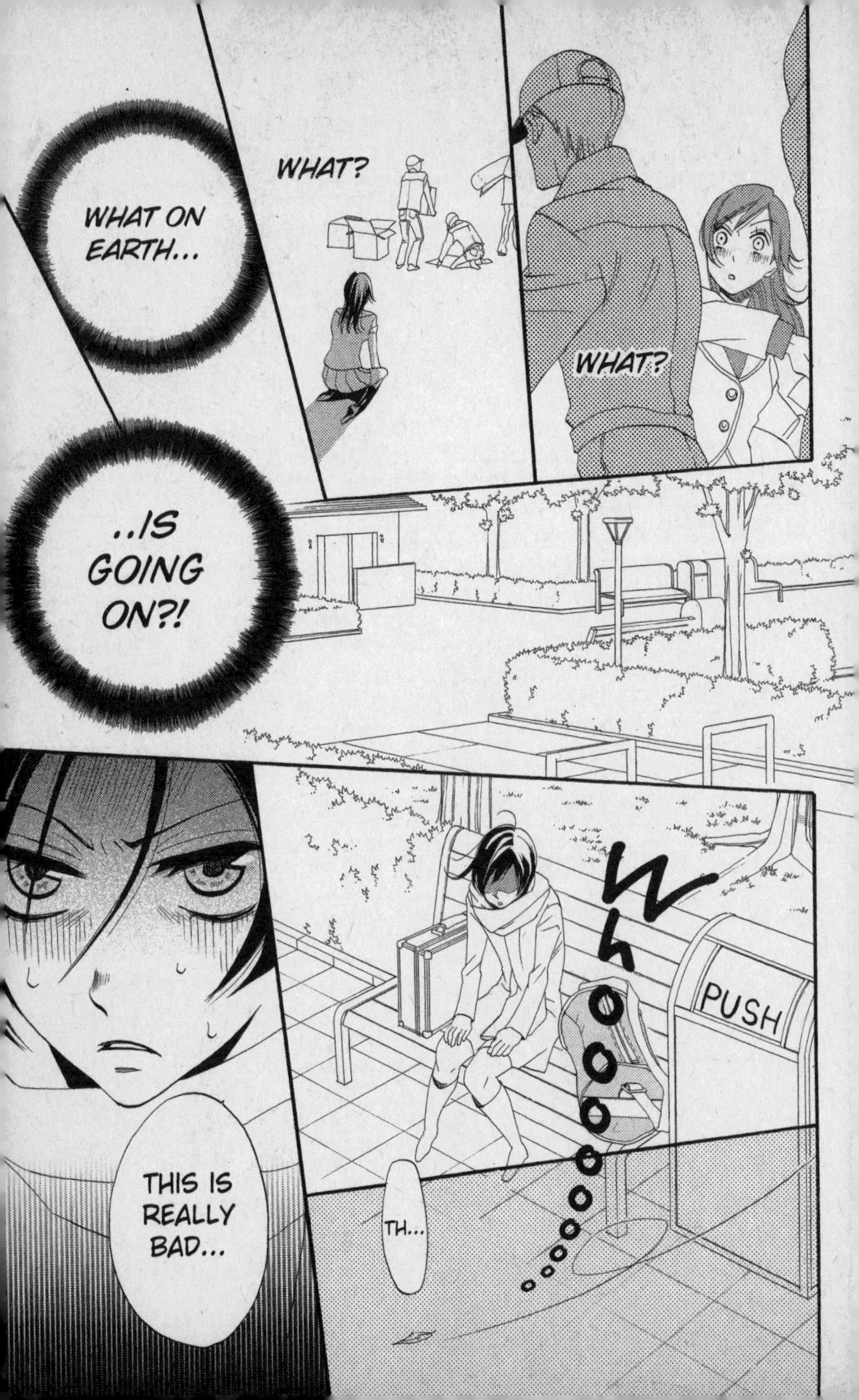
WHAT?
WHAT?
WHAT ON EARTH...
..IS GOING ON?!
PUSH
Whoooooooooo
TH...
THIS IS REALLY BAD...

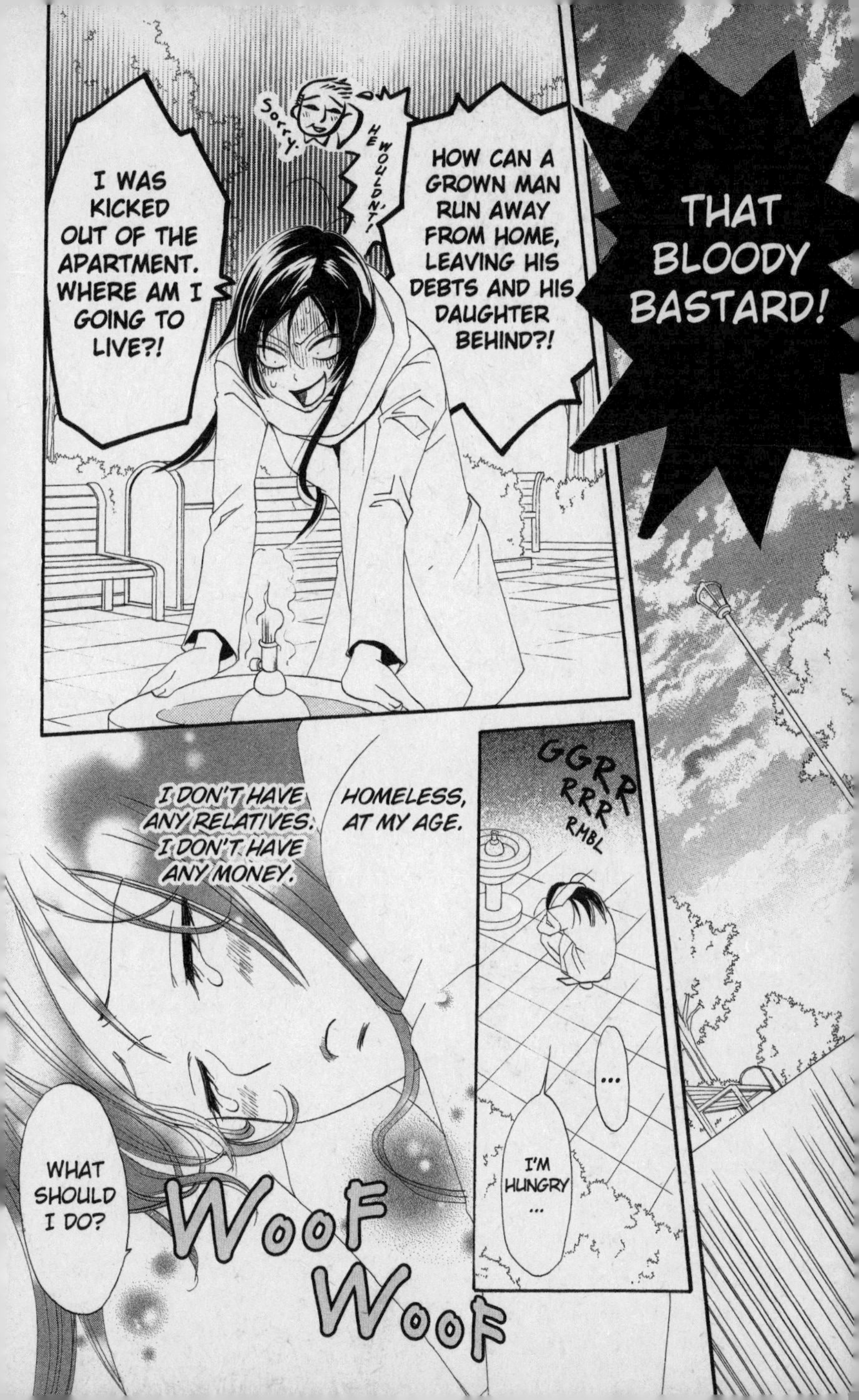
THAT BLOODY BASTARD!
HOW CAN A GROWN MAN RUN AWAY FROM HOME, LEAVING HIS DEBTS AND HIS DAUGHTER BEHIND?!
HE WOULDN'T!
Sorry.
I WAS KICKED OUT OF THE APARTMENT. WHERE AM I GOING TO LIVE?!
GGRRRRRR RMBL
...
I'M HUNGRY...
HOMELESS, AT MY AGE.
I DON'T HAVE ANY RELATIVES. I DON'T HAVE ANY MONEY.
WHAT SHOULD I DO?
WOOF WOOF

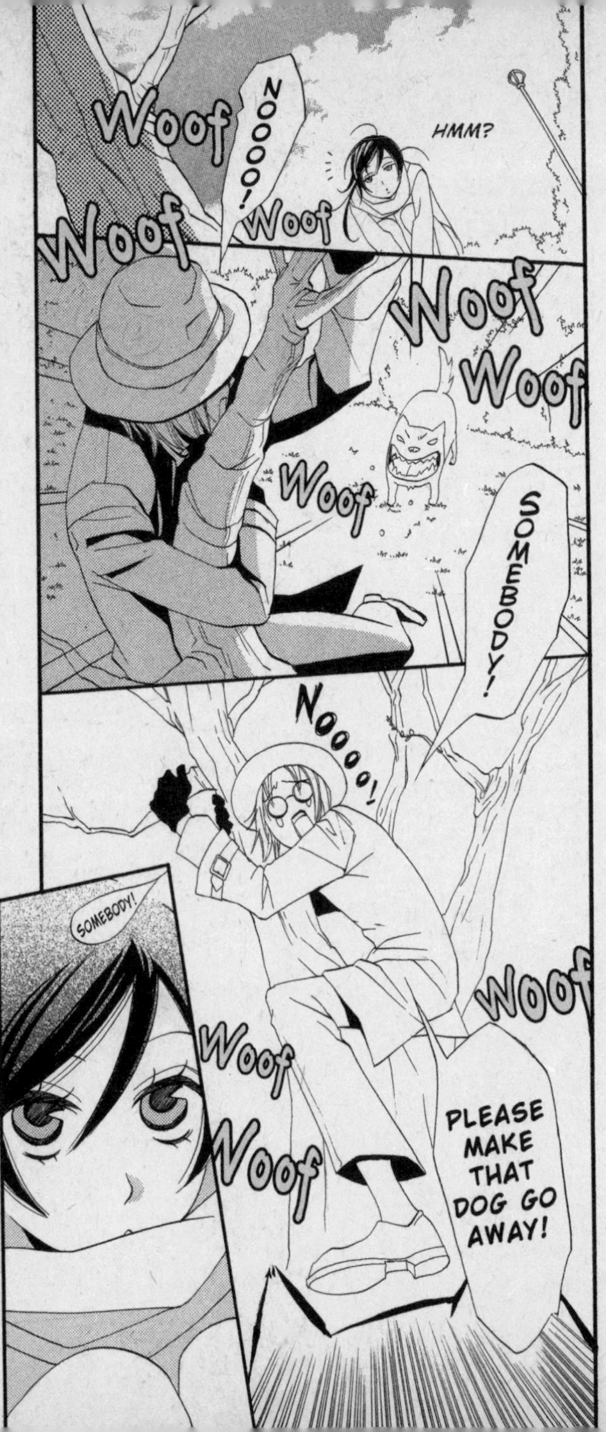
HMM?
NOOOOO!
Woof
Woof
Woof
Woof
Woof
Woof
SOMEBODY!
Noooooo!
Woof
Woof
Woof
PLEASE MAKE THAT DOG GO AWAY!
SOMEBODY!

Hello, or how do you do? I'm Julietta Suzuki. Thank you for picking up this volume! I'll be happy if you enjoy reading it.

I started visiting shrines often after I began drawing this manga. When I was a child, there was a large shrine in my neighborhood, and I played there with my friends and went to festivals. After I came to Tokyo, I didn't visit shrines much, but this year I've visited many and got a lot of paper fortunes.

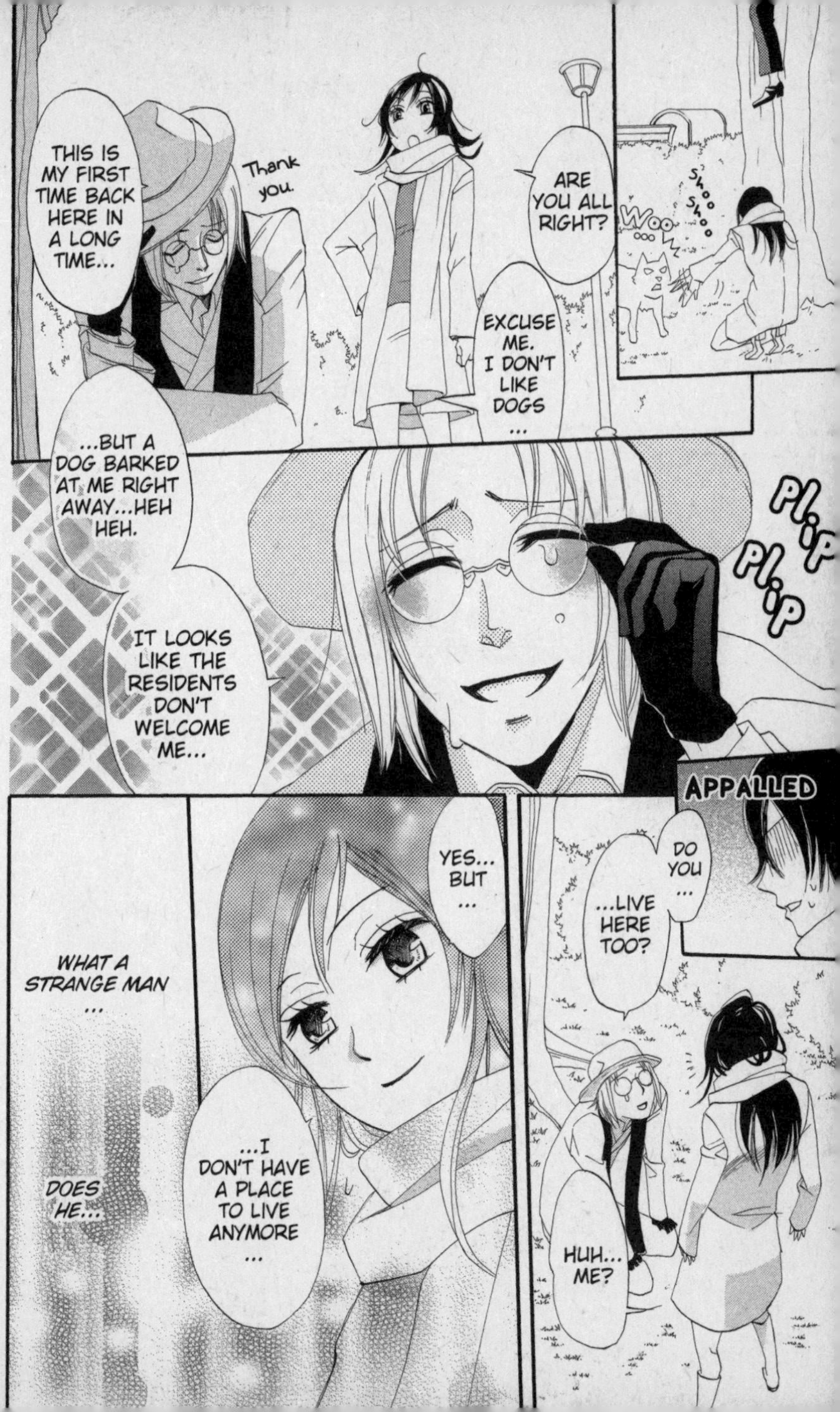
Shoo Shoo
Woooo
ARE YOU ALL RIGHT?
EXCUSE ME. I DON'T LIKE DOGS ...
Thank you.
THIS IS MY FIRST TIME BACK HERE IN A LONG TIME...
Plip Plip
...BUT A DOG BARKED AT ME RIGHT AWAY...HEH HEH.
IT LOOKS LIKE THE RESIDENTS DON'T WELCOME ME...
APPALLED
DO YOU ...
...LIVE HERE TOO?
HUH... ME?
YES... BUT ...
...I DON'T HAVE A PLACE TO LIVE ANYMORE ...
WHAT A STRANGE MAN ...
DOES HE...

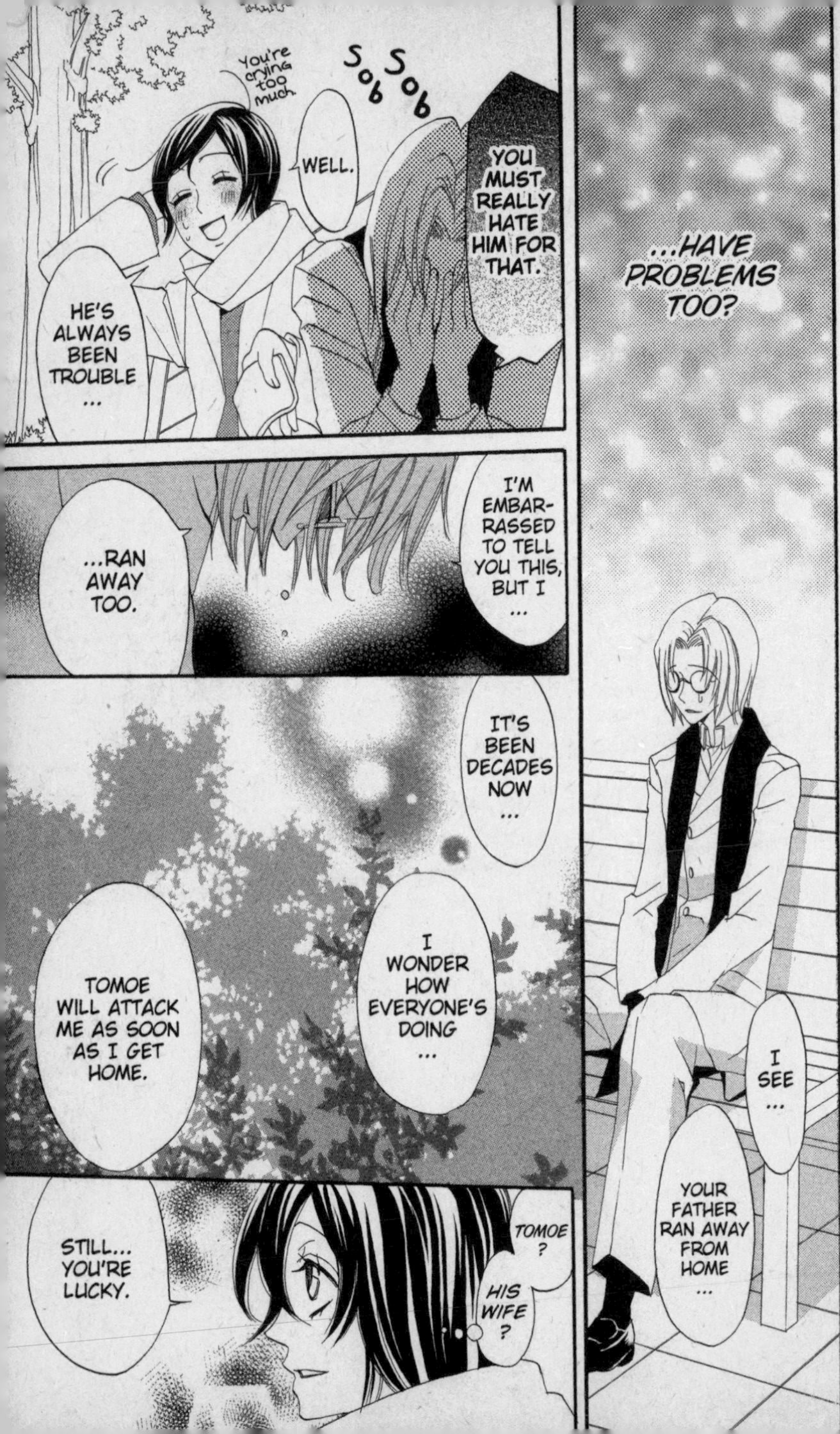
...HAVE PROBLEMS TOO?
I SEE...
YOUR FATHER RAN AWAY FROM HOME...
YOU MUST REALLY HATE HIM FOR THAT.
Sob Sob
WELL.
You're crying too much
HE'S ALWAYS BEEN TROUBLE...
I'M EMBARRASSED TO TELL YOU THIS, BUT I...
...RAN AWAY TOO.
IT'S BEEN DECADES NOW...
I WONDER HOW EVERYONE'S DOING...
TOMOE WILL ATTACK ME AS SOON AS I GET HOME.
TOMOE?
HIS WIFE?
STILL... YOU'RE LUCKY.

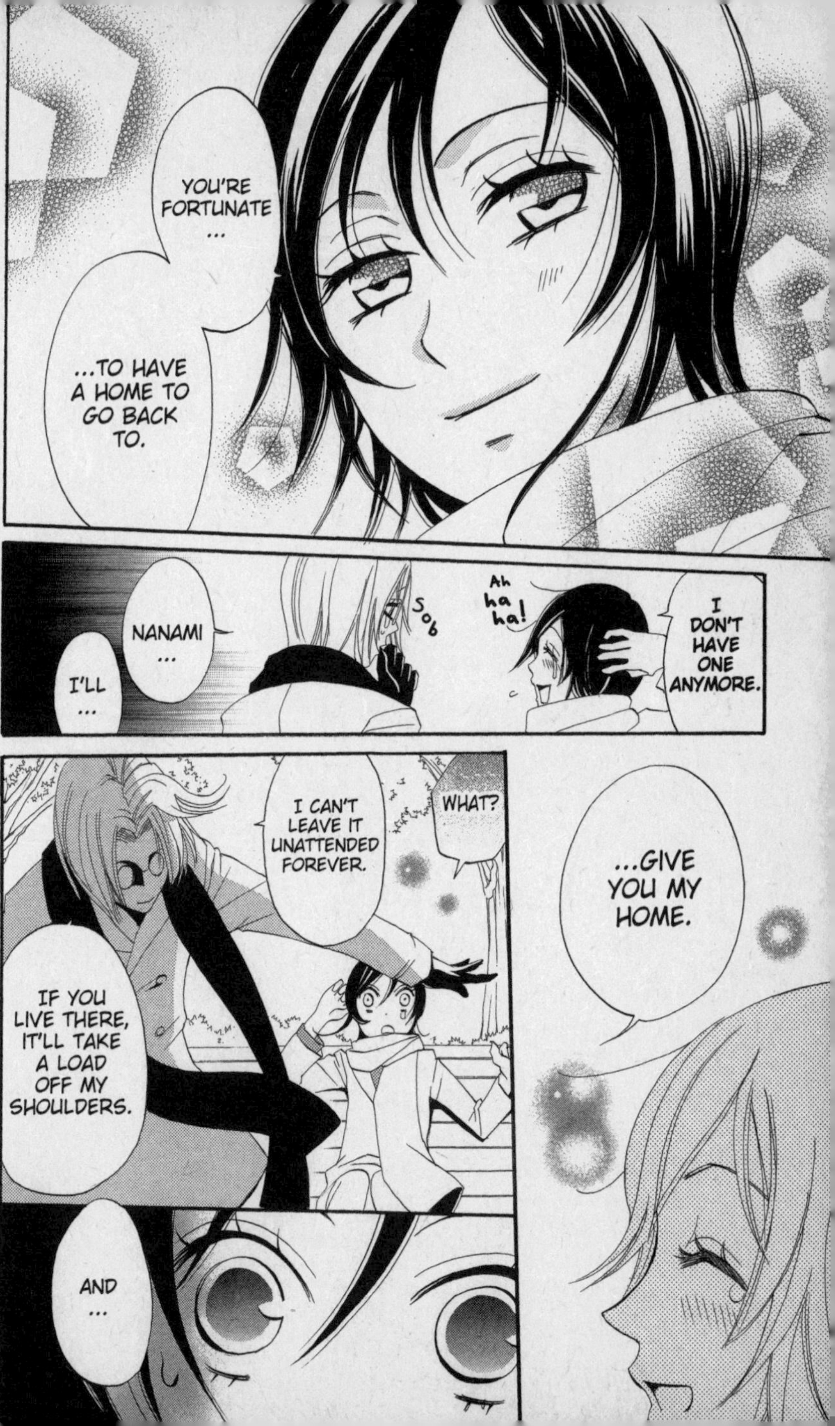
YOU'RE FORTUNATE ...
...TO HAVE A HOME TO GO BACK TO.
I DON'T HAVE ONE ANYMORE.
Ah ha ha!
Sob
NANAMI ...
I'LL ...
...GIVE YOU MY HOME.
WHAT?
I CAN'T LEAVE IT UNATTENDED FOREVER.
IF YOU LIVE THERE, IT'LL TAKE A LOAD OFF MY SHOULDERS.
AND ...

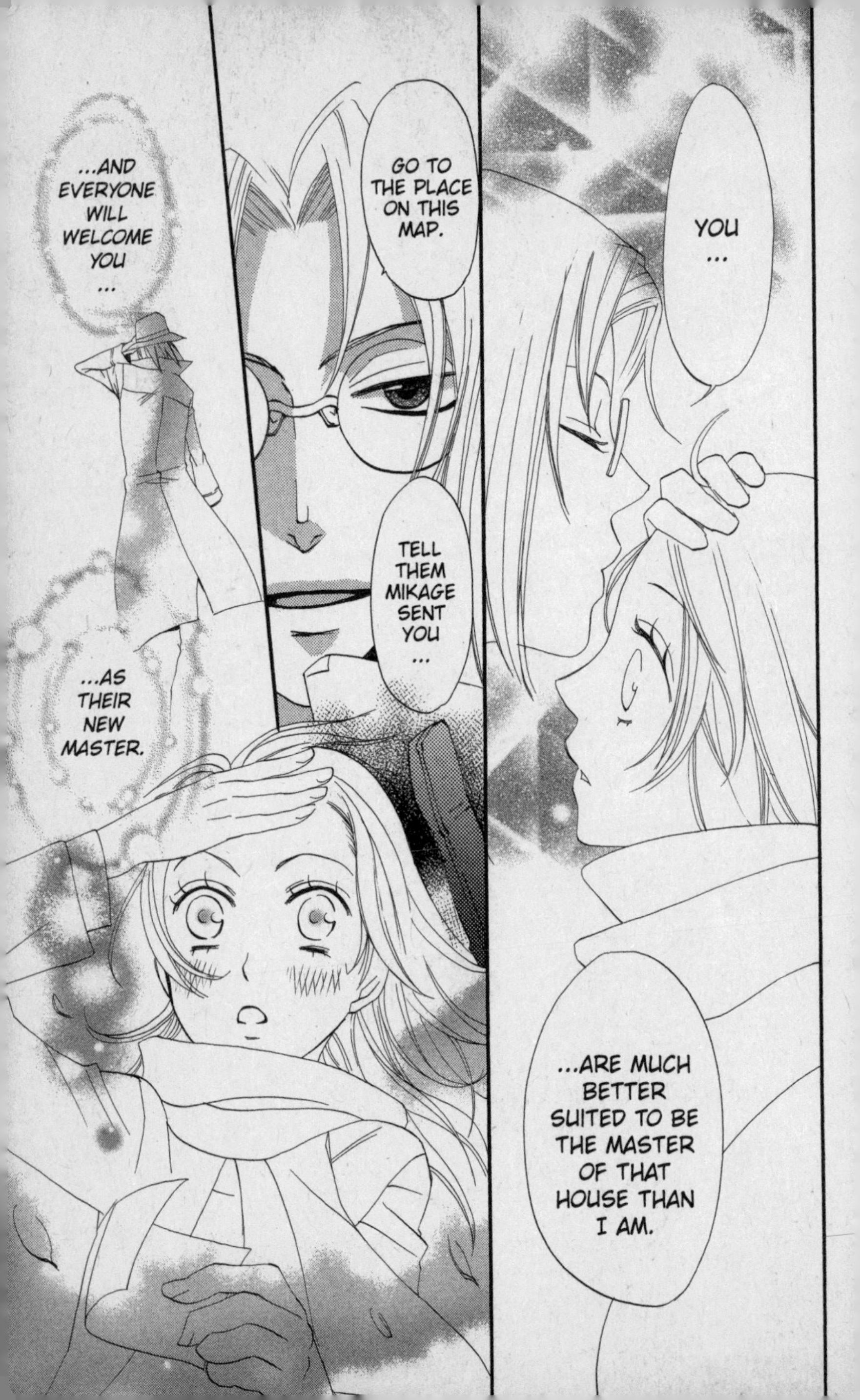
YOU ...
...ARE MUCH BETTER SUITED TO BE THE MASTER OF THAT HOUSE THAN I AM.
GO TO THE PLACE ON THIS MAP.
TELL THEM MIKAGE SENT YOU ...
...AND EVERYONE WILL WELCOME YOU ...
...AS THEIR NEW MASTER.

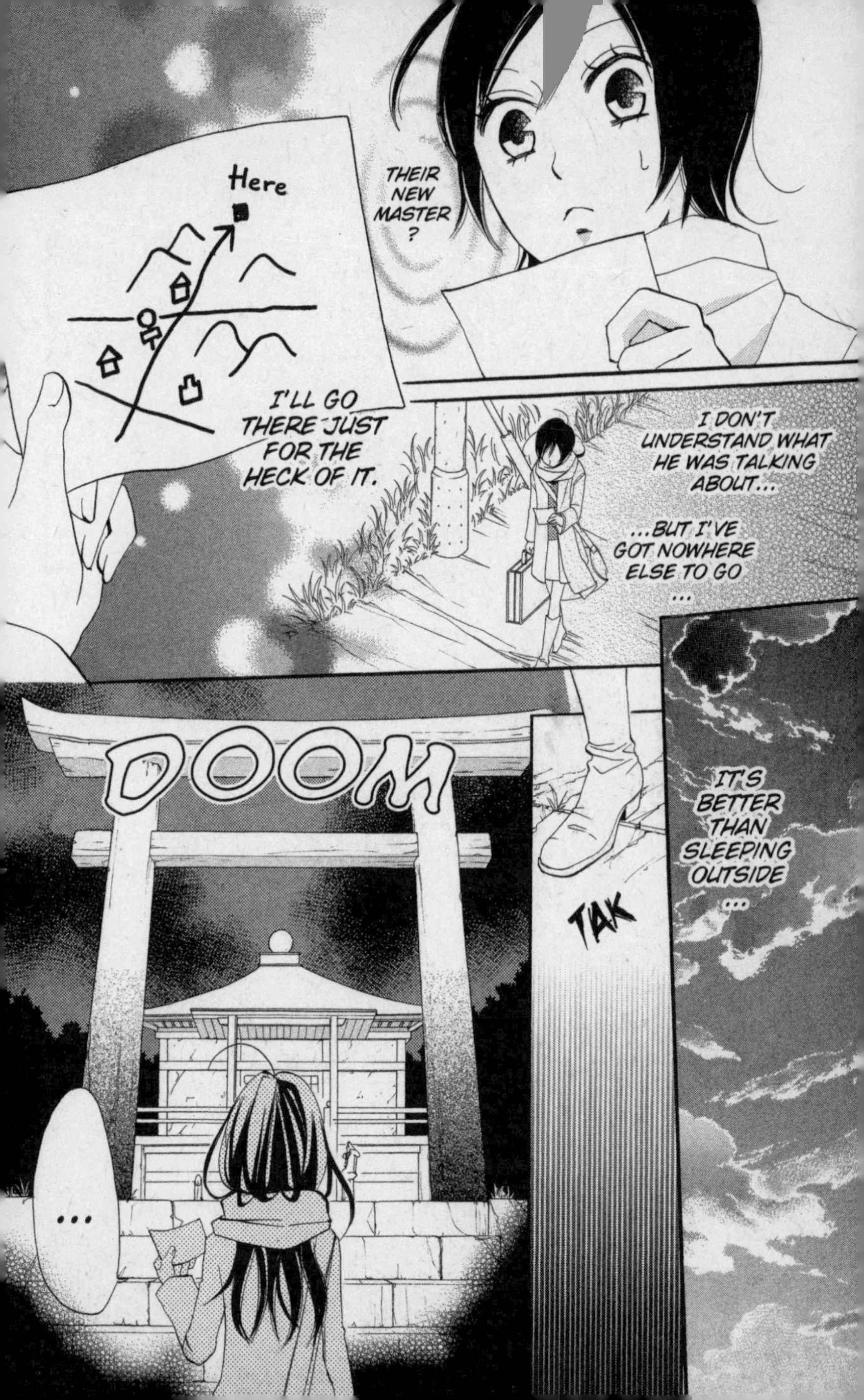
THEIR NEW MASTER ?
Here
I'LL GO THERE JUST FOR THE HECK OF IT.
I DON'T UNDERSTAND WHAT HE WAS TALKING ABOUT...
...BUT I'VE GOT NOWHERE ELSE TO GO ...
IT'S BETTER THAN SLEEPING OUTSIDE ...
TAK
DOOM
...

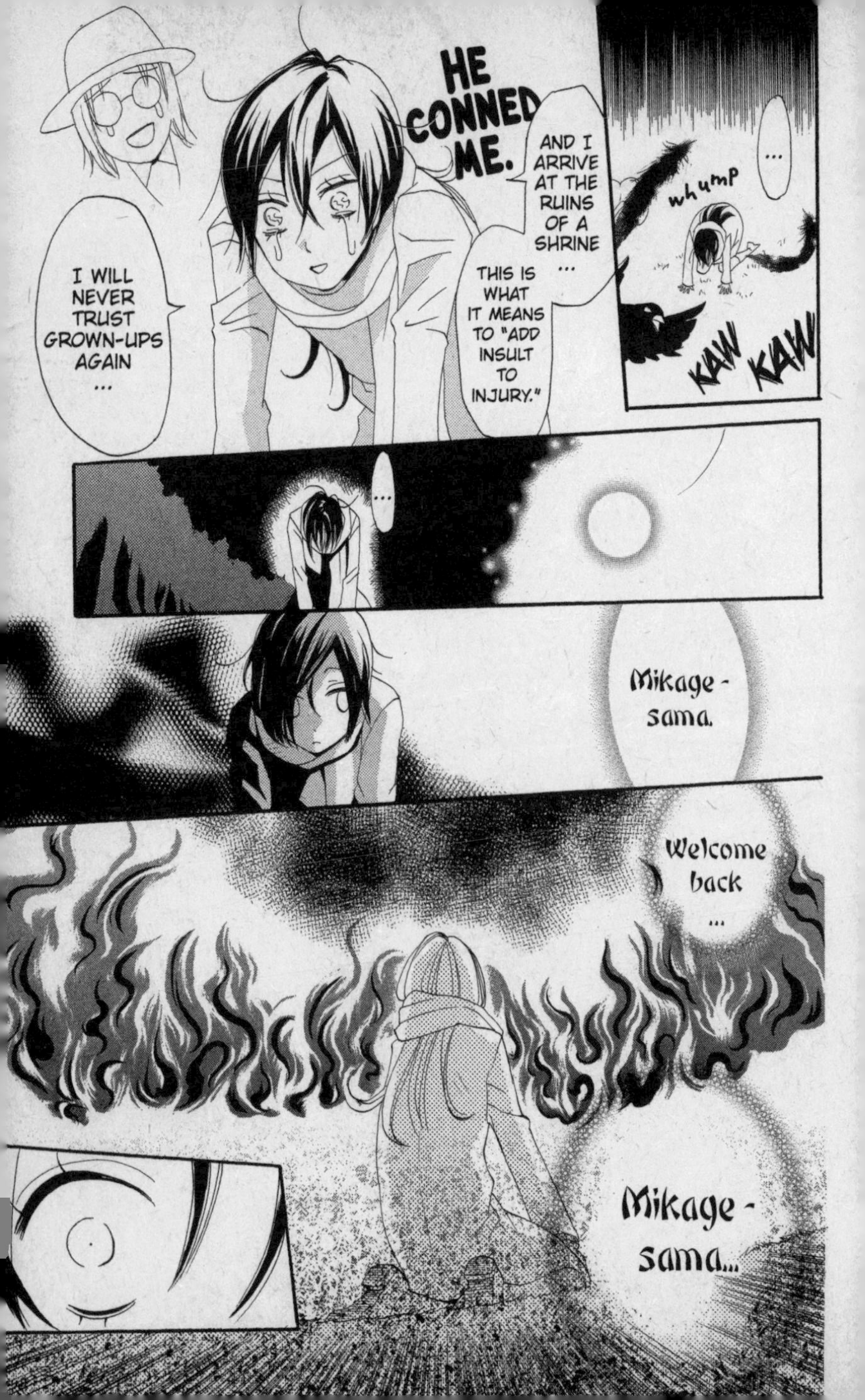
...
whump
KAW KAW
AND I ARRIVE AT THE RUINS OF A SHRINE ...
HE CONNED ME.
THIS IS WHAT IT MEANS TO "ADD INSULT TO INJURY."
I WILL NEVER TRUST GROWN-UPS AGAIN ...
...
Mikage-sama.
Welcome back ...
Mikage-sama...

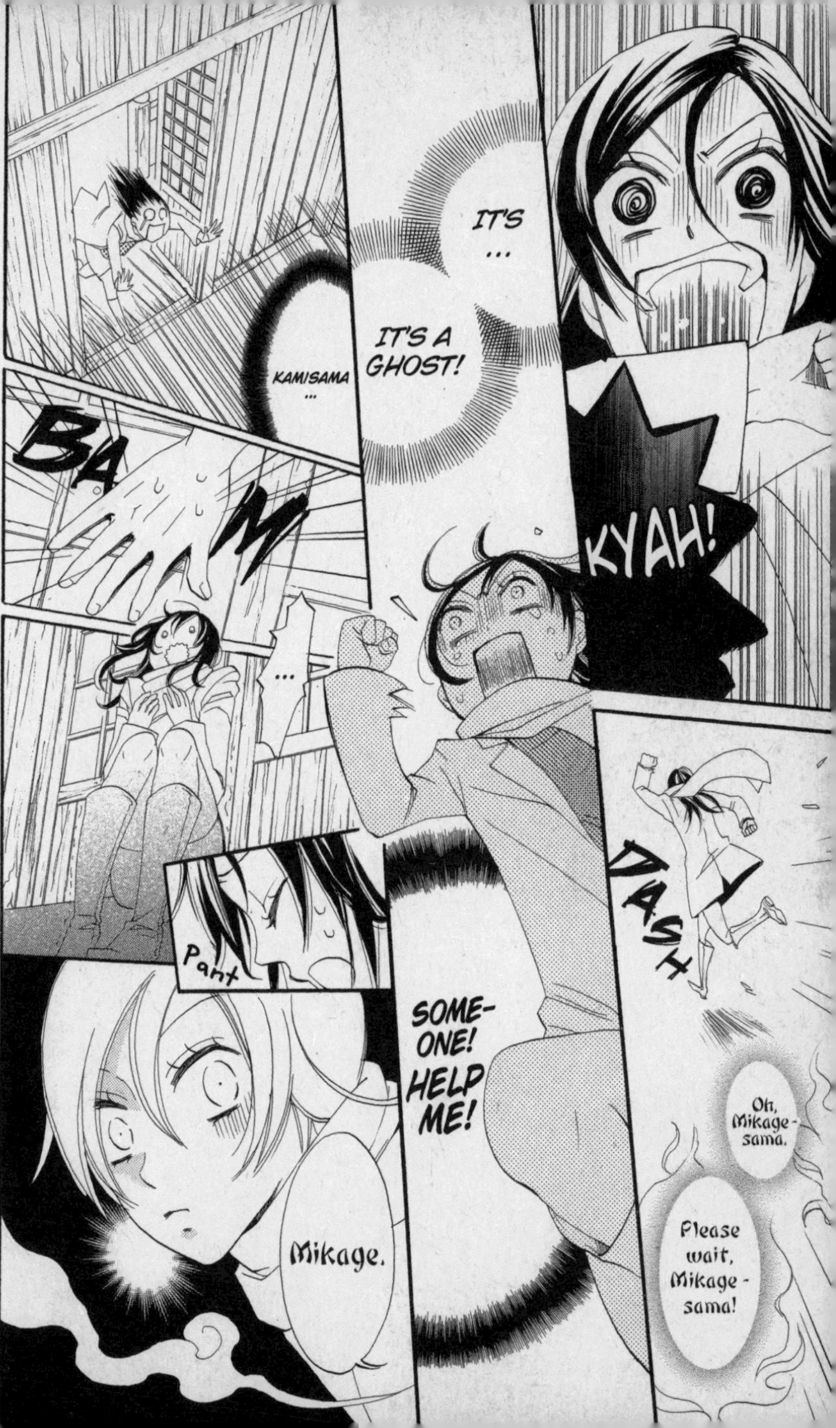
IT'S ...
IT'S A GHOST!
KYAH!
KAMISAMA ...
BAM
...
DASH
SOME-ONE! HELP ME!
Oh, Mikage-sama.
Please wait, Mikage-sama!
Pant
Mikage.

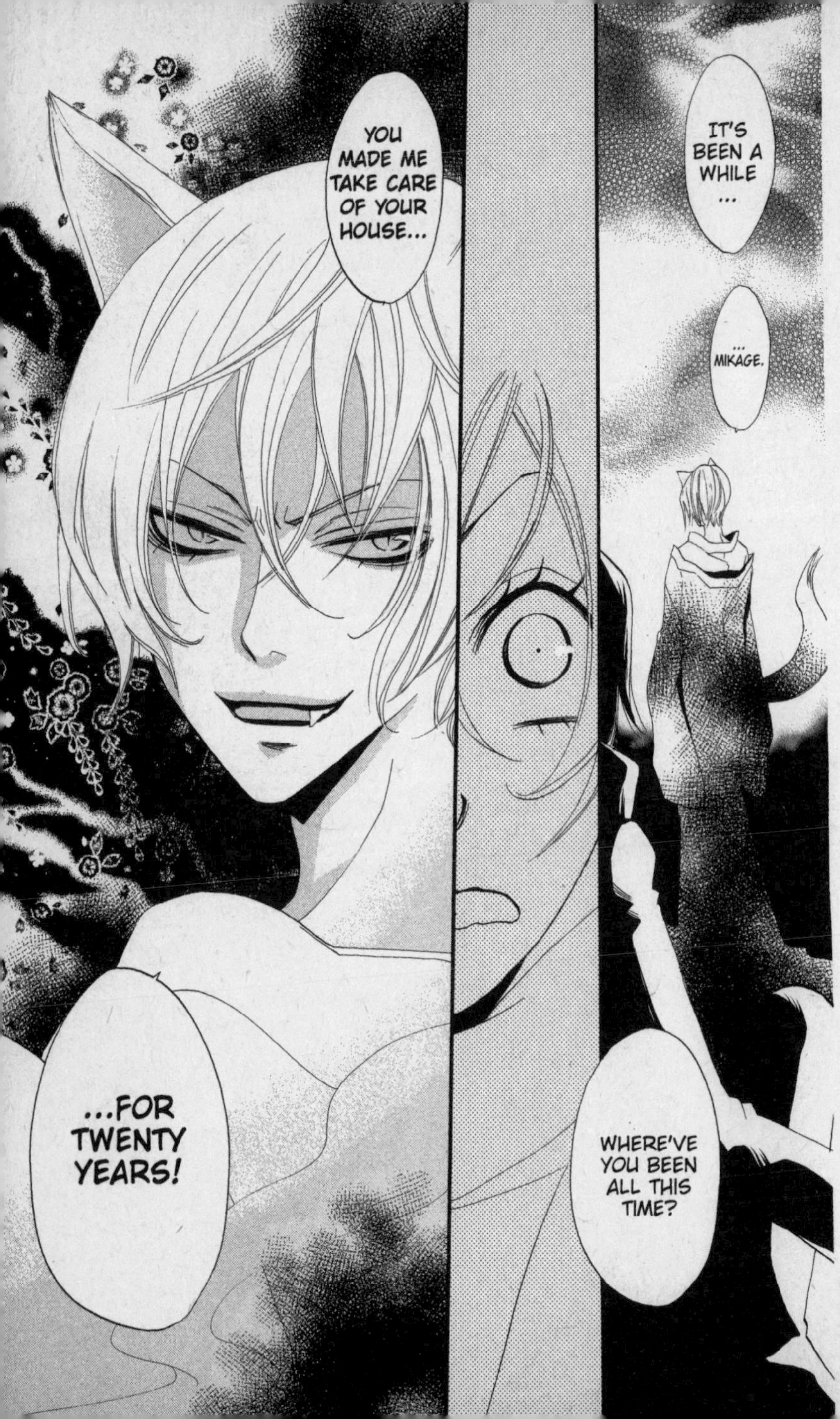
IT'S BEEN A WHILE ...
... MIKAGE.
WHERE'VE YOU BEEN ALL THIS TIME?
YOU MADE ME TAKE CARE OF YOUR HOUSE...
...FOR TWENTY YEARS!

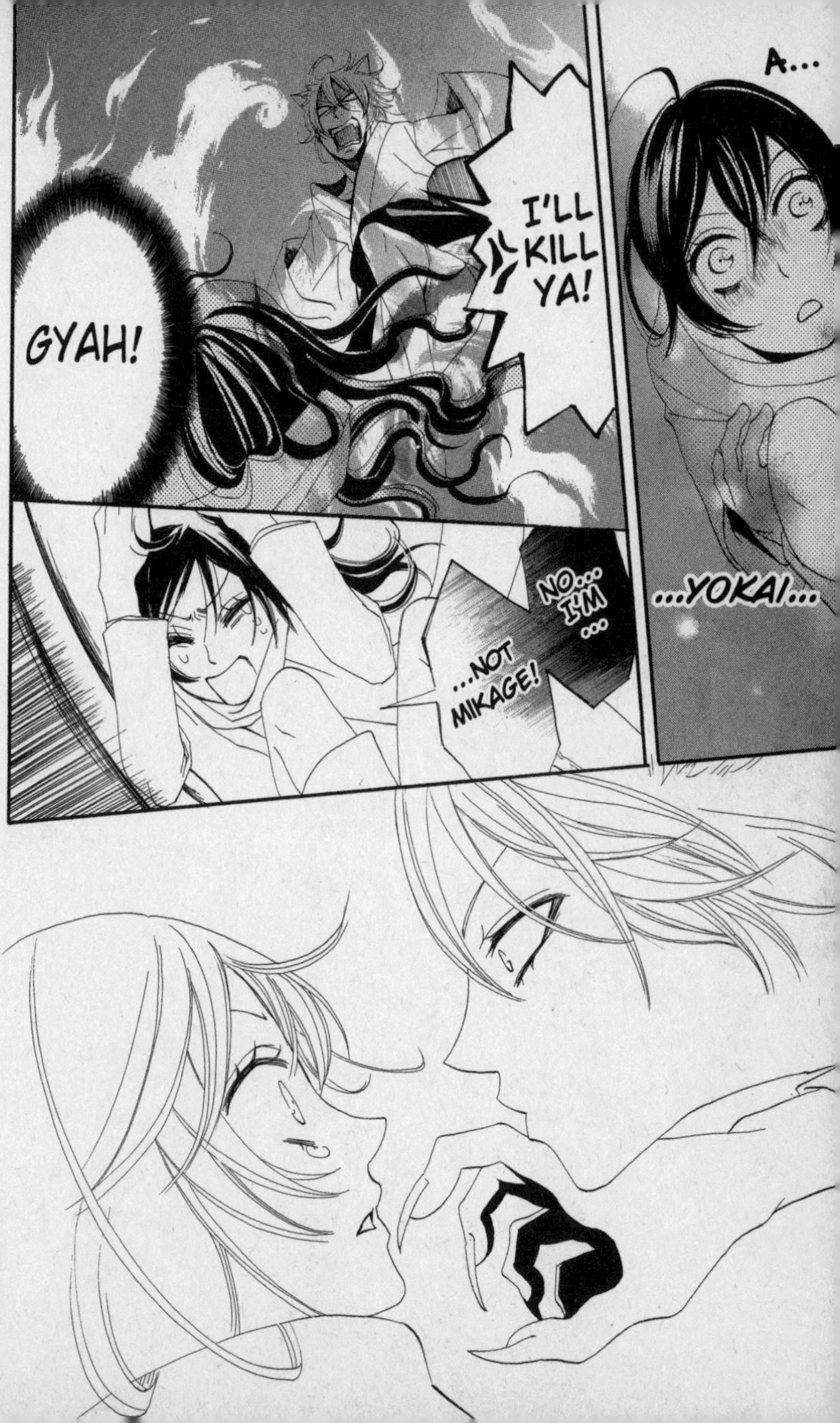
A...
...YOKAI...
I'LL KILL YA!
GYAH!
NO... I'M...
...NOT MIKAGE!

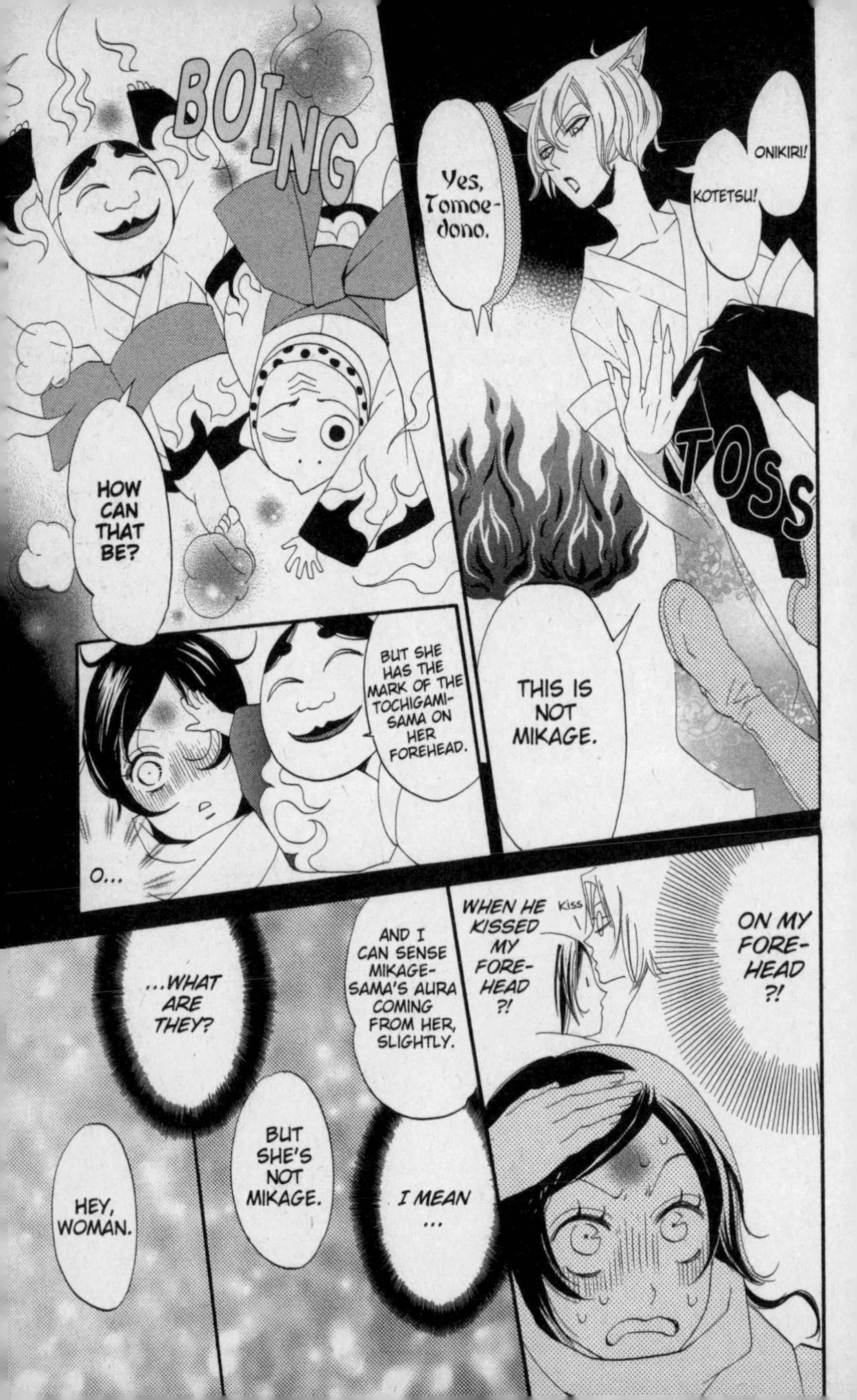
ONIKIRI!
KOTETSU!
Yes, Tomoe-dono.
TOSS
THIS IS NOT MIKAGE.
BOING
HOW CAN THAT BE?
BUT SHE HAS THE MARK OF THE TOCHIGAMI-SAMA ON HER FOREHEAD.
O...
ON MY FOREHEAD?!
Kiss
WHEN HE KISSED MY FOREHEAD?!
I MEAN ...
AND I CAN SENSE MIKAGE-SAMA'S AURA COMING FROM HER, SLIGHTLY.
...WHAT ARE THEY?
BUT SHE'S NOT MIKAGE.
HEY, WOMAN.

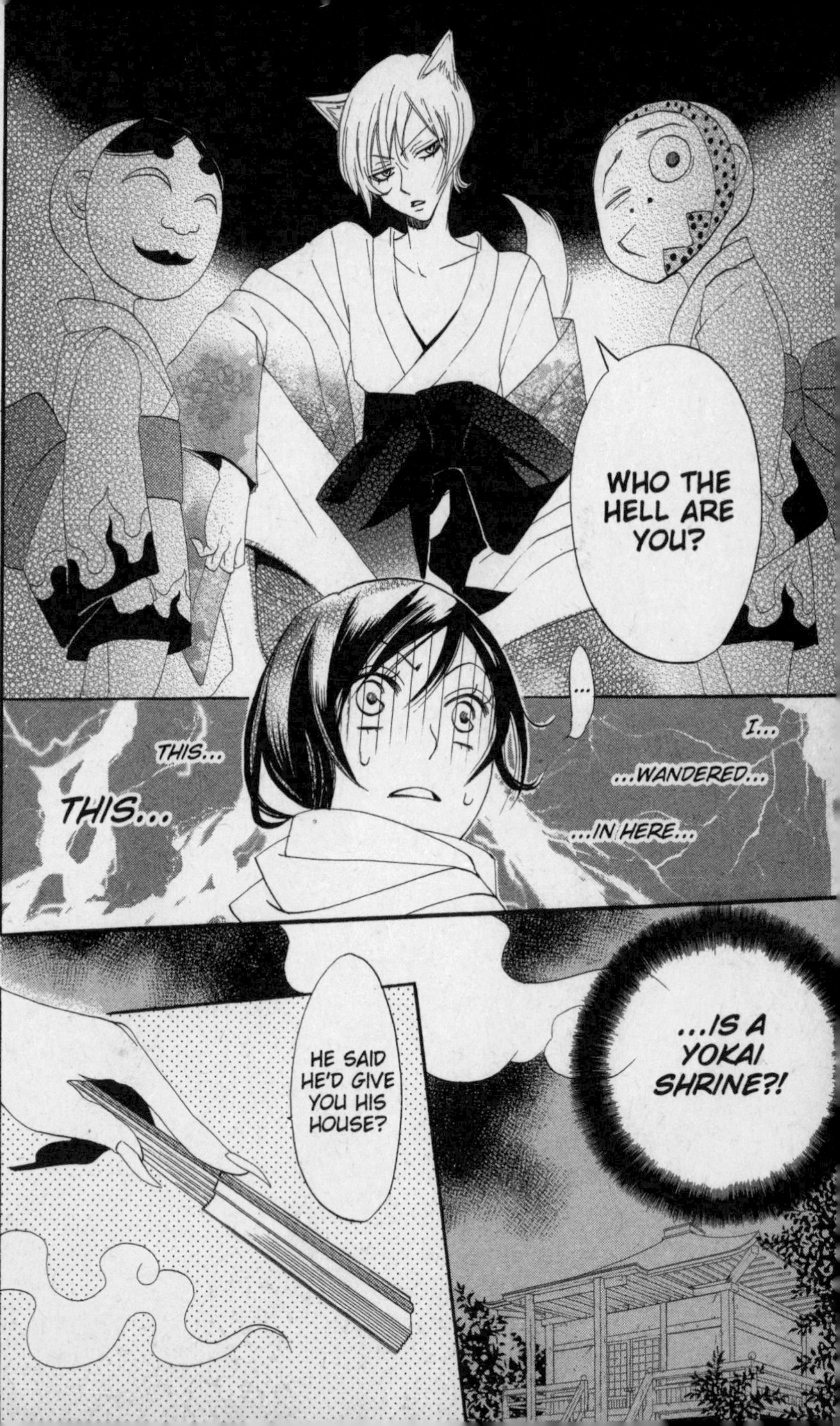
WHO THE HELL ARE YOU?
...
I...
...WANDERED...
...IN HERE...
THIS...
THIS...
...IS A YOKAI SHRINE?!
HE SAID HE'D GIVE YOU HIS HOUSE?

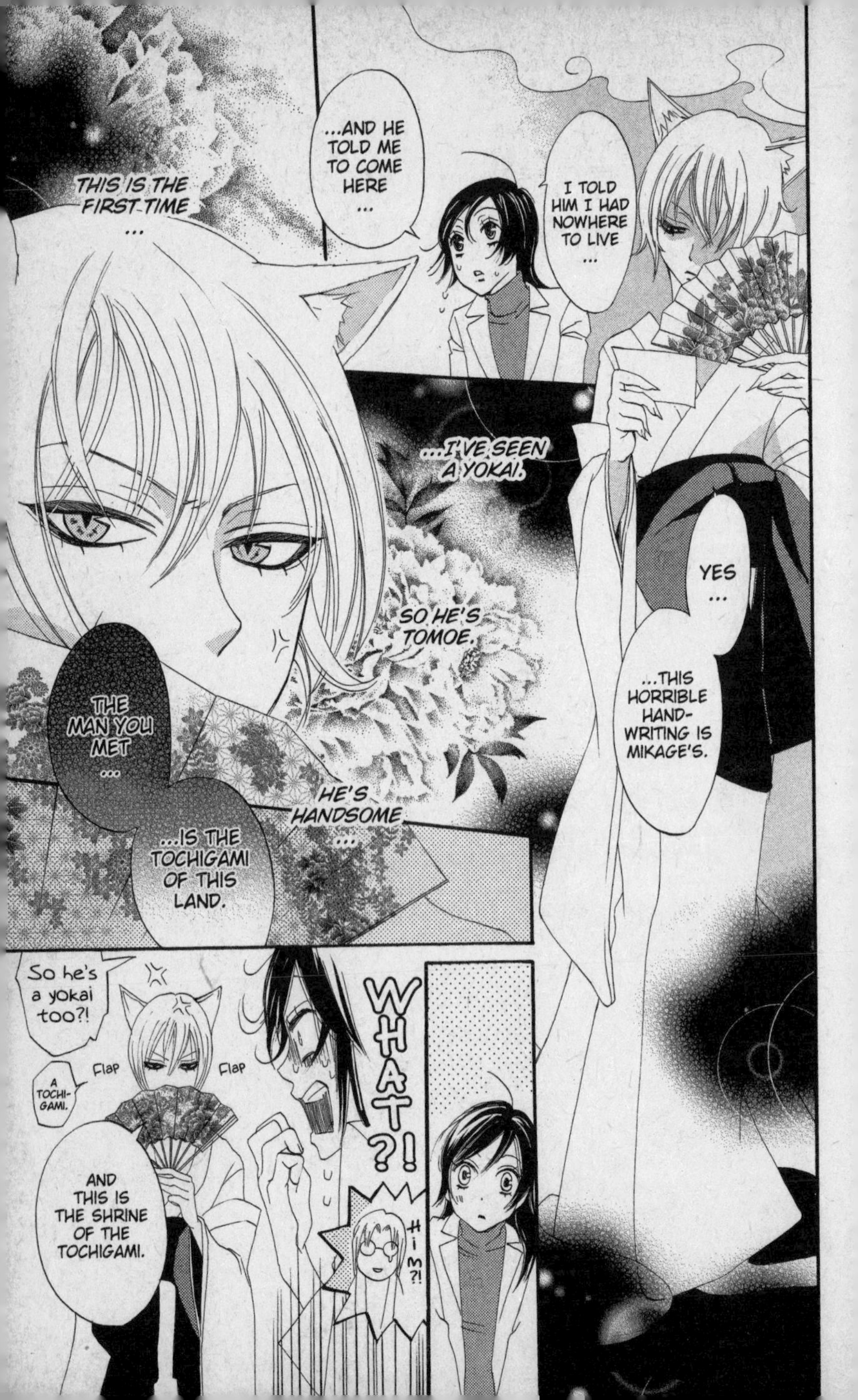
I TOLD HIM I HAD NOWHERE TO LIVE ...
...AND HE TOLD ME TO COME HERE ...
YES ...
...THIS HORRIBLE HAND-WRITING IS MIKAGE'S.
THIS IS THE FIRST TIME ...
...I'VE SEEN A YOKAI.
SO HE'S TOMOE.
HE'S HANDSOME ...
THE MAN YOU MET ...
...IS THE TOCHIGAMI OF THIS LAND.
WHAT?!
Him?!
So he's a yokai too?!
Flap
Flap
A TOCHI-GAMI.
AND THIS IS THE SHRINE OF THE TOCHIGAMI.

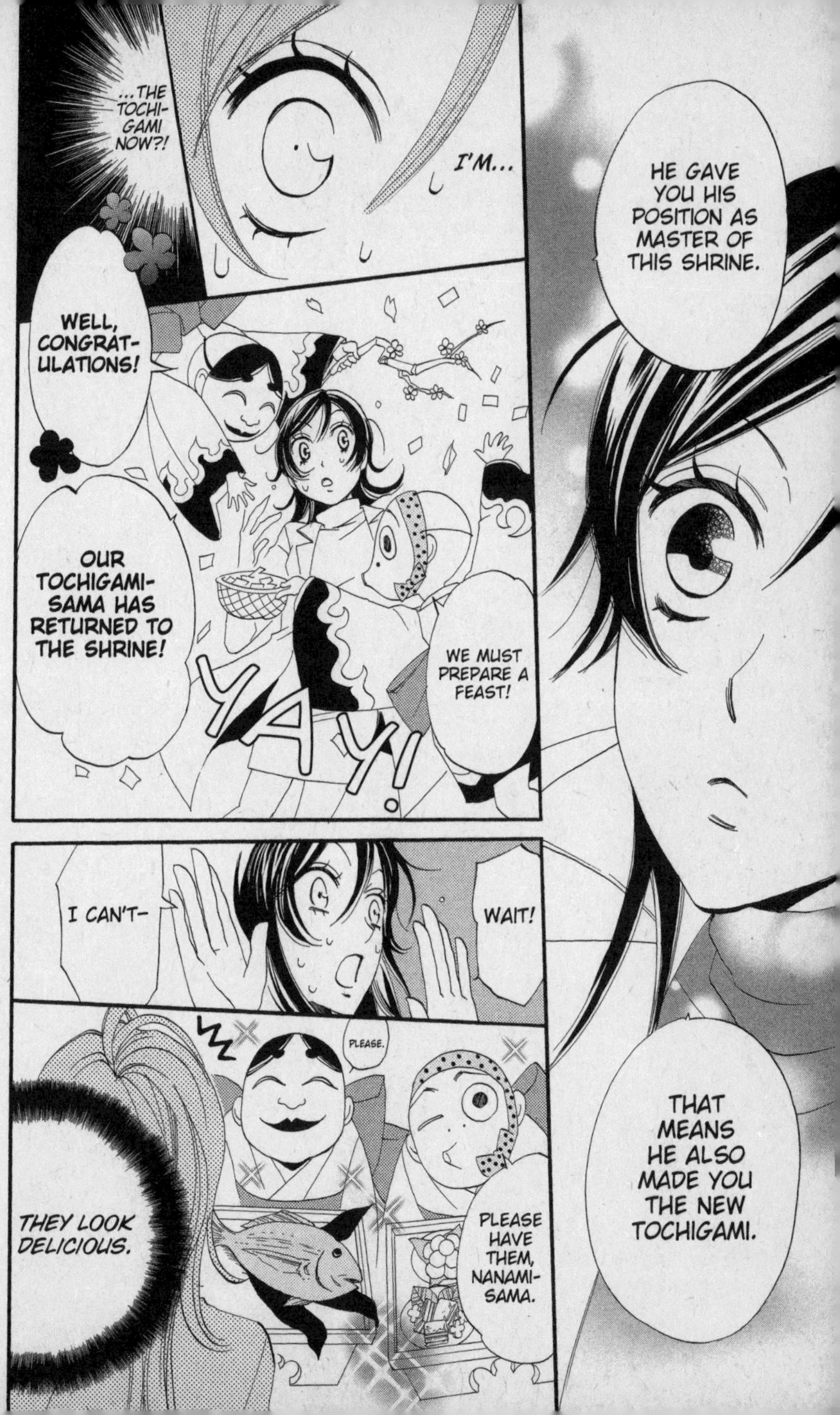
HE GAVE YOU HIS POSITION AS MASTER OF THIS SHRINE.
THAT MEANS HE ALSO MADE YOU THE NEW TOCHIGAMI.
I'M...
...THE TOCHI-GAMI NOW?!
WELL, CONGRAT-ULATIONS!
OUR TOCHIGAMI-SAMA HAS RETURNED TO THE SHRINE!
WE MUST PREPARE A FEAST!
YAY!
WAIT!
I CAN'T-
PLEASE.
PLEASE HAVE THEM, NANAMI-SAMA.
THEY LOOK DELICIOUS.

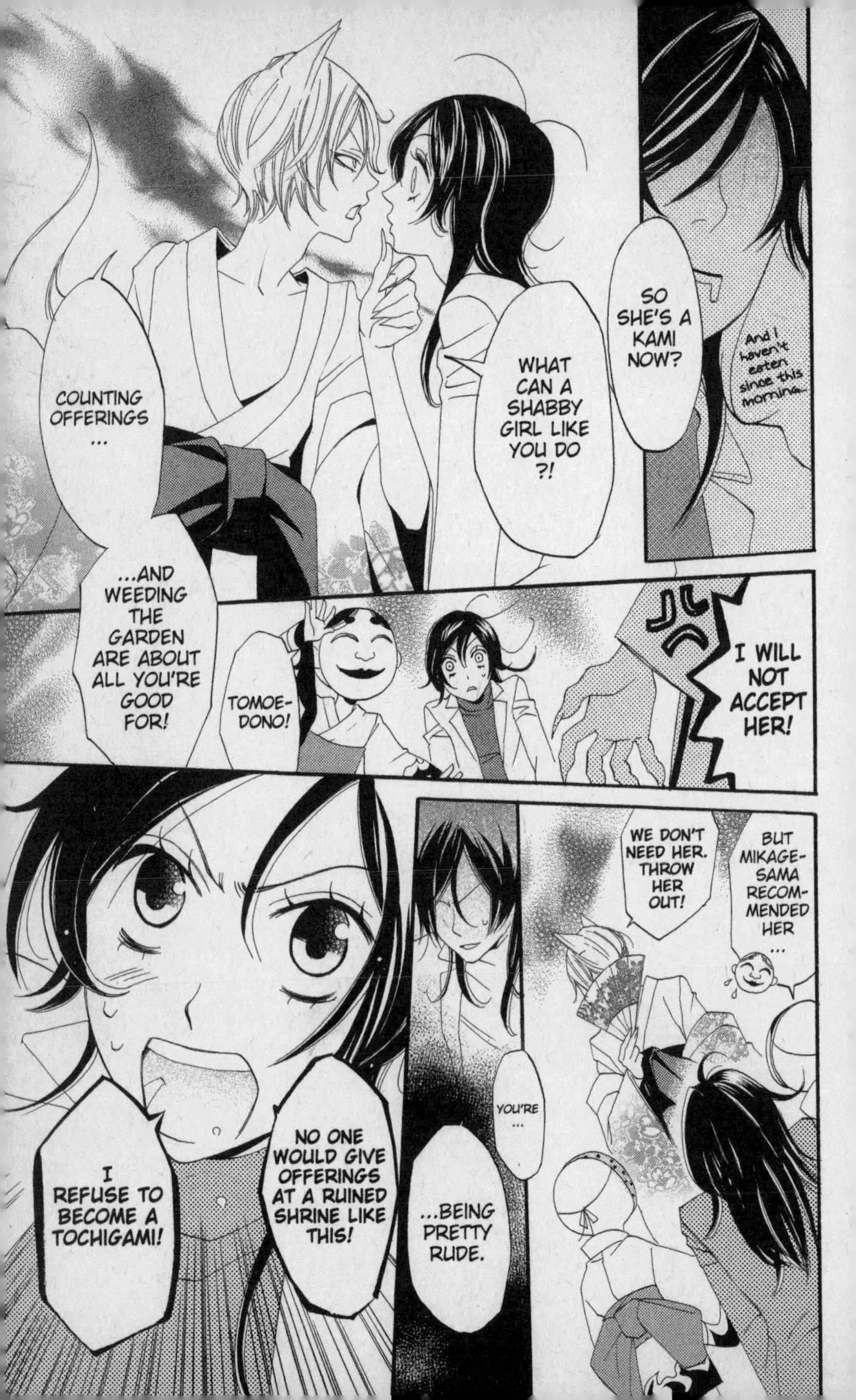
SO SHE'S A KAMI NOW?
And I haven't eaten since this morning.
WHAT CAN A SHABBY GIRL LIKE YOU DO ?!
COUNTING OFFERINGS ...
...AND WEEDING THE GARDEN ARE ABOUT ALL YOU'RE GOOD FOR!
I WILL NOT ACCEPT HER!
TOMOE-DONO!
BUT MIKAGE-SAMA RECOMMENDED HER ...
WE DON'T NEED HER. THROW HER OUT!
YOU'RE ...
...BEING PRETTY RUDE.
NO ONE WOULD GIVE OFFERINGS AT A RUINED SHRINE LIKE THIS!
I REFUSE TO BECOME A TOCHIGAMI!

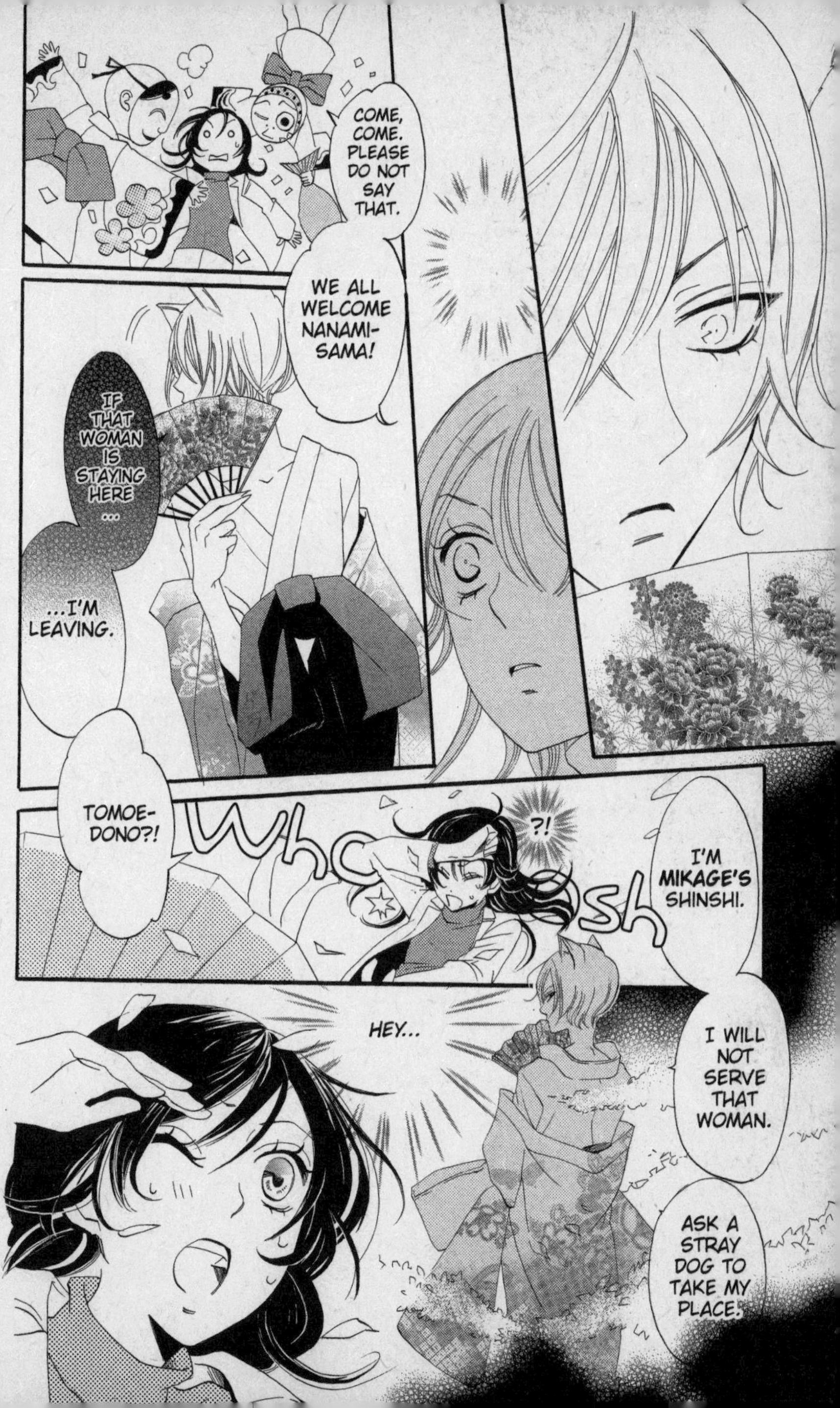
COME, COME. PLEASE DO NOT SAY THAT.
WE ALL WELCOME NANAMI-SAMA!
IF THAT WOMAN IS STAYING HERE...
...I'M LEAVING.
TOMOE-DONO?!
I'M MIKAGE'S SHINSHI.
?!
Whoosh
I WILL NOT SERVE THAT WOMAN.
ASK A STRAY DOG TO TAKE MY PLACE.
HEY...

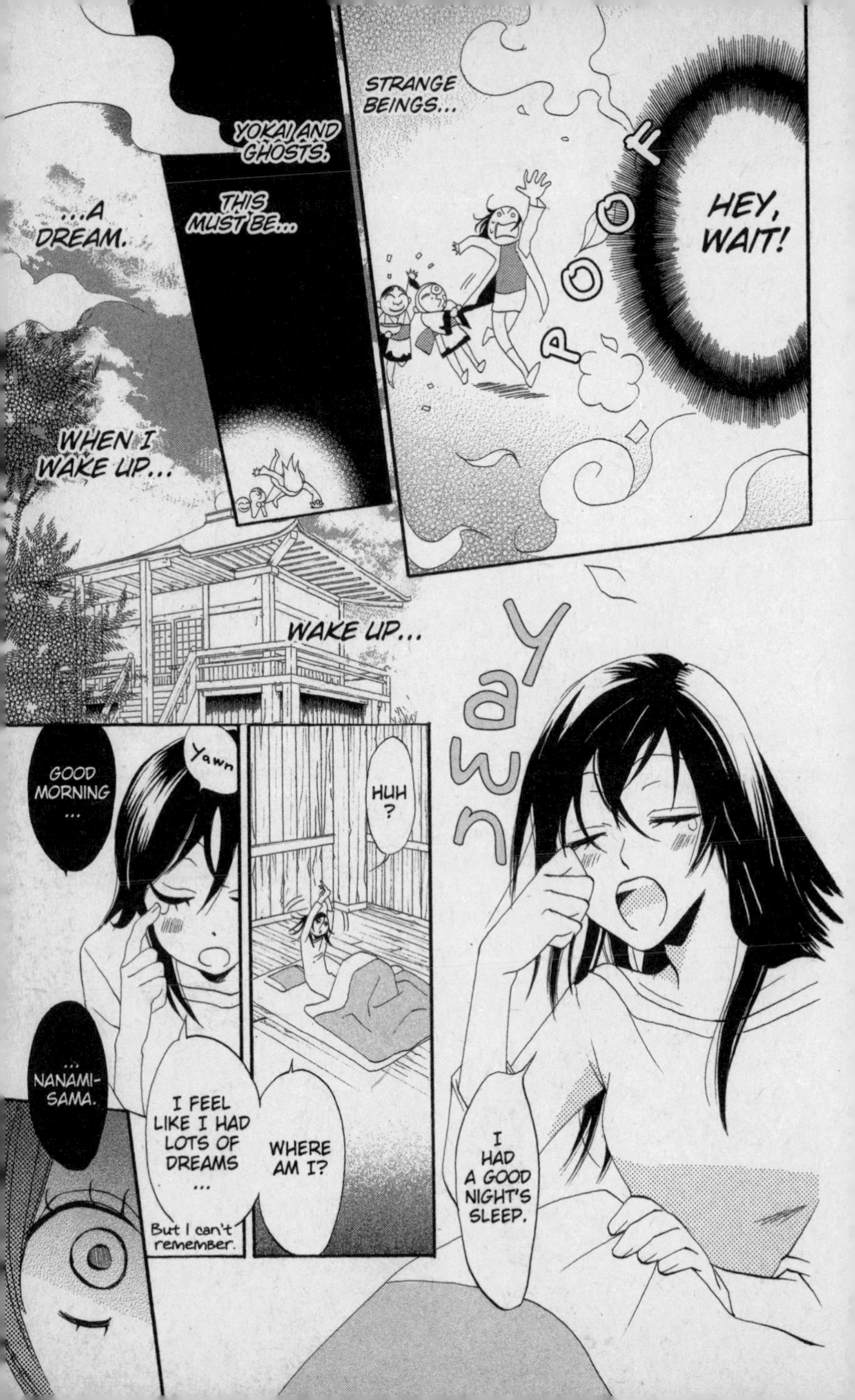
STRANGE BEINGS...
HEY, WAIT!
POOF
YOKAI AND GHOSTS.
THIS MUST BE...
...A DREAM.
WHEN I WAKE UP...
WAKE UP...
yawn
I HAD A GOOD NIGHT'S SLEEP.
HUH?
WHERE AM I?
Yawn
GOOD MORNING...
I FEEL LIKE I HAD LOTS OF DREAMS...
But I can't remember.
...NANAMI-SAMA.

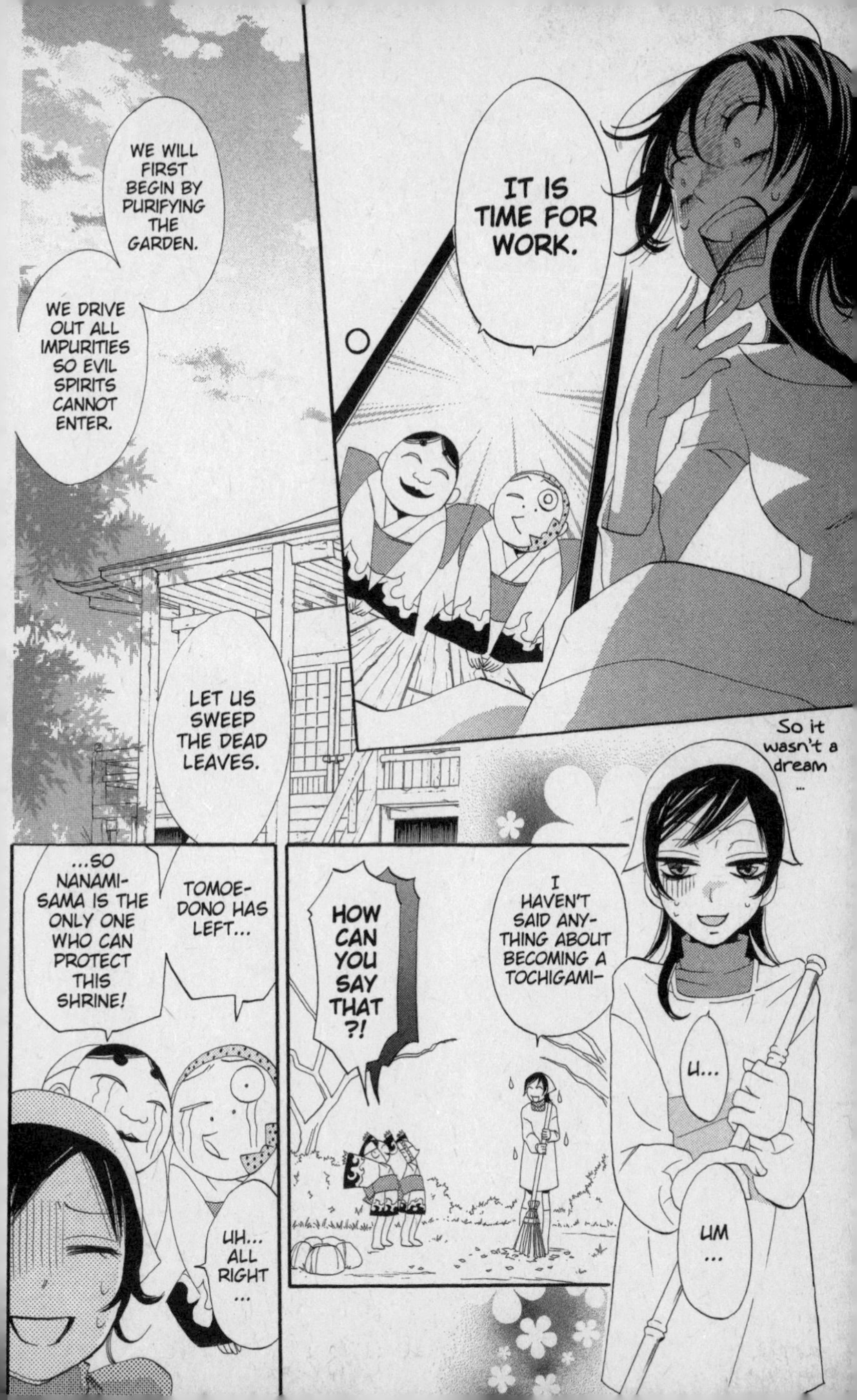
IT IS TIME FOR WORK.
WE WILL FIRST BEGIN BY PURIFYING THE GARDEN.
WE DRIVE OUT ALL IMPURITIES SO EVIL SPIRITS CANNOT ENTER.
LET US SWEEP THE DEAD LEAVES.
So it wasn't a dream ...
I HAVEN'T SAID ANY-THING ABOUT BECOMING A TOCHIGAMI-
U...
UM ...
HOW CAN YOU SAY THAT?!
TOMOE-DONO HAS LEFT...
...SO NANAMI-SAMA IS THE ONLY ONE WHO CAN PROTECT THIS SHRINE!
UH... ALL RIGHT ...

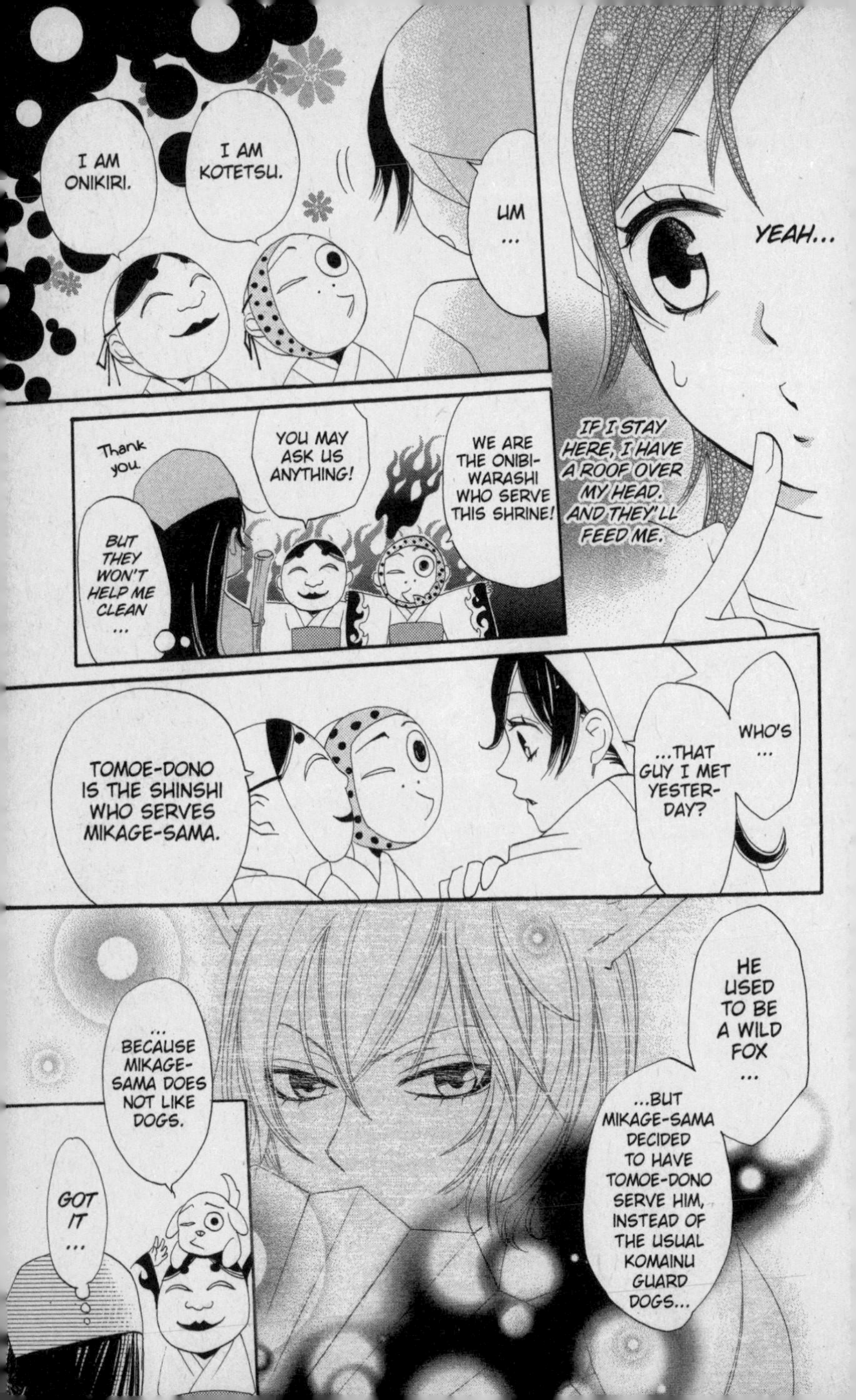
YEAH...
IF I STAY HERE, I HAVE A ROOF OVER MY HEAD. AND THEY'LL FEED ME.
UM ...
I AM KOTETSU.
I AM ONIKIRI.
WE ARE THE ONIBI-WARASHI WHO SERVE THIS SHRINE!
YOU MAY ASK US ANYTHING!
Thank you.
BUT THEY WON'T HELP ME CLEAN ...
WHO'S ...
...THAT GUY I MET YESTER-DAY?
TOMOE-DONO IS THE SHINSHI WHO SERVES MIKAGE-SAMA.
HE USED TO BE A WILD FOX ...
...BUT MIKAGE-SAMA DECIDED TO HAVE TOMOE-DONO SERVE HIM, INSTEAD OF THE USUAL KOMAINU GUARD DOGS...
... BECAUSE MIKAGE-SAMA DOES NOT LIKE DOGS.
GOT IT ...

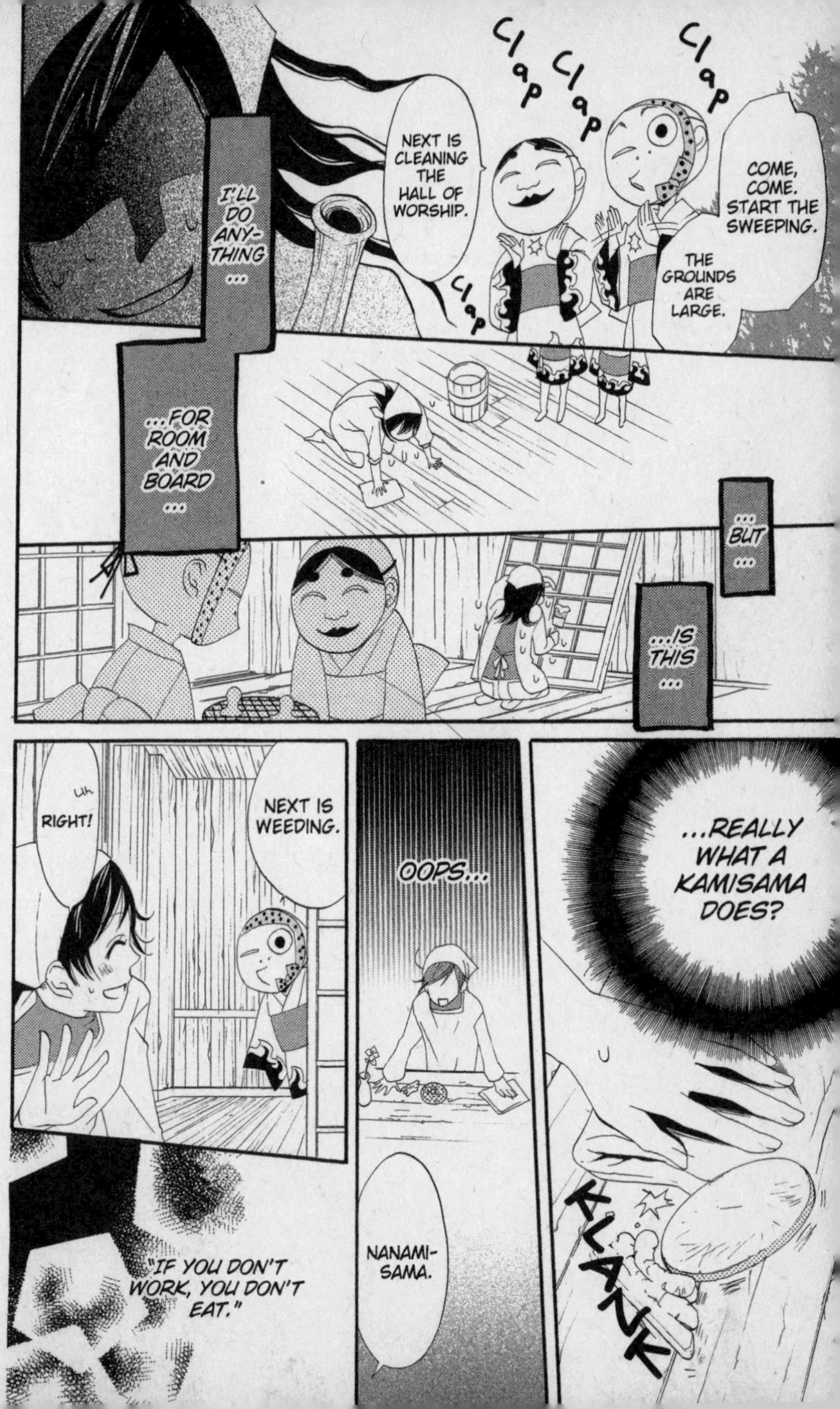
Clap Clap Clap
COME, COME. START THE SWEEPING.
THE GROUNDS ARE LARGE.
NEXT IS CLEANING THE HALL OF WORSHIP.
Clap
I'LL DO ANYTHING...
...FOR ROOM AND BOARD...
...BUT...
...IS THIS...
...REALLY WHAT A KAMISAMA DOES?
KLANK
OOPS...
NANAMI-SAMA.
NEXT IS WEEDING.
Uh.
RIGHT!
"IF YOU DON'T WORK, YOU DON'T EAT."

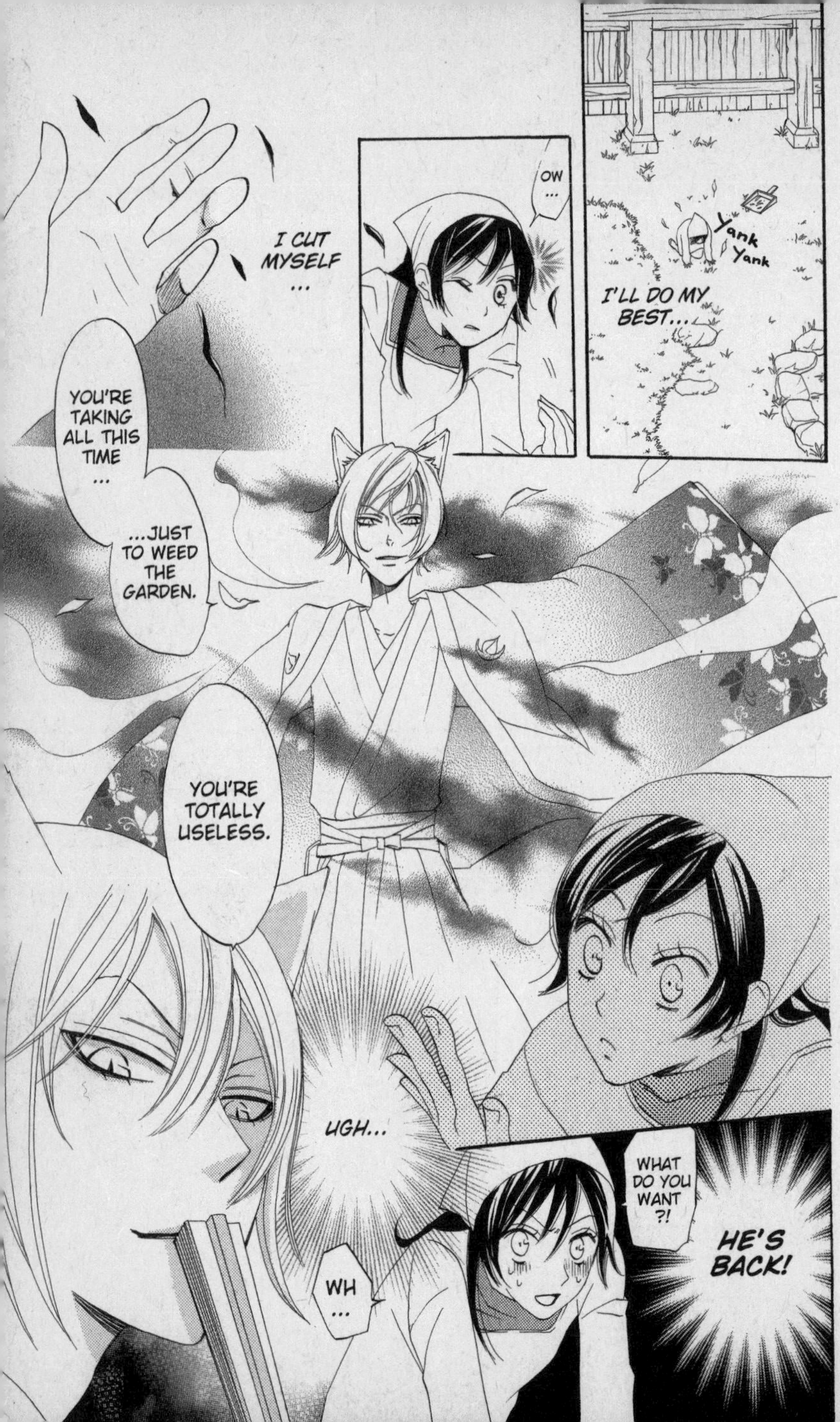
Yank Yank
I'LL DO MY BEST...
OW...
I CUT MYSELF...
YOU'RE TAKING ALL THIS TIME...
...JUST TO WEED THE GARDEN.
YOU'RE TOTALLY USELESS.
UGH...
HE'S BACK!
WH...
WHAT DO YOU WANT?!

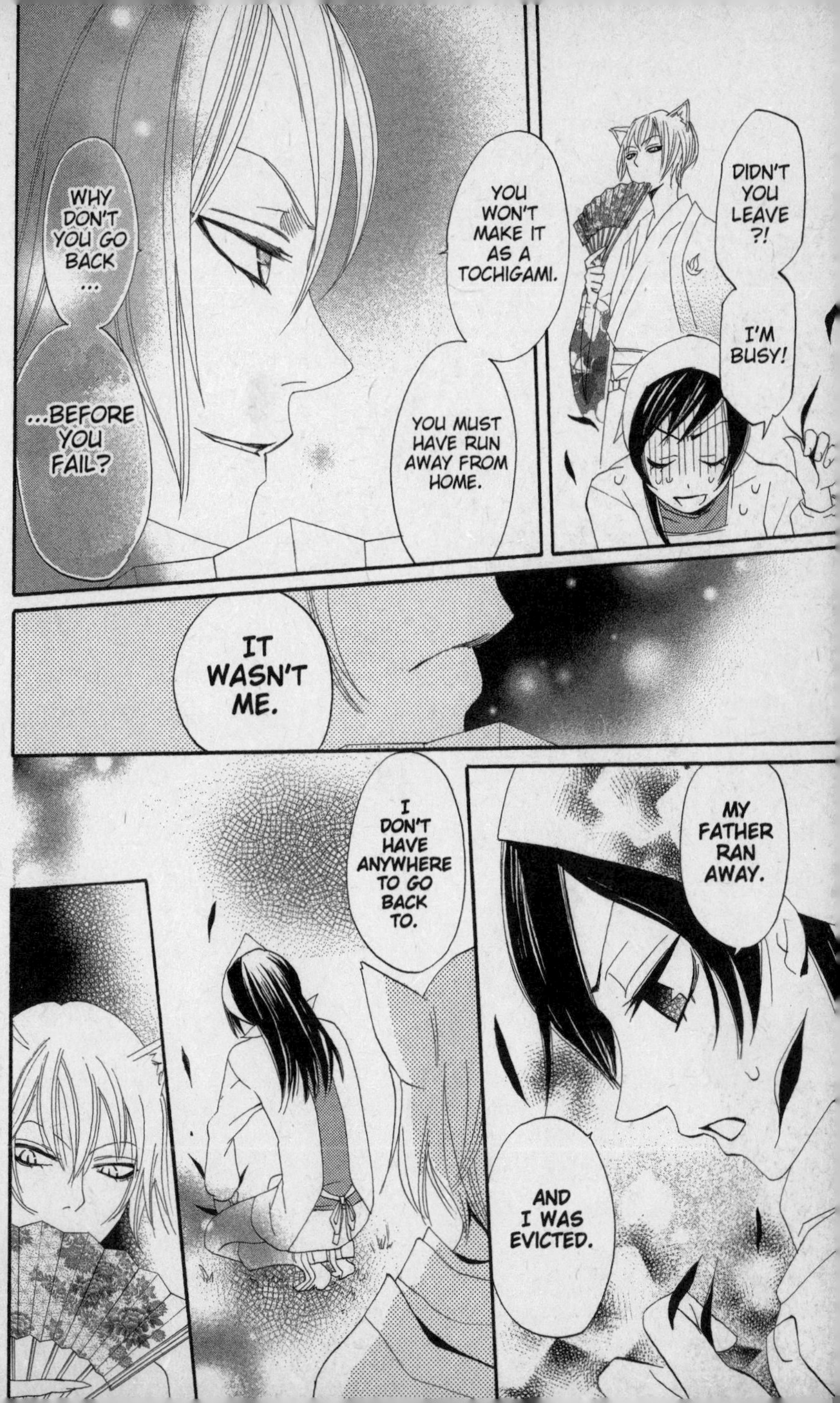
DIDN'T YOU LEAVE ?!
I'M BUSY!
YOU WON'T MAKE IT AS A TOCHIGAMI.
YOU MUST HAVE RUN AWAY FROM HOME.
WHY DON'T YOU GO BACK ...
...BEFORE YOU FAIL?
IT WASN'T ME.
MY FATHER RAN AWAY.
AND I WAS EVICTED.
I DON'T HAVE ANYWHERE TO GO BACK TO.

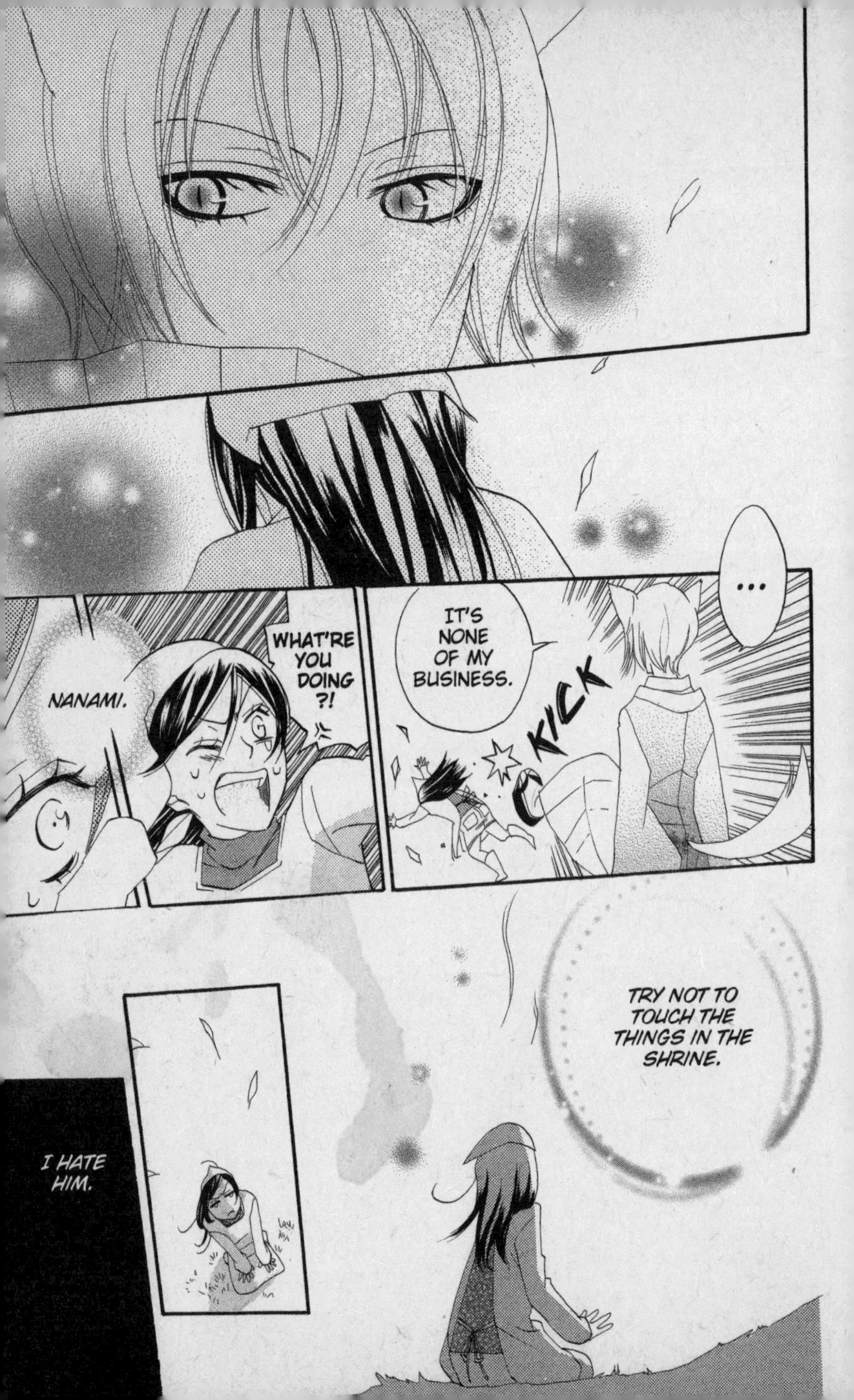
...
IT'S NONE OF MY BUSINESS.
KICK
WHAT'RE YOU DOING ?!
NANAMI.
TRY NOT TO TOUCH THE THINGS IN THE SHRINE.
I HATE HIM.

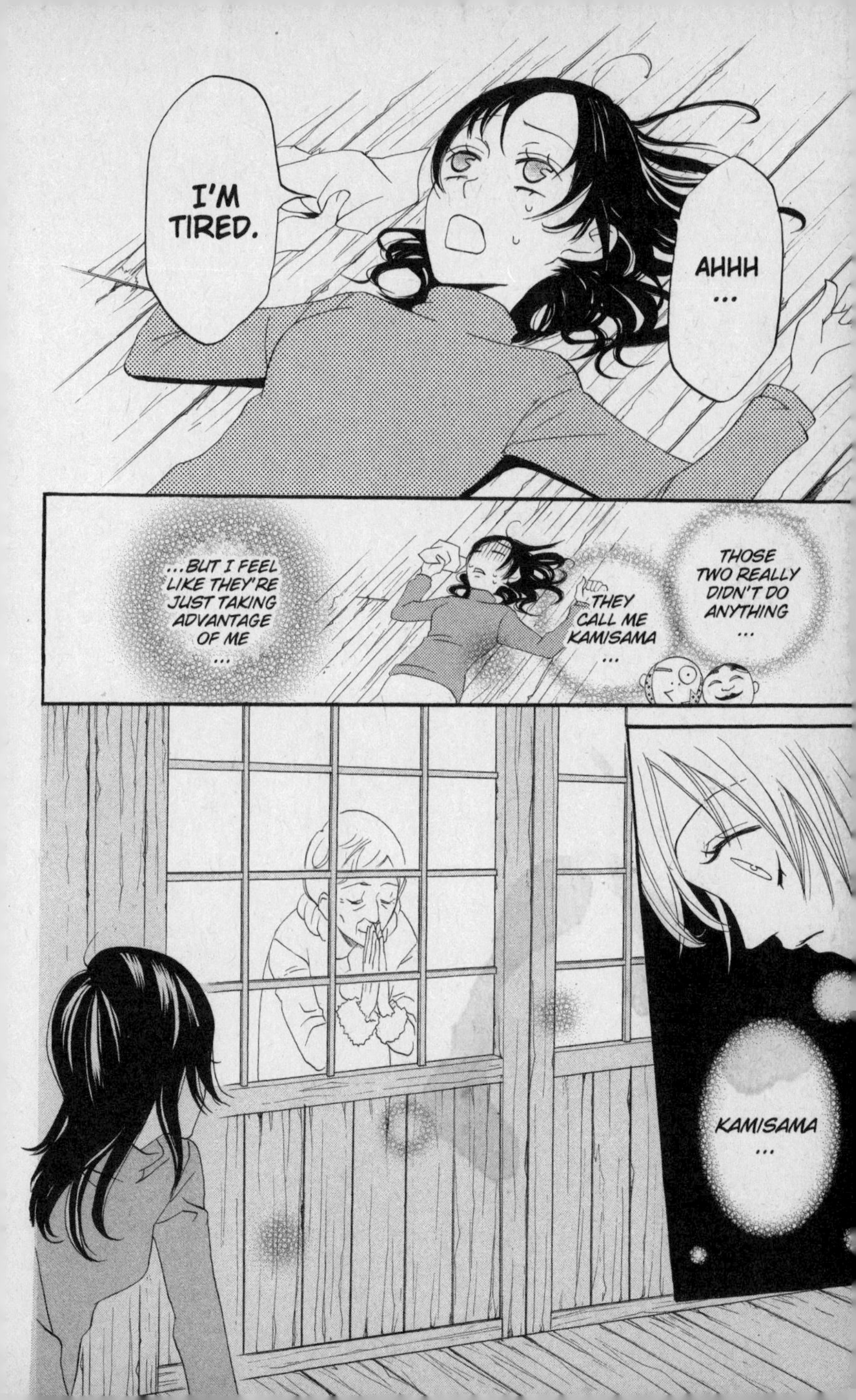
AHHH ...
I'M TIRED.
THOSE TWO REALLY DIDN'T DO ANYTHING ...
THEY CALL ME KAMISAMA ...
...BUT I FEEL LIKE THEY'RE JUST TAKING ADVANTAGE OF ME ...
KAMISAMA ...

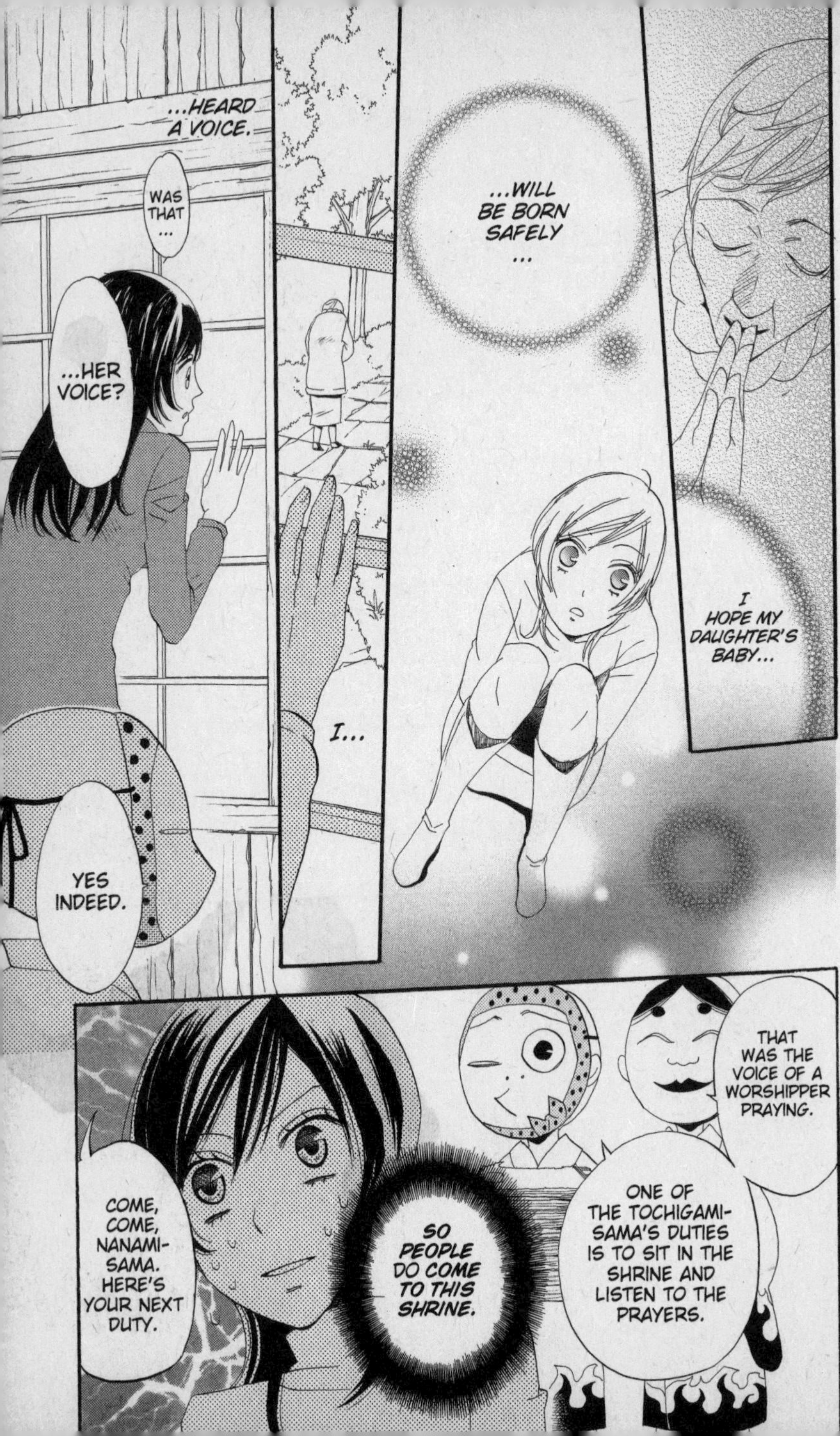
I HOPE MY DAUGHTER'S BABY...
...WILL BE BORN SAFELY ...
I...
...HEARD A VOICE.
WAS THAT ...
...HER VOICE?
YES INDEED.
THAT WAS THE VOICE OF A WORSHIPPER PRAYING.
ONE OF THE TOCHIGAMI-SAMA'S DUTIES IS TO SIT IN THE SHRINE AND LISTEN TO THE PRAYERS.
SO PEOPLE DO COME TO THIS SHRINE.
COME, COME, NANAMI-SAMA. HERE'S YOUR NEXT DUTY.

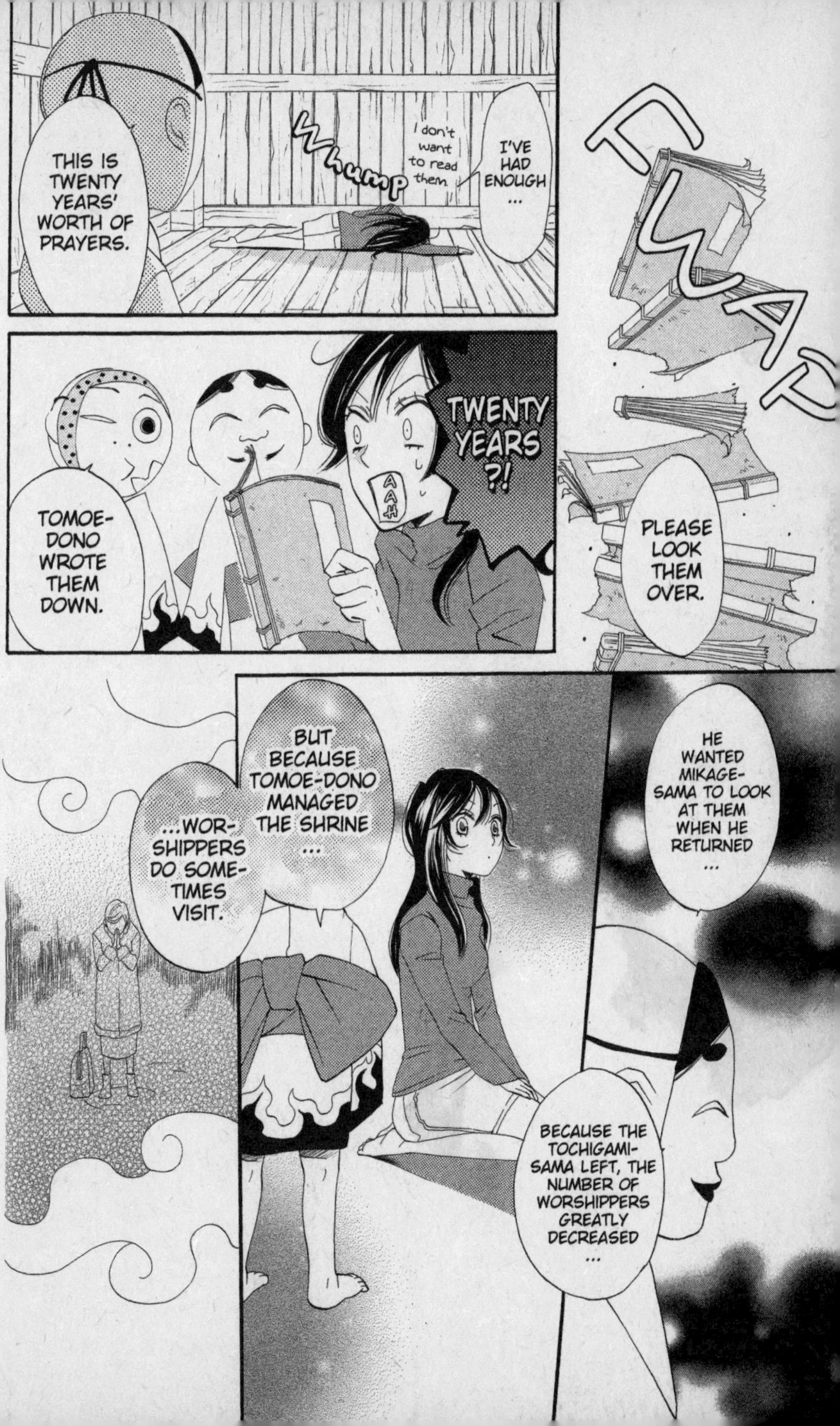
FWAP
PLEASE LOOK THEM OVER.
I'VE HAD ENOUGH ...
I don't want to read them.
WHUMP
THIS IS TWENTY YEARS' WORTH OF PRAYERS.
TWENTY YEARS ?!
AAH
TOMOE-DONO WROTE THEM DOWN.
HE WANTED MIKAGE-SAMA TO LOOK AT THEM WHEN HE RETURNED ...
BECAUSE THE TOCHIGAMI-SAMA LEFT, THE NUMBER OF WORSHIPPERS GREATLY DECREASED ...
BUT BECAUSE TOMOE-DONO MANAGED THE SHRINE ...
...WOR-SHIPPERS DO SOME-TIMES VISIT.

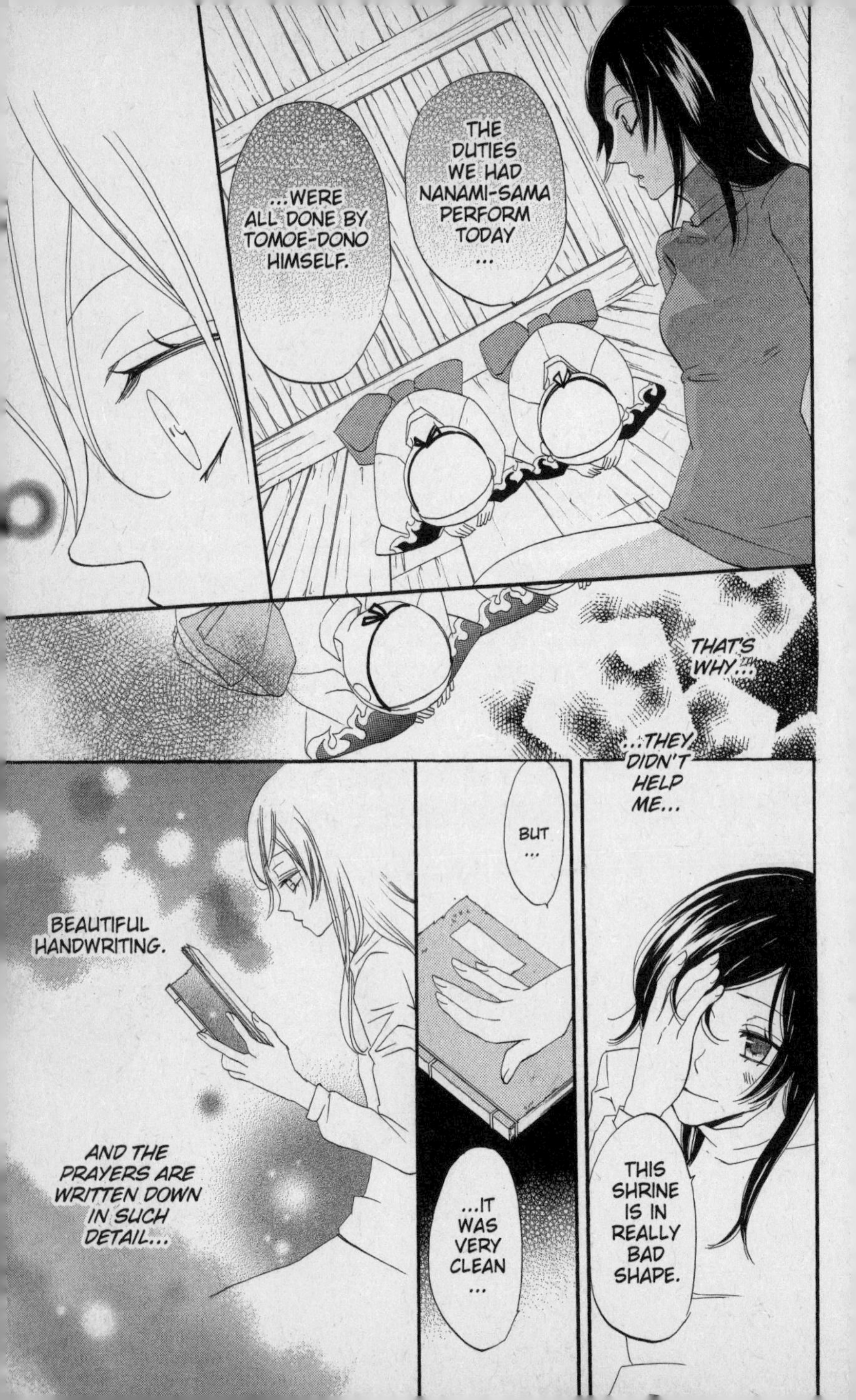
THE DUTIES WE HAD NANAMI-SAMA PERFORM TODAY...
...WERE ALL DONE BY TOMOE-DONO HIMSELF.
THAT'S WHY...
...THEY DIDN'T HELP ME...
THIS SHRINE IS IN REALLY BAD SHAPE.
BUT...
...IT WAS VERY CLEAN...
BEAUTIFUL HANDWRITING.
AND THE PRAYERS ARE WRITTEN DOWN IN SUCH DETAIL...

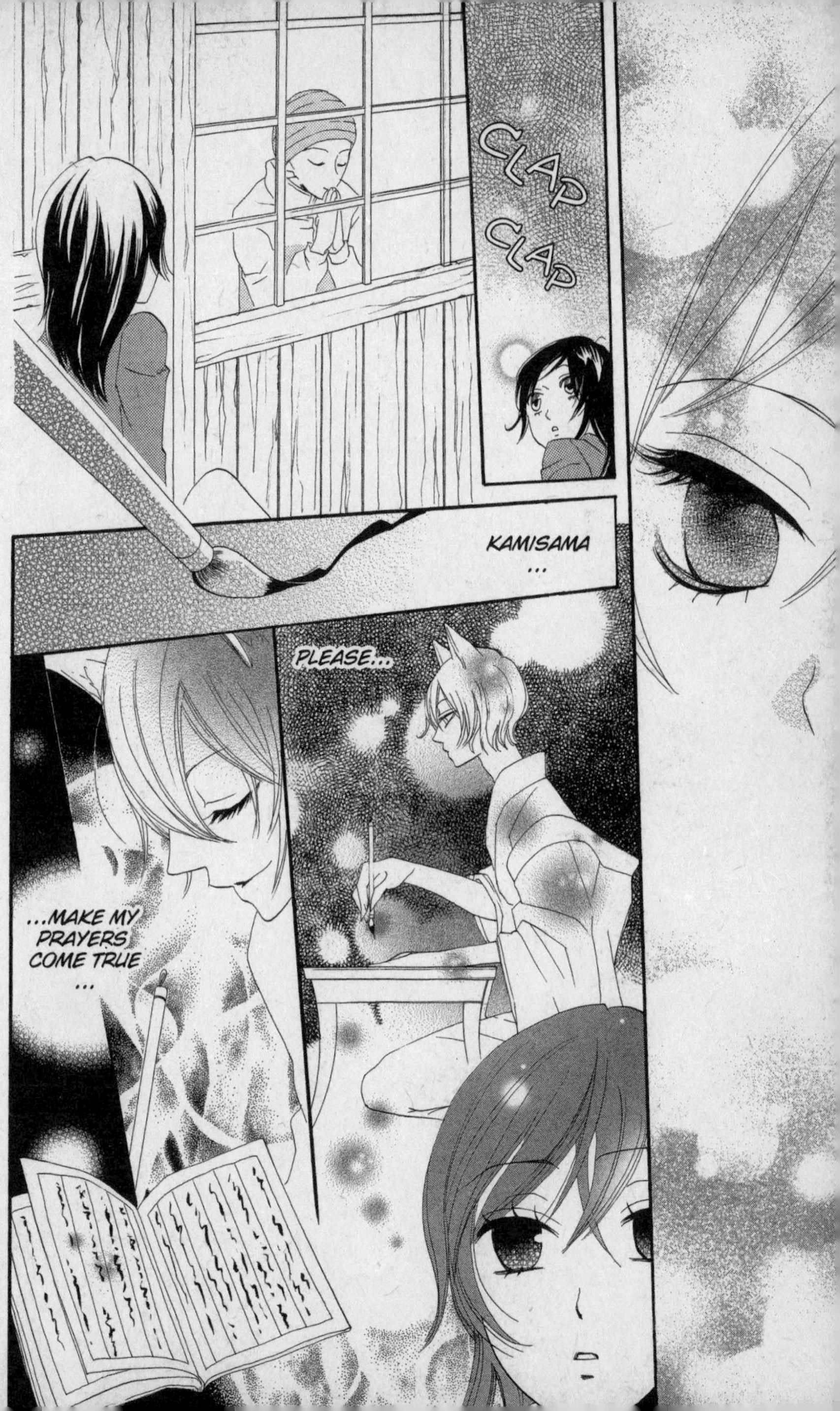
CLAP CLAP
KAMISAMA ...
PLEASE...
...MAKE MY PRAYERS COME TRUE ...

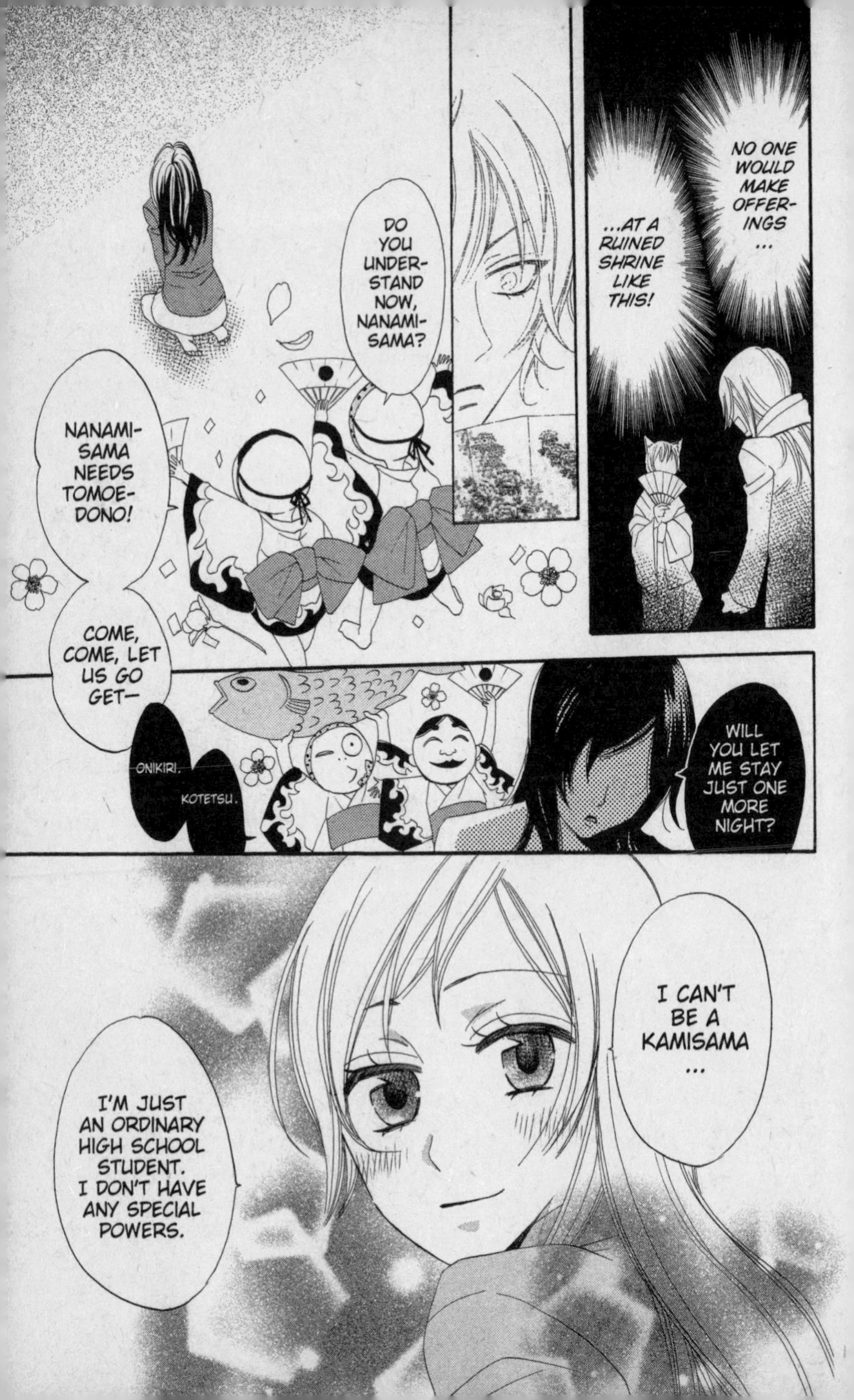
NO ONE WOULD MAKE OFFERINGS...
...AT A RUINED SHRINE LIKE THIS!
DO YOU UNDERSTAND NOW, NANAMI-SAMA?
NANAMI-SAMA NEEDS TOMOE-DONO!
COME, COME, LET US GO GET—
WILL YOU LET ME STAY JUST ONE MORE NIGHT?
ONIKIRI.
KOTETSU.
I CAN'T BE A KAMISAMA...
I'M JUST AN ORDINARY HIGH SCHOOL STUDENT. I DON'T HAVE ANY SPECIAL POWERS.

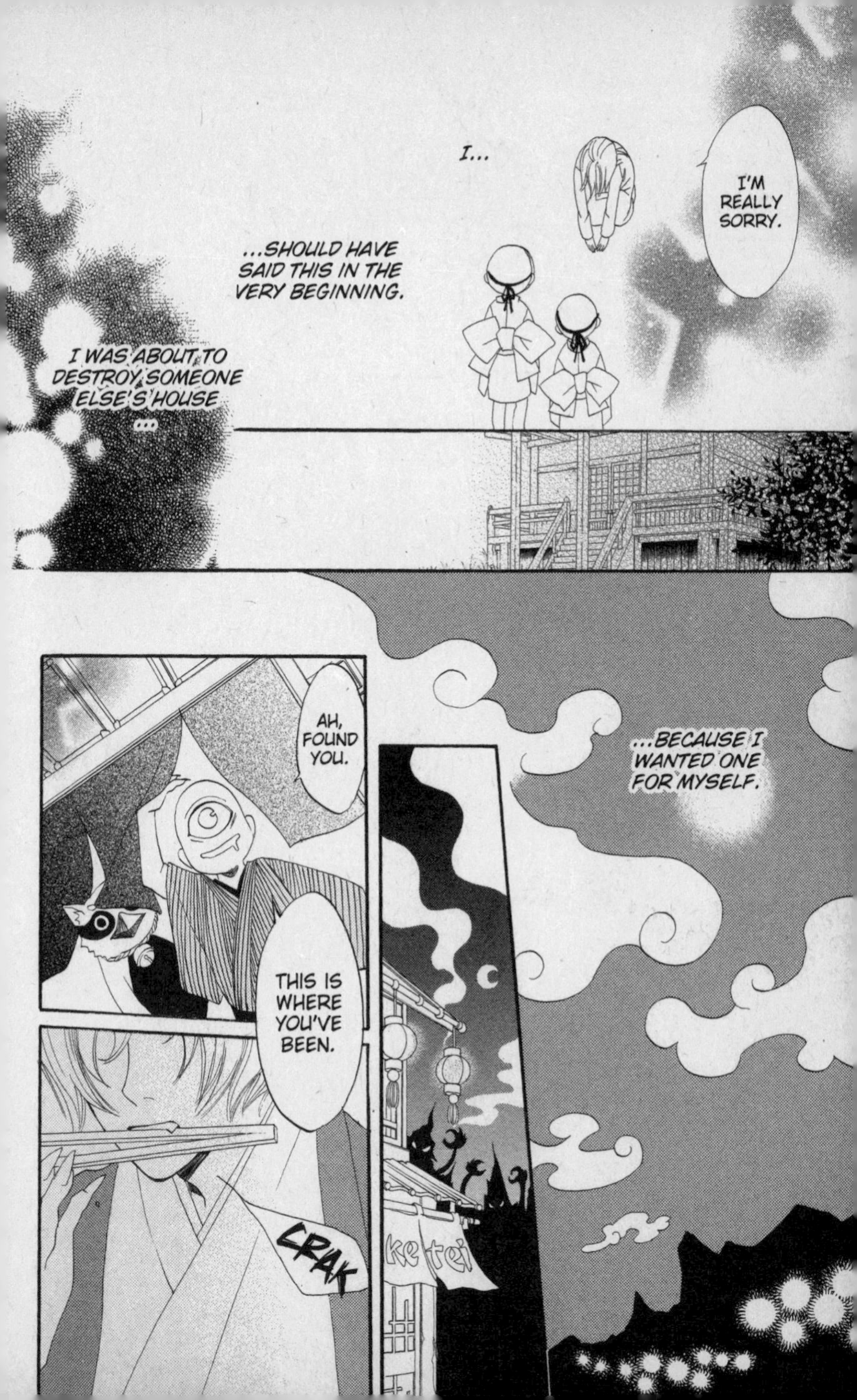
I'M REALLY SORRY.
I...
...SHOULD HAVE SAID THIS IN THE VERY BEGINNING.
I WAS ABOUT TO DESTROY SOMEONE ELSE'S HOUSE ...
...BECAUSE I WANTED ONE FOR MYSELF.
ke tei
AH, FOUND YOU.
THIS IS WHERE YOU'VE BEEN.
CRAK

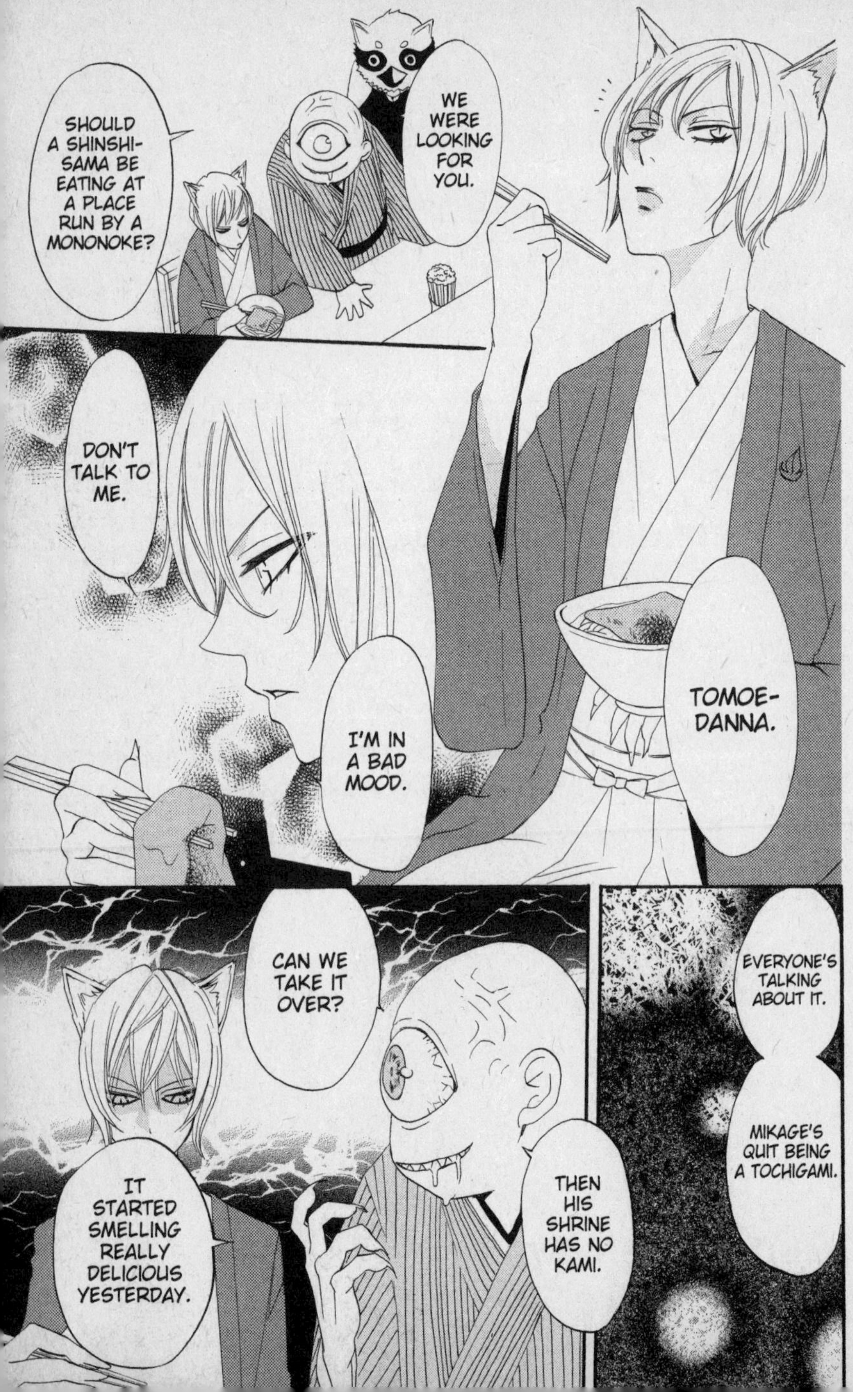
WE WERE LOOKING FOR YOU.
TOMOE-DANNA.
SHOULD A SHINSHI-SAMA BE EATING AT A PLACE RUN BY A MONONOKE?
I'M IN A BAD MOOD.
DON'T TALK TO ME.
EVERYONE'S TALKING ABOUT IT.
MIKAGE'S QUIT BEING A TOCHIGAMI.
THEN HIS SHRINE HAS NO KAMI.
CAN WE TAKE IT OVER?
IT STARTED SMELLING REALLY DELICIOUS YESTERDAY.

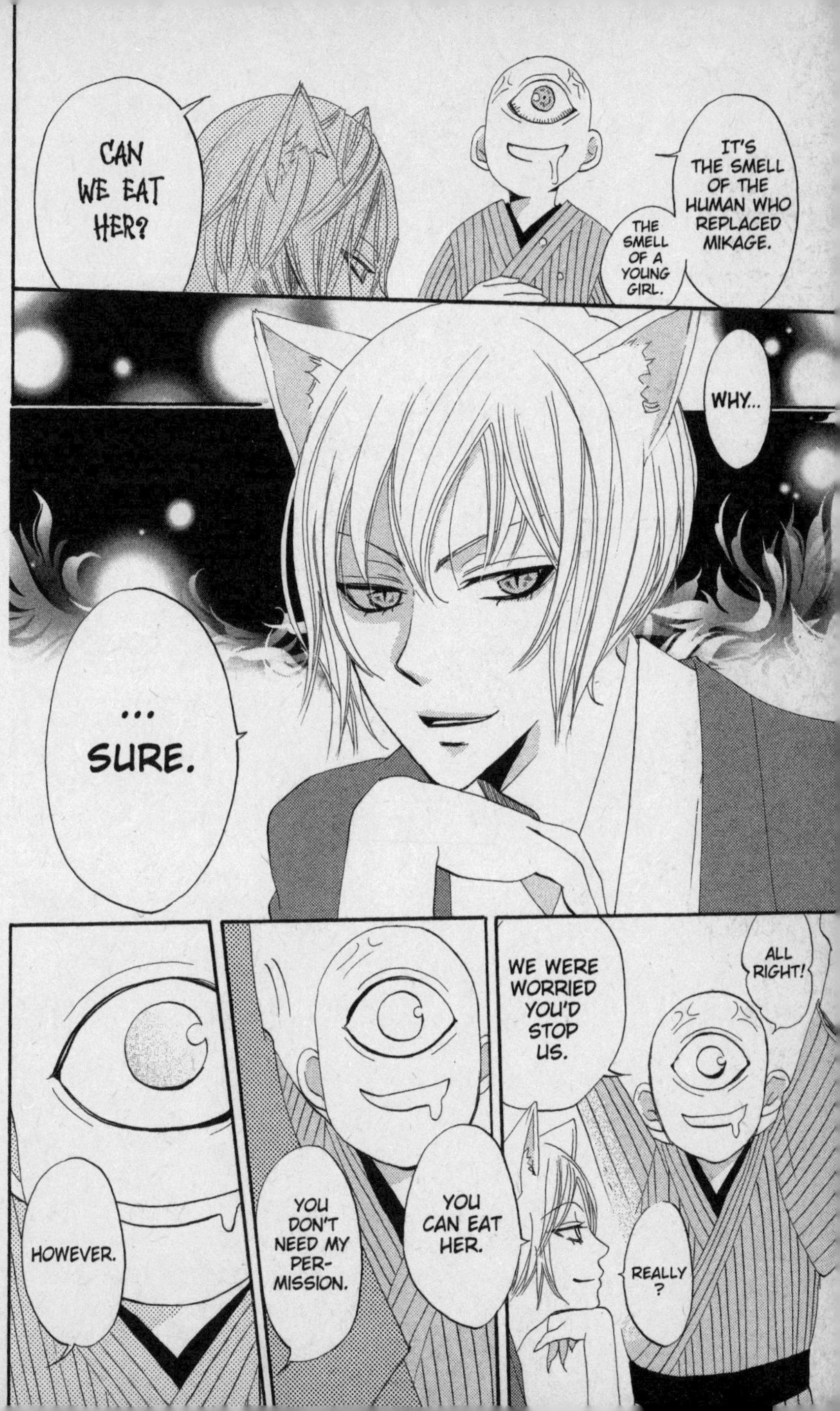
IT'S THE SMELL OF THE HUMAN WHO REPLACED MIKAGE.
THE SMELL OF A YOUNG GIRL.
CAN WE EAT HER?
WHY...
... SURE.
ALL RIGHT!
WE WERE WORRIED YOU'D STOP US.
REALLY?
YOU CAN EAT HER.
YOU DON'T NEED MY PER-MISSION.
HOWEVER.

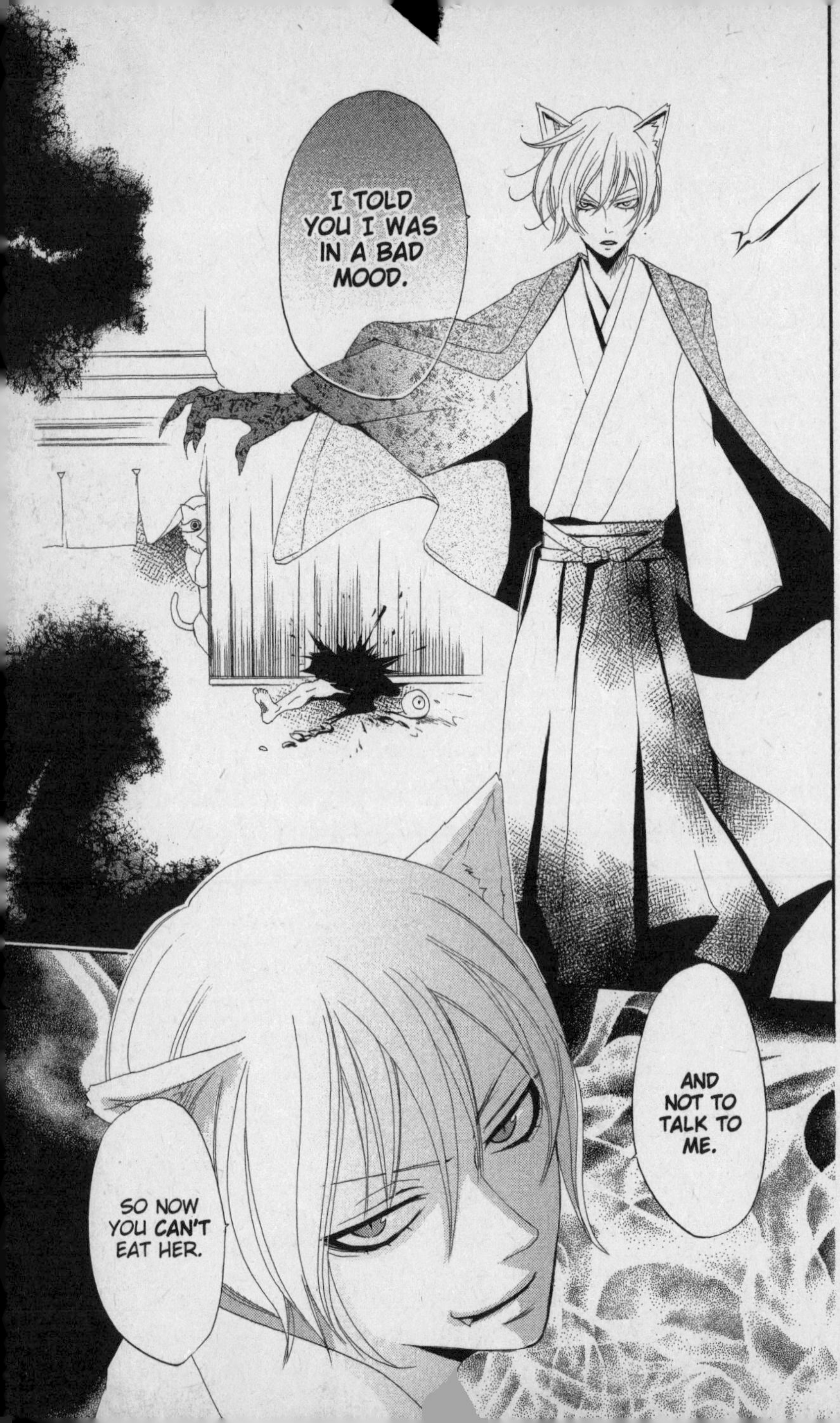
I TOLD YOU I WAS IN A BAD MOOD.
AND NOT TO TALK TO ME.
SO NOW YOU CAN'T EAT HER.

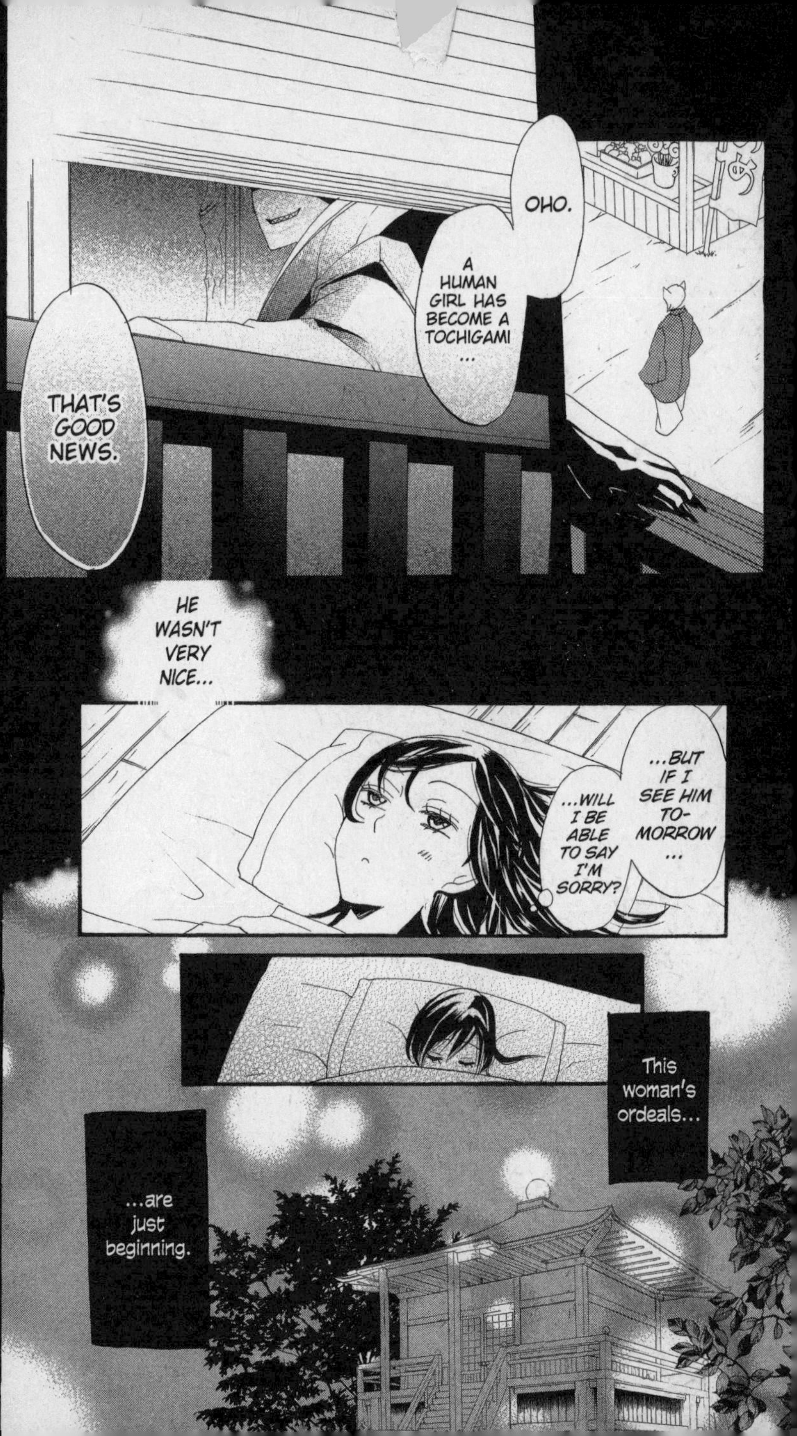
OHO.
A HUMAN GIRL HAS BECOME A TOCHIGAMI...
THAT'S GOOD NEWS.
HE WASN'T VERY NICE...
...BUT IF I SEE HIM TO-MORROW...
...WILL I BE ABLE TO SAY I'M SORRY?
This woman's ordeals...
...are just beginning.

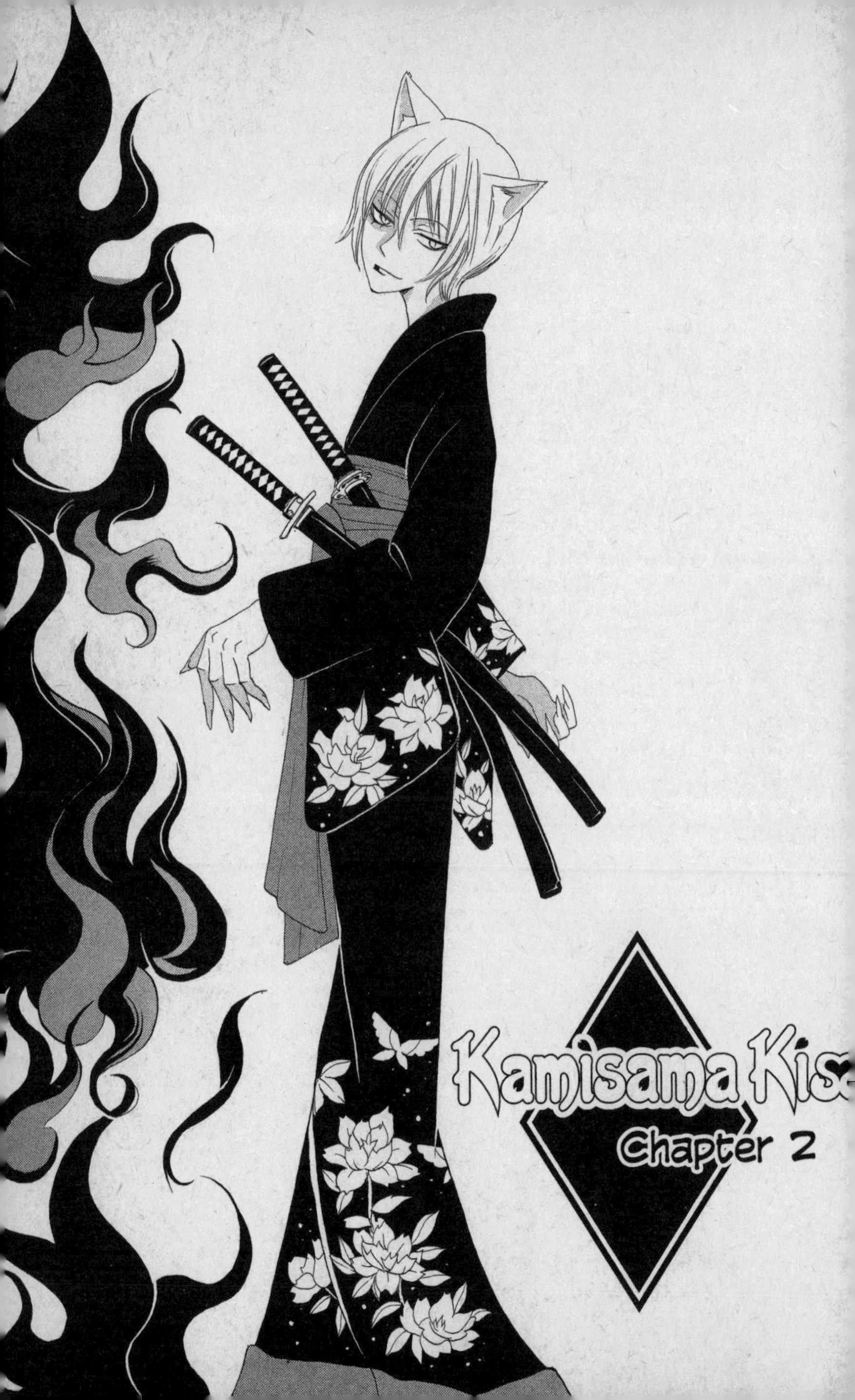
Kamisama Kis
Chapter 2

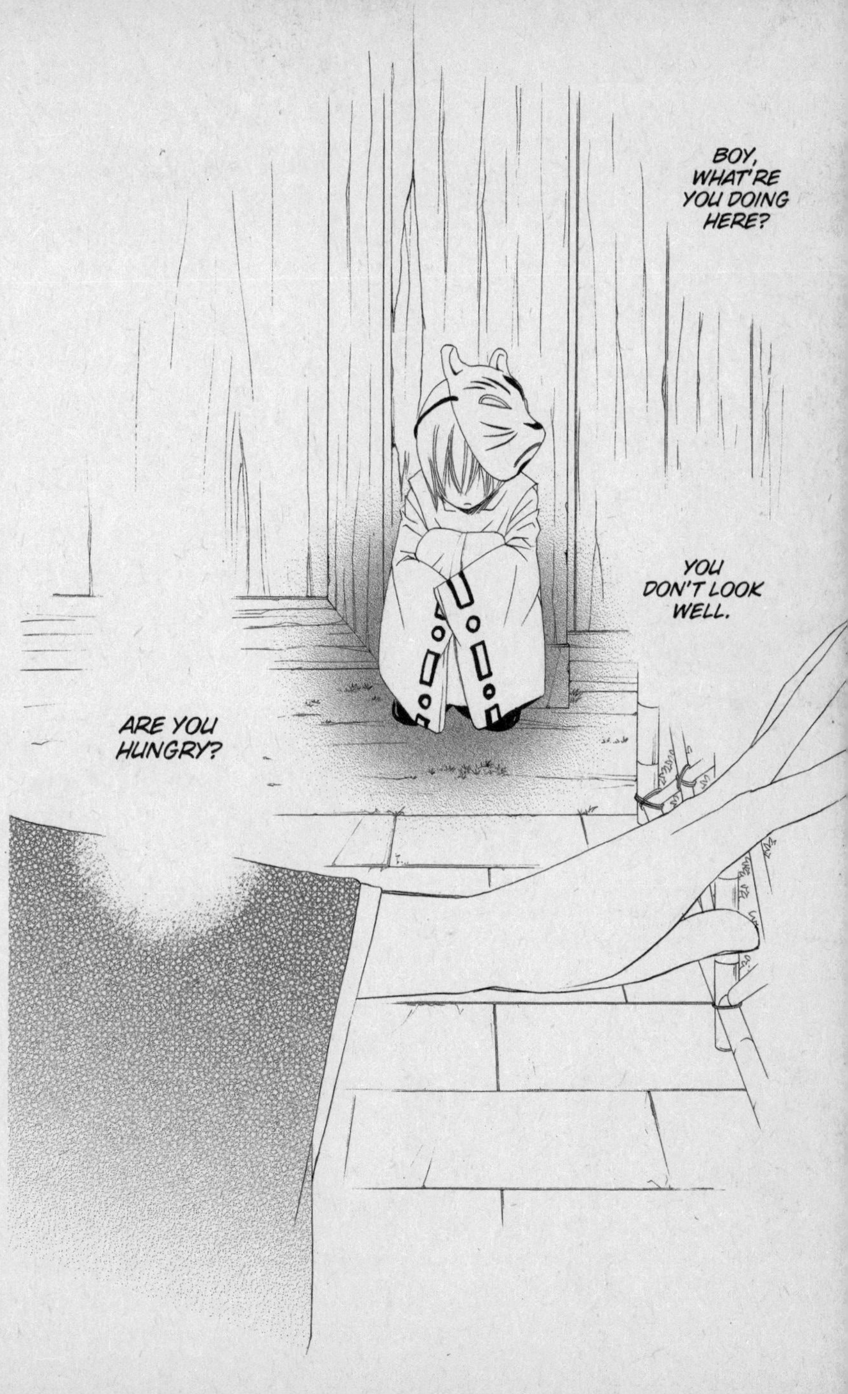
BOY, WHAT'RE YOU DOING HERE?
YOU DON'T LOOK WELL.
ARE YOU HUNGRY?

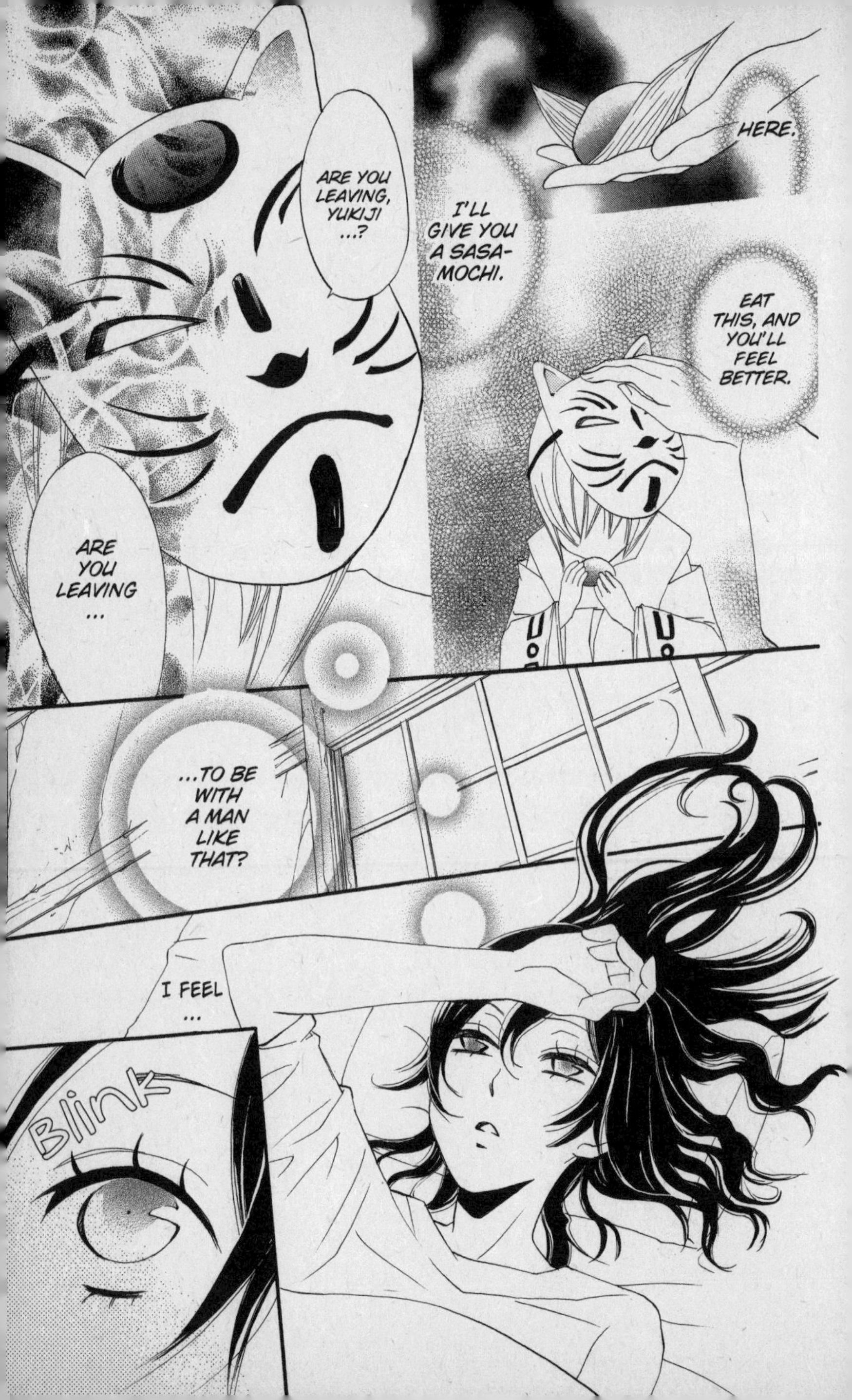
HERE.
I'LL GIVE YOU A SASA-MOCHI.
EAT THIS, AND YOU'LL FEEL BETTER.
ARE YOU LEAVING, YUKIJI ...?
ARE YOU LEAVING ...
...TO BE WITH A MAN LIKE THAT?
I FEEL ...
Blink

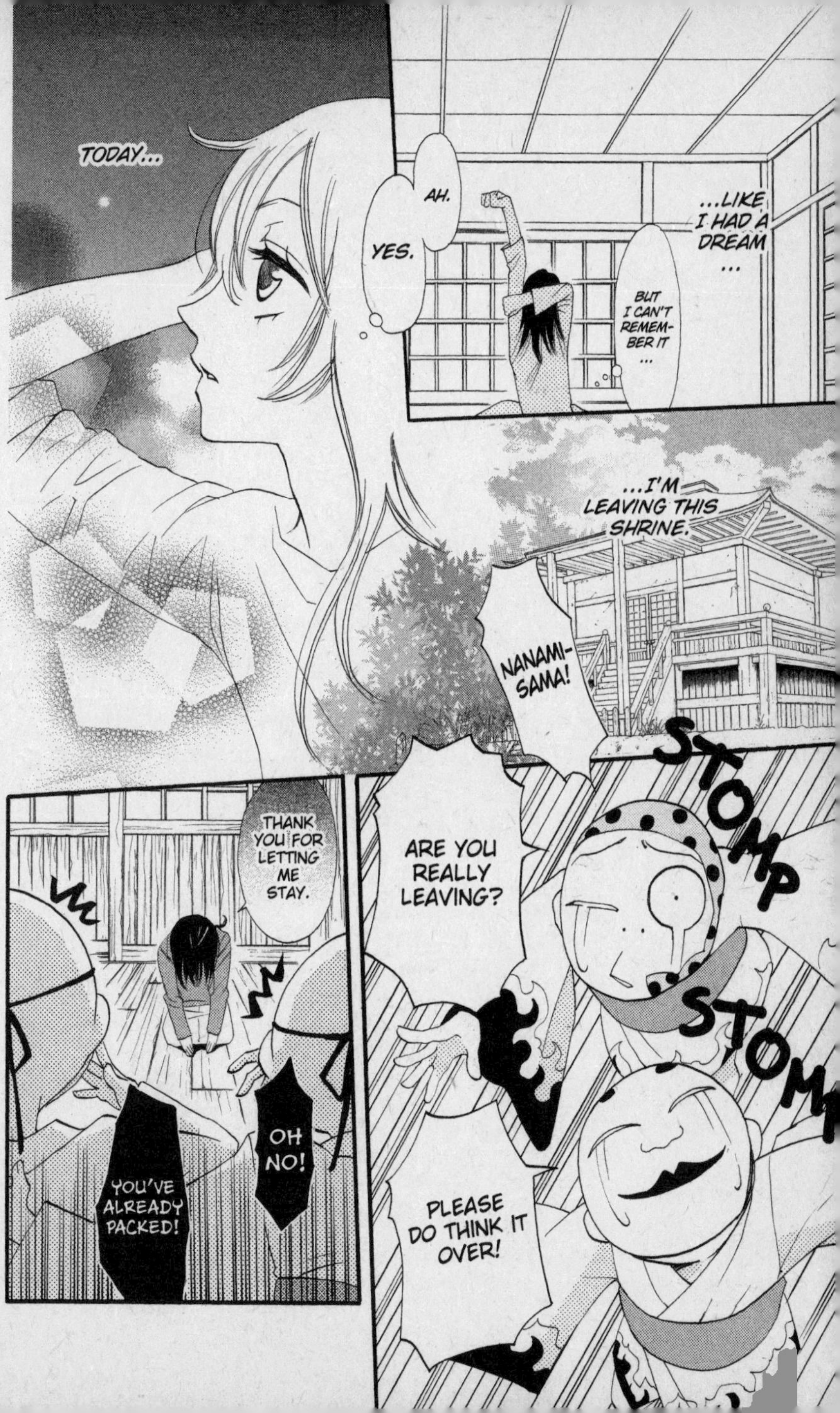
...LIKE I HAD A DREAM ...
BUT I CAN'T REMEMBER IT ...
AH.
YES.
...I'M LEAVING THIS SHRINE.
NANAMI-SAMA!
TODAY...
STOMP
STOMP
ARE YOU REALLY LEAVING?
PLEASE DO THINK IT OVER!
THANK YOU FOR LETTING ME STAY.
OH NO!
YOU'VE ALREADY PACKED!

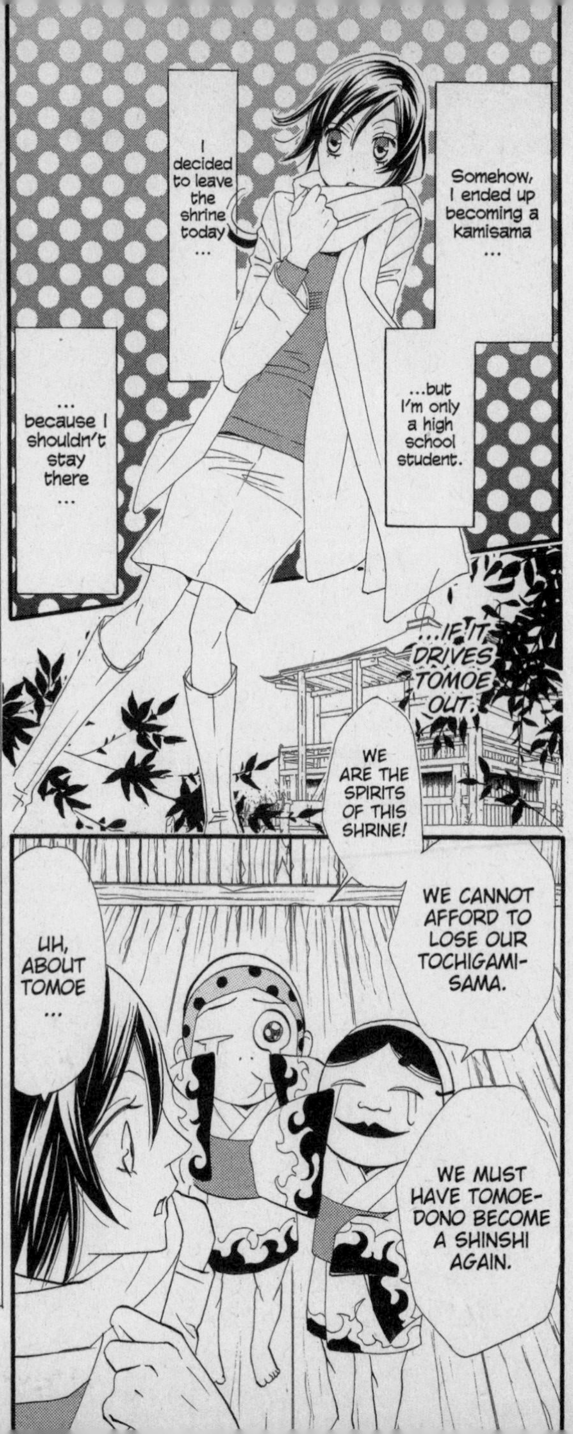
Somehow, I ended up becoming a kamisama ...
...but I'm only a high school student.
I decided to leave the shrine today ...
... because I shouldn't stay there ...
...IF IT DRIVES TOMOE OUT.
WE ARE THE SPIRITS OF THIS SHRINE!
WE CANNOT AFFORD TO LOSE OUR TOCHIGAMI-SAMA.
UH, ABOUT TOMOE ...
WE MUST HAVE TOMOE-DONO BECOME A SHINSHI AGAIN.

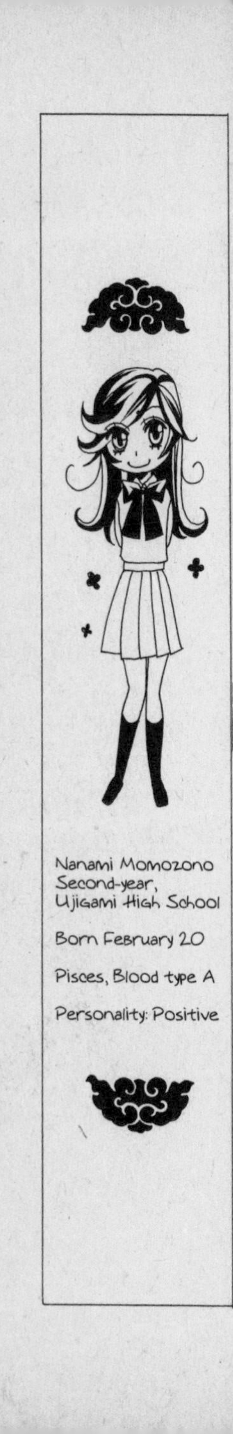

Nanami Momozono
Second-year,
Ujigami High School

Born February 20

Pisces, Blood type A

Personality: Positive

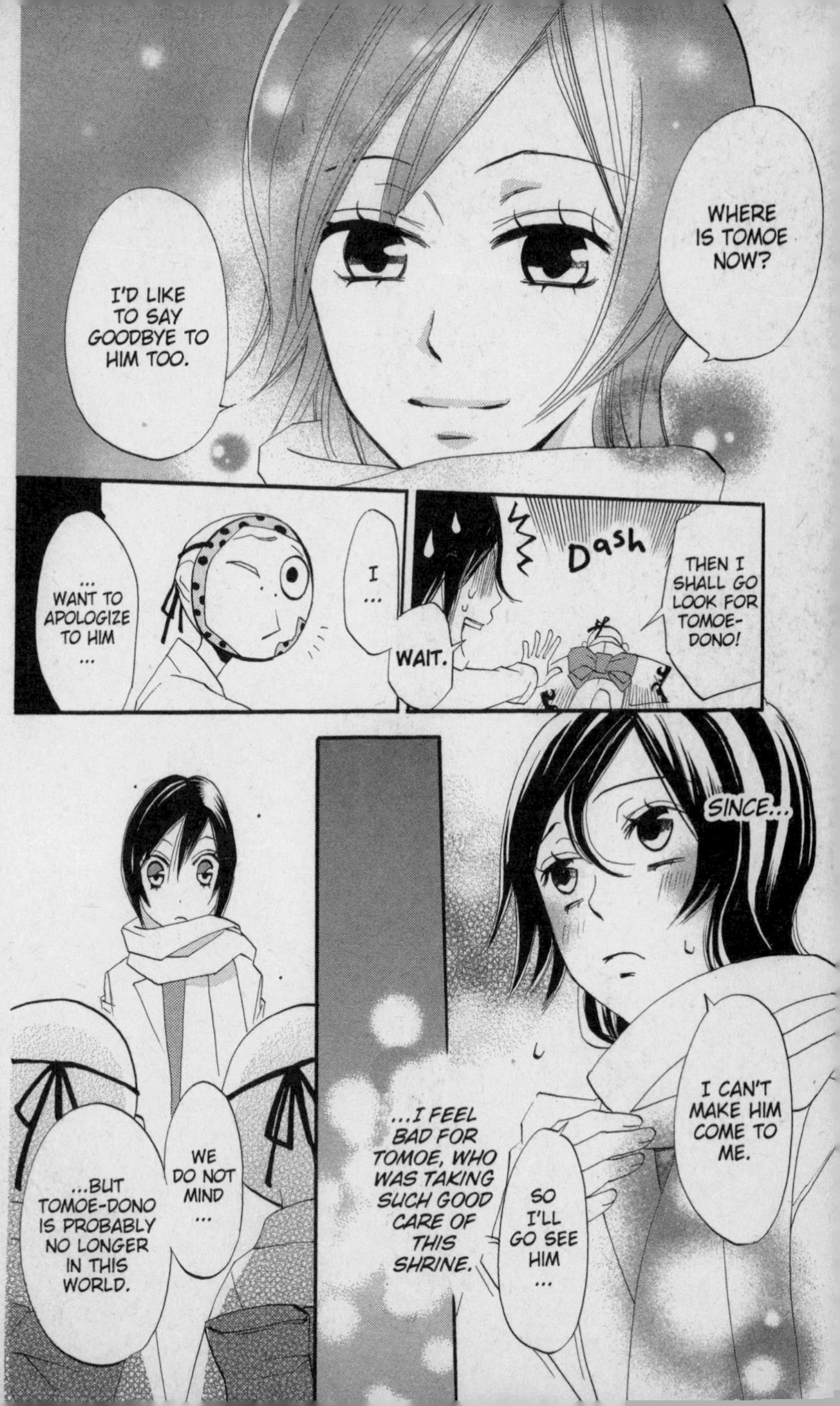
WHERE IS TOMOE NOW?
I'D LIKE TO SAY GOODBYE TO HIM TOO.
THEN I SHALL GO LOOK FOR TOMOE-DONO!
Dash
WAIT.
I ...
... WANT TO APOLOGIZE TO HIM ...
SINCE...
I CAN'T MAKE HIM COME TO ME.
SO I'LL GO SEE HIM ...
...I FEEL BAD FOR TOMOE, WHO WAS TAKING SUCH GOOD CARE OF THIS SHRINE.
WE DO NOT MIND ...
...BUT TOMOE-DONO IS PROBABLY NO LONGER IN THIS WORLD.

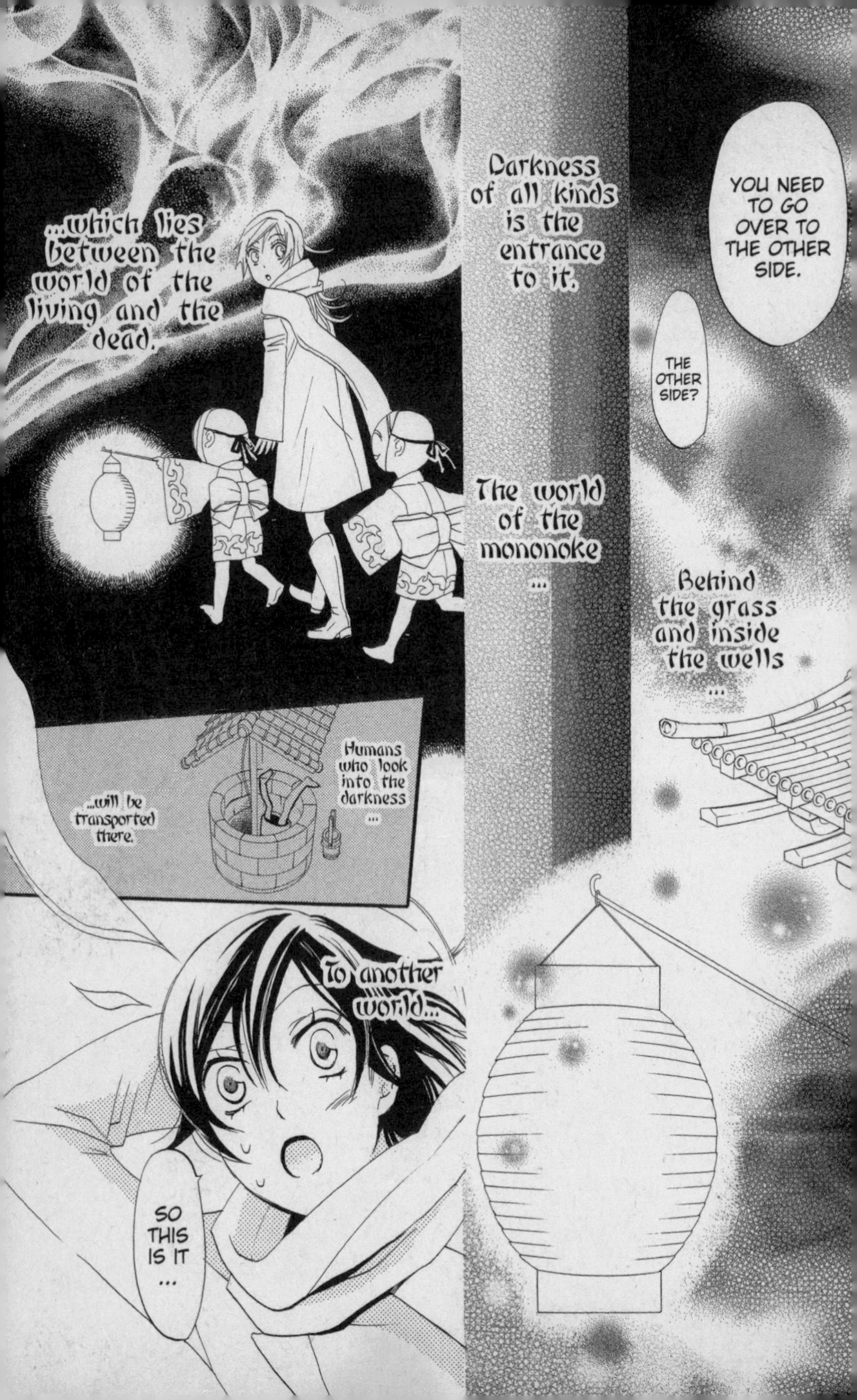

YOU NEED TO GO OVER TO THE OTHER SIDE.
THE OTHER SIDE?
Darkness of all kinds is the entrance to it.
The world of the mononoke...
Behind the grass and inside the wells...
...which lies between the world of the living and the dead.
Humans who look into the darkness...
...will be transported there.
To another world...
SO THIS IS IT...

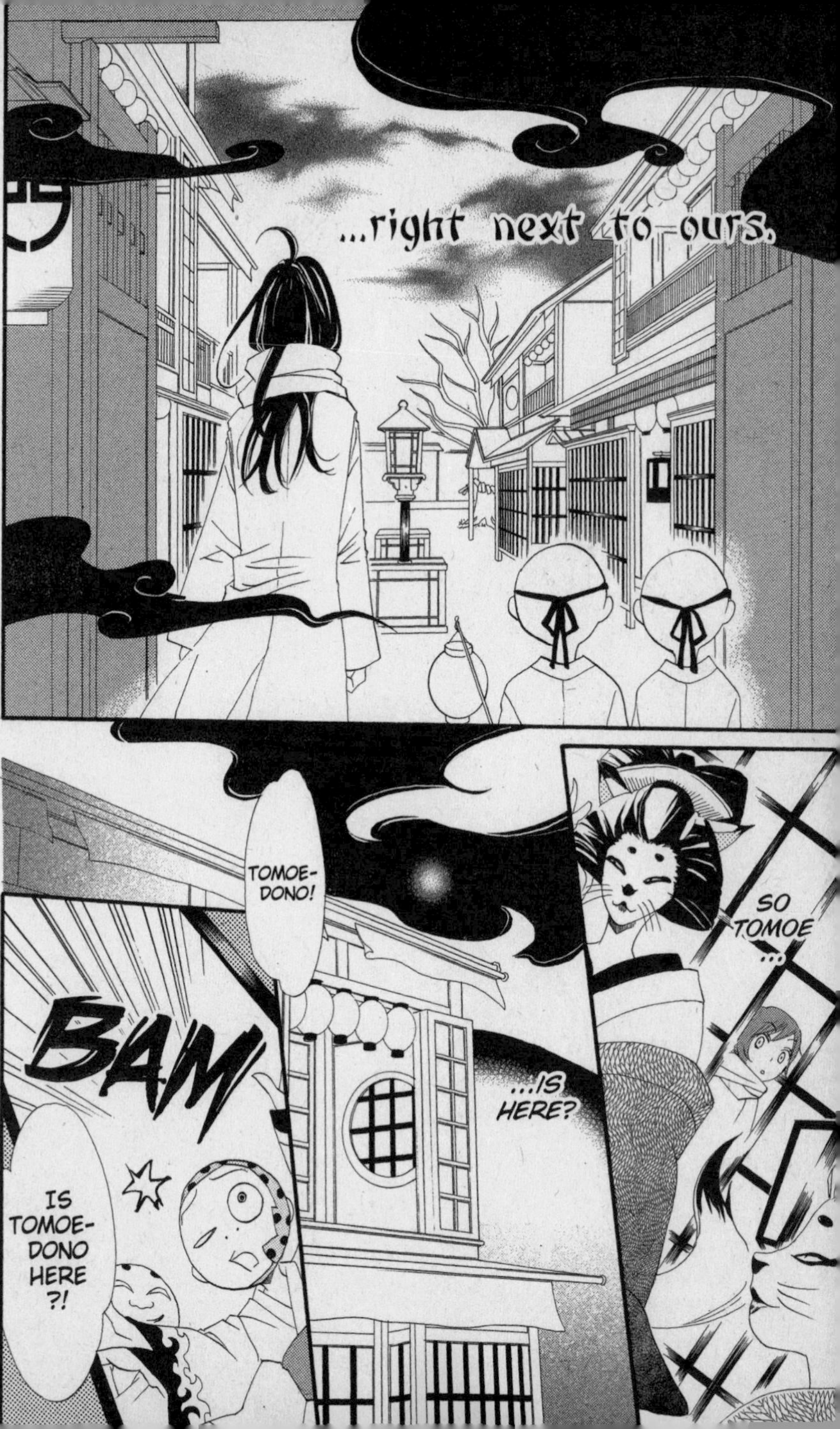
...right next to ours.
SO TOMOE ...
...IS HERE?
TOMOE-DONO!
BAM
IS TOMOE-DONO HERE?!

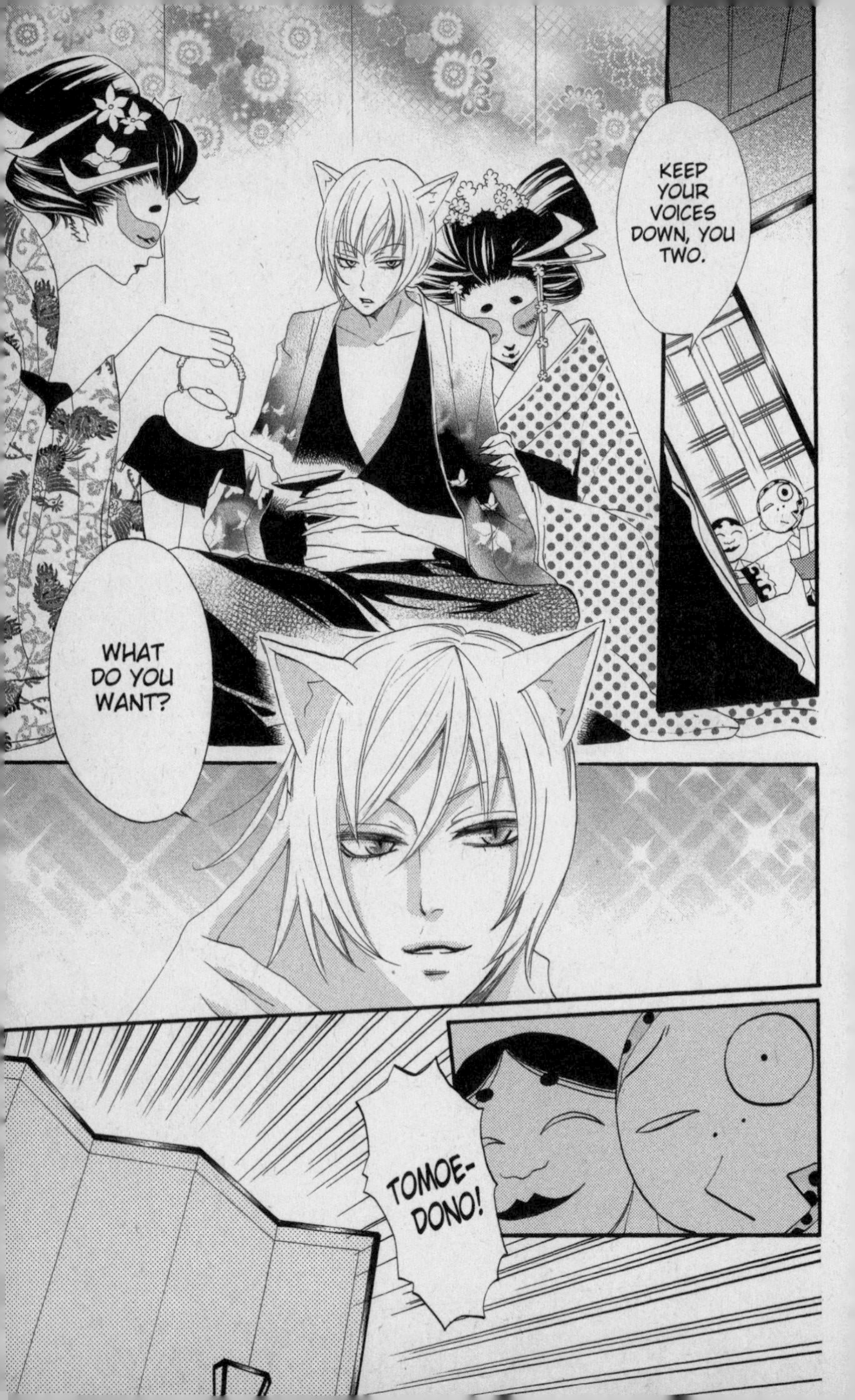
KEEP YOUR VOICES DOWN, YOU TWO.
WHAT DO YOU WANT?
TOMOE-DONO!

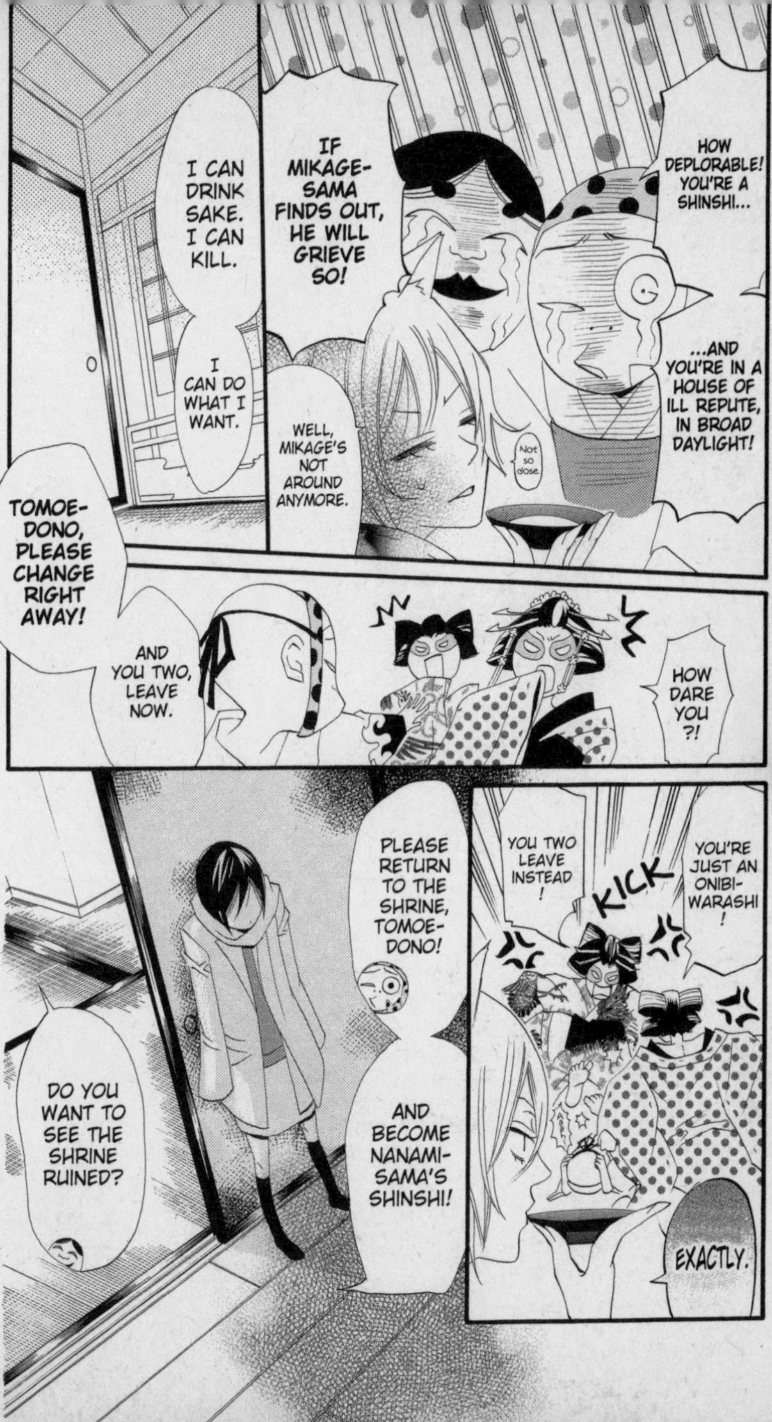
HOW DEPLORABLE! YOU'RE A SHINSHI...
...AND YOU'RE IN A HOUSE OF ILL REPUTE, IN BROAD DAYLIGHT!
IF MIKAGE-SAMA FINDS OUT, HE WILL GRIEVE SO!
Not so close.
WELL, MIKAGE'S NOT AROUND ANYMORE.
I CAN DRINK SAKE. I CAN KILL.
I CAN DO WHAT I WANT.
TOMOE-DONO, PLEASE CHANGE RIGHT AWAY!
HOW DARE YOU?!
AND YOU TWO, LEAVE NOW.
YOU'RE JUST AN ONIBI-WARASHI!
YOU TWO LEAVE INSTEAD!
KICK
EXACTLY.
PLEASE RETURN TO THE SHRINE, TOMOE-DONO!
AND BECOME NANAMI-SAMA'S SHINSHI!
DO YOU WANT TO SEE THE SHRINE RUINED?

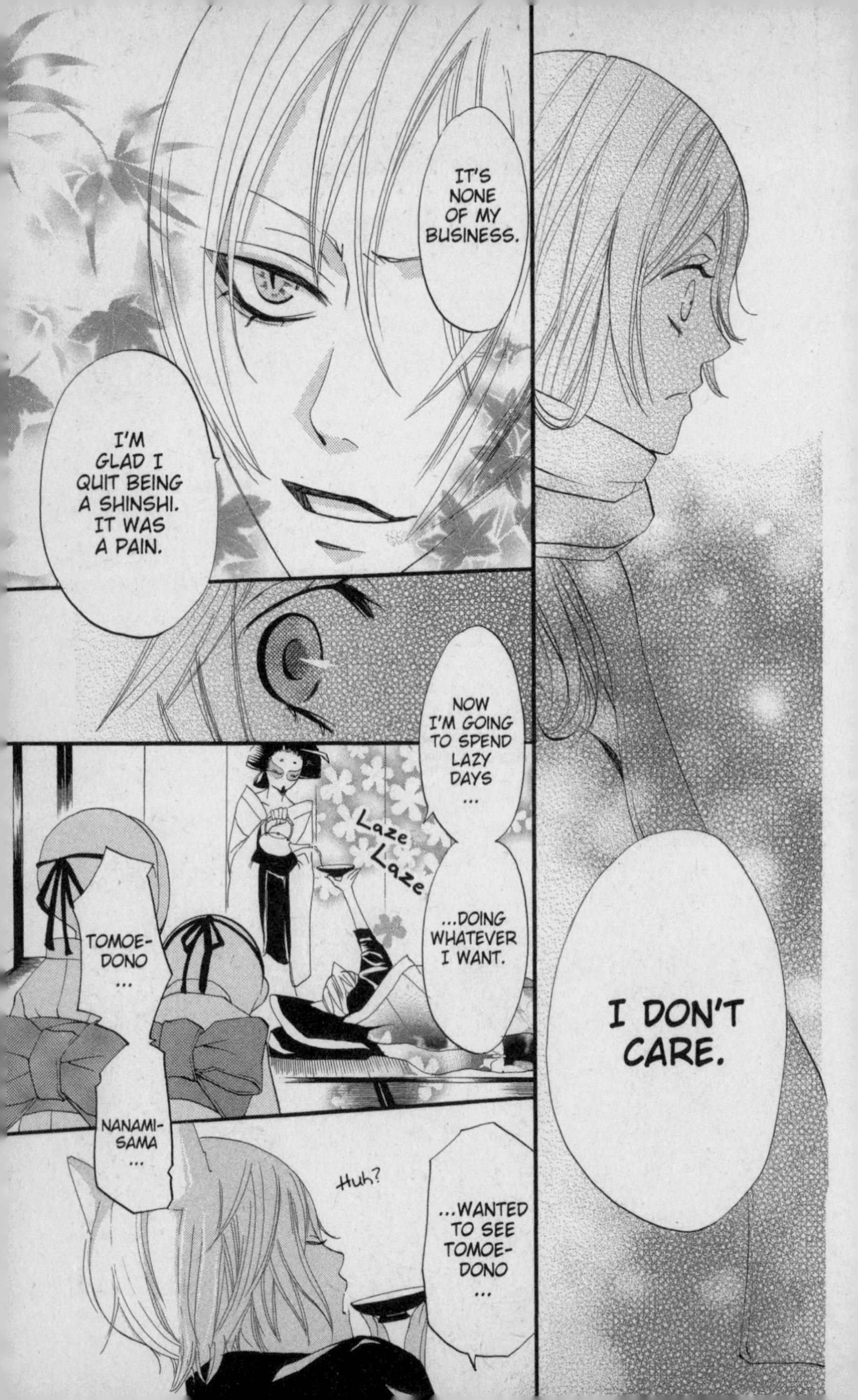
I DON'T CARE.
IT'S NONE OF MY BUSINESS.
I'M GLAD I QUIT BEING A SHINSHI. IT WAS A PAIN.
NOW I'M GOING TO SPEND LAZY DAYS ...
...DOING WHATEVER I WANT.
Laze Laze
TOMOE-DONO ...
NANAMI-SAMA ...
...WANTED TO SEE TOMOE-DONO ...
Huh?

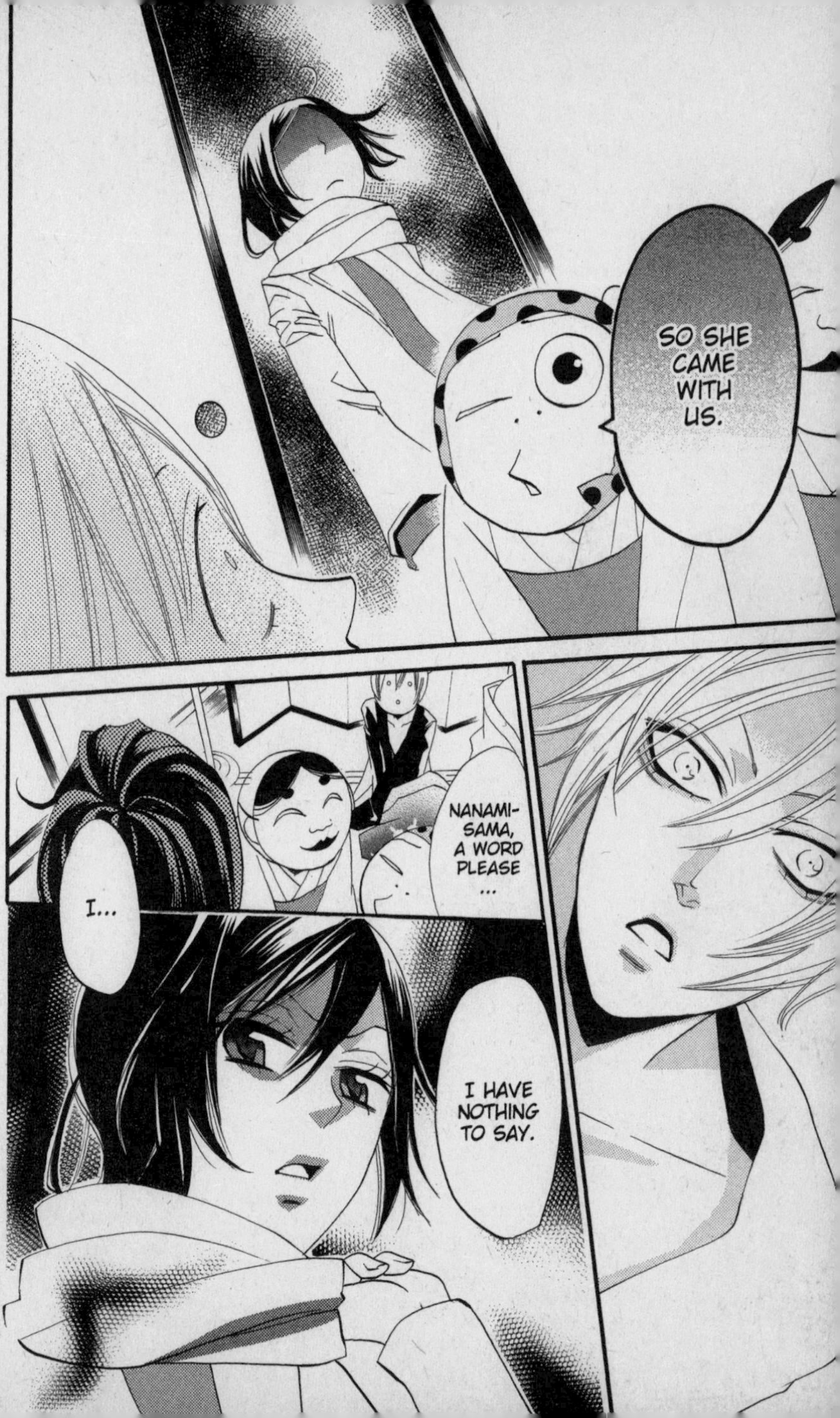
SO SHE CAME WITH US.
NANAMI-SAMA, A WORD PLEASE ...
I...
I HAVE NOTHING TO SAY.

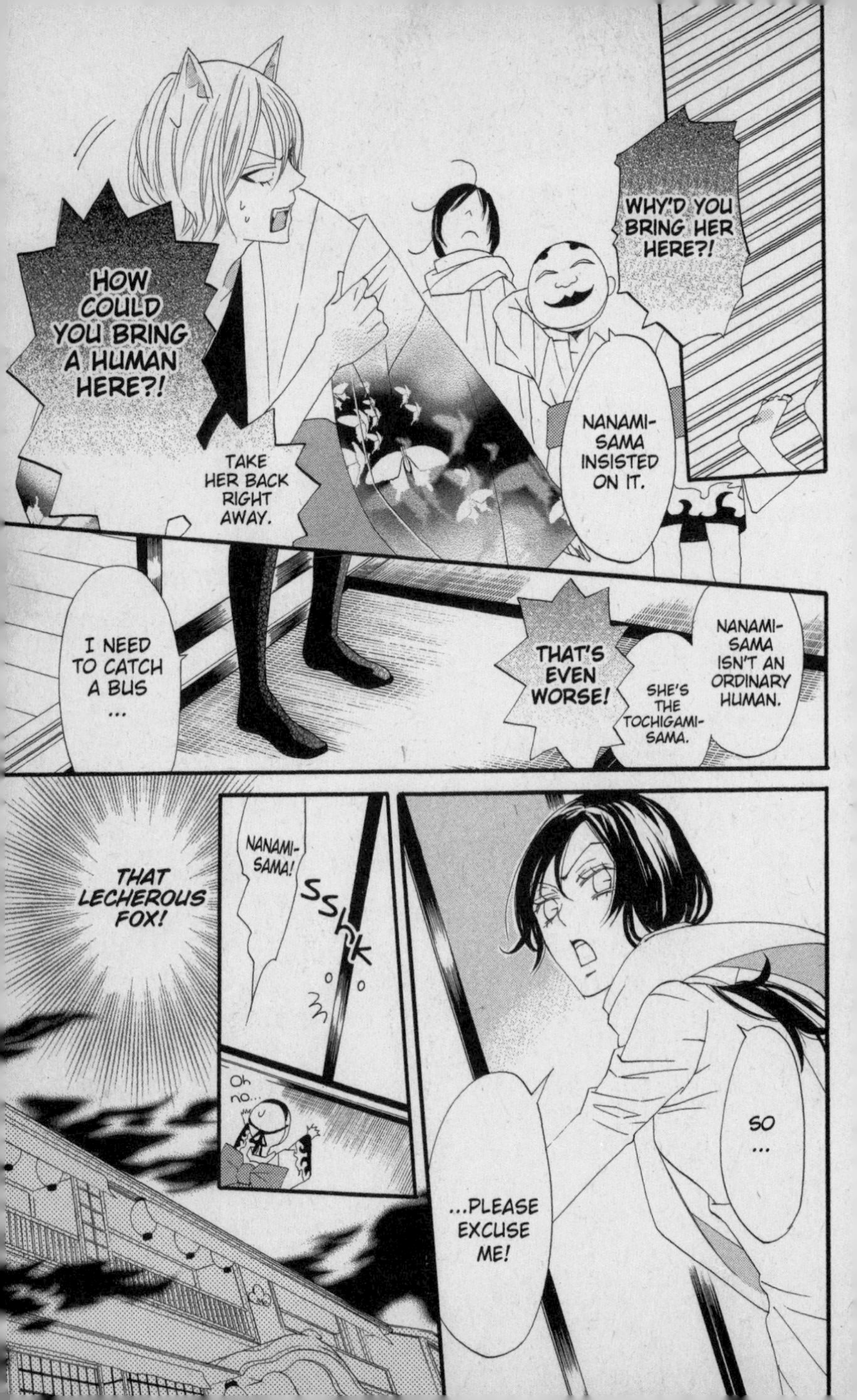
WHY'D YOU BRING HER HERE?!
HOW COULD YOU BRING A HUMAN HERE?!
NANAMI-SAMA INSISTED ON IT.
TAKE HER BACK RIGHT AWAY.
NANAMI-SAMA ISN'T AN ORDINARY HUMAN.
SHE'S THE TOCHIGAMI-SAMA.
THAT'S EVEN WORSE!
I NEED TO CATCH A BUS ...
SO ...
...PLEASE EXCUSE ME!
NANAMI-SAMA!
SSHK
Oh no...
THAT LECHEROUS FOX!

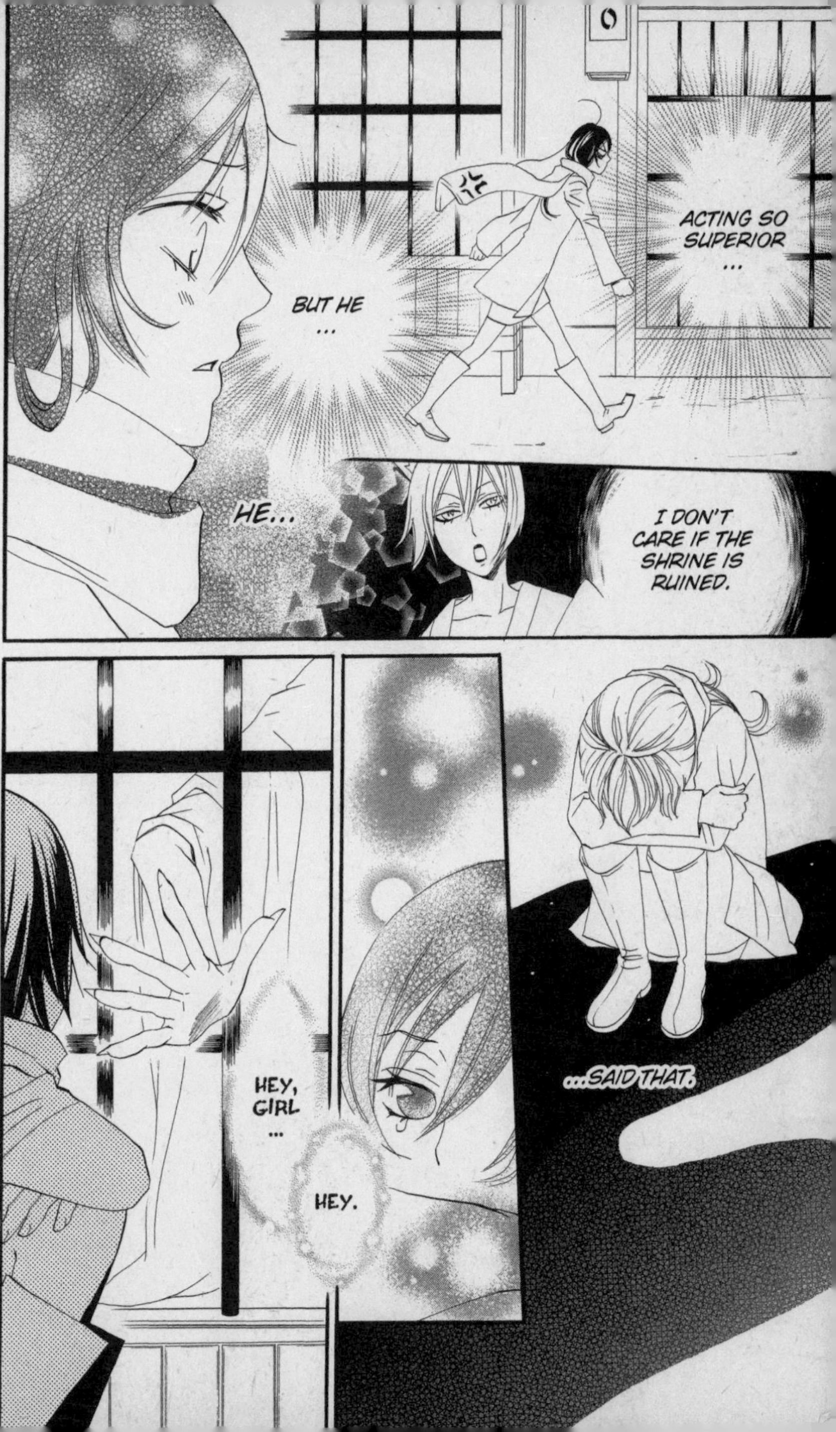
ACTING SO SUPERIOR ...
BUT HE ...
I DON'T CARE IF THE SHRINE IS RUINED.
HE...
...SAID THAT.
HEY, GIRL ...
HEY.

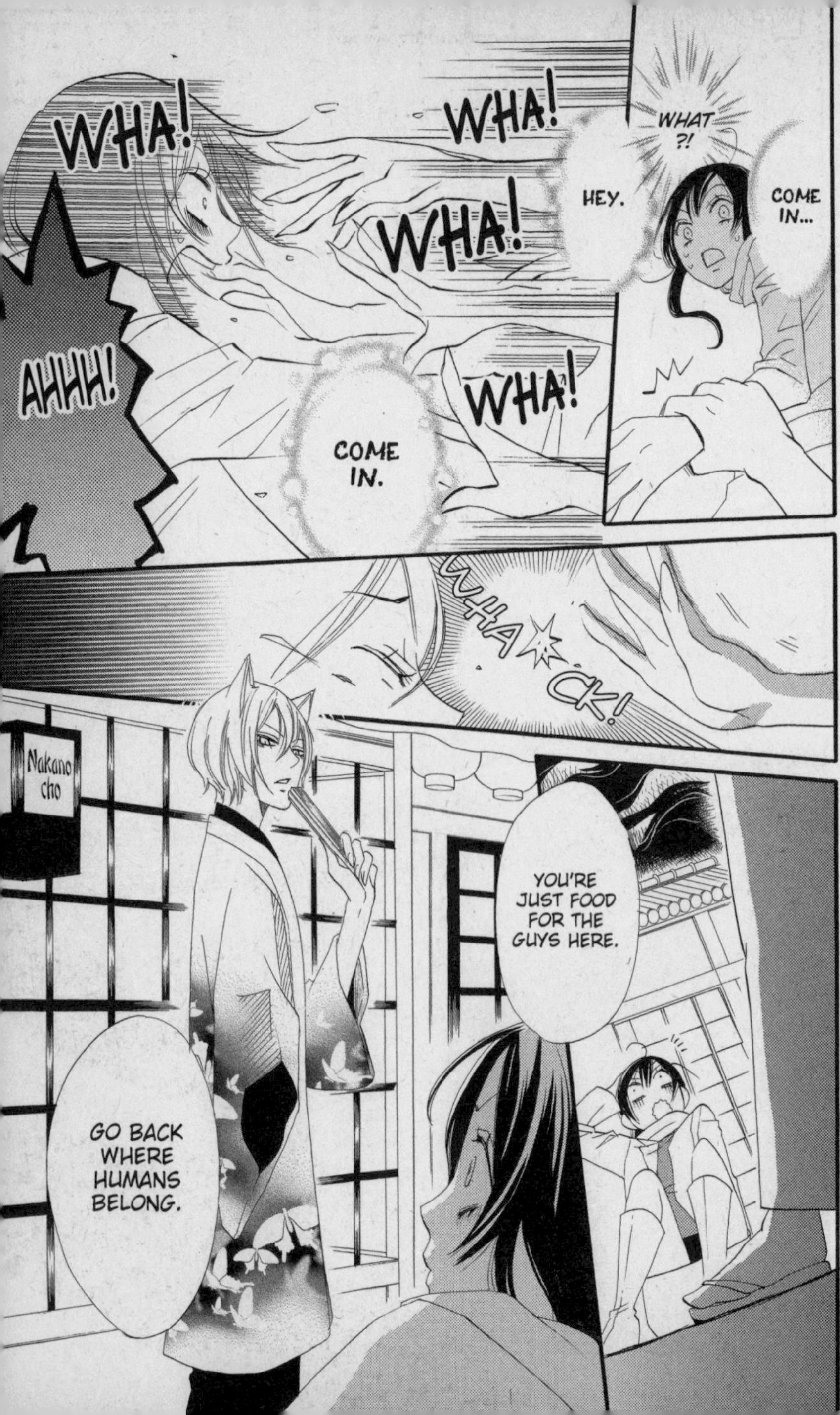
WHAT ?!
COME IN...
HEY.
WHA!
WHA!
WHA!
WHA!
AHHH!
COME IN.
WHACK!
YOU'RE JUST FOOD FOR THE GUYS HERE.
Nakano cho
GO BACK WHERE HUMANS BELONG.

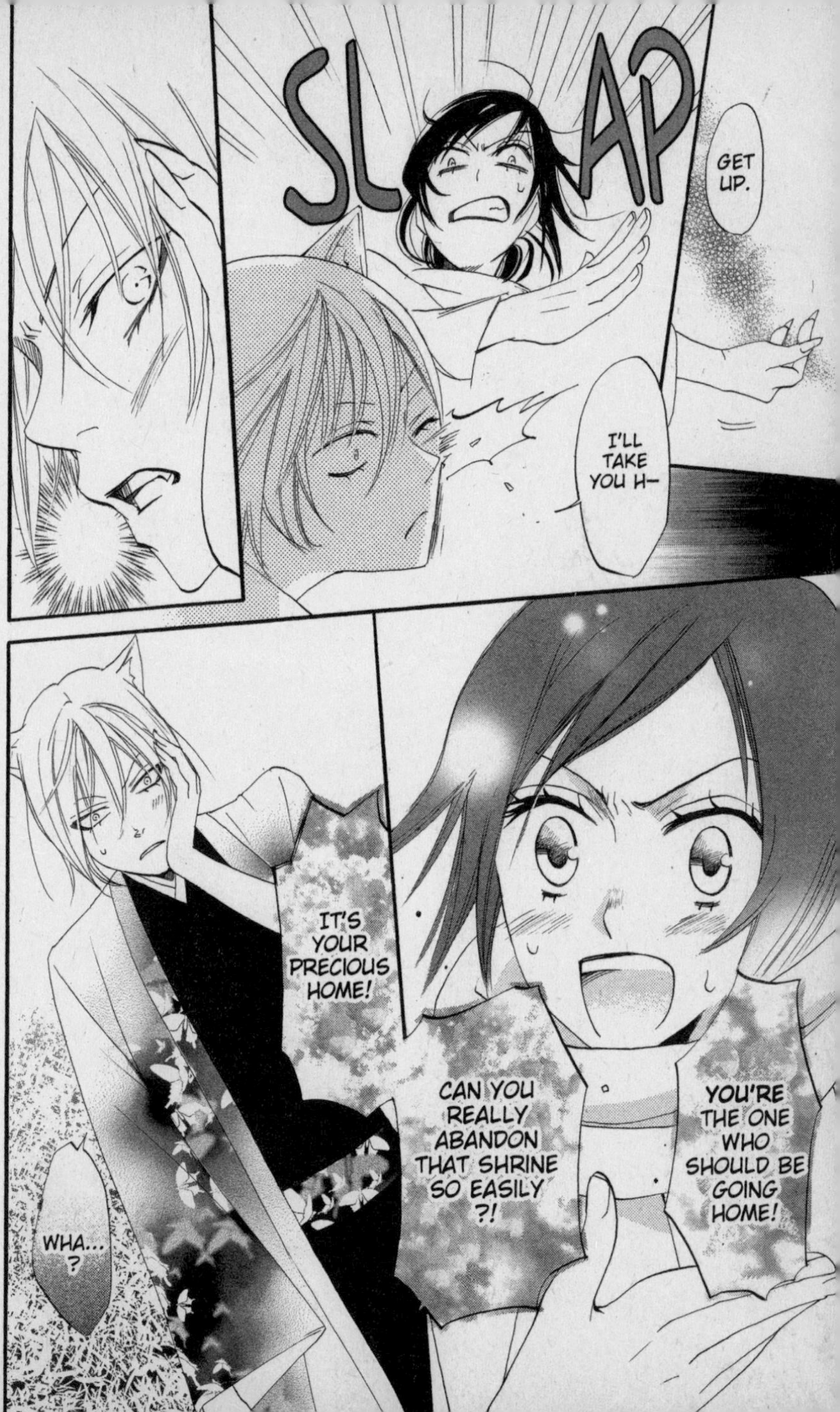
GET UP.
SLAP
I'LL TAKE YOU H—
YOU'RE THE ONE WHO SHOULD BE GOING HOME!
CAN YOU REALLY ABANDON THAT SHRINE SO EASILY ?!
IT'S YOUR PRECIOUS HOME!
WHA... ?

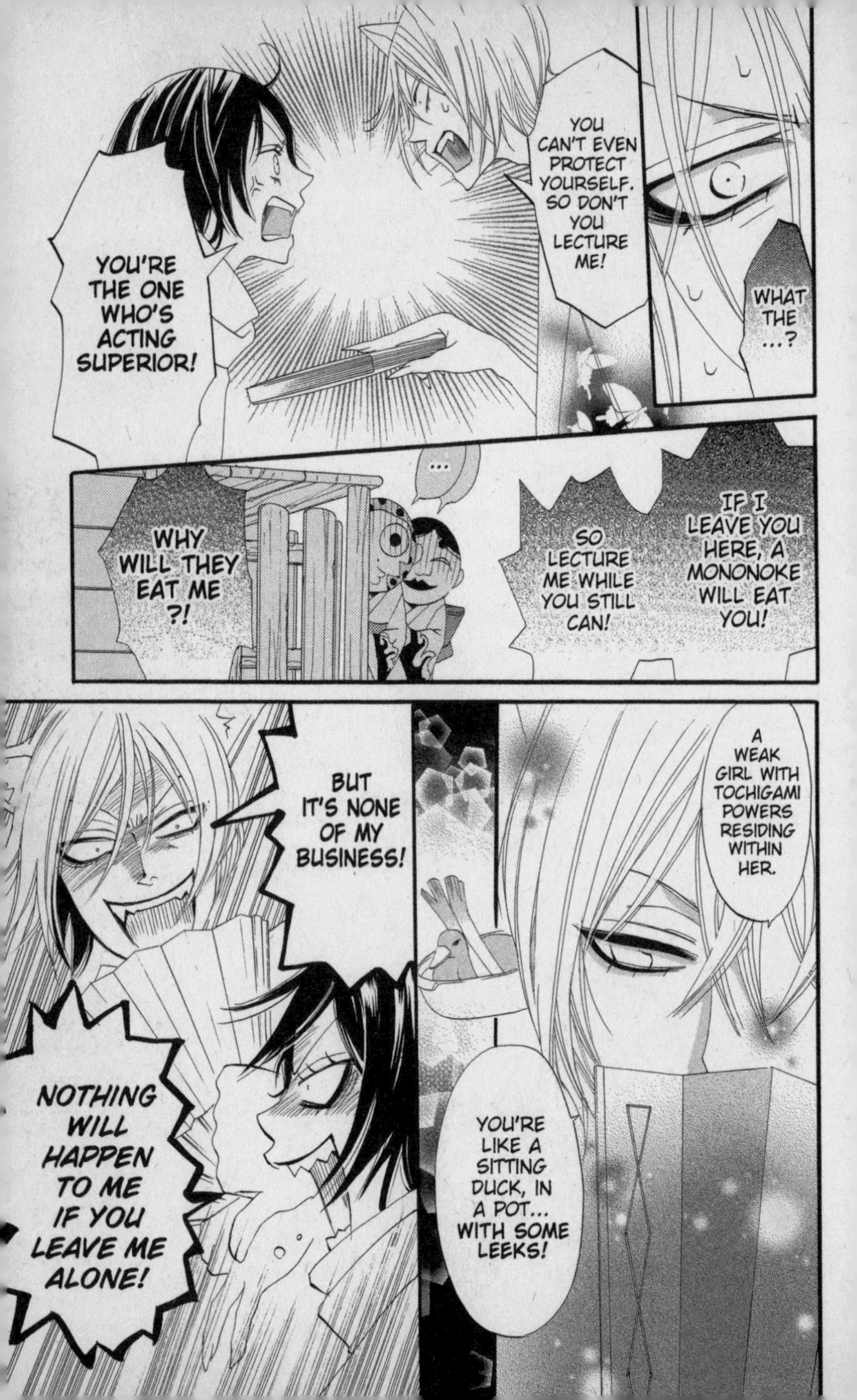
WHAT THE ...?
YOU CAN'T EVEN PROTECT YOURSELF. SO DON'T YOU LECTURE ME!
YOU'RE THE ONE WHO'S ACTING SUPERIOR!
IF I LEAVE YOU HERE, A MONONOKE WILL EAT YOU!
SO LECTURE ME WHILE YOU STILL CAN!
...
WHY WILL THEY EAT ME ?!
A WEAK GIRL WITH TOCHIGAMI POWERS RESIDING WITHIN HER.
YOU'RE LIKE A SITTING DUCK, IN A POT... WITH SOME LEEKS!
BUT IT'S NONE OF MY BUSINESS!
NOTHING WILL HAPPEN TO ME IF YOU LEAVE ME ALONE!

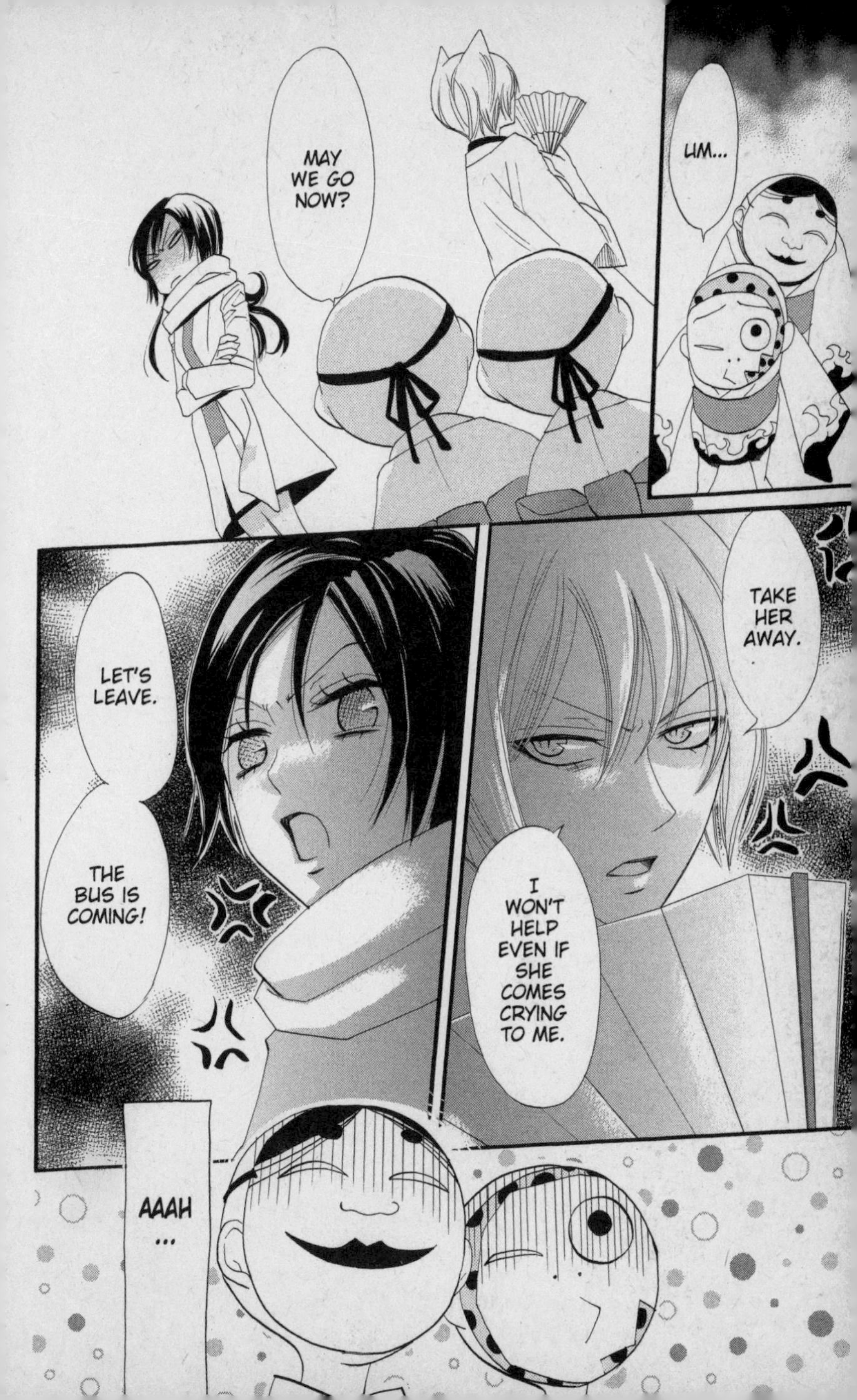
UM...
MAY WE GO NOW?
TAKE HER AWAY.
I WON'T HELP EVEN IF SHE COMES CRYING TO ME.
LET'S LEAVE.
THE BUS IS COMING!
AAAH ...

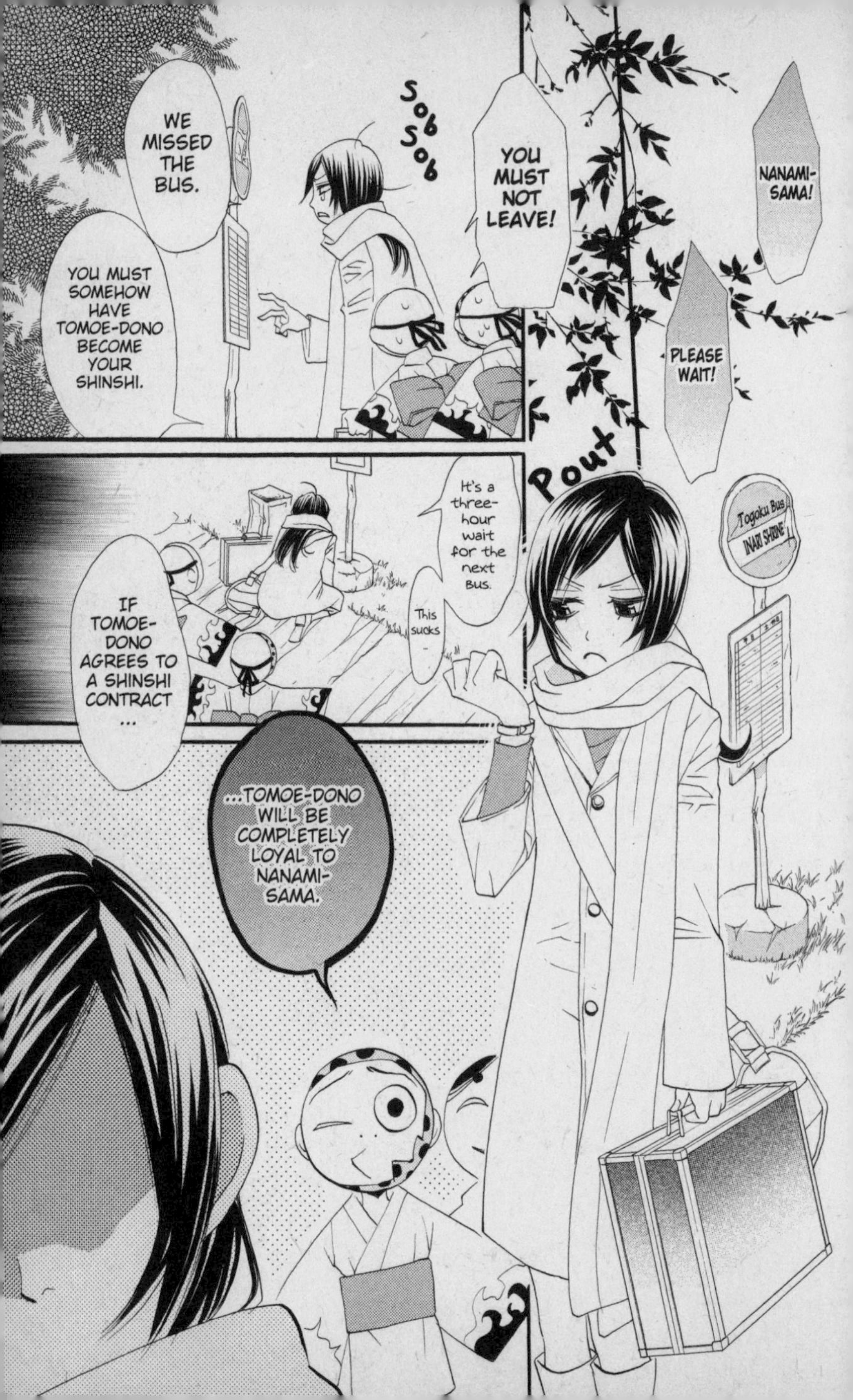

NANAMI-SAMA!
PLEASE WAIT!
YOU MUST NOT LEAVE!
Sob Sob
WE MISSED THE BUS.
YOU MUST SOMEHOW HAVE TOMOE-DONO BECOME YOUR SHINSHI.
Pout
Togoku Bus
INARI SHRINE
It's a three-hour wait for the next bus.
This sucks...
IF TOMOE-DONO AGREES TO A SHINSHI CONTRACT...
...TOMOE-DONO WILL BE COMPLETELY LOYAL TO NANAMI-SAMA.

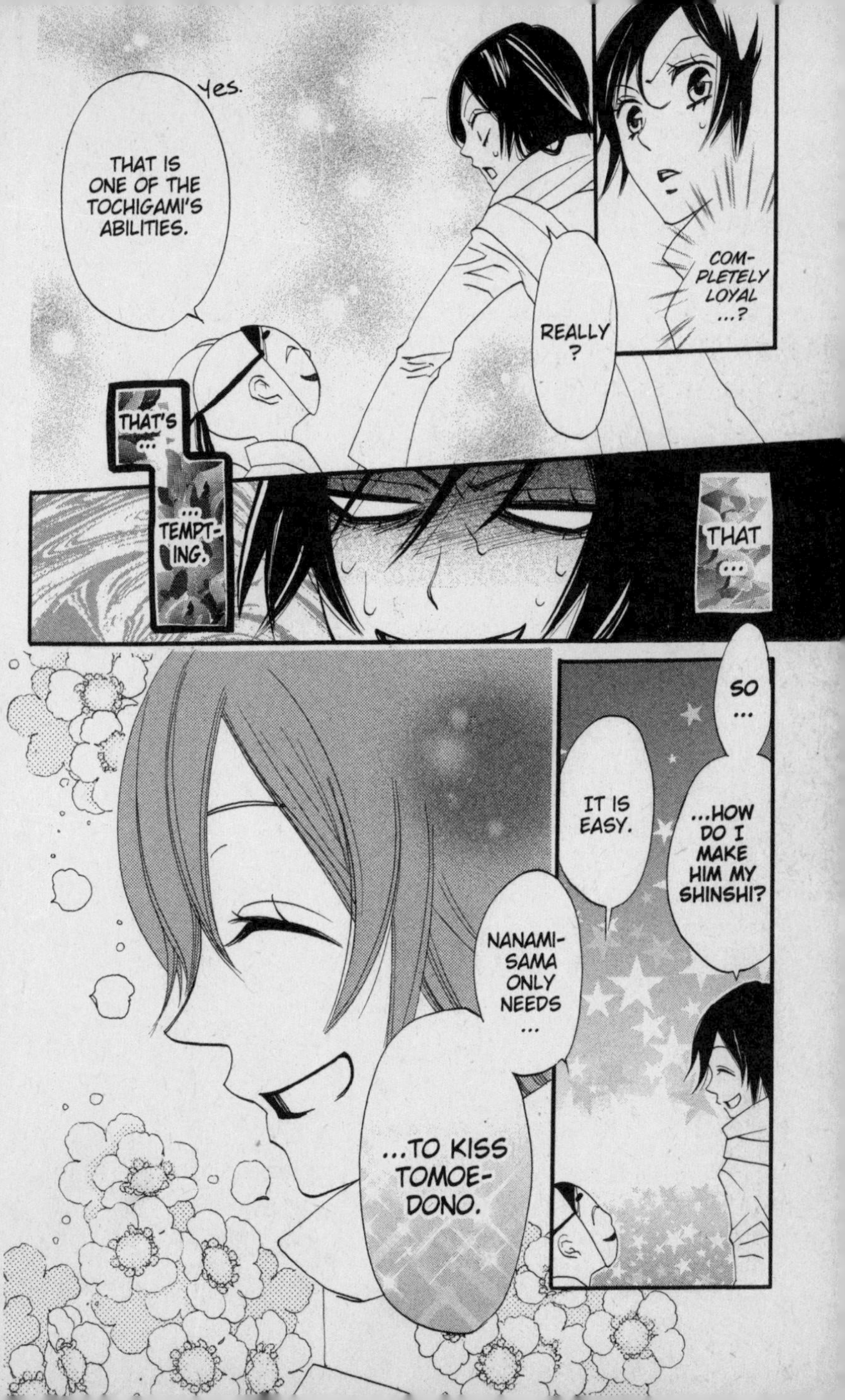
COMPLETELY LOYAL ...?
Yes.
THAT IS ONE OF THE TOCHIGAMI'S ABILITIES.
REALLY?
THAT ...
THAT'S ...
... TEMPTING.
SO ...
...HOW DO I MAKE HIM MY SHINSHI?
IT IS EASY.
NANAMI-SAMA ONLY NEEDS ...
...TO KISS TOMOE-DONO.

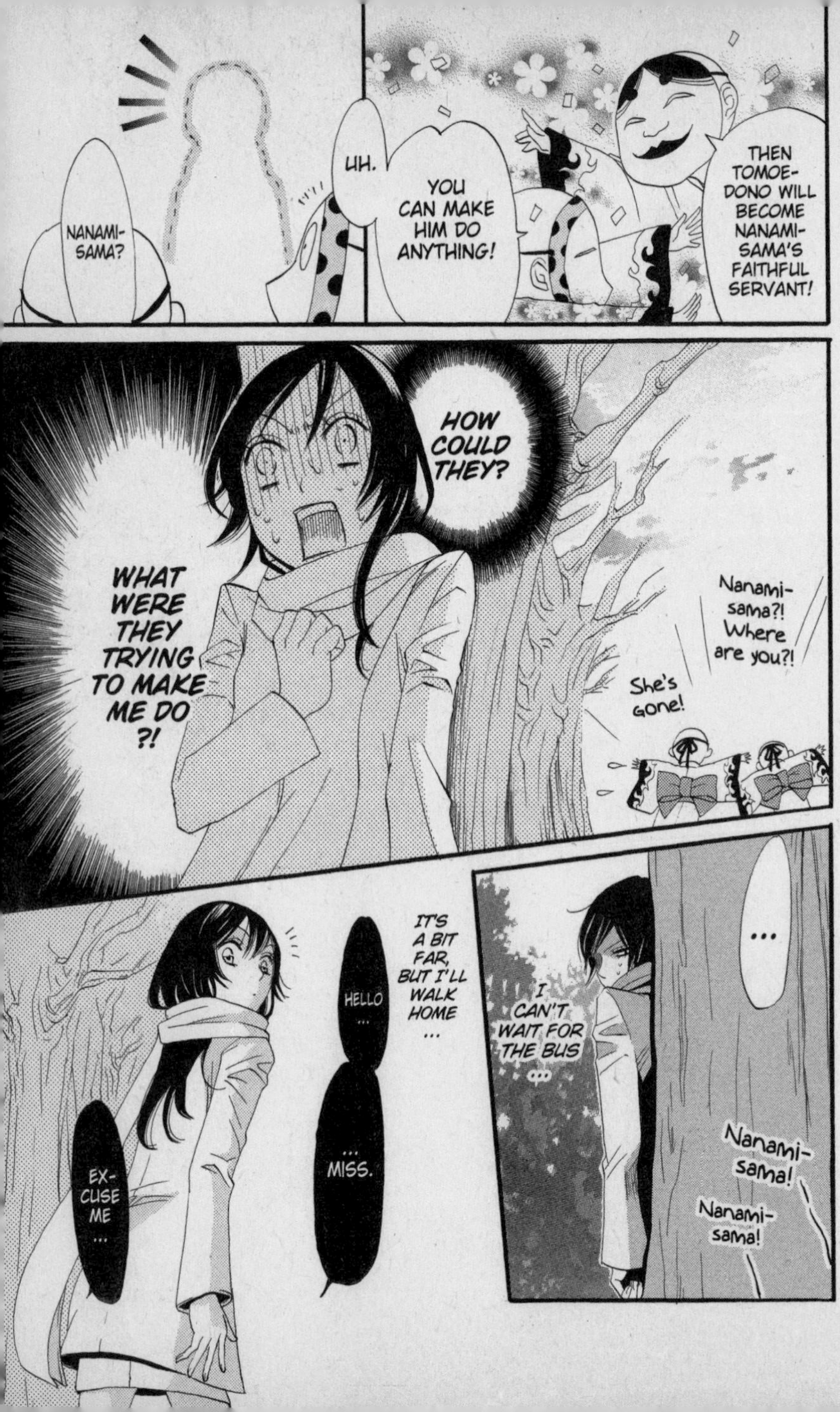
THEN TOMOE-DONO WILL BECOME NANAMI-SAMA'S FAITHFUL SERVANT!
YOU CAN MAKE HIM DO ANYTHING!
UH.
NANAMI-SAMA?
Nanami-sama?! Where are you?!
She's gone!
HOW COULD THEY?
WHAT WERE THEY TRYING TO MAKE ME DO ?!
...
I CAN'T WAIT FOR THE BUS ...
Nanami-sama!
Nanami-sama!
IT'S A BIT FAR, BUT I'LL WALK HOME ...
HELLO ...
... MISS.
EX-CUSE ME ...

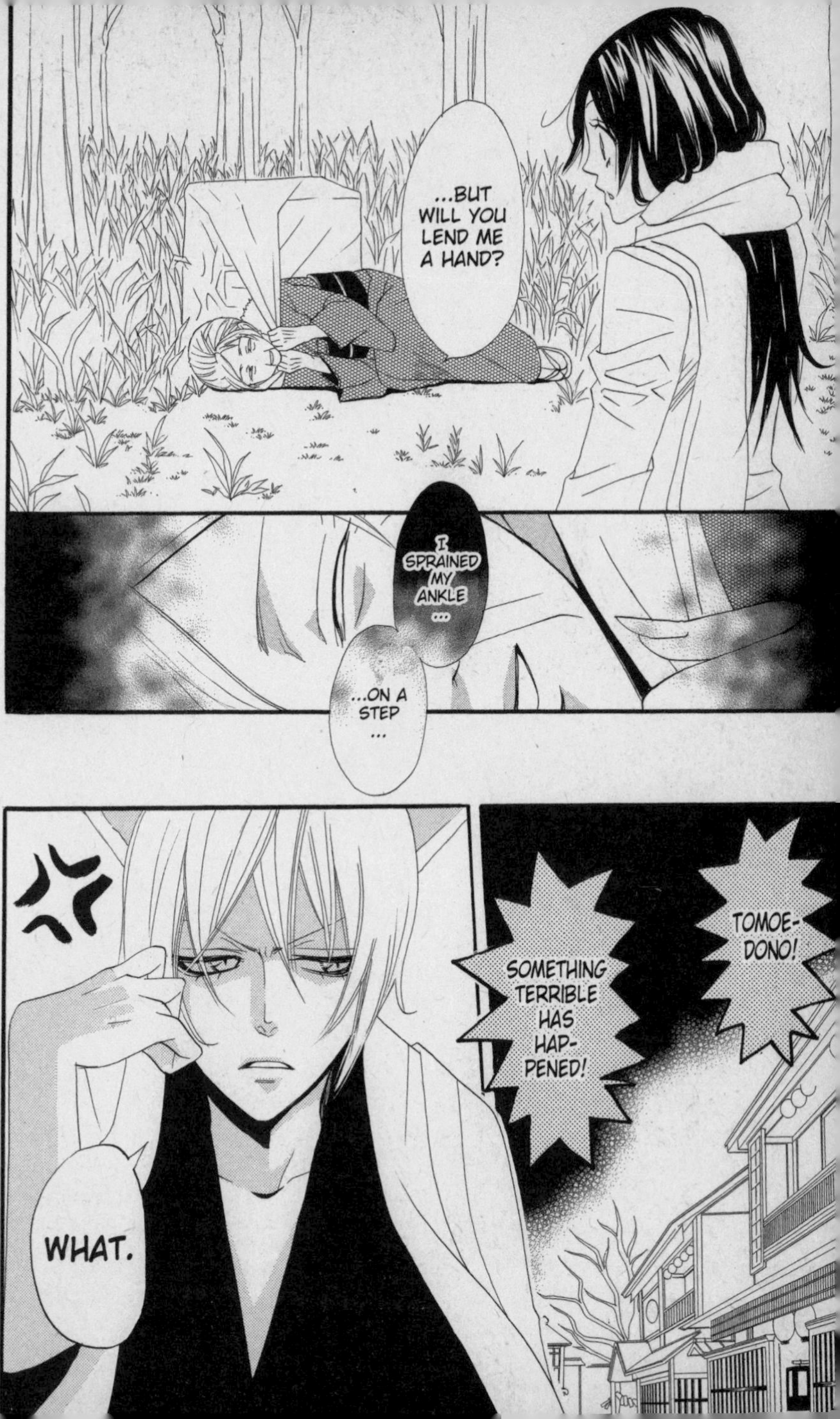
...BUT WILL YOU LEND ME A HAND?
I SPRAINED MY ANKLE...
...ON A STEP...
TOMOE-DONO!
SOMETHING TERRIBLE HAS HAP-PENED!
WHAT.

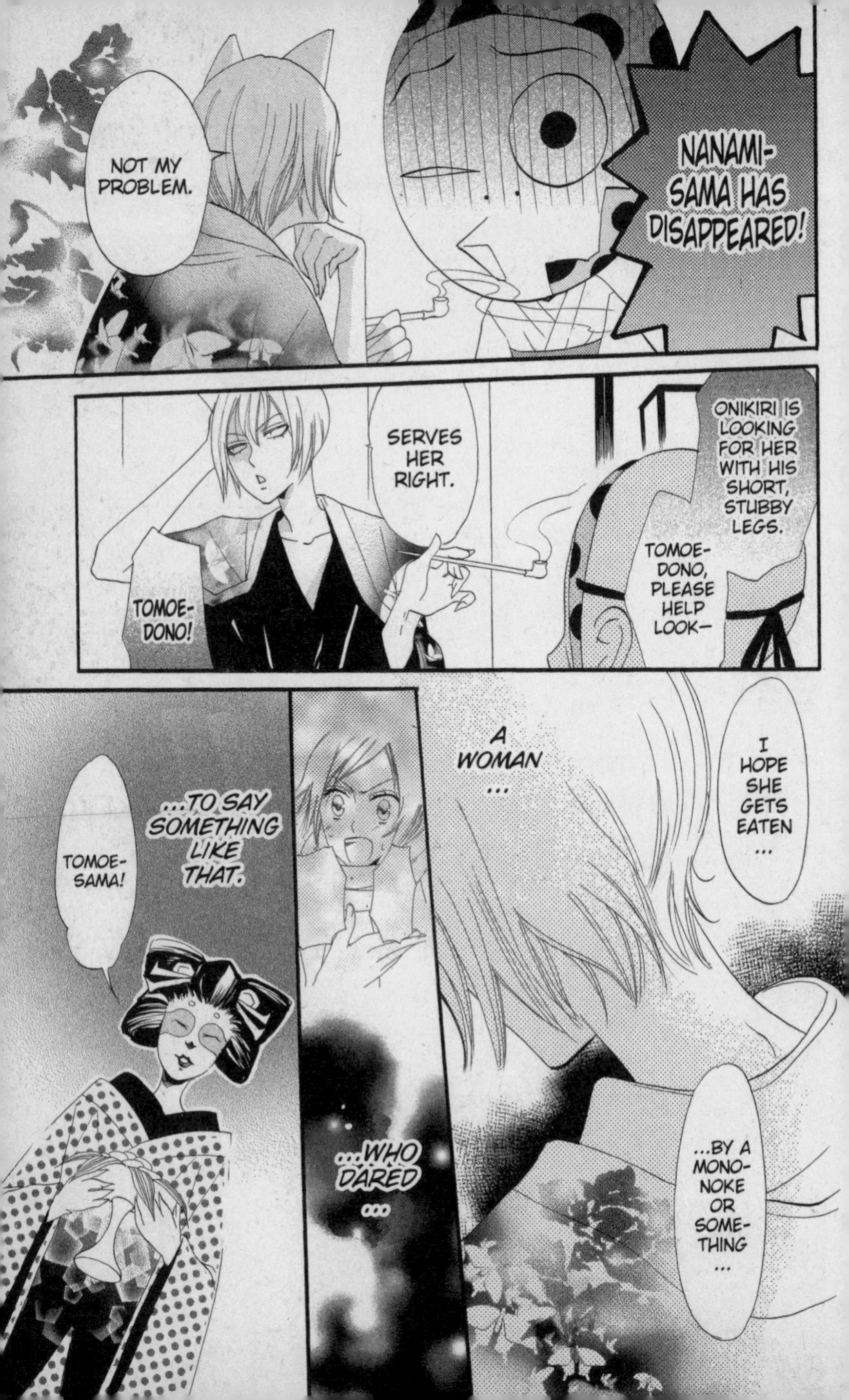
NANAMI-SAMA HAS DISAPPEARED!
NOT MY PROBLEM.
ONIKIRI IS LOOKING FOR HER WITH HIS SHORT, STUBBY LEGS.
TOMOE-DONO, PLEASE HELP LOOK—
SERVES HER RIGHT.
TOMOE-DONO!
I HOPE SHE GETS EATEN...
A WOMAN...
...BY A MONONOKE OR SOMETHING...
...WHO DARED...
...TO SAY SOMETHING LIKE THAT.
TOMOE-SAMA!

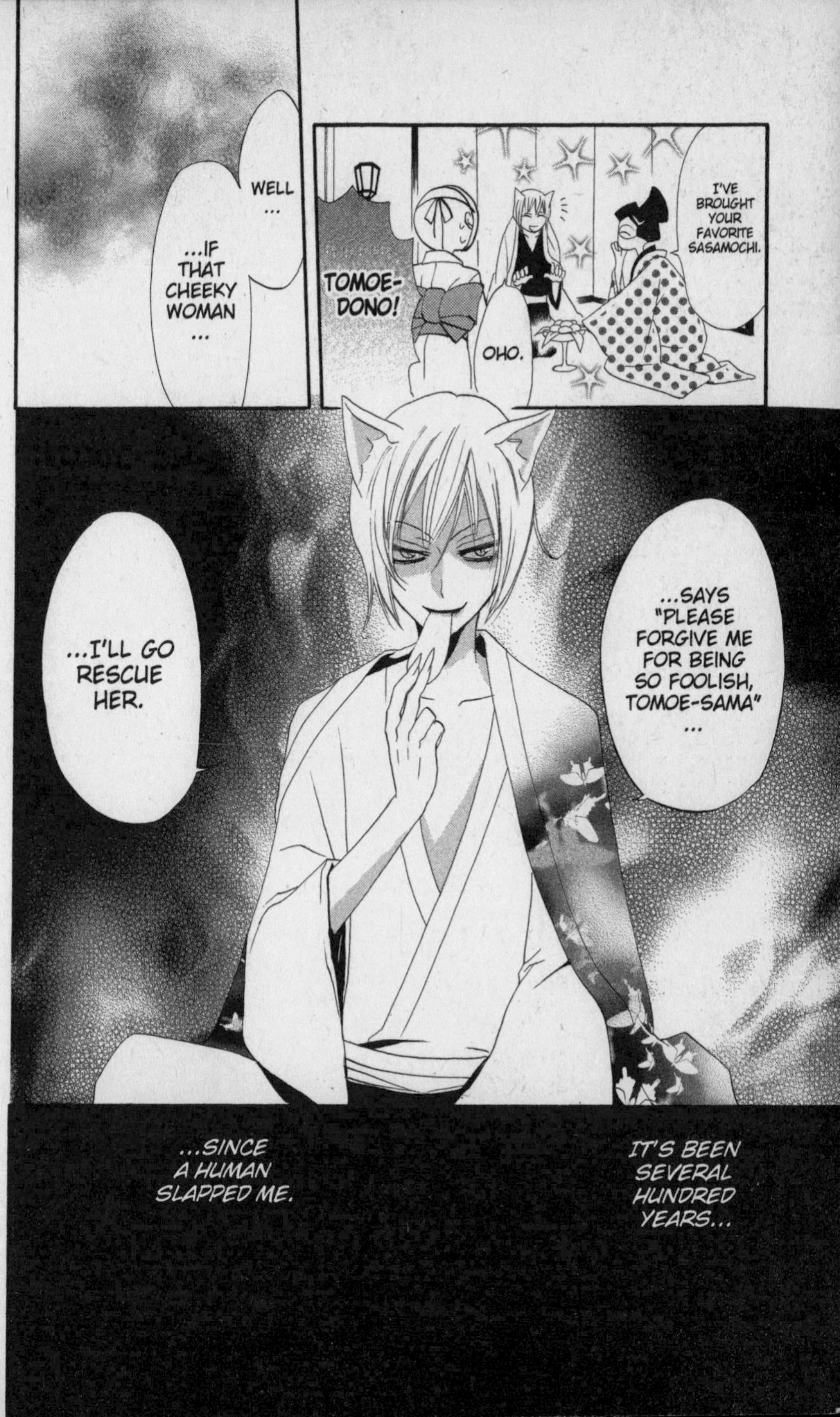
I'VE BROUGHT YOUR FAVORITE SASAMOCHI.
TOMOE-DONO!
OHO.
WELL ...
...IF THAT CHEEKY WOMAN ...
...SAYS "PLEASE FORGIVE ME FOR BEING SO FOOLISH, TOMOE-SAMA" ...
...I'LL GO RESCUE HER.
IT'S BEEN SEVERAL HUNDRED YEARS...
...SINCE A HUMAN SLAPPED ME.

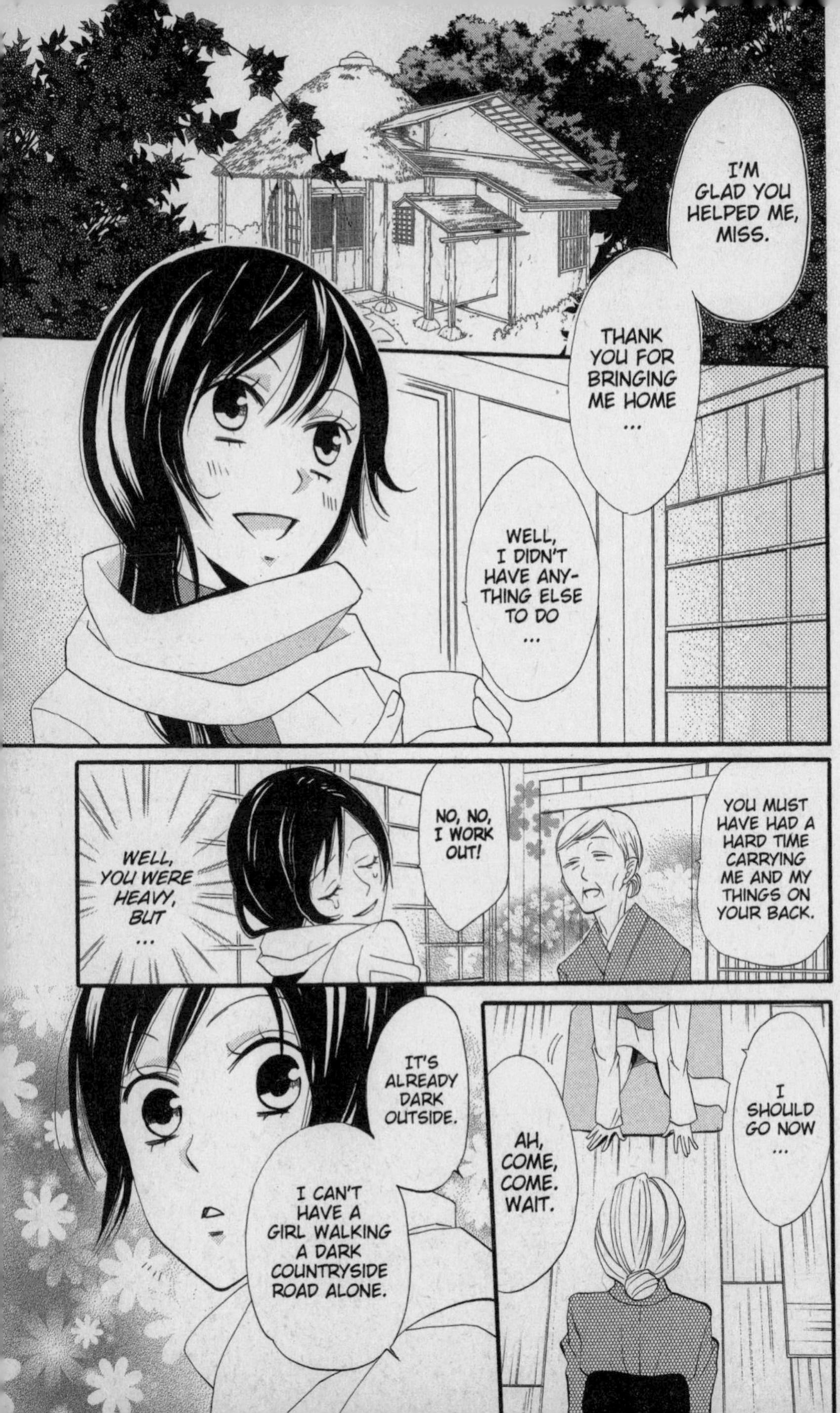
I'M GLAD YOU HELPED ME, MISS.
THANK YOU FOR BRINGING ME HOME ...
WELL, I DIDN'T HAVE ANY-THING ELSE TO DO ...
YOU MUST HAVE HAD A HARD TIME CARRYING ME AND MY THINGS ON YOUR BACK.
NO, NO, I WORK OUT!
WELL, YOU WERE HEAVY, BUT ...
I SHOULD GO NOW ...
AH, COME, COME. WAIT.
IT'S ALREADY DARK OUTSIDE.
I CAN'T HAVE A GIRL WALKING A DARK COUNTRYSIDE ROAD ALONE.

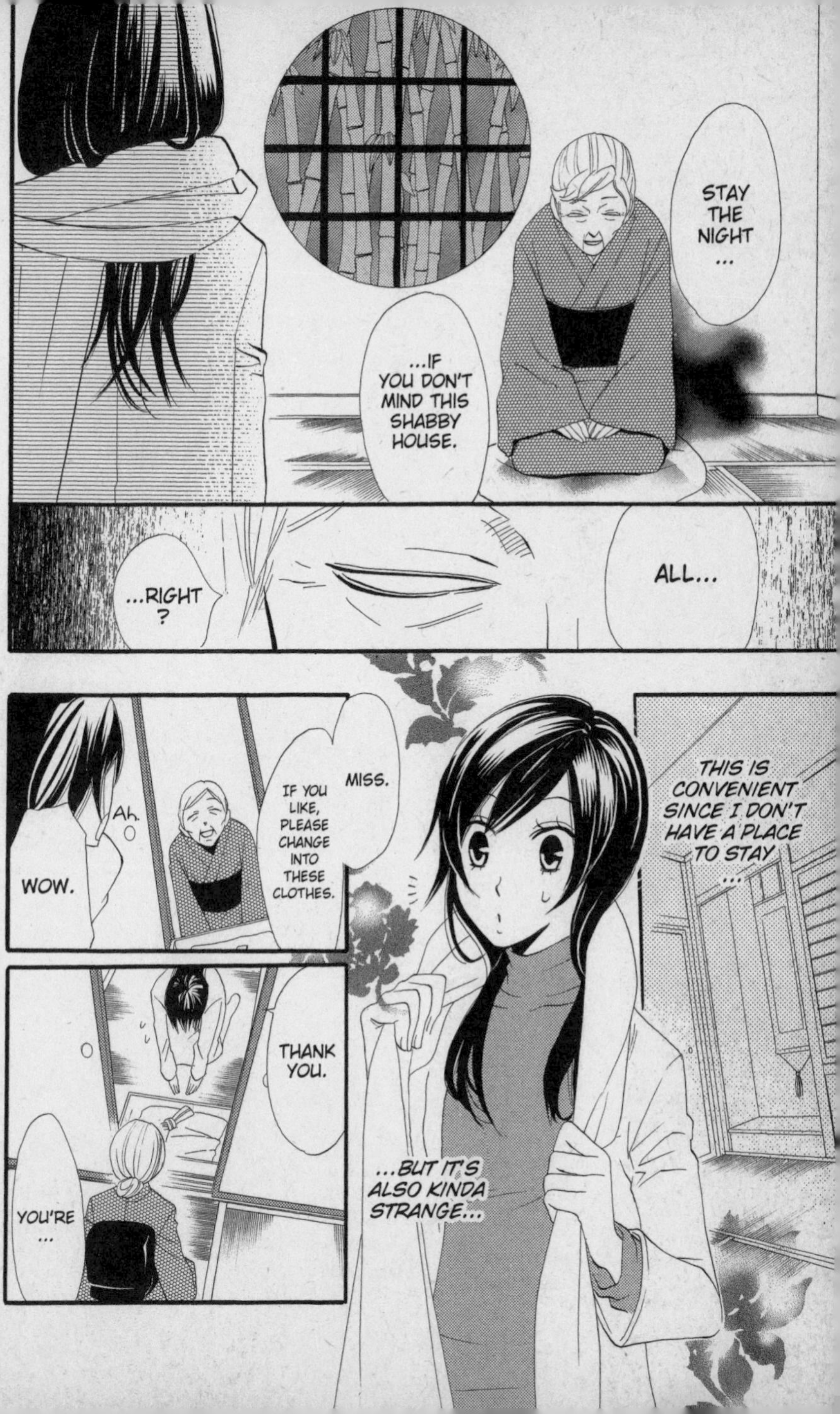
STAY THE NIGHT ...
...IF YOU DON'T MIND THIS SHABBY HOUSE.
ALL...
...RIGHT?
THIS IS CONVENIENT SINCE I DON'T HAVE A PLACE TO STAY ...
...BUT IT'S ALSO KINDA STRANGE...
MISS.
IF YOU LIKE, PLEASE CHANGE INTO THESE CLOTHES.
Ah.
WOW.
THANK YOU.
YOU'RE ...

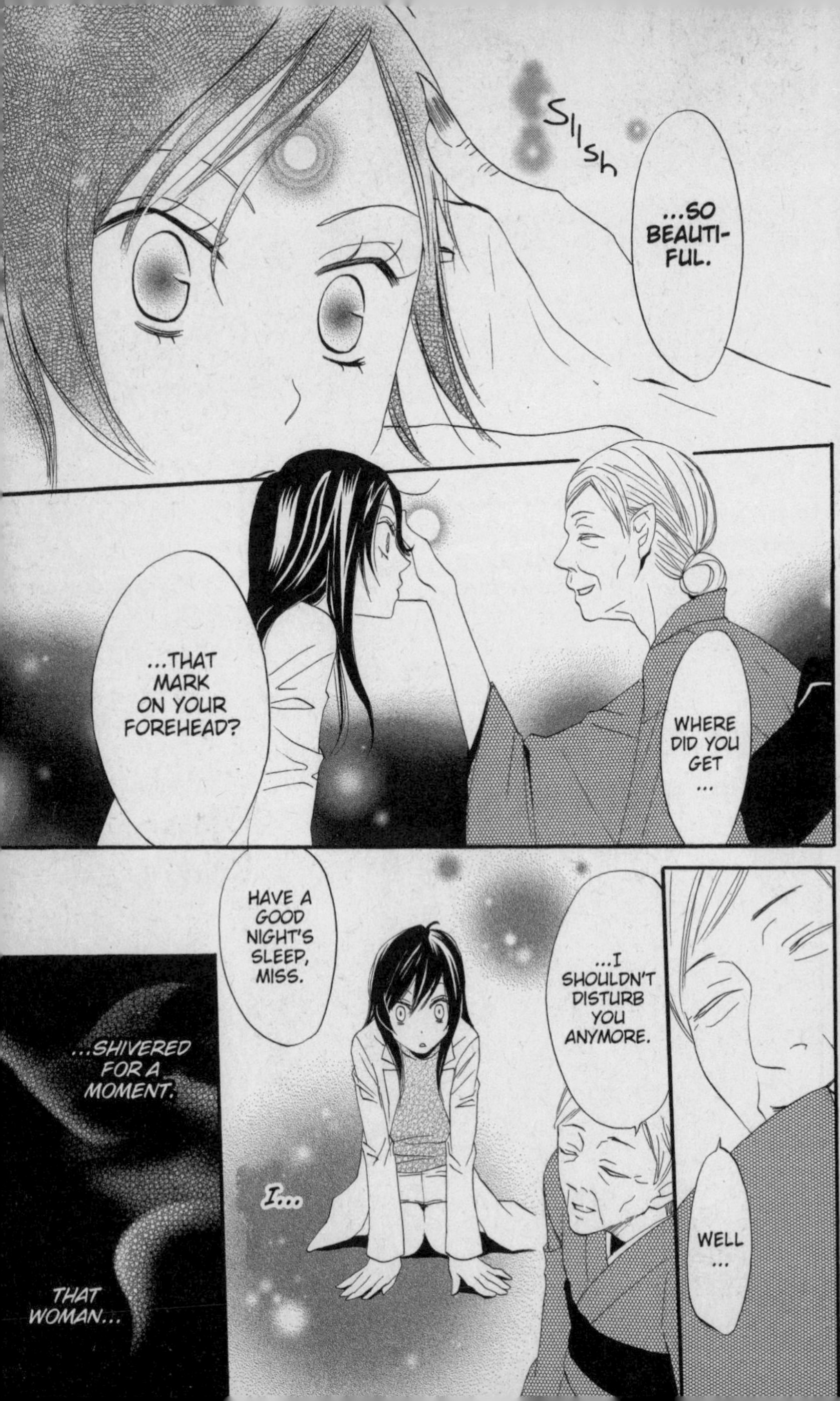
Sllsh
...SO BEAUTIFUL.
WHERE DID YOU GET ...
...THAT MARK ON YOUR FOREHEAD?
WELL ...
...I SHOULDN'T DISTURB YOU ANYMORE.
HAVE A GOOD NIGHT'S SLEEP, MISS.
I...
THAT WOMAN...
...SHIVERED FOR A MOMENT.

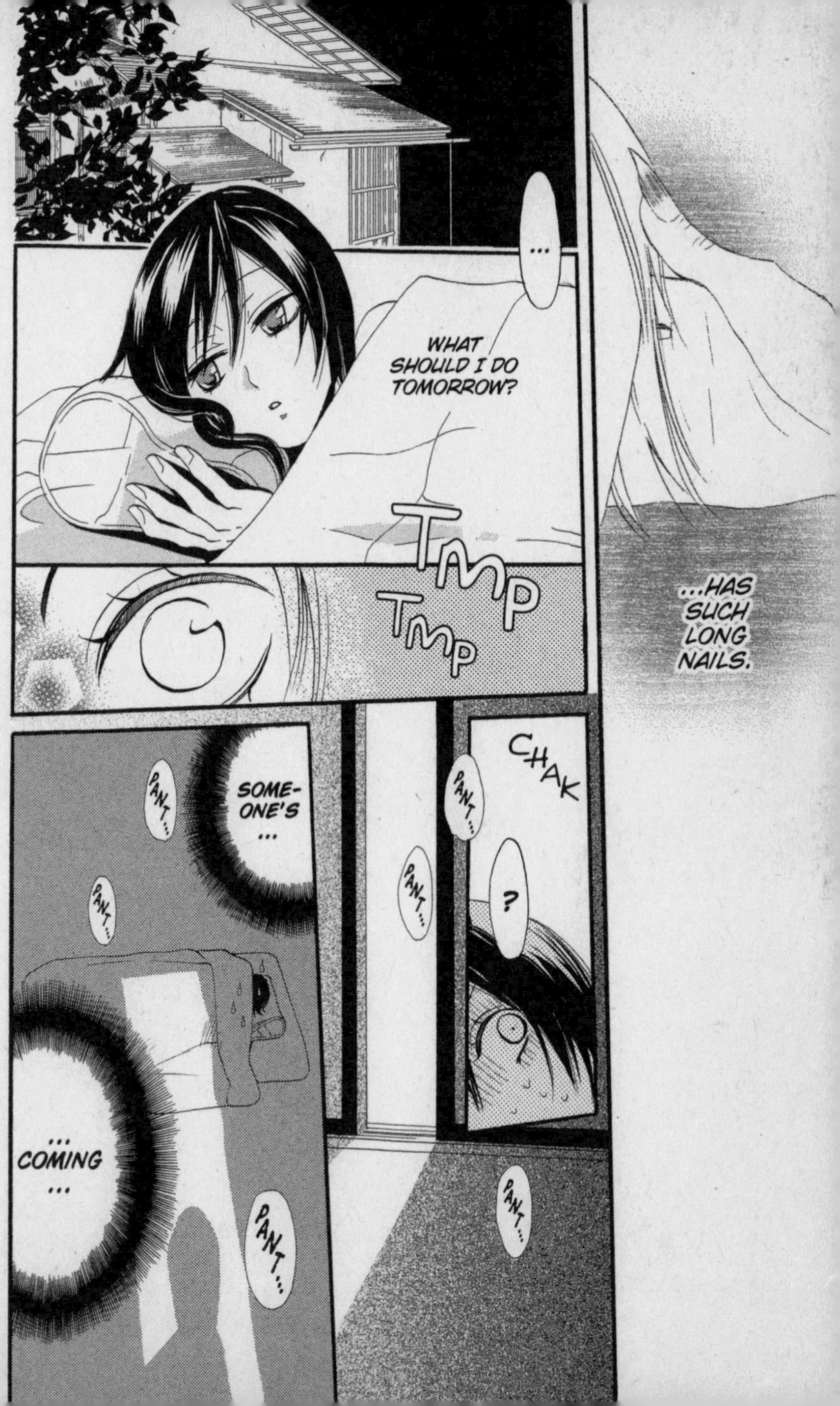

...HAS SUCH LONG NAILS.
...
WHAT SHOULD I DO TOMORROW?
TMP
TMP
CHAK
PANT...
?
PANT...
PANT...
SOME-ONE'S ...
PANT...
... COMING ...
PANT...

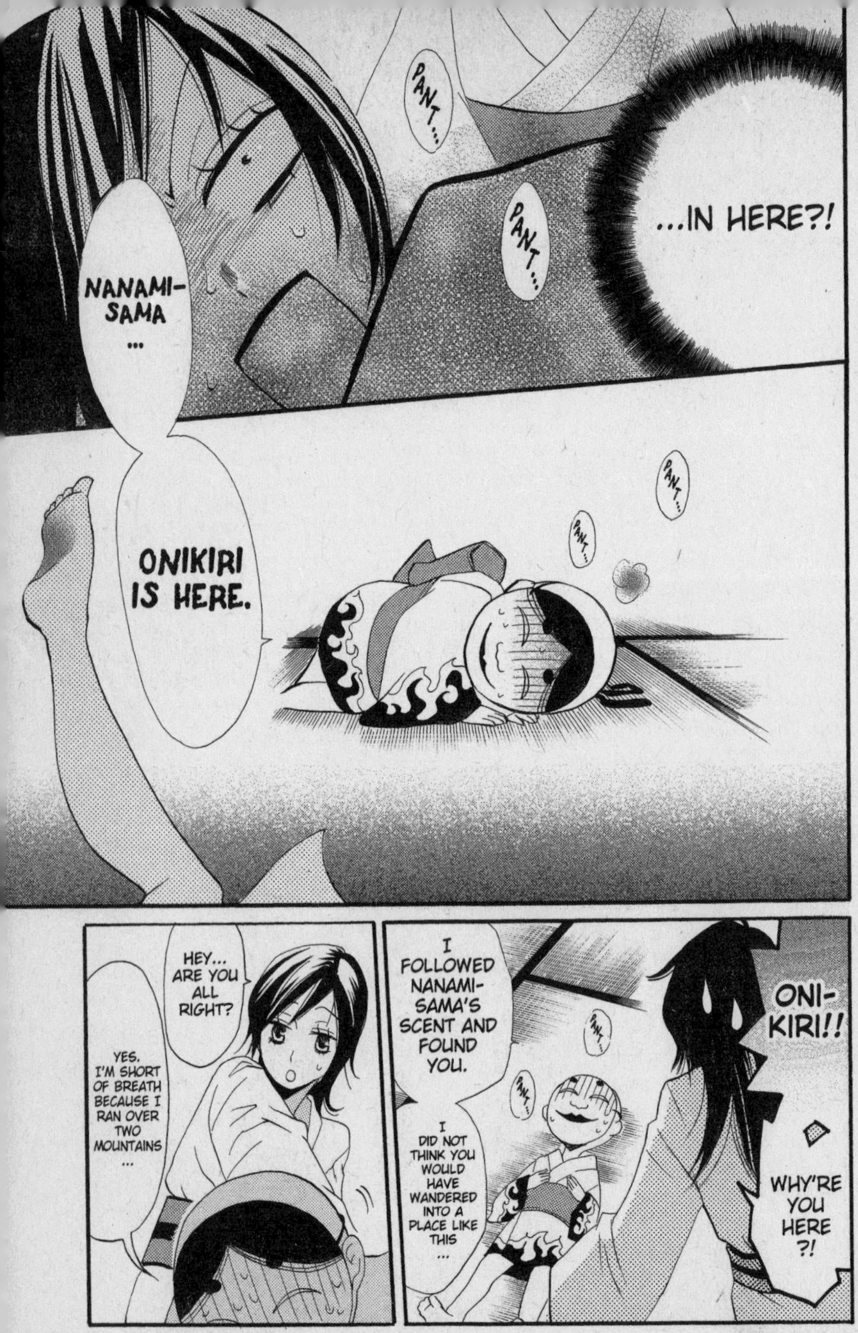
...IN HERE?!
PANT...
PANT...
NANAMI-SAMA ... ONIKIRI IS HERE.
PANT...
PANT...
ONI-KIRI!!
WHY'RE YOU HERE ?!
I FOLLOWED NANAMI-SAMA'S SCENT AND FOUND YOU.
PANT...
PANT...
I DID NOT THINK YOU WOULD HAVE WANDERED INTO A PLACE LIKE THIS ...
HEY... ARE YOU ALL RIGHT?
YES. I'M SHORT OF BREATH BECAUSE I RAN OVER TWO MOUNTAINS ...

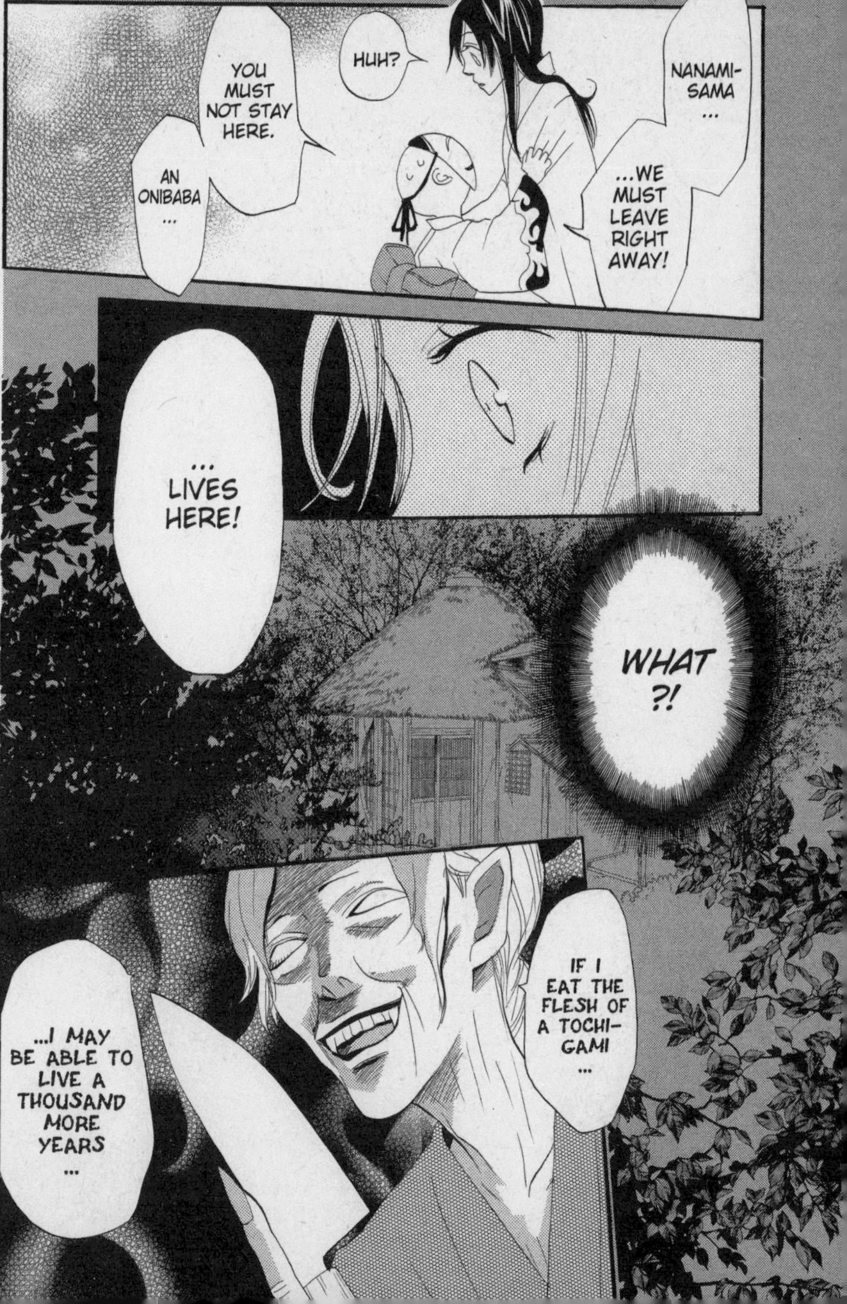
NANAMI-SAMA ...
...WE MUST LEAVE RIGHT AWAY!
HUH?
YOU MUST NOT STAY HERE.
AN ONIBABA ...
... LIVES HERE!
WHAT ?!
IF I EAT THE FLESH OF A TOCHI-GAMI ...
...I MAY BE ABLE TO LIVE A THOUSAND MORE YEARS ...

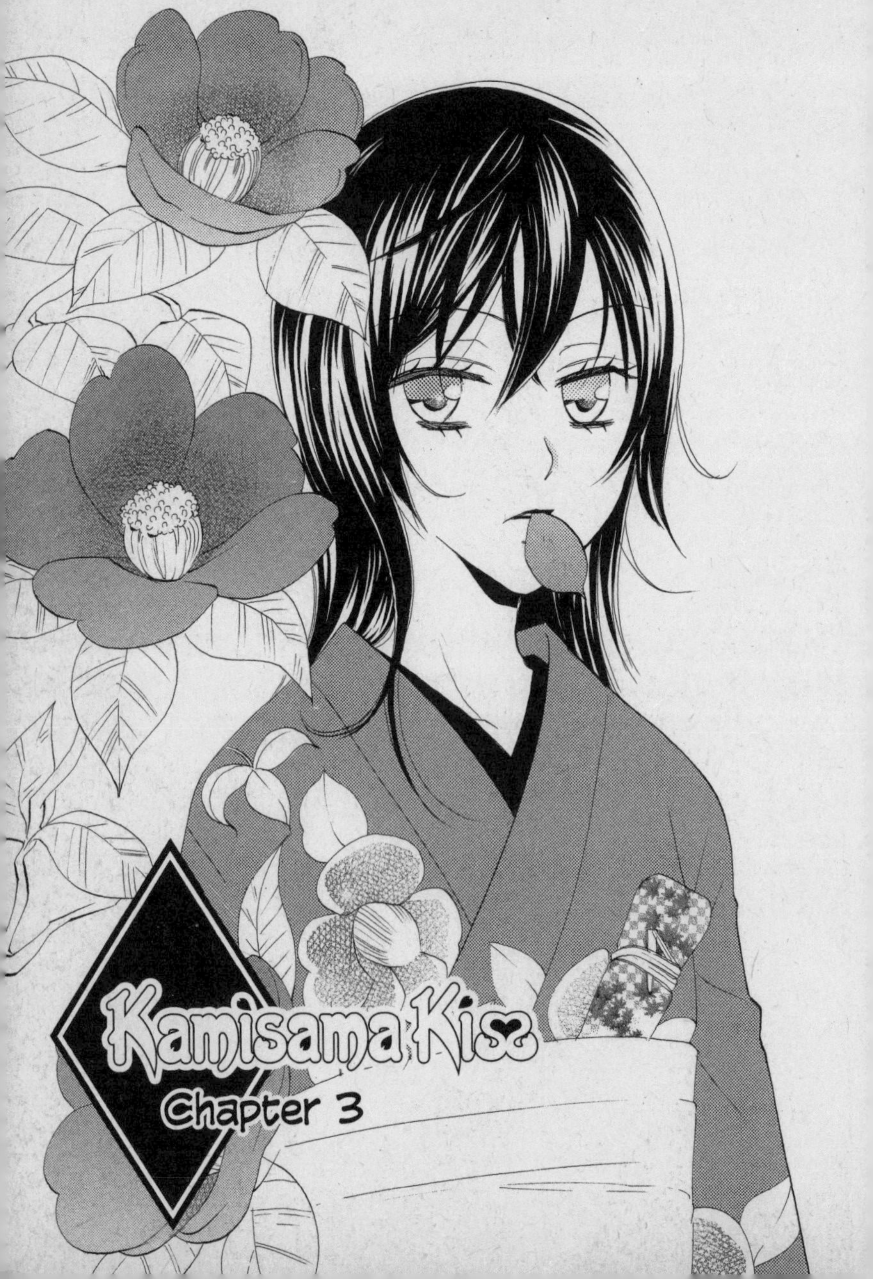
Kamisama Kiss
Chapter 3

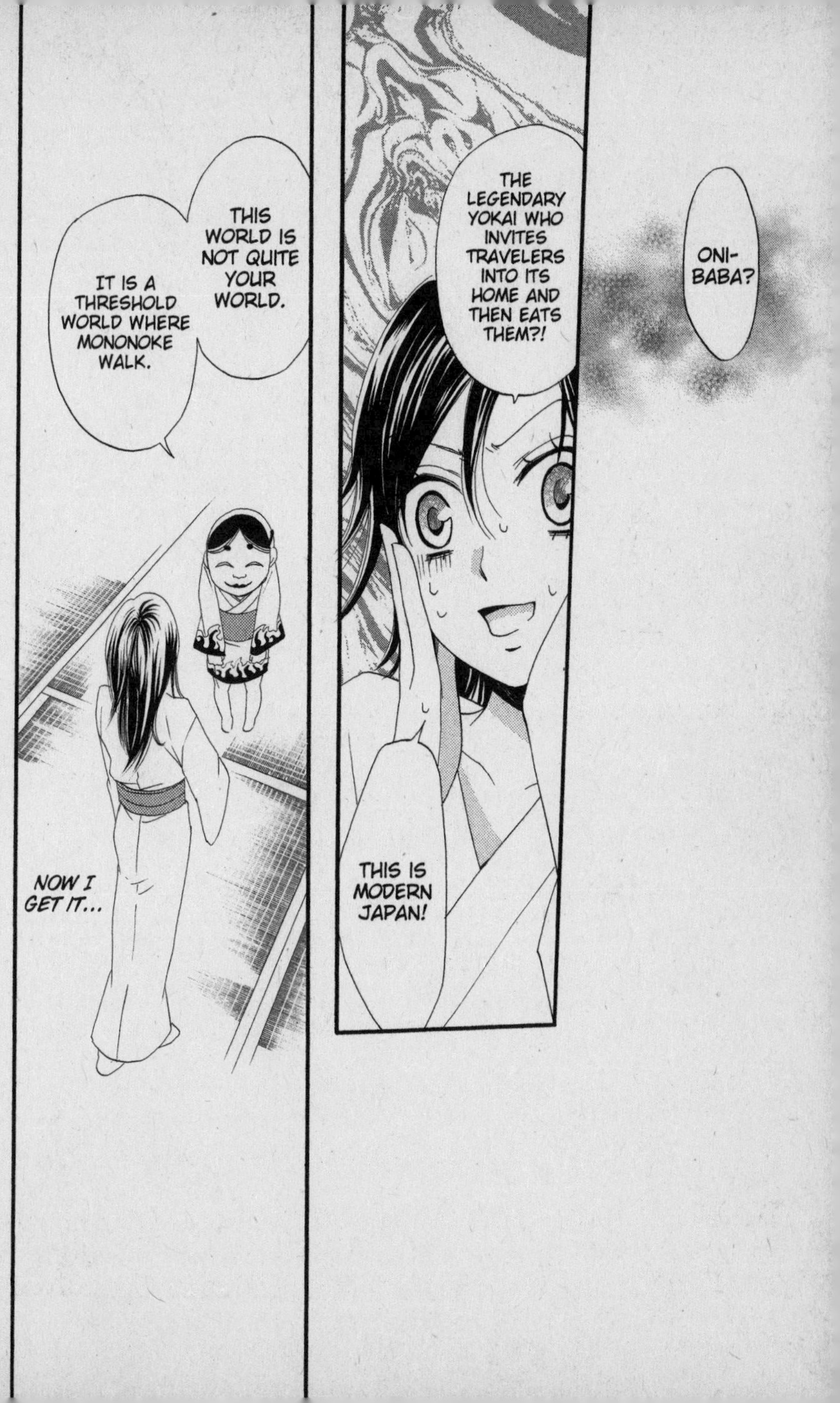
ONI-BABA?
THE LEGENDARY YOKAI WHO INVITES TRAVELERS INTO ITS HOME AND THEN EATS THEM?!
THIS IS MODERN JAPAN!
THIS WORLD IS NOT QUITE YOUR WORLD.
IT IS A THRESHOLD WORLD WHERE MONONOKE WALK.
NOW I GET IT...

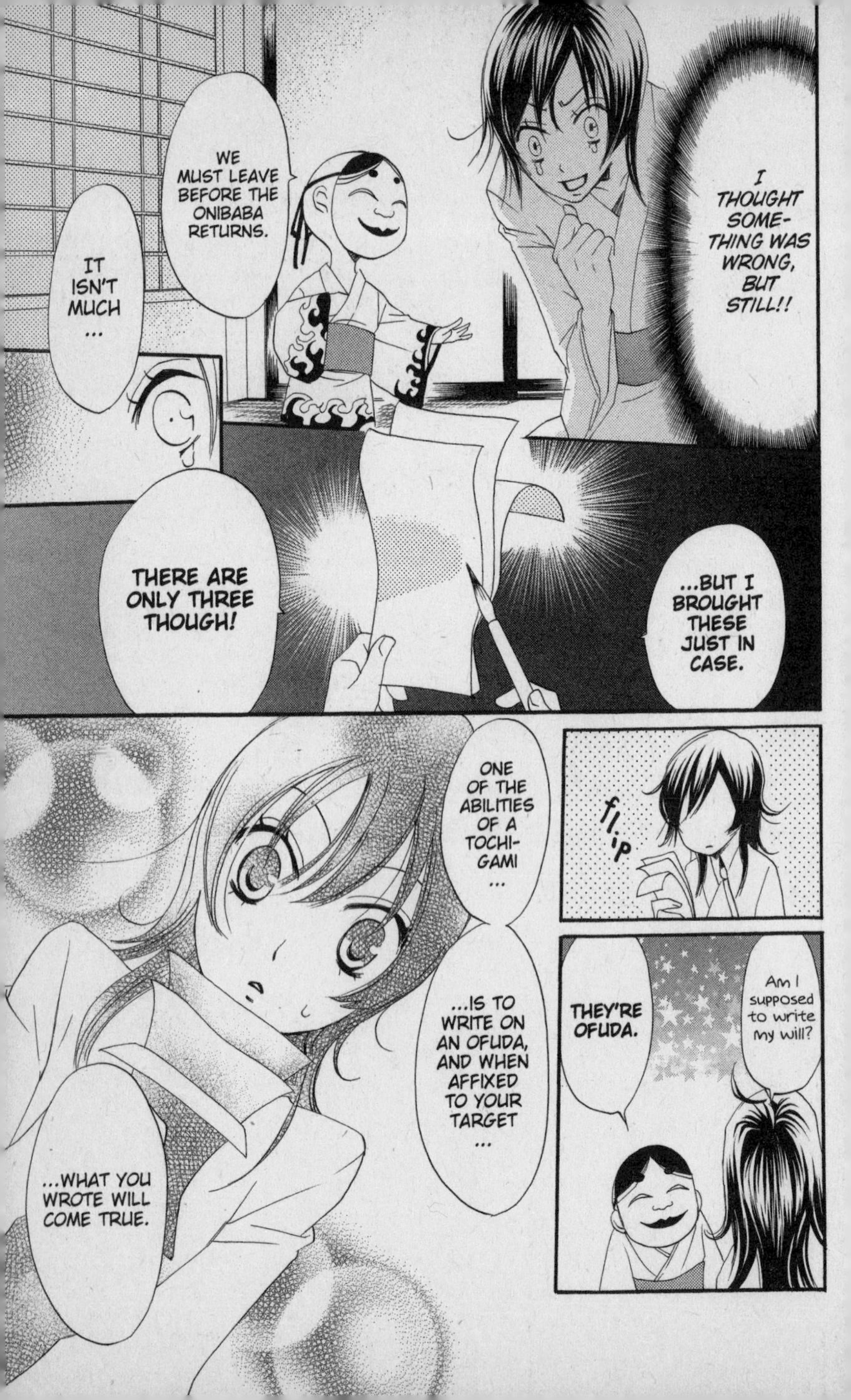
I THOUGHT SOMETHING WAS WRONG, BUT STILL!!
WE MUST LEAVE BEFORE THE ONIBABA RETURNS.
IT ISN'T MUCH...
...BUT I BROUGHT THESE JUST IN CASE.
THERE ARE ONLY THREE THOUGH!
flip
Am I supposed to write my will?
THEY'RE OFUDA.
ONE OF THE ABILITIES OF A TOCHI-GAMI...
...IS TO WRITE ON AN OFUDA, AND WHEN AFFIXED TO YOUR TARGET...
...WHAT YOU WROTE WILL COME TRUE.

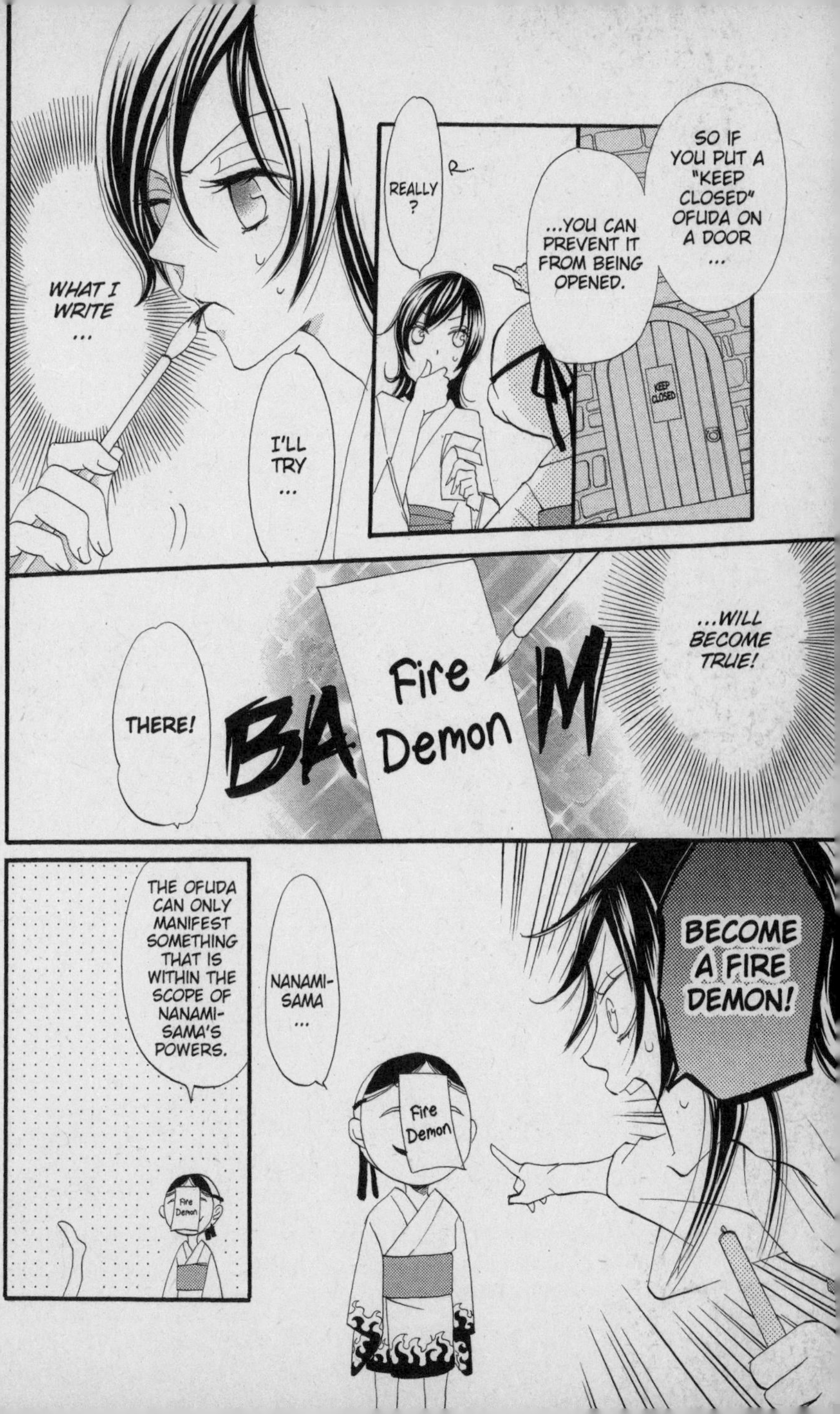
SO IF YOU PUT A "KEEP CLOSED" OFUDA ON A DOOR ...
...YOU CAN PREVENT IT FROM BEING OPENED.
R...
REALLY ?
KEEP CLOSED
I'LL TRY ...
WHAT I WRITE ...
...WILL BECOME TRUE!
Fire Demon
BAM
THERE!
BECOME A FIRE DEMON!
Fire Demon
NANAMI-SAMA ...
THE OFUDA CAN ONLY MANIFEST SOMETHING THAT IS WITHIN THE SCOPE OF NANAMI-SAMA'S POWERS.
Fire Demon

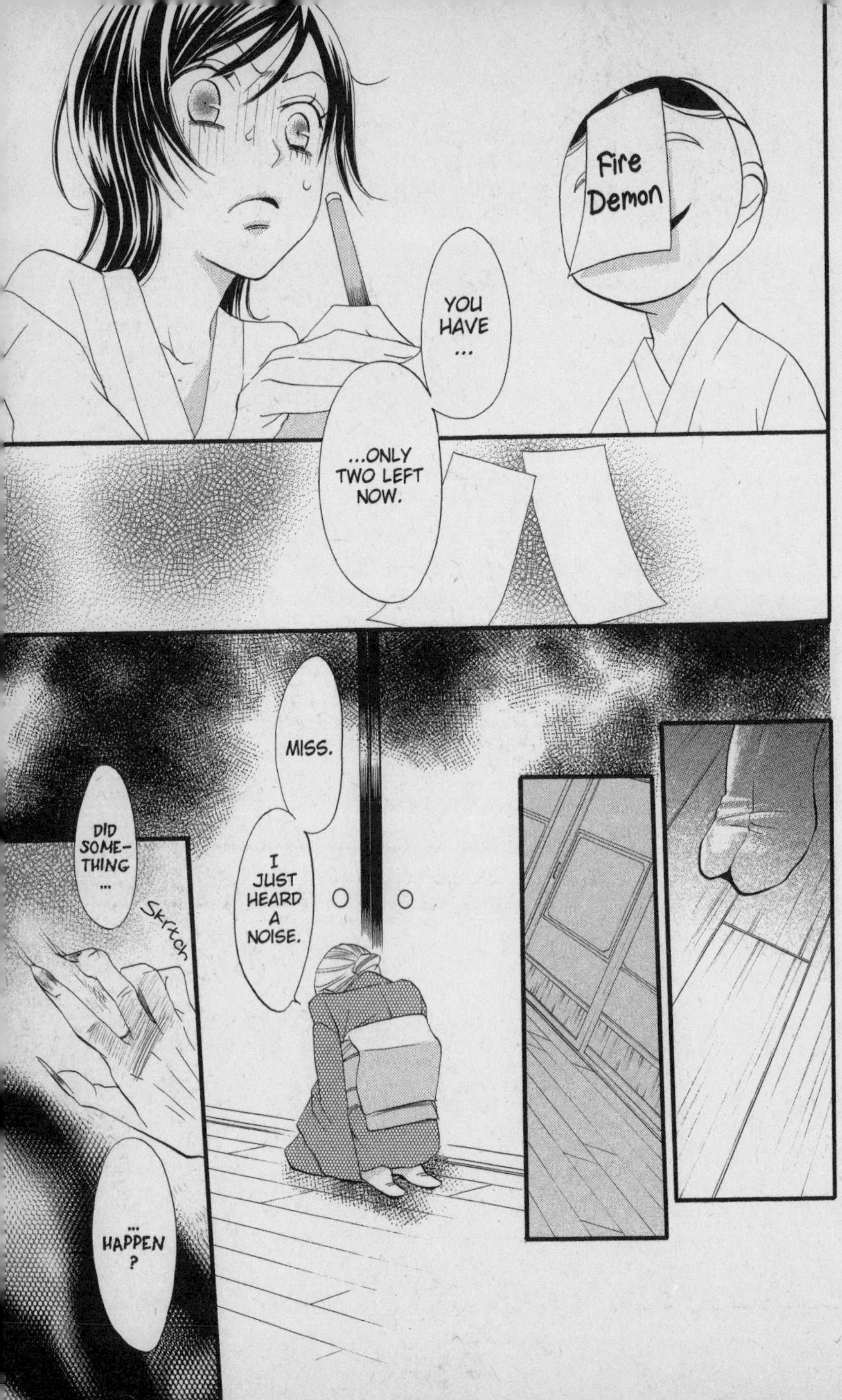
Fire Demon
YOU HAVE ...
...ONLY TWO LEFT NOW.
MISS.
I JUST HEARD A NOISE.
DID SOME-THING ...
Skrtch
... HAPPEN?

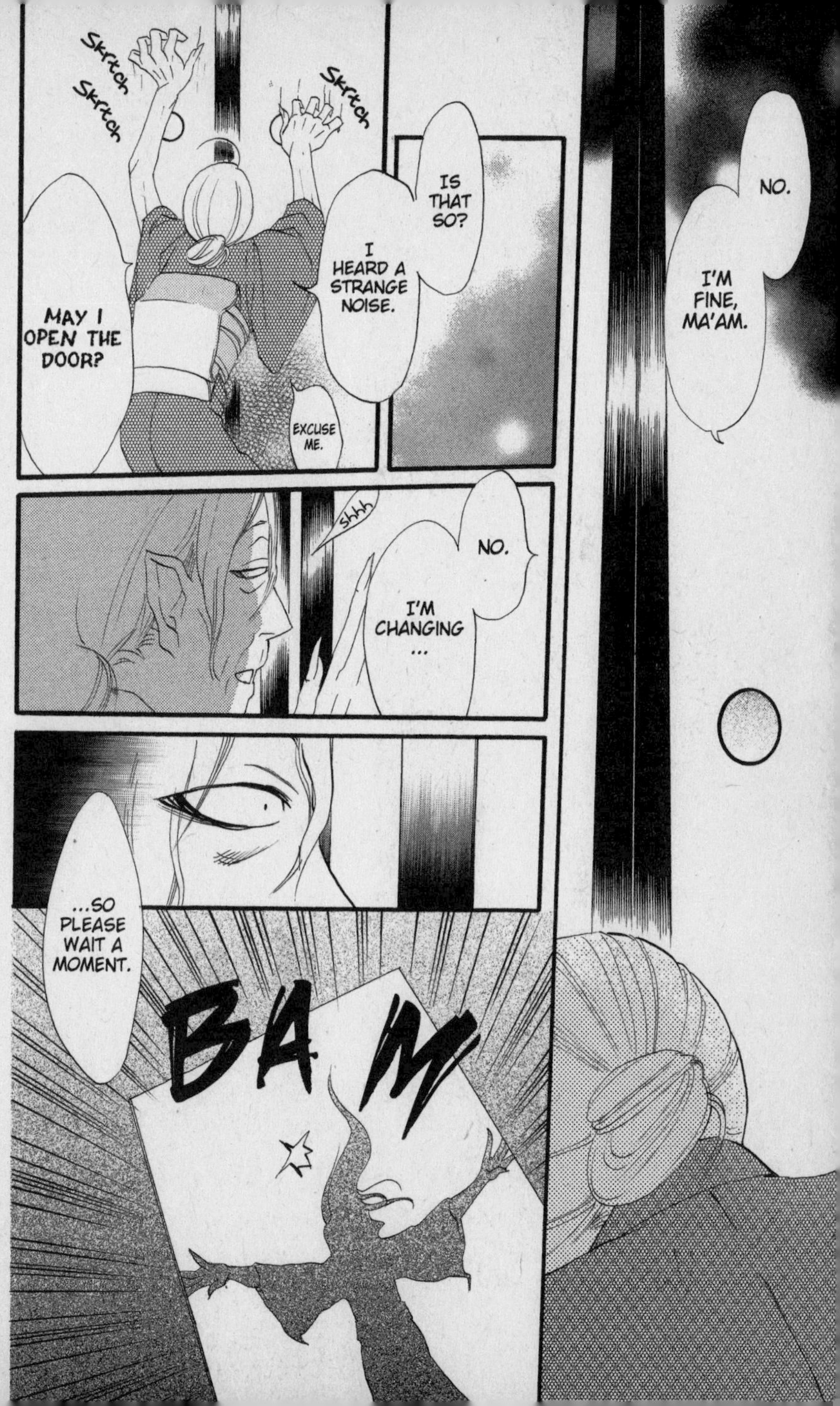
NO.
I'M FINE, MA'AM.
IS THAT SO?
I HEARD A STRANGE NOISE.
EXCUSE ME.
Skrtch
Skrtch
Skrtch
MAY I OPEN THE DOOR?
NO.
I'M CHANGING ...
shhh
...SO PLEASE WAIT A MOMENT.
BAM

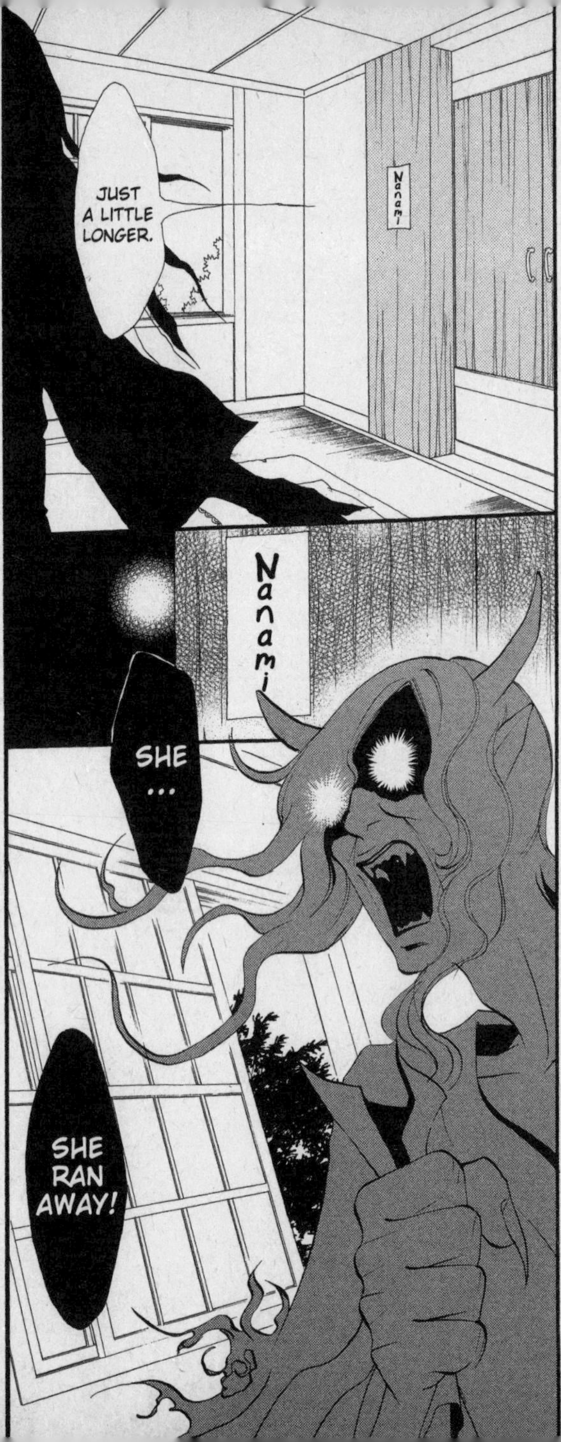
JUST A LITTLE LONGER.
Nanami
Nanami
SHE ...
SHE RAN AWAY!

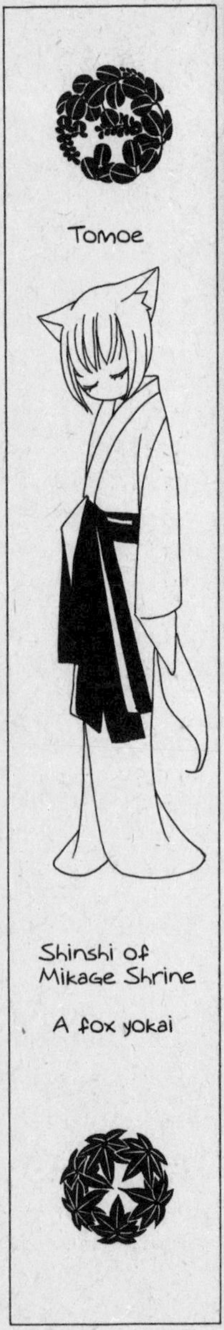
Tomoe
Shinshi of Mikage Shrine
A fox yokai

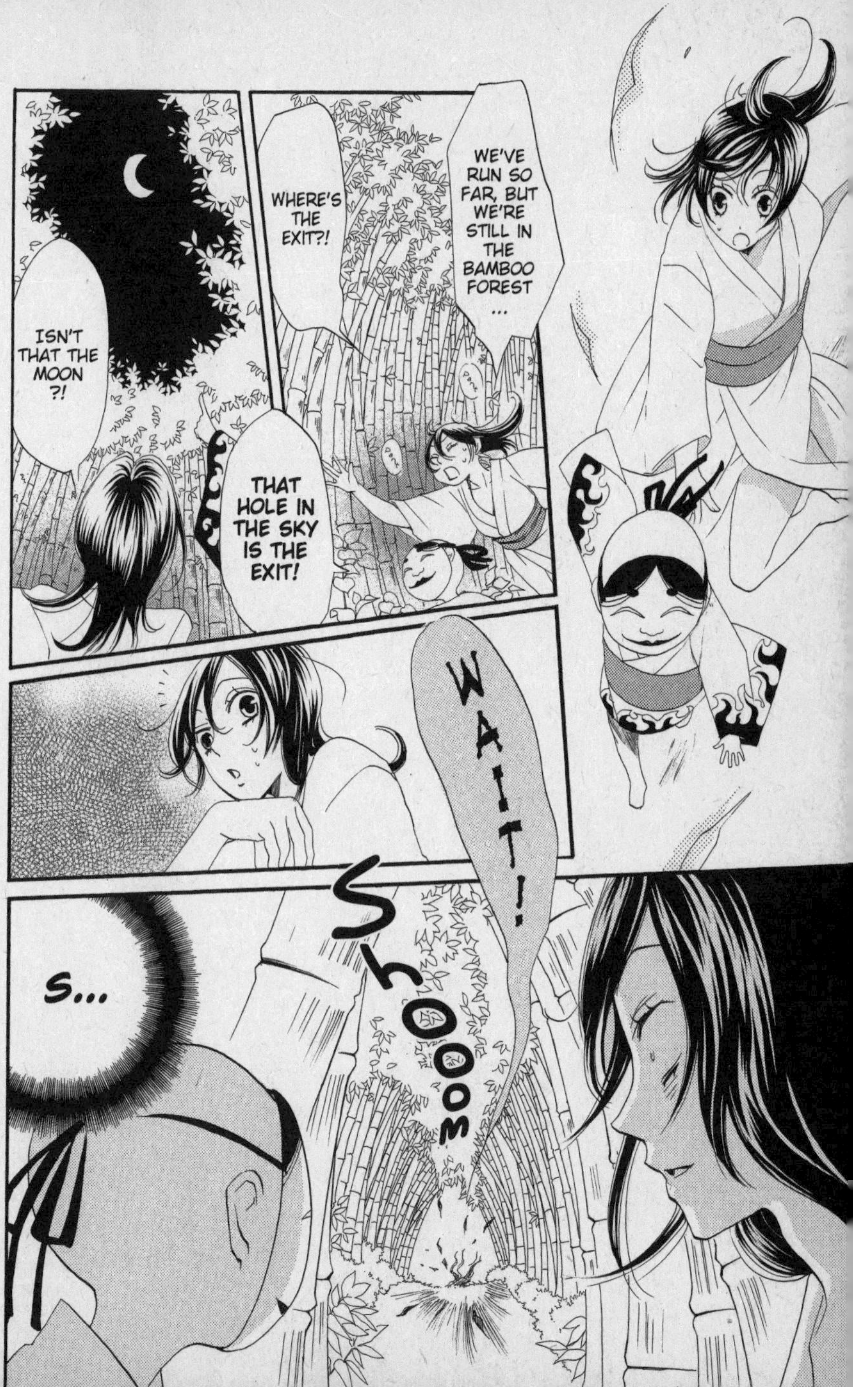
WE'VE RUN SO FAR, BUT WE'RE STILL IN THE BAMBOO FOREST ...
WHERE'S THE EXIT?!
THAT HOLE IN THE SKY IS THE EXIT!
ISN'T THAT THE MOON ?!
WAIT!!
Shoooom
S...

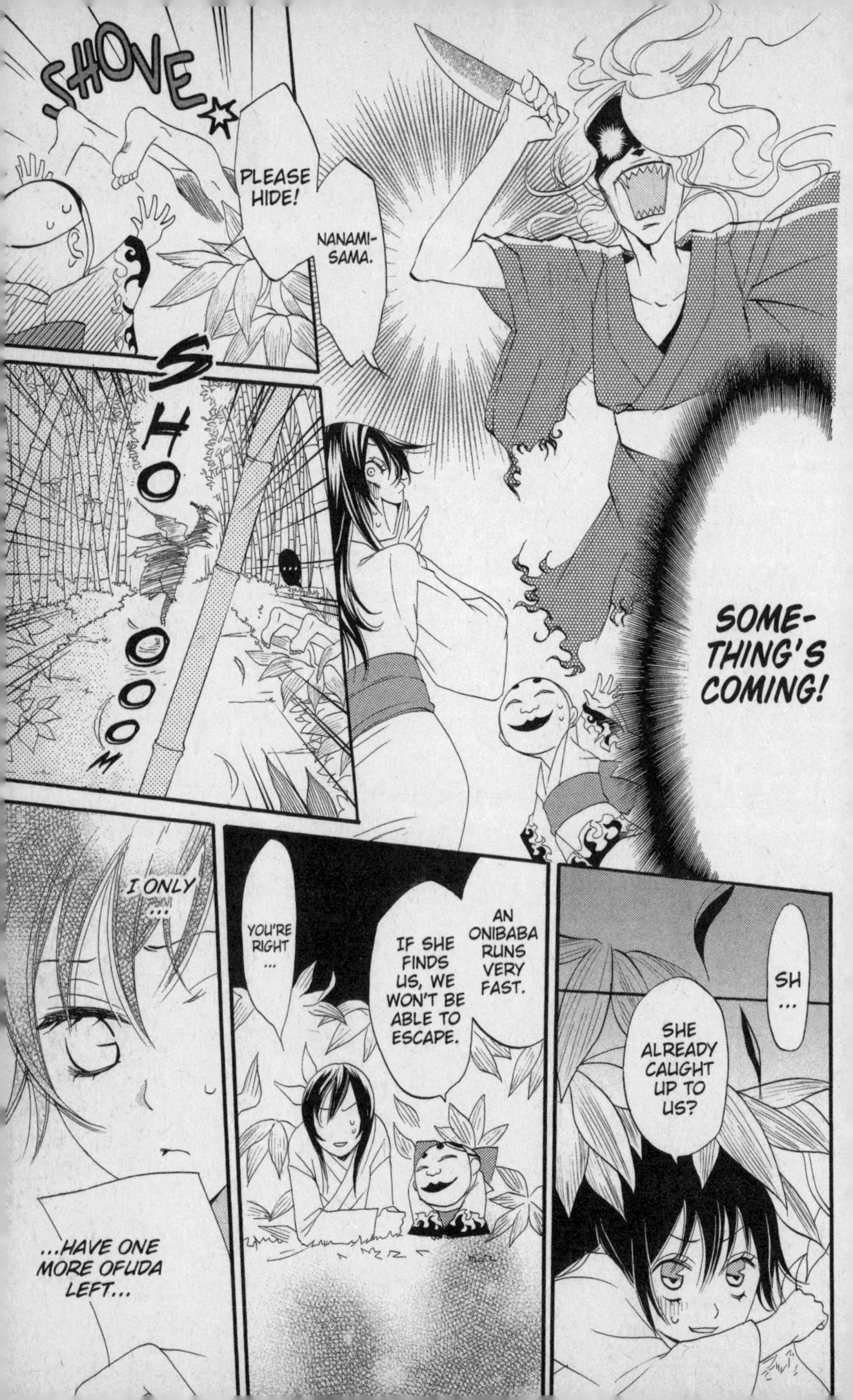
SOMETHING'S COMING!
SHOVE
PLEASE HIDE!
NANAMI-SAMA.
SHOOOOOM
SH...
SHE ALREADY CAUGHT UP TO US?
AN ONIBABA RUNS VERY FAST.
IF SHE FINDS US, WE WON'T BE ABLE TO ESCAPE.
YOU'RE RIGHT...
I ONLY...
...HAVE ONE MORE OFUDA LEFT...

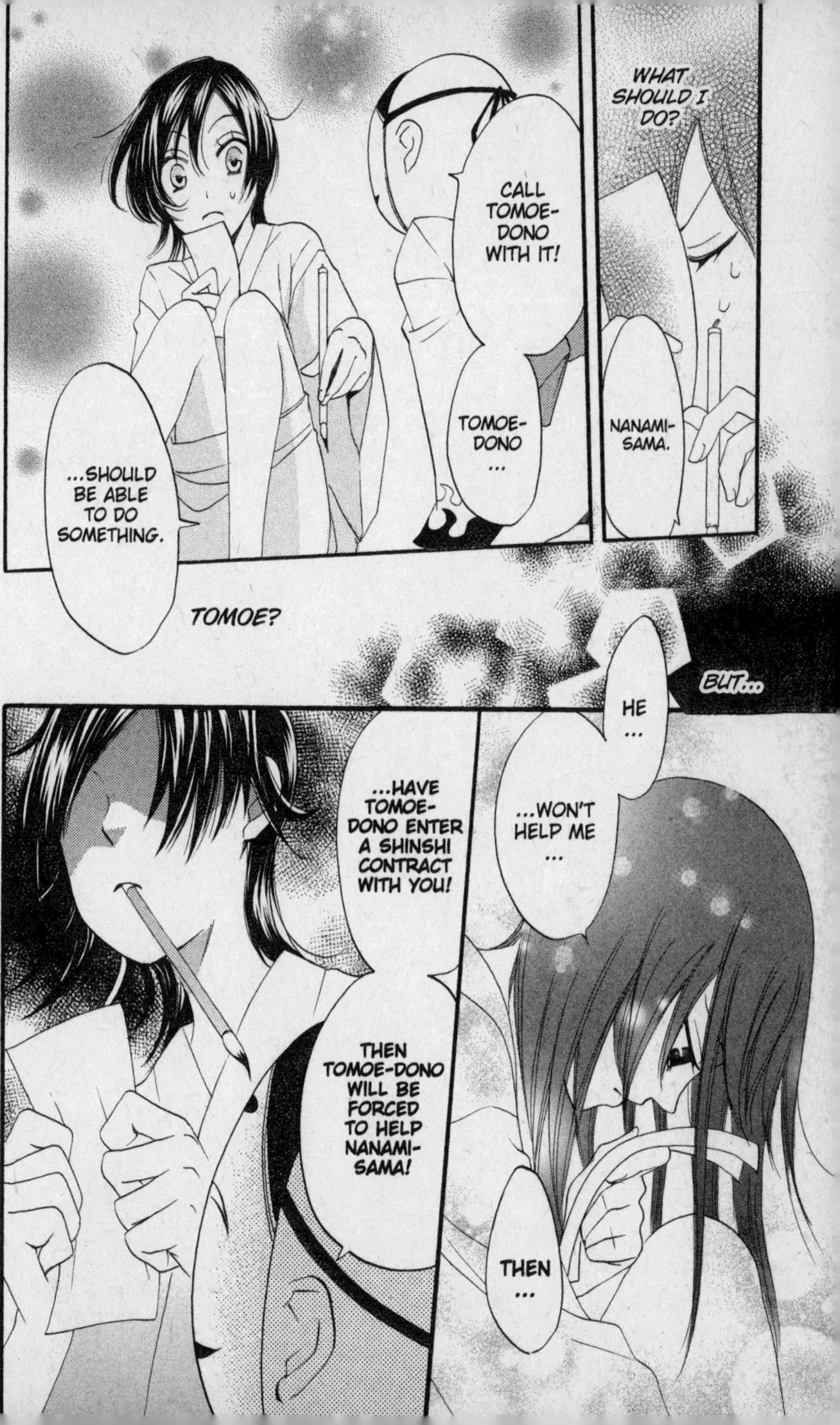
WHAT SHOULD I DO?
NANAMI-SAMA.
CALL TOMOE-DONO WITH IT!
TOMOE-DONO ...
...SHOULD BE ABLE TO DO SOMETHING.
TOMOE?
BUT...
HE ...
...WON'T HELP ME ...
THEN ...
...HAVE TOMOE-DONO ENTER A SHINSHI CONTRACT WITH YOU!
THEN TOMOE-DONO WILL BE FORCED TO HELP NANAMI-SAMA!

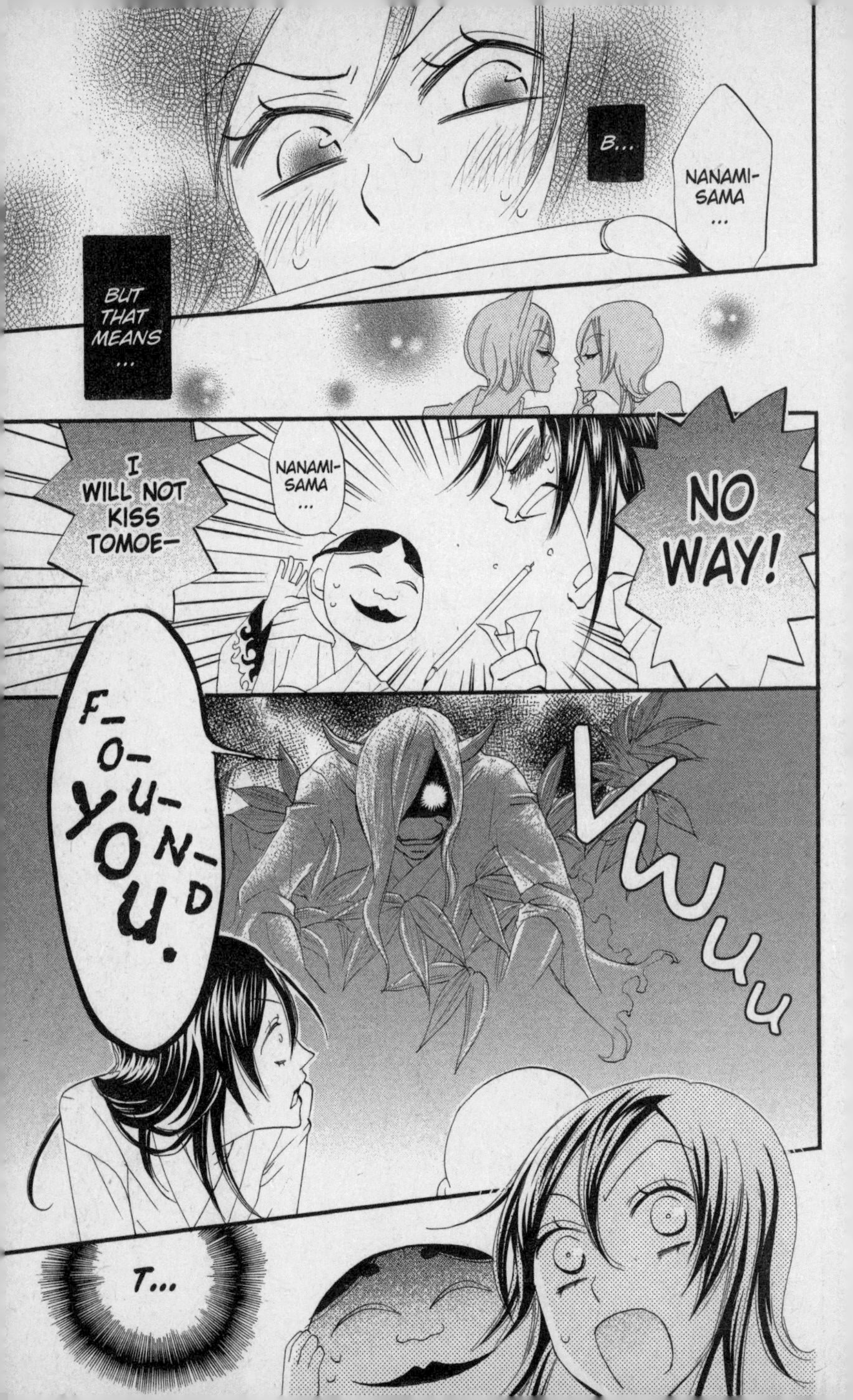
NANAMI-SAMA ...
B...
BUT THAT MEANS ...
NO WAY!
NANAMI-SAMA ...
I WILL NOT KISS TOMOE—
VWUUU
F—O—U—N—D YOU.
T...

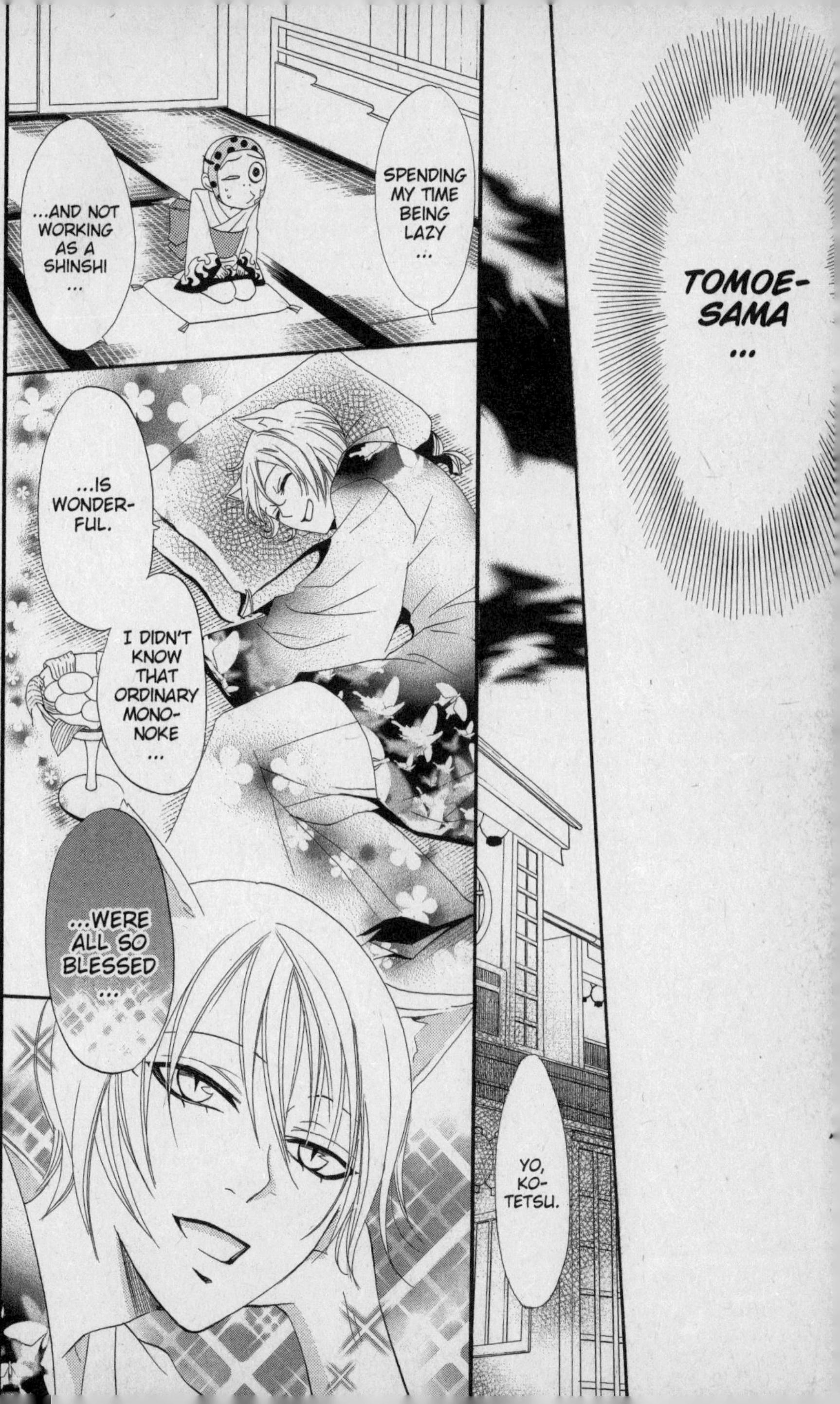
TOMOE-SAMA ...
YO, KO-TETSU.
SPENDING MY TIME BEING LAZY ...
...AND NOT WORKING AS A SHINSHI ...
...IS WONDER-FUL.
I DIDN'T KNOW THAT ORDINARY MONO-NOKE ...
...WERE ALL SO BLESSED ...

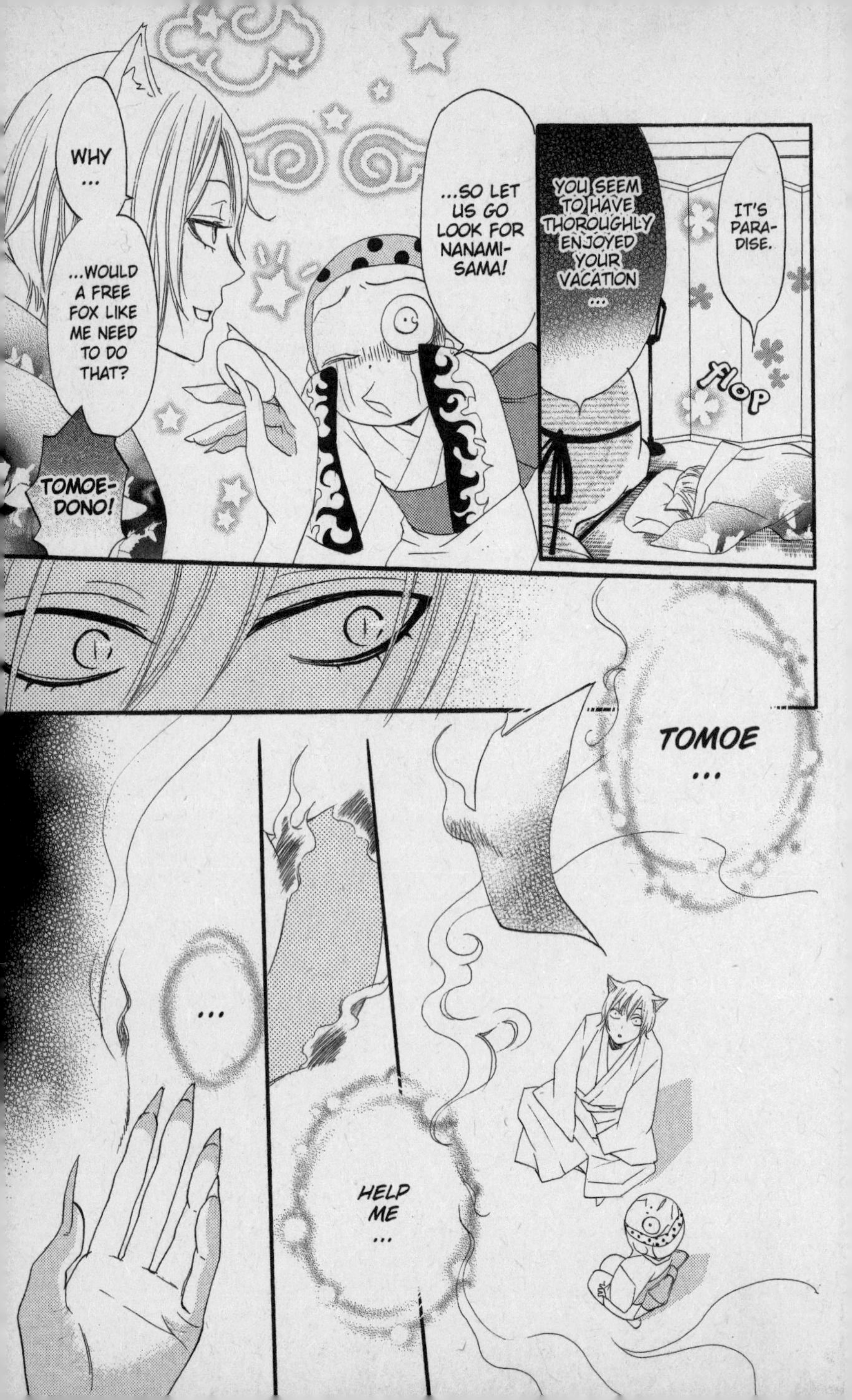
IT'S PARA-DISE.
FLOP
YOU SEEM TO HAVE THOROUGHLY ENJOYED YOUR VACATION ...
...SO LET US GO LOOK FOR NANAMI-SAMA!
WHY ...
...WOULD A FREE FOX LIKE ME NEED TO DO THAT?
TOMOE-DONO!
TOMOE ...
HELP ME ...
...

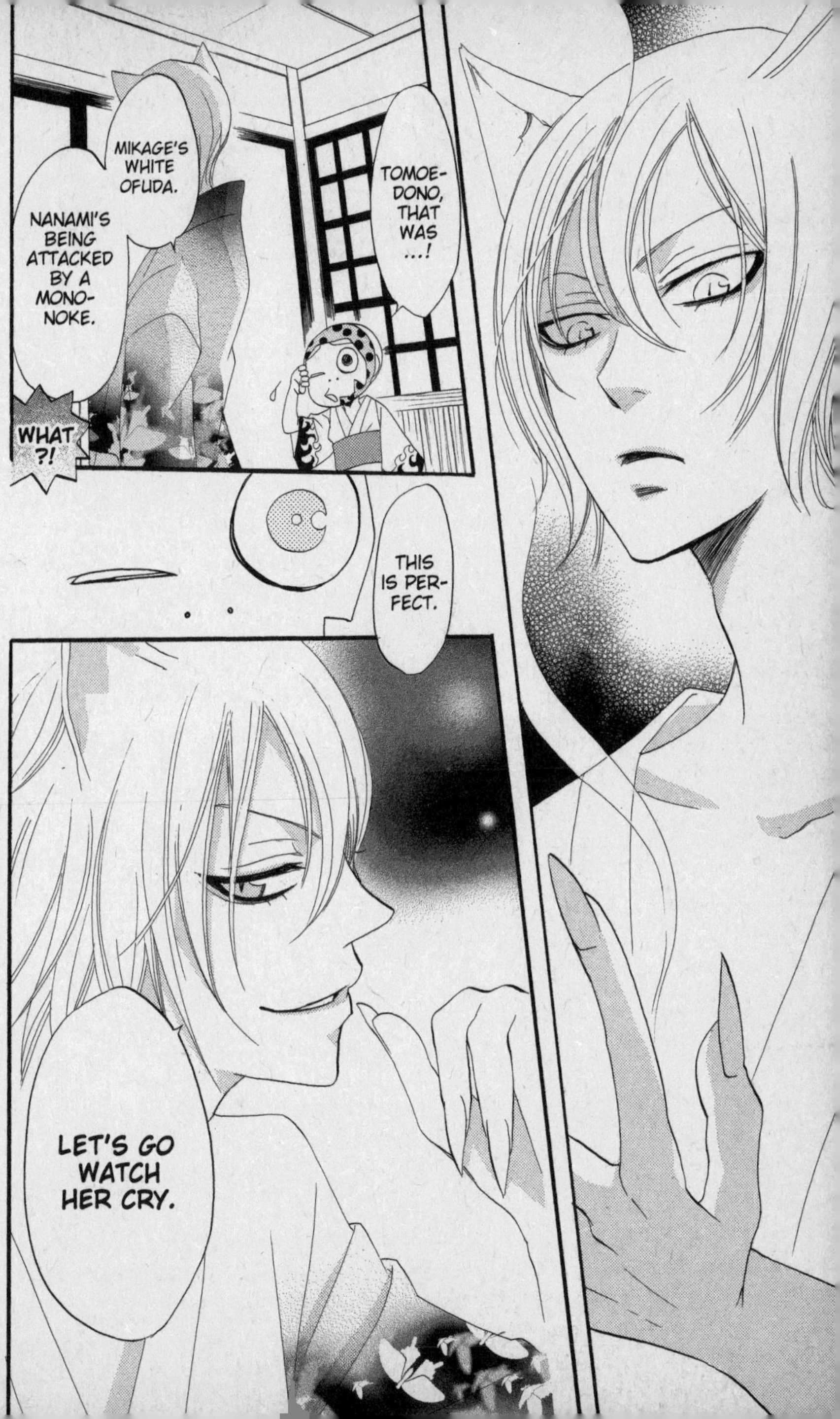
TOMOE-DONO, THAT WAS ...!
MIKAGE'S WHITE OFUDA.
NANAMI'S BEING ATTACKED BY A MONO-NOKE.
WHAT?!
THIS IS PER-FECT.
LET'S GO WATCH HER CRY.

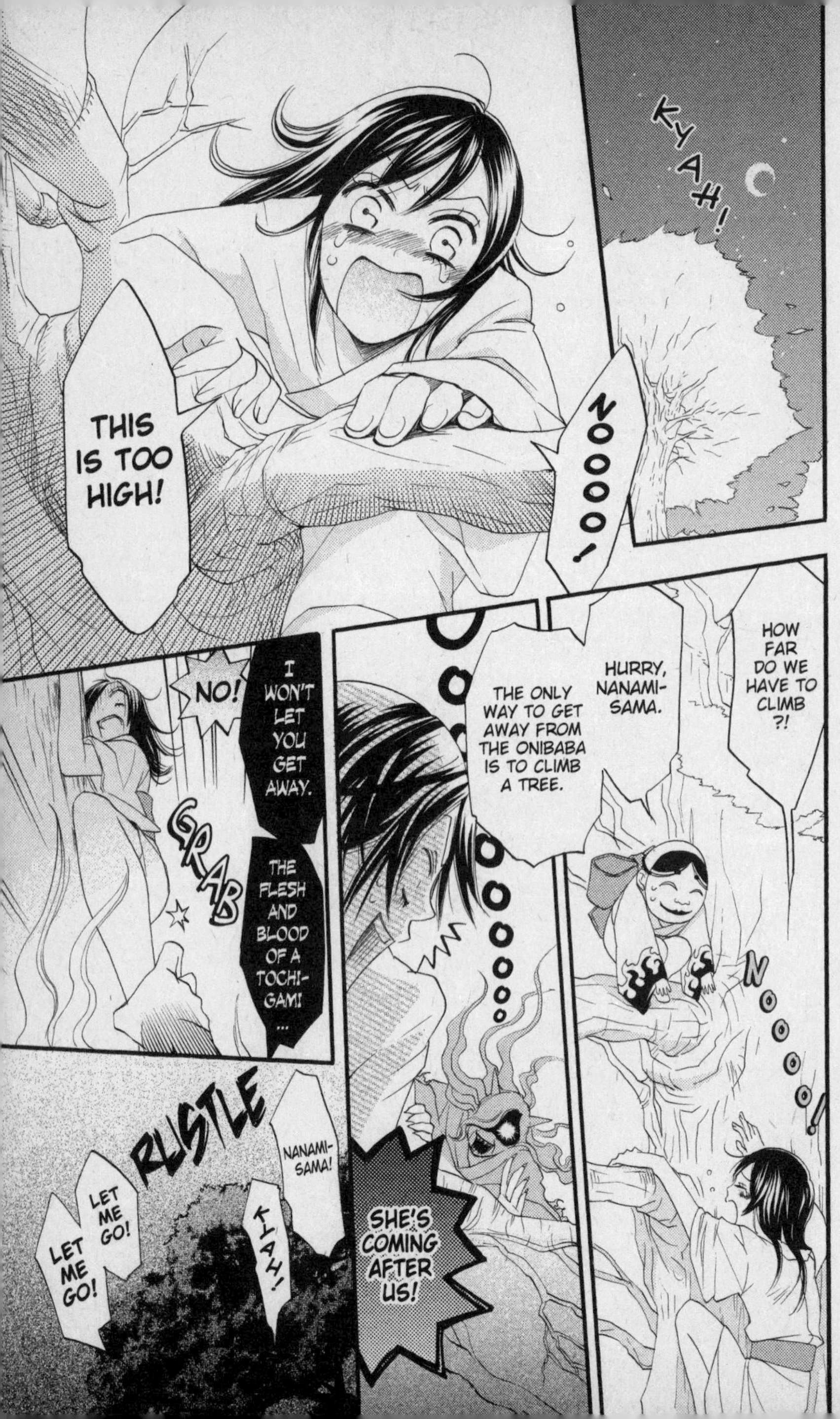
KYAH!
NOOOO!
THIS IS TOO HIGH!
HOW FAR DO WE HAVE TO CLIMB ?!
HURRY, NANAMI-SAMA.
THE ONLY WAY TO GET AWAY FROM THE ONIBABA IS TO CLIMB A TREE.
NOOOO!
OOOOOOOOOOOO
I WON'T LET YOU GET AWAY.
THE FLESH AND BLOOD OF A TOCHI-GAMI ...
NO!
GRAB
SHE'S COMING AFTER US!
KYAH!
NANAMI-SAMA!
RUSTLE
LET ME GO!
LET ME GO!

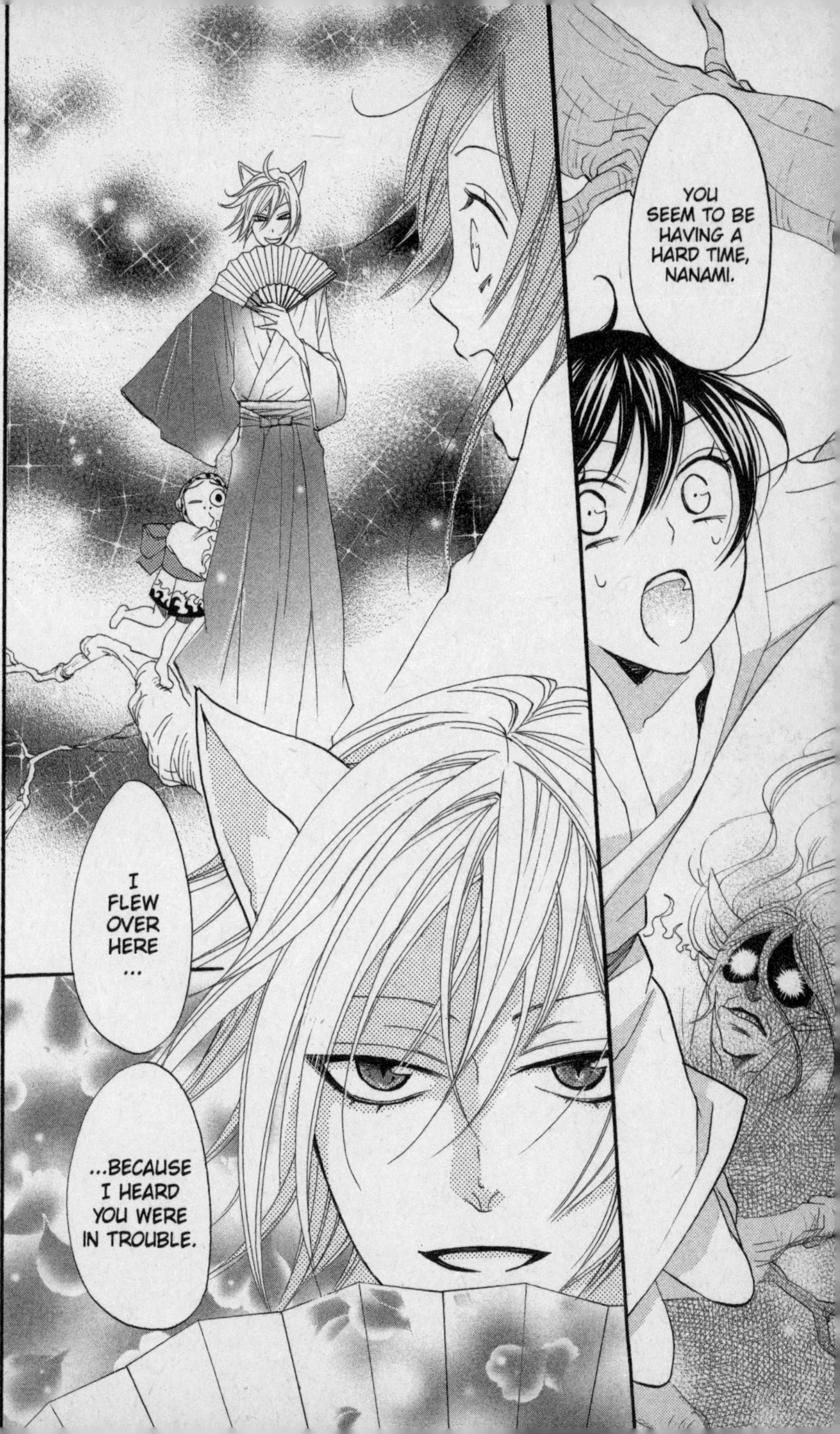

YOU SEEM TO BE HAVING A HARD TIME, NANAMI.
I FLEW OVER HERE...
...BECAUSE I HEARD YOU WERE IN TROUBLE.

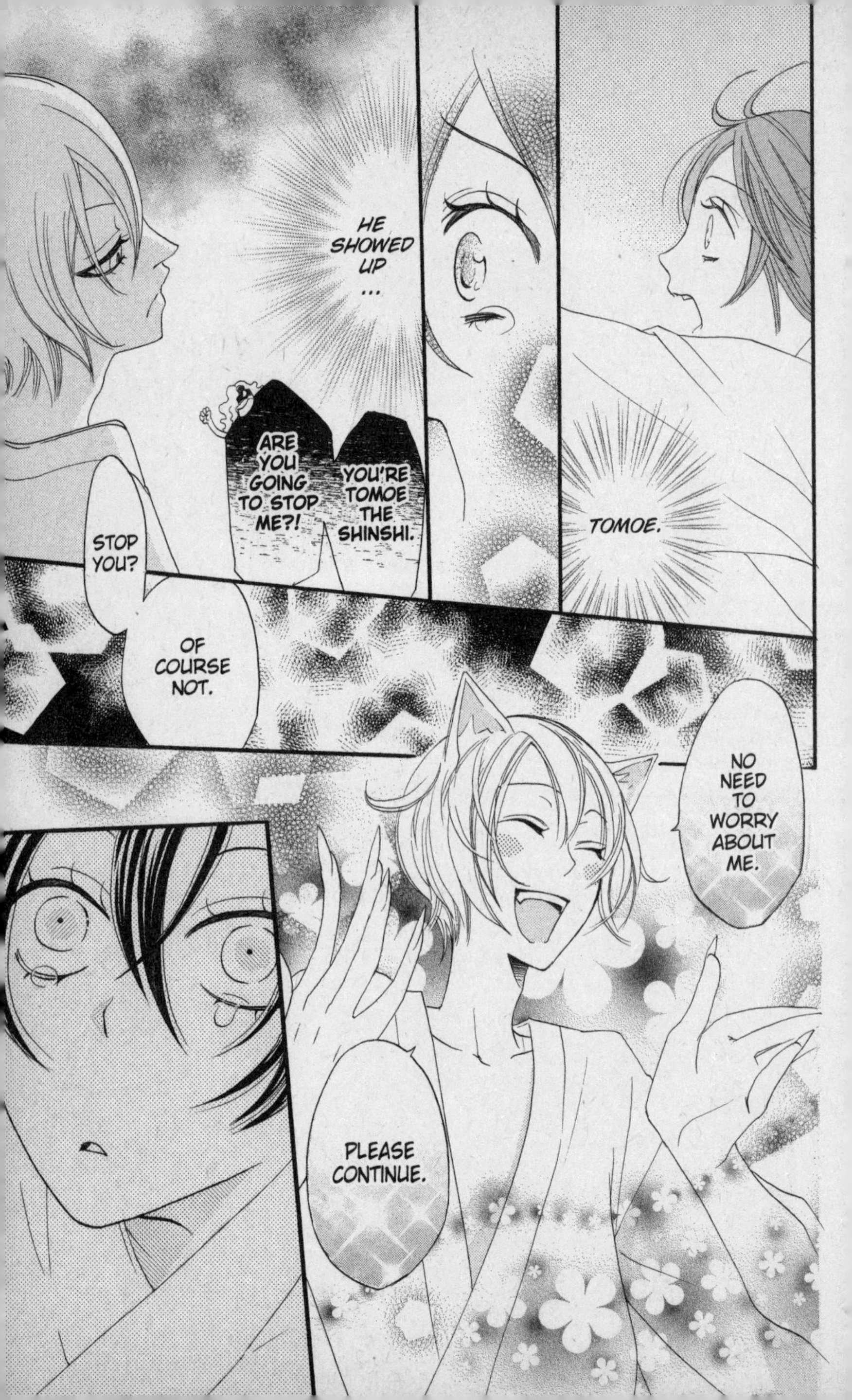
TOMOE.
HE SHOWED UP ...
YOU'RE TOMOE THE SHINSHI.
ARE YOU GOING TO STOP ME?!
STOP YOU?
OF COURSE NOT.
NO NEED TO WORRY ABOUT ME.
PLEASE CONTINUE.

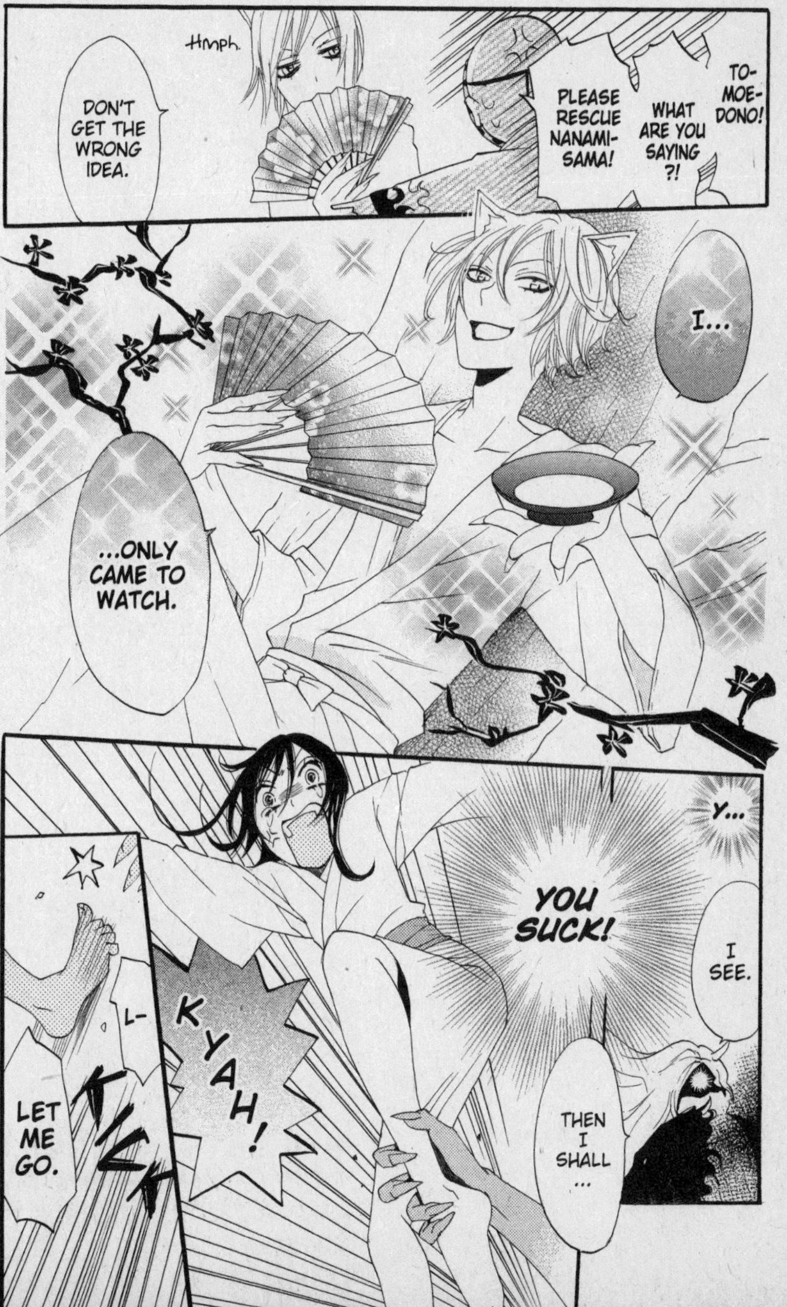
TO-MOE-DONO!
WHAT ARE YOU SAYING ?!
PLEASE RESCUE NANAMI-SAMA!
Hmph.
DON'T GET THE WRONG IDEA.
I...
...ONLY CAME TO WATCH.
Y...
YOU SUCK!
I SEE.
THEN I SHALL ...
KYAH!
L-
KICK
LET ME GO.

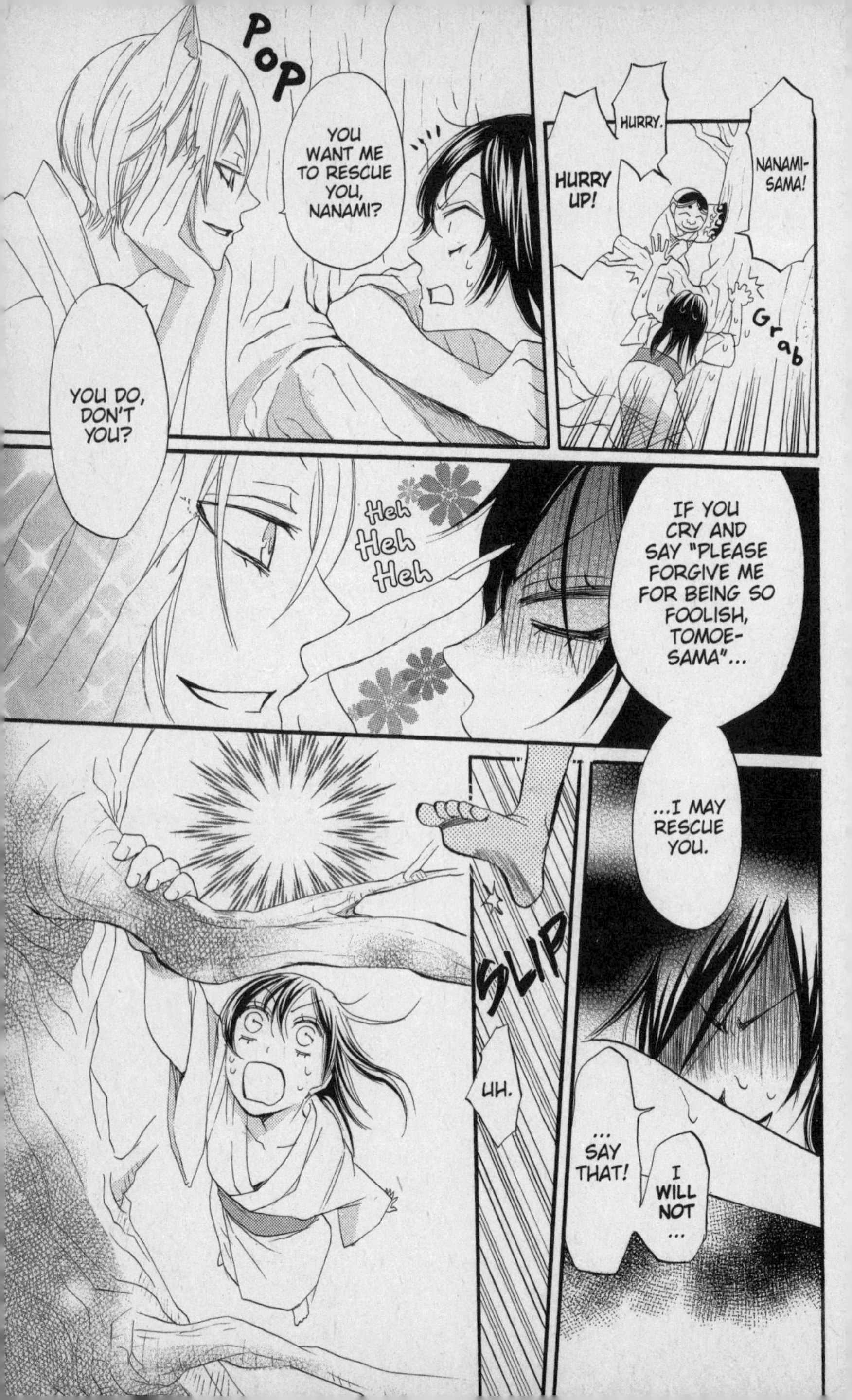
NANAMI-SAMA!
HURRY.
HURRY UP!
Grab
POP
YOU WANT ME TO RESCUE YOU, NANAMI?
YOU DO, DON'T YOU?
IF YOU CRY AND SAY "PLEASE FORGIVE ME FOR BEING SO FOOLISH, TOMOE-SAMA"...
Heh Heh Heh
...I MAY RESCUE YOU.
I WILL NOT ...
... SAY THAT!
SLIP
UH.

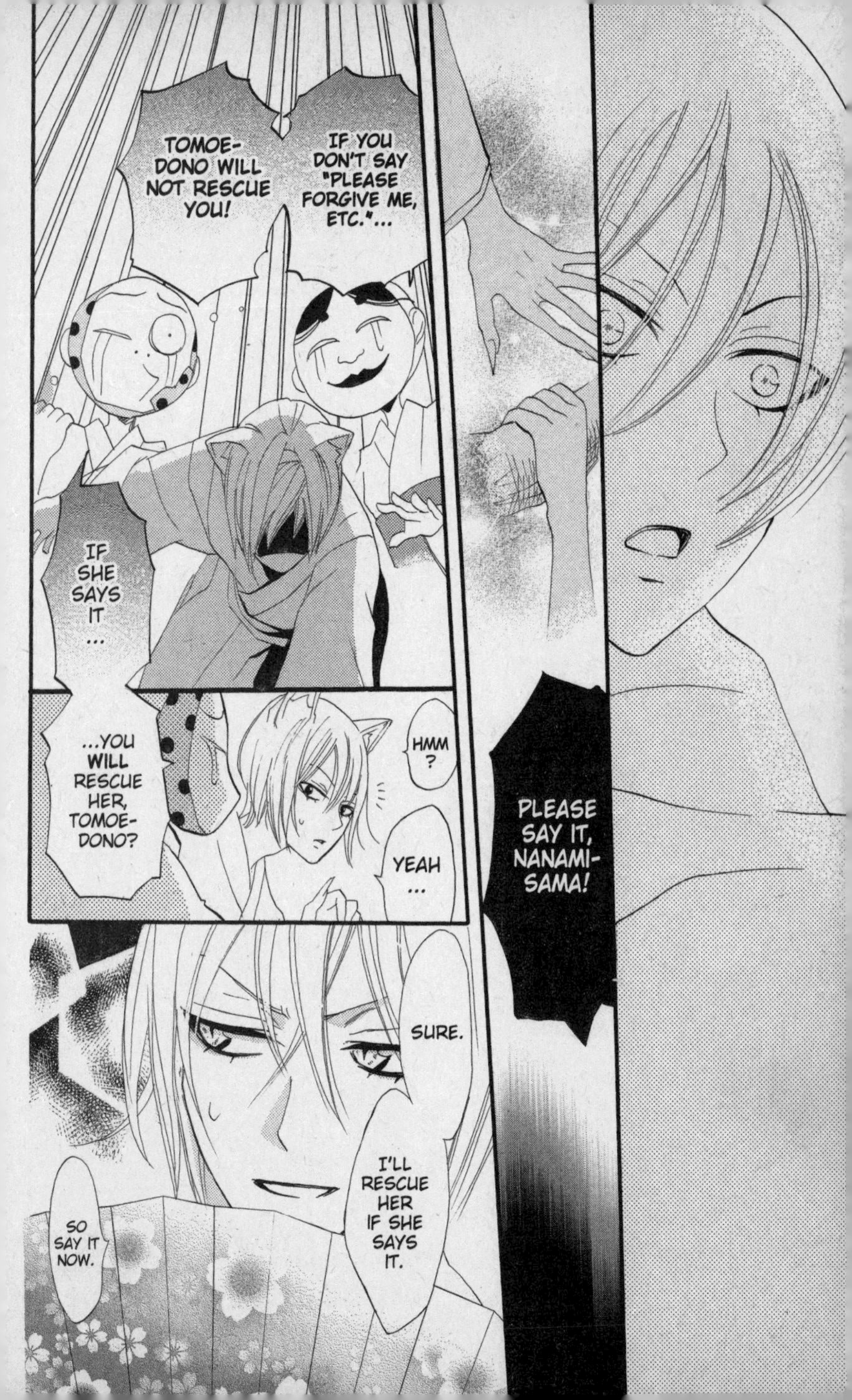
PLEASE SAY IT, NANAMI-SAMA!
IF YOU DON'T SAY "PLEASE FORGIVE ME, ETC."...
TOMOE-DONO WILL NOT RESCUE YOU!
IF SHE SAYS IT...
HMM?
...YOU WILL RESCUE HER, TOMOE-DONO?
YEAH...
SURE.
I'LL RESCUE HER IF SHE SAYS IT.
SO SAY IT NOW.

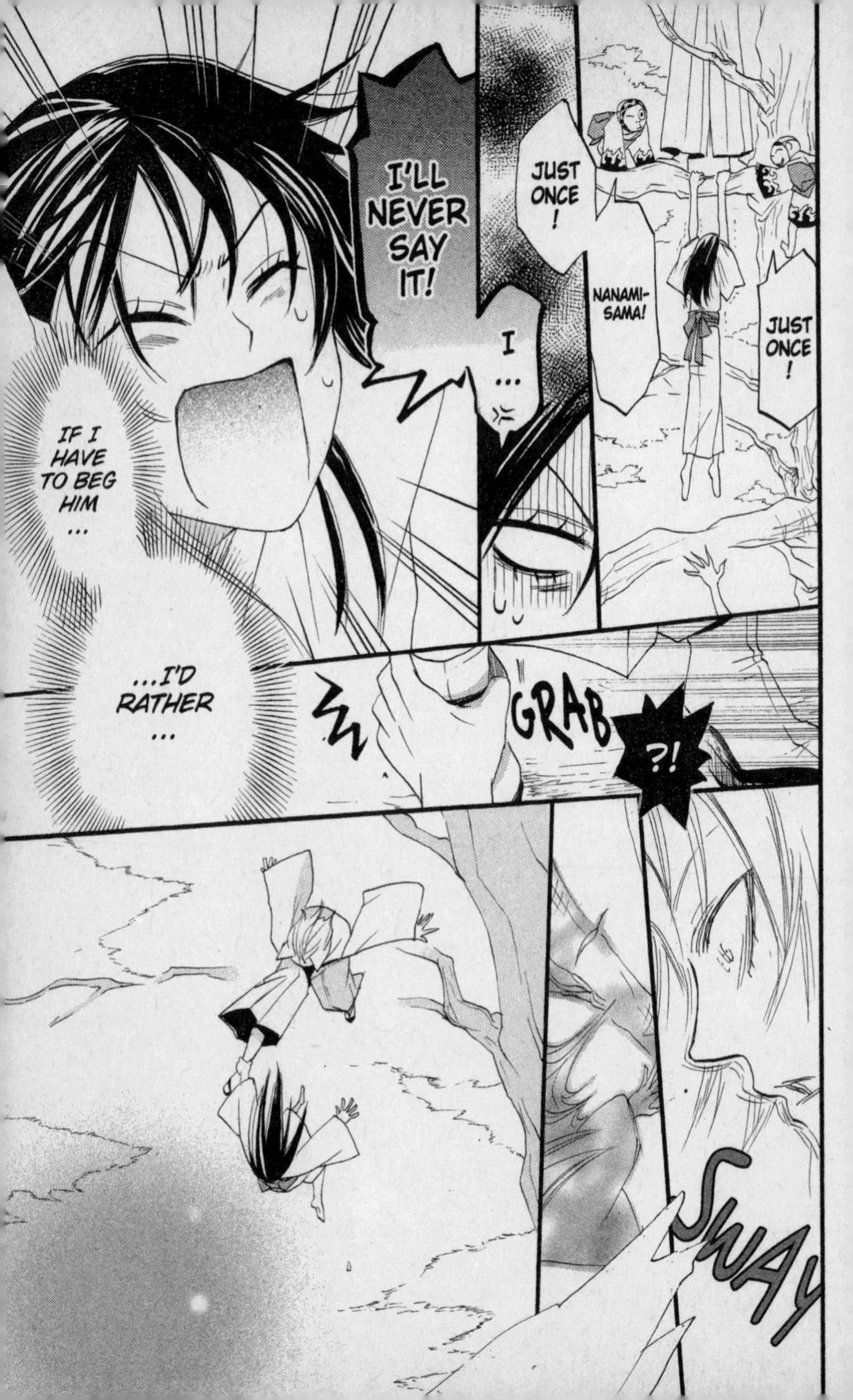
JUST ONCE!
NANAMI-SAMA!
JUST ONCE!
I...
I'LL NEVER SAY IT!
IF I HAVE TO BEG HIM...
...I'D RATHER...
GRAB
?!
SWAY

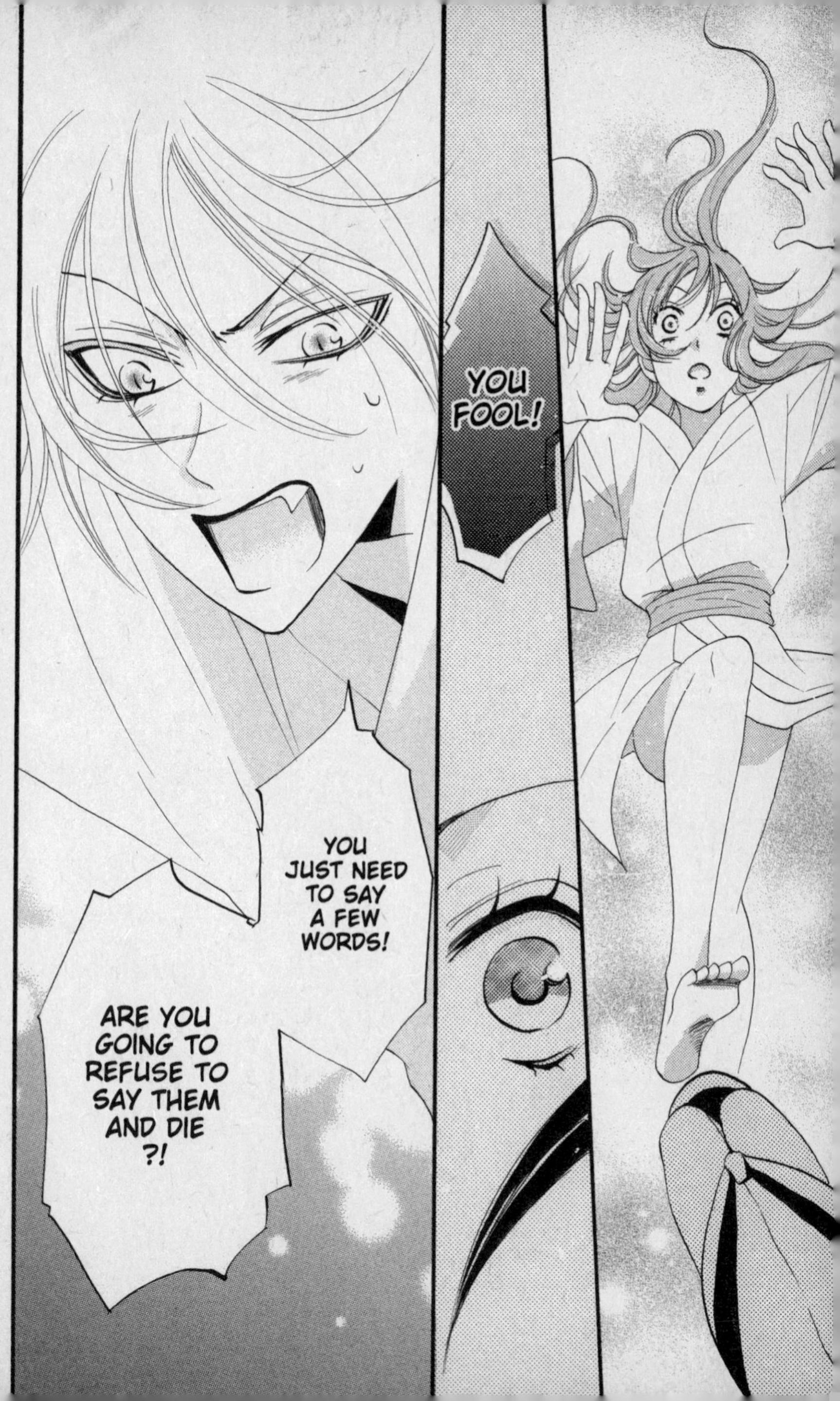
YOU FOOL!
YOU JUST NEED TO SAY A FEW WORDS!
ARE YOU GOING TO REFUSE TO SAY THEM AND DIE?!

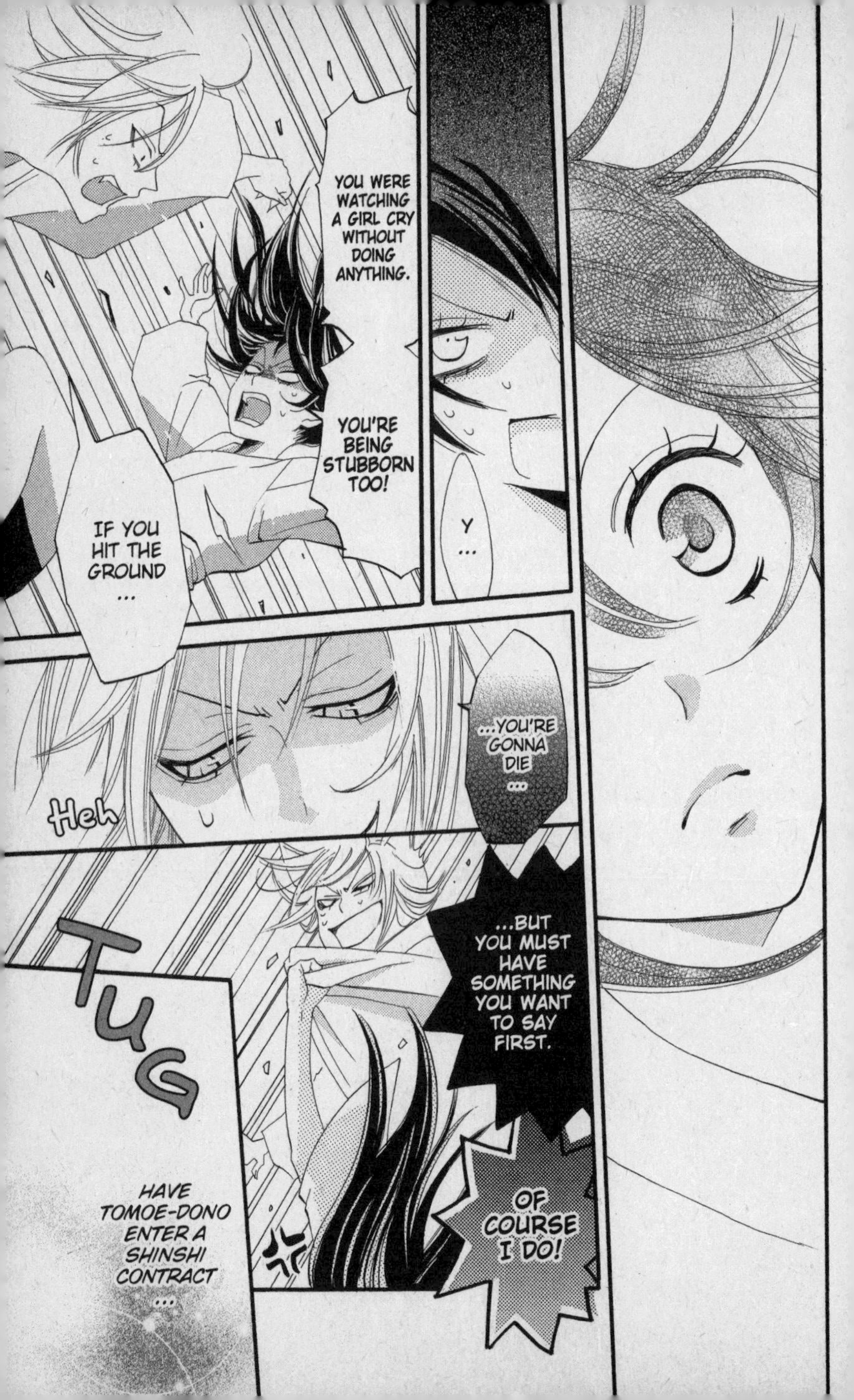
Y ...
YOU WERE WATCHING A GIRL CRY WITHOUT DOING ANYTHING.
YOU'RE BEING STUBBORN TOO!
IF YOU HIT THE GROUND ...
...YOU'RE GONNA DIE ...
Heh
...BUT YOU MUST HAVE SOMETHING YOU WANT TO SAY FIRST.
TUG
OF COURSE I DO!
HAVE TOMOE-DONO ENTER A SHINSHI CONTRACT ...

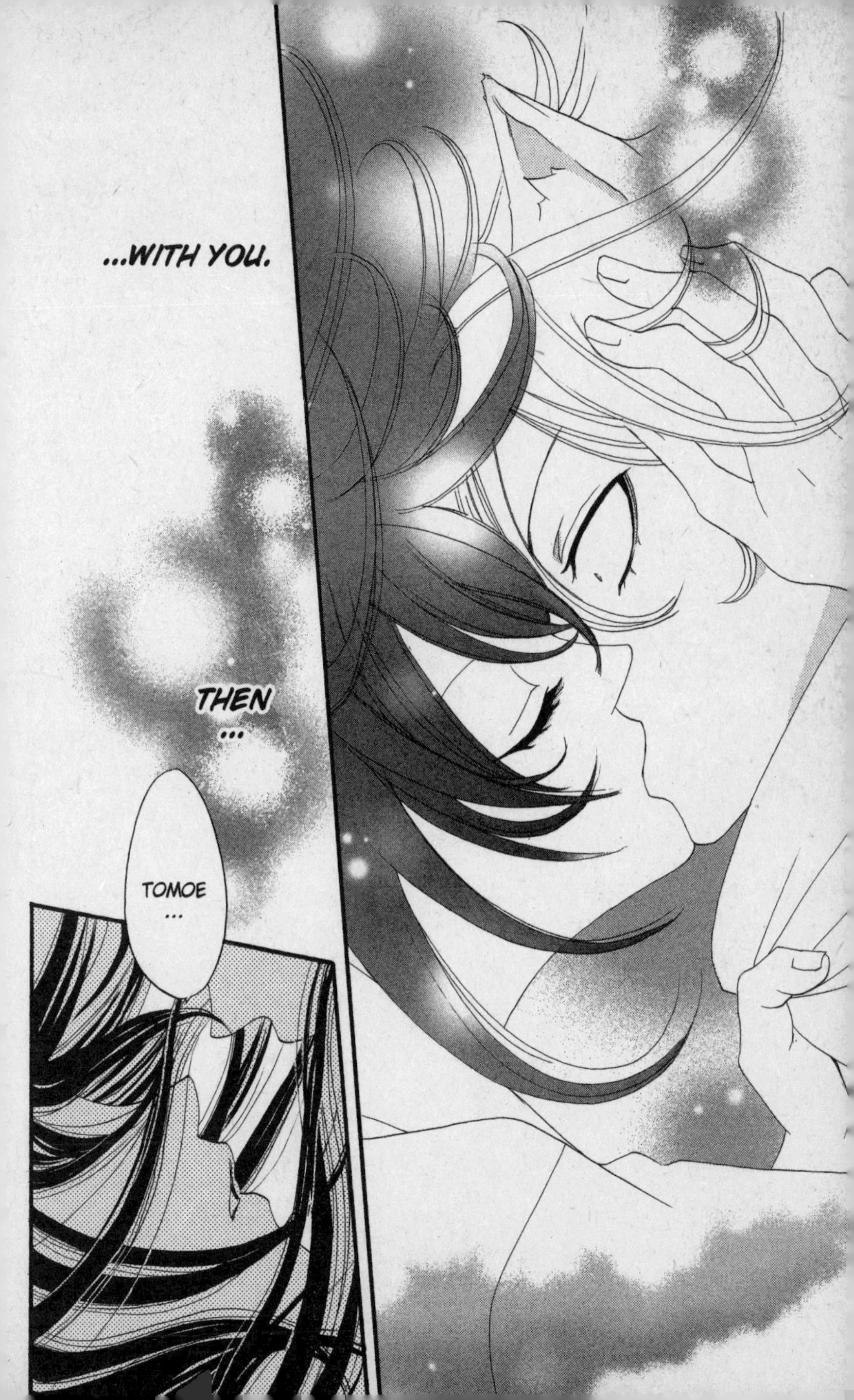
...WITH YOU.
THEN ...
TOMOE ...

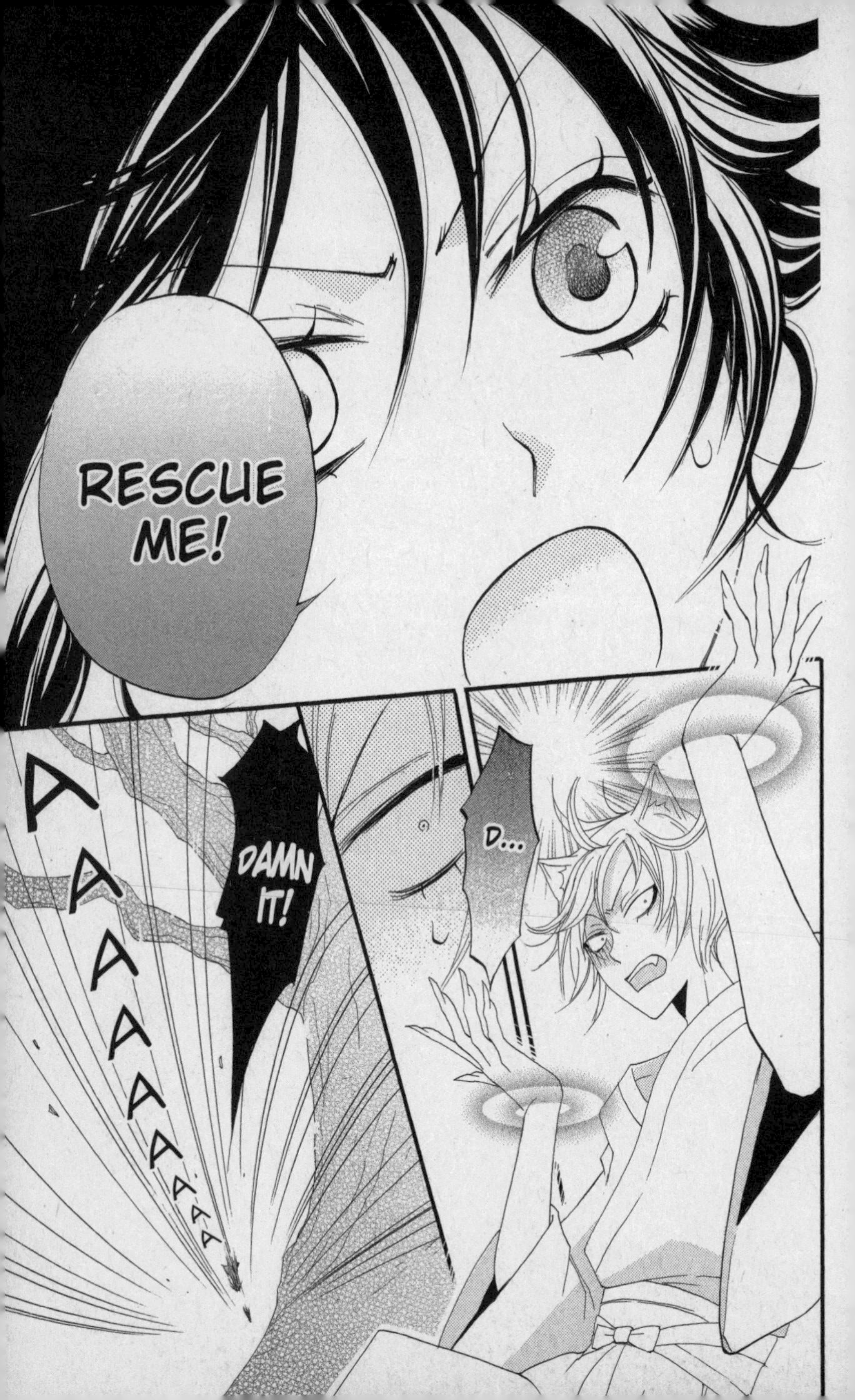
RESCUE ME!
D...
DAMN IT!
AAAAAAAAAA

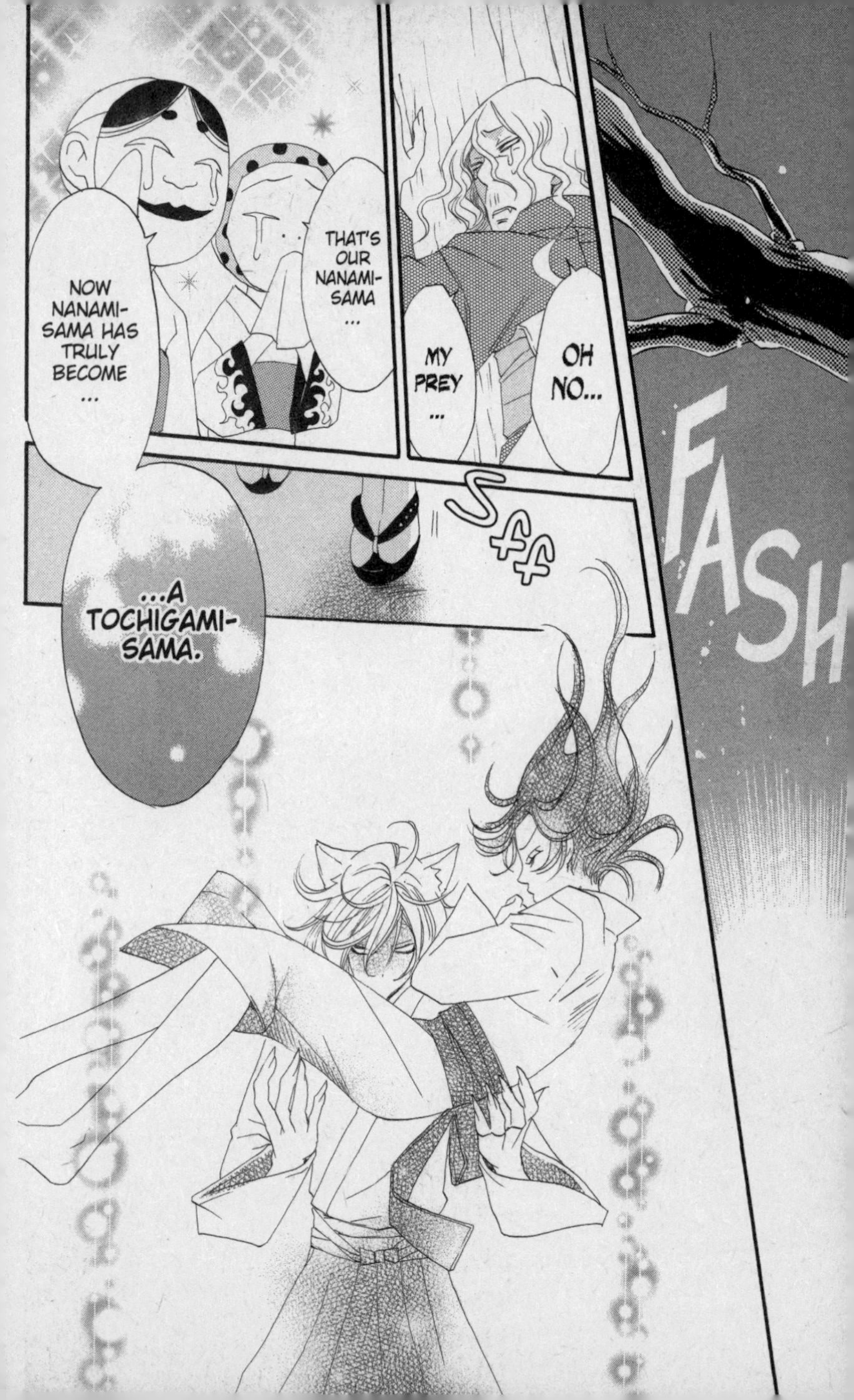
FASH
OH NO...
MY PREY ...
THAT'S OUR NANAMI-SAMA ...
NOW NANAMI-SAMA HAS TRULY BECOME ...
...A TOCHIGAMI-SAMA.
Sff

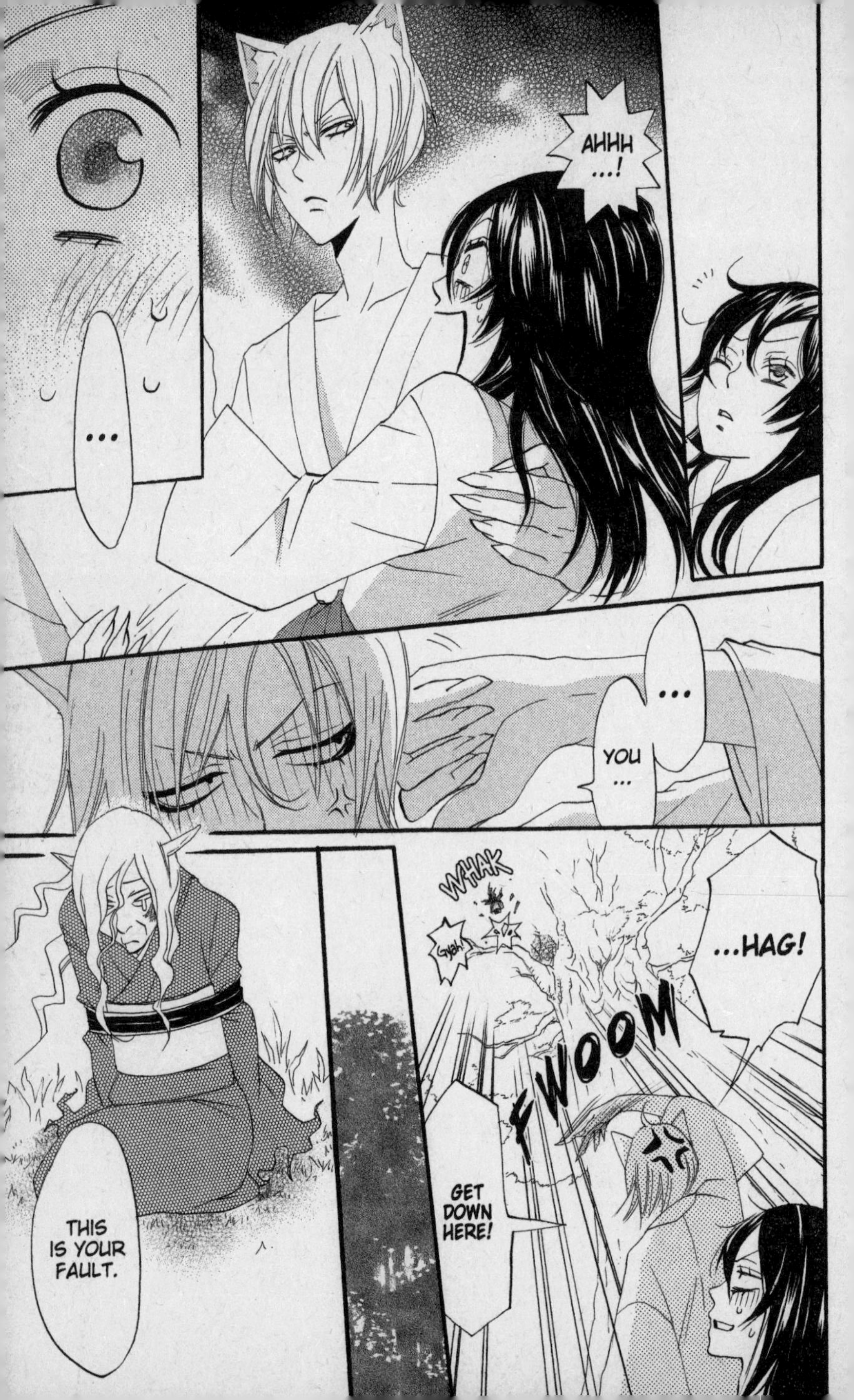
AHHH ...!
...
... YOU ...
...HAG!
FWOOM
WHAK
Gyah!
GET DOWN HERE!
THIS IS YOUR FAULT.

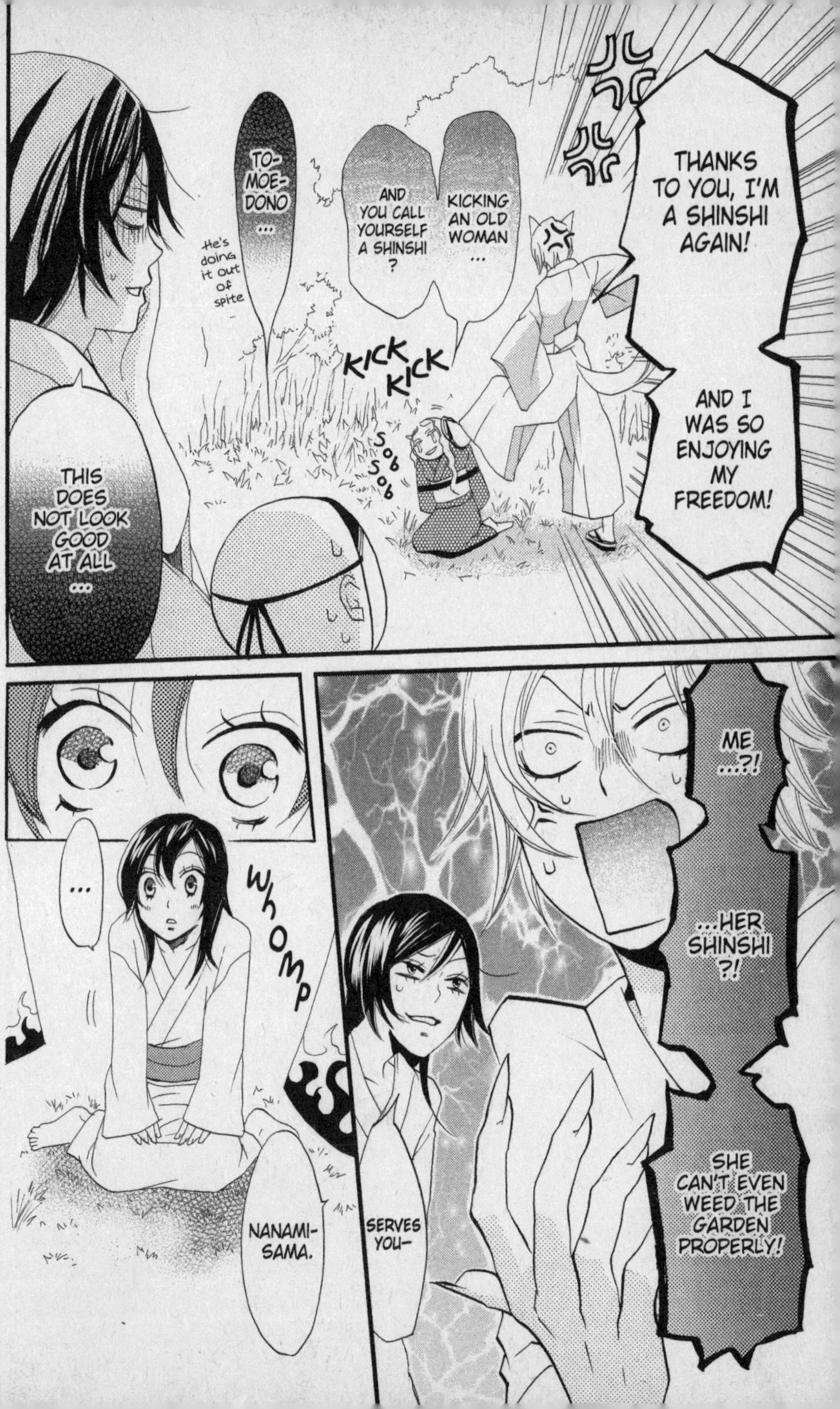
THANKS TO YOU, I'M A SHINSHI AGAIN!
AND I WAS SO ENJOYING MY FREEDOM!
KICKING AN OLD WOMAN...
AND YOU CALL YOURSELF A SHINSHI?
KICK KICK
Sob Sob
TO-MOE-DONO...
He's doing it out of spite...
THIS DOES NOT LOOK GOOD AT ALL...
ME...?!
...HER SHINSHI?!
SHE CAN'T EVEN WEED THE GARDEN PROPERLY!
SERVES YOU-
...
WHOMP
NANAMI-SAMA.

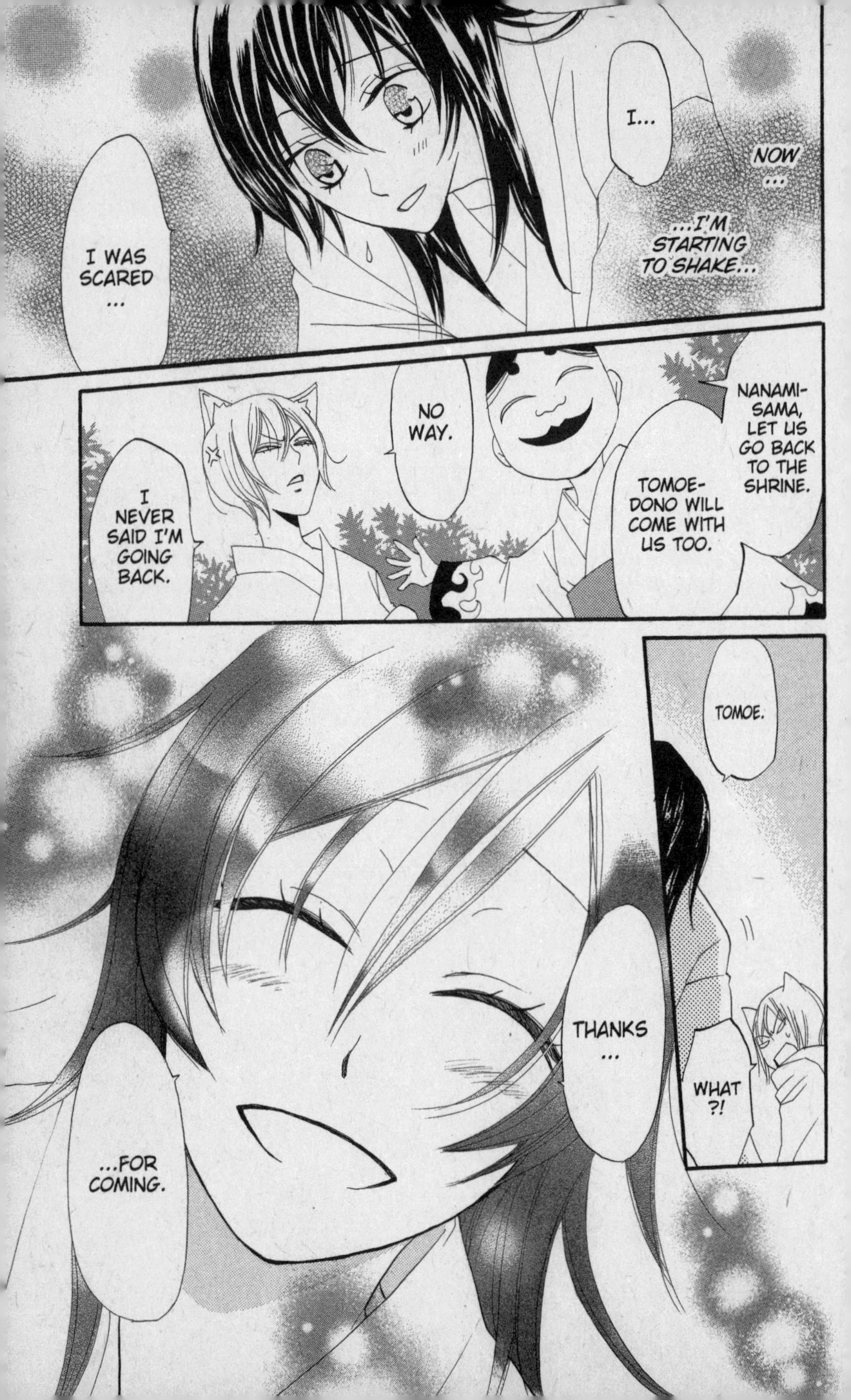
NOW... ...I'M STARTING TO SHAKE...
I...
I WAS SCARED...
NANAMI-SAMA, LET US GO BACK TO THE SHRINE.
TOMOE-DONO WILL COME WITH US TOO.
NO WAY.
I NEVER SAID I'M GOING BACK.
TOMOE.
WHAT?!
THANKS...
...FOR COMING.

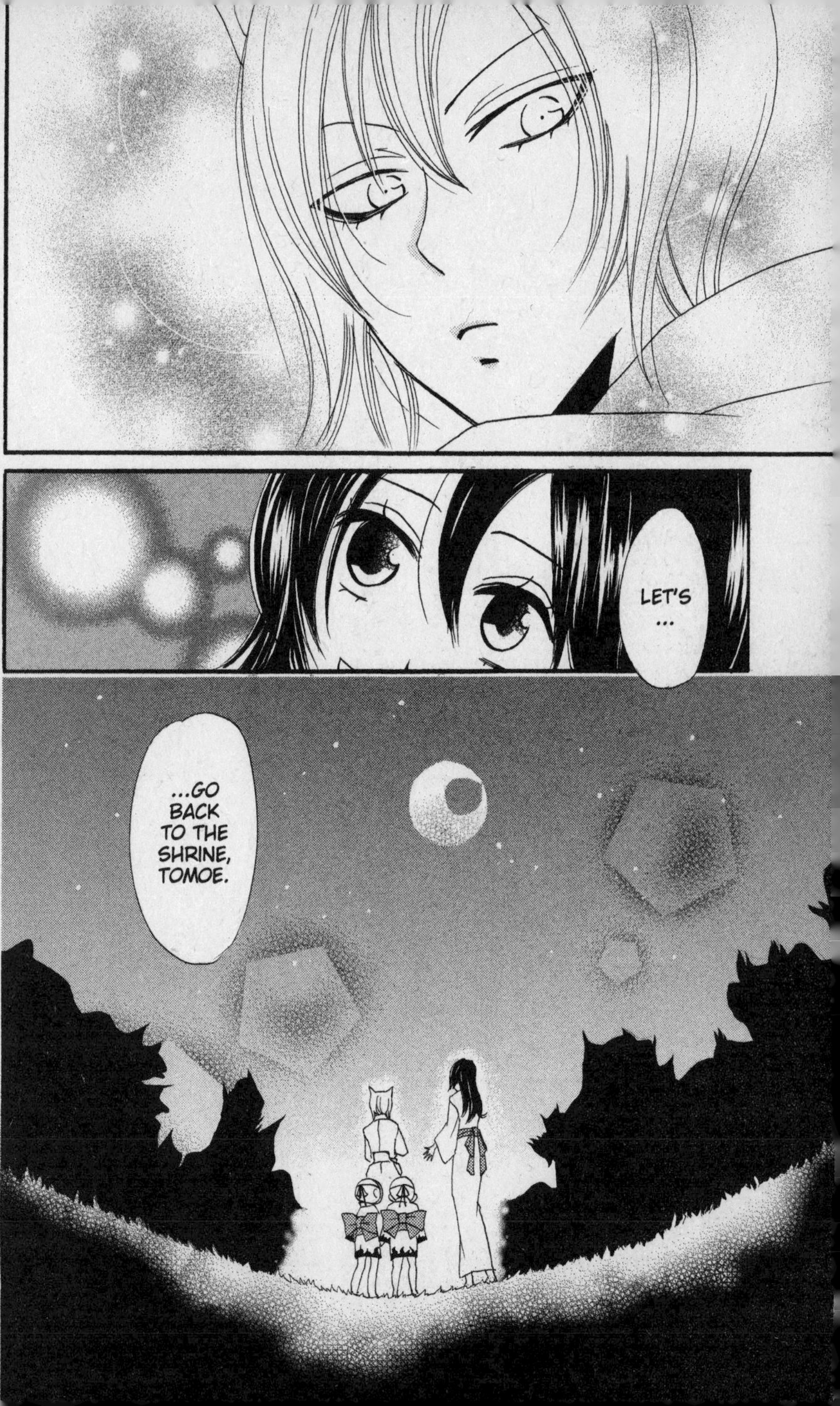
LET'S ...
...GO BACK TO THE SHRINE, TOMOE.

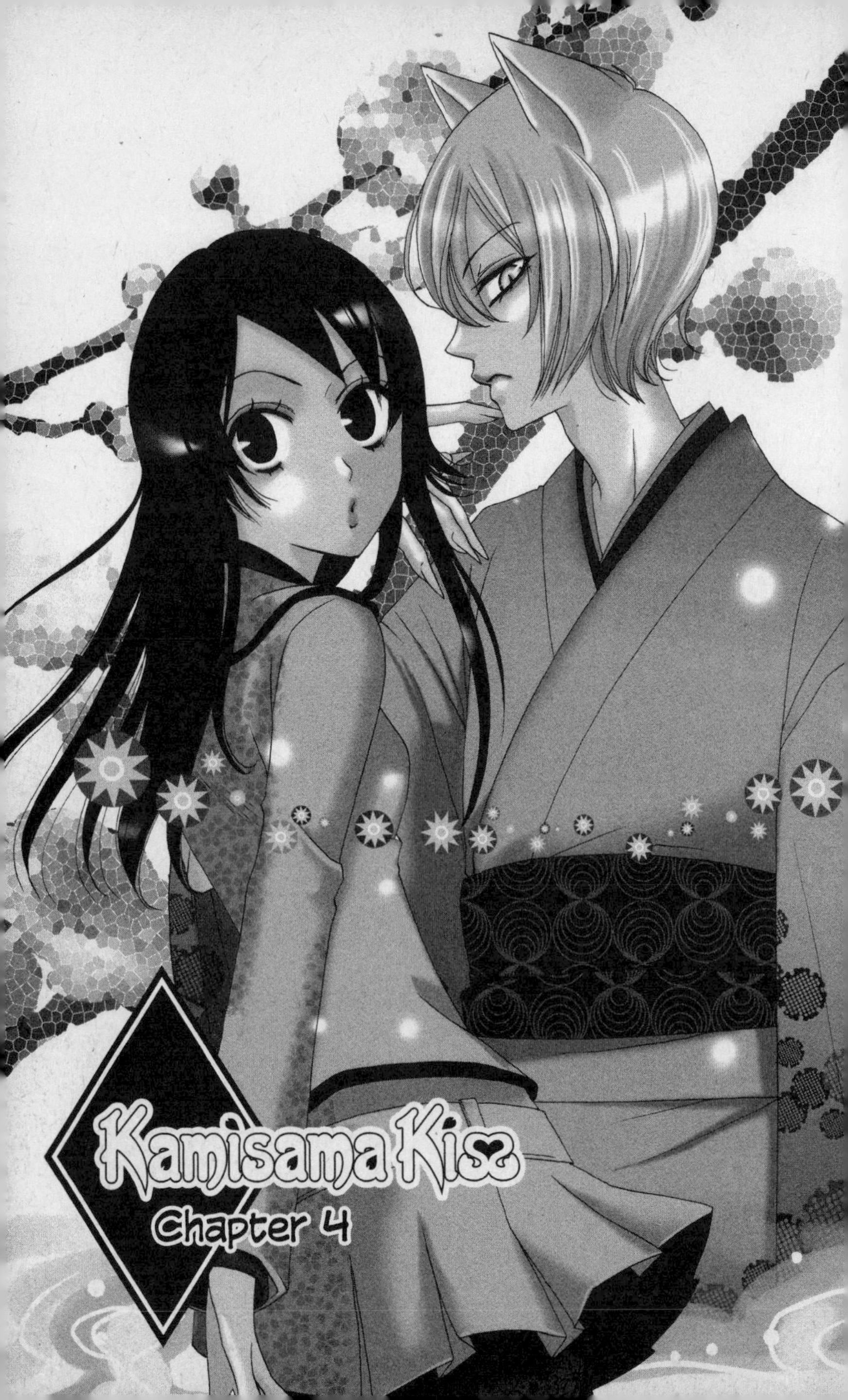
Kamisama Kiss
Chapter 4

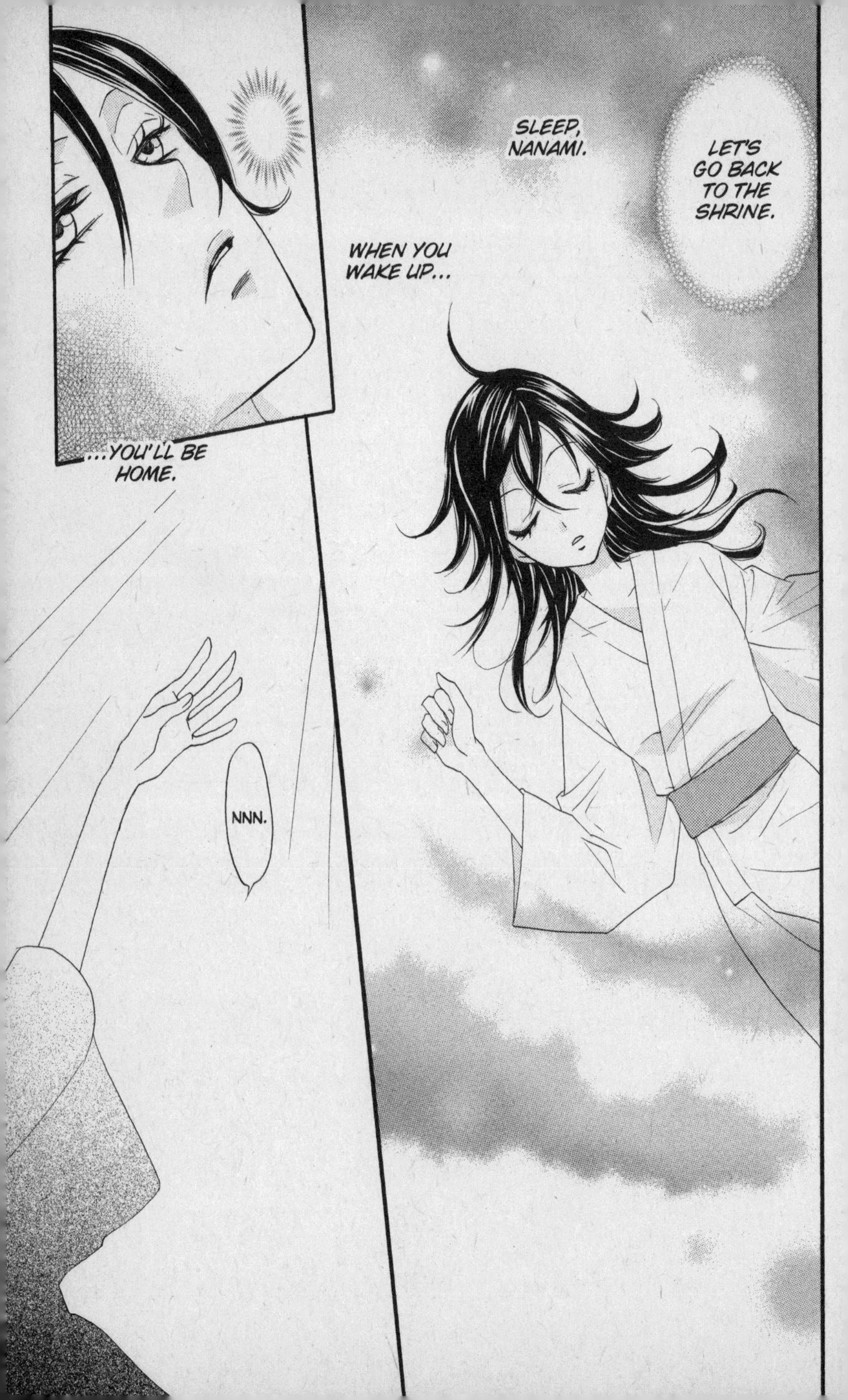
LET'S GO BACK TO THE SHRINE.
SLEEP, NANAMI.
WHEN YOU WAKE UP...
...YOU'LL BE HOME.
NNN.

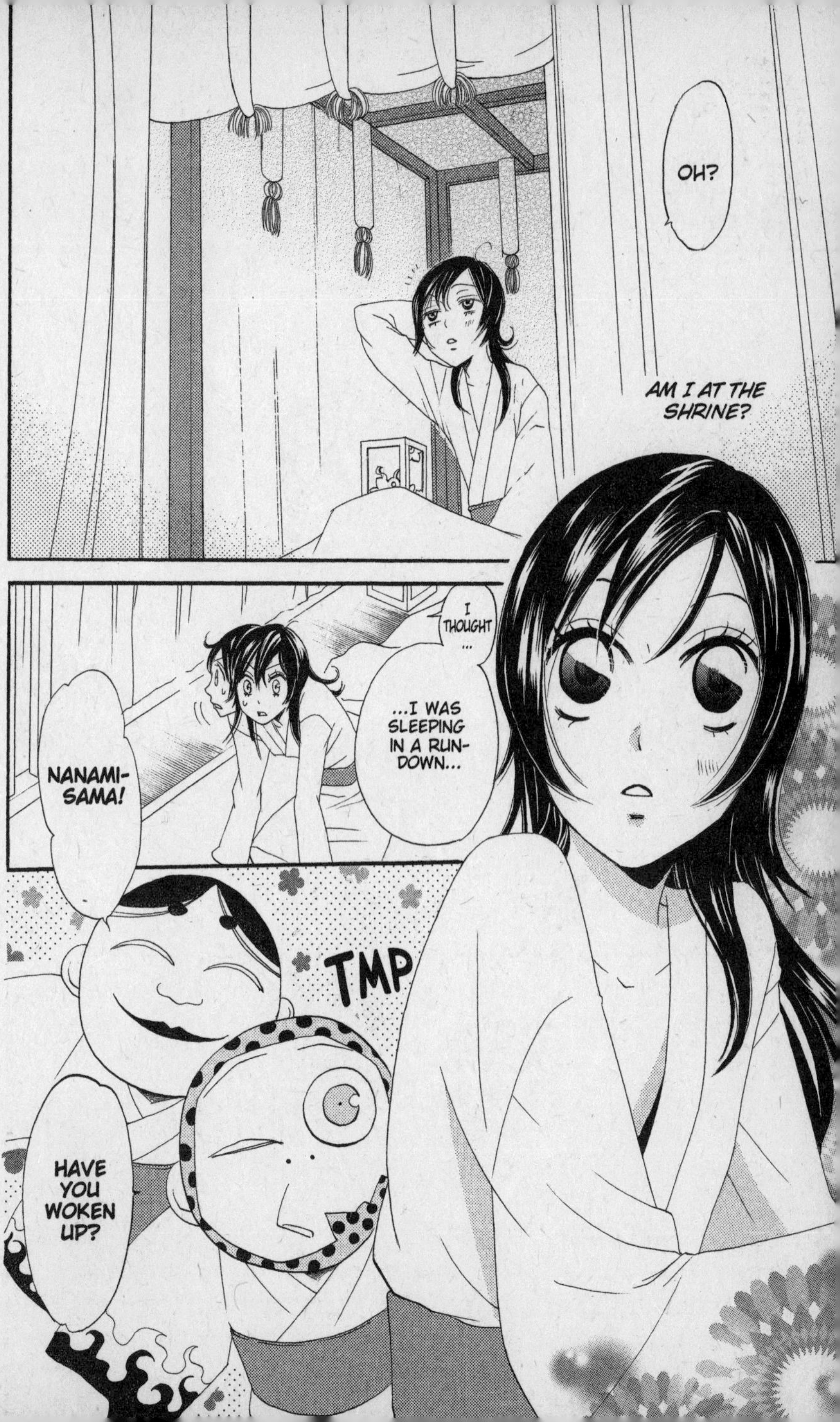
OH?
AM I AT THE SHRINE?
I THOUGHT...
...I WAS SLEEPING IN A RUN-DOWN...
NANAMI-SAMA!
TMP
HAVE YOU WOKEN UP?

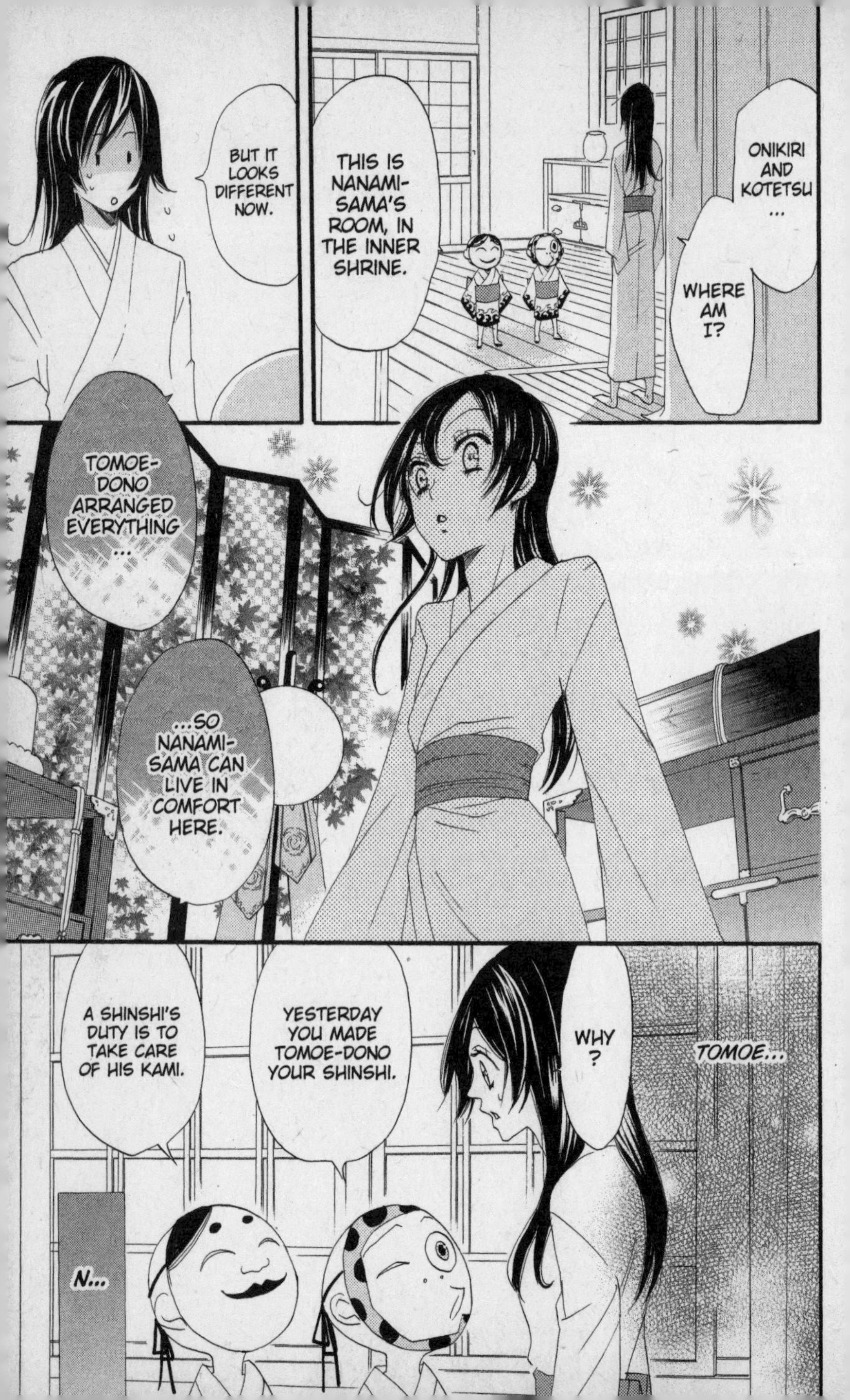
ONIKIRI AND KOTETSU ...
WHERE AM I?
THIS IS NANAMI-SAMA'S ROOM, IN THE INNER SHRINE.
BUT IT LOOKS DIFFERENT NOW.
TOMOE-DONO ARRANGED EVERYTHING ...
...SO NANAMI-SAMA CAN LIVE IN COMFORT HERE.
TOMOE...
WHY ?
YESTERDAY YOU MADE TOMOE-DONO YOUR SHINSHI.
A SHINSHI'S DUTY IS TO TAKE CARE OF HIS KAMI.
N...

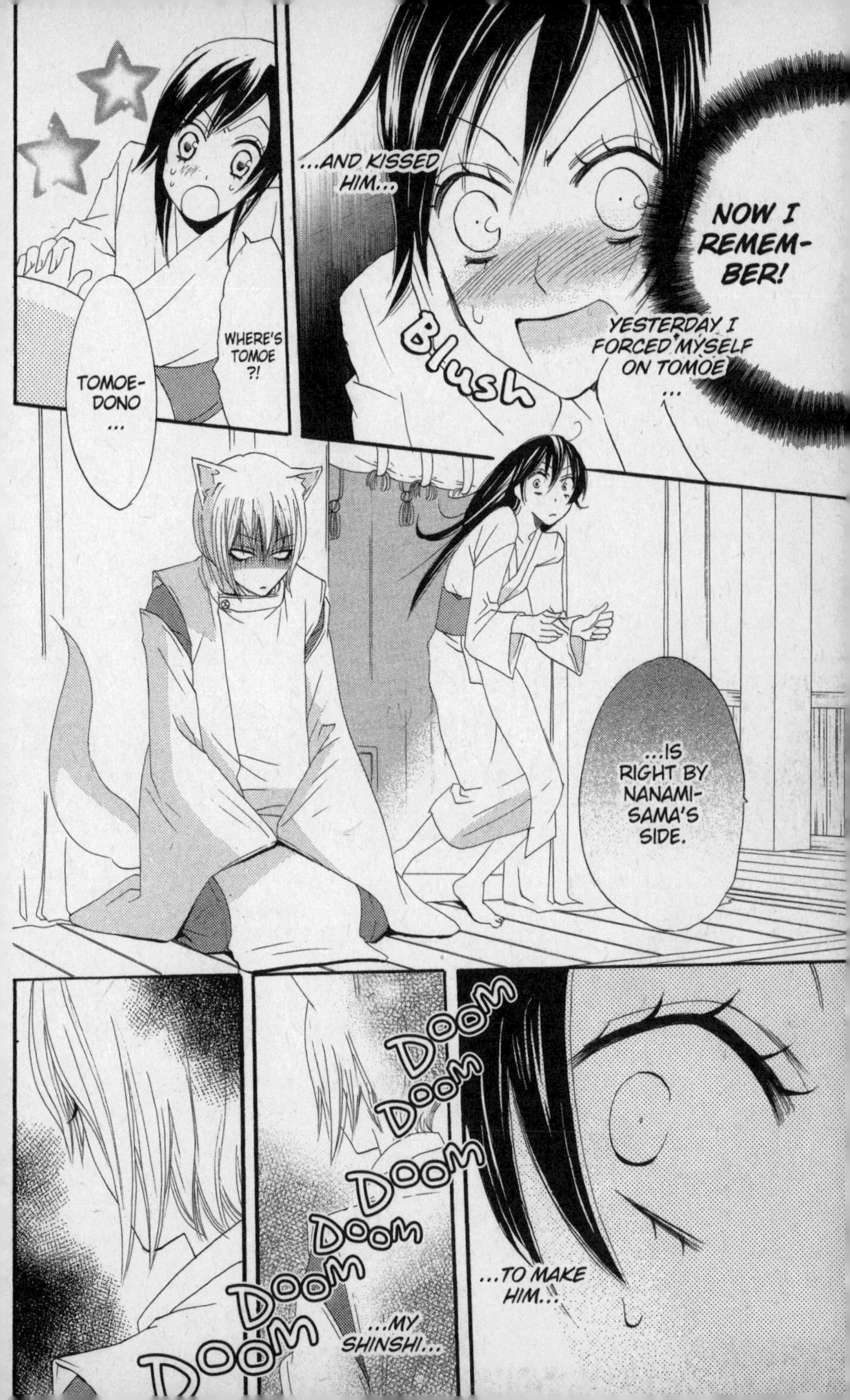
NOW I REMEMBER!
YESTERDAY I FORCED MYSELF ON TOMOE...
Blush
...AND KISSED HIM...
WHERE'S TOMOE?!
TOMOE-DONO...
...IS RIGHT BY NANAMI-SAMA'S SIDE.
...TO MAKE HIM...
...MY SHINSHI...
Doom Doom Doom Doom Doom Doom

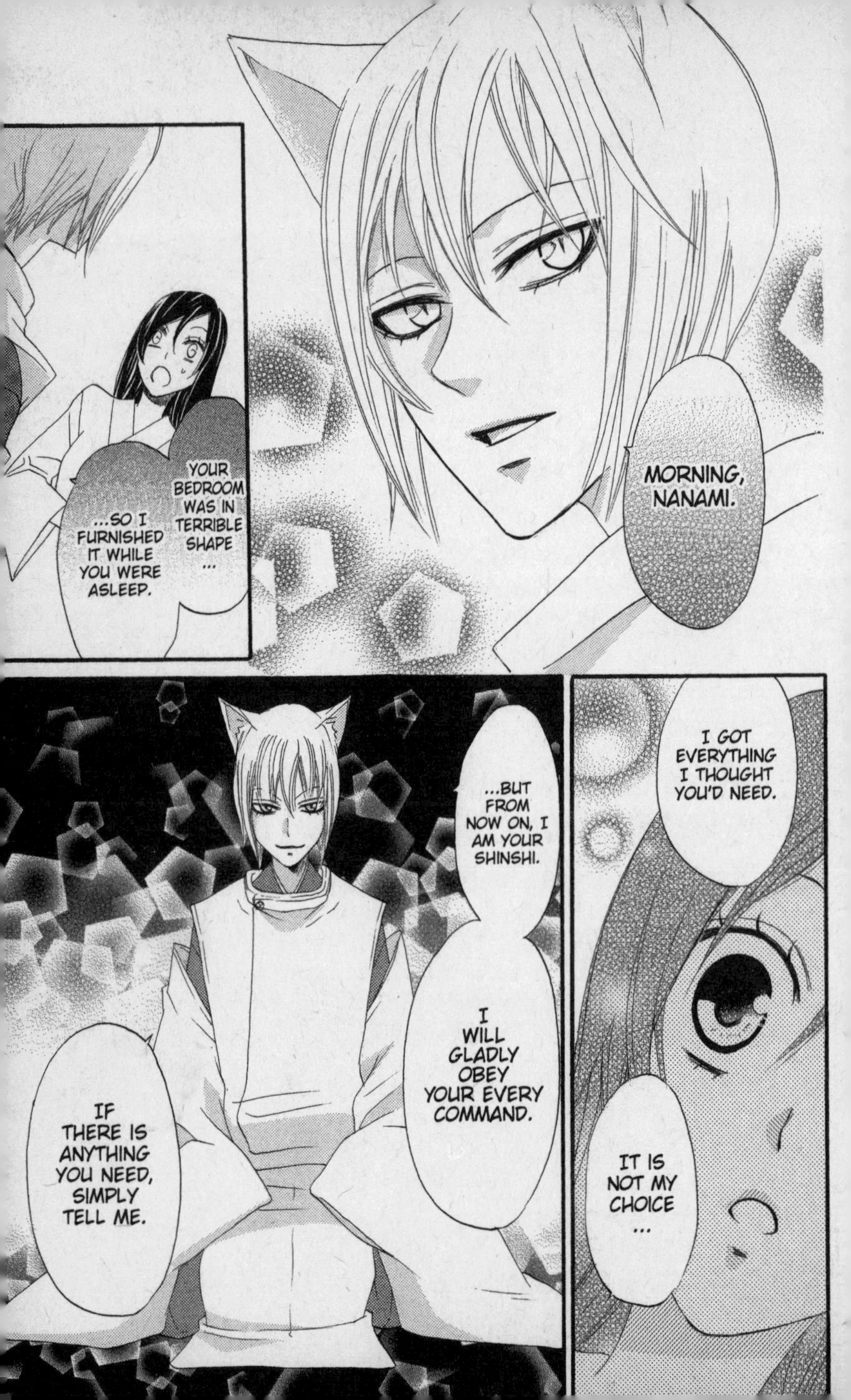
MORNING, NANAMI.
YOUR BEDROOM WAS IN TERRIBLE SHAPE...
...SO I FURNISHED IT WHILE YOU WERE ASLEEP.
I GOT EVERYTHING I THOUGHT YOU'D NEED.
IT IS NOT MY CHOICE...
...BUT FROM NOW ON, I AM YOUR SHINSHI.
I WILL GLADLY OBEY YOUR EVERY COMMAND.
IF THERE IS ANYTHING YOU NEED, SIMPLY TELL ME.

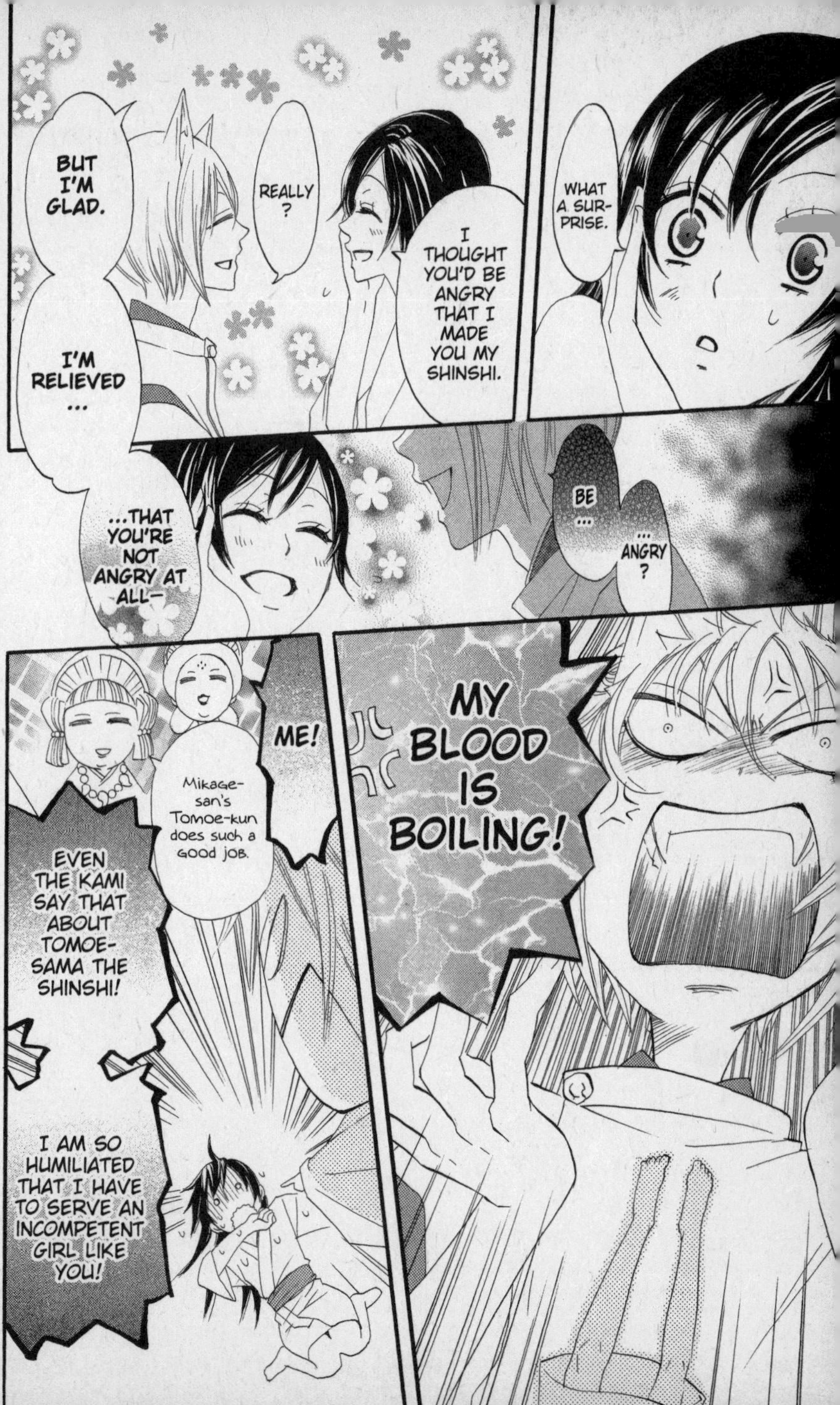
WHAT A SUR-PRISE.
I THOUGHT YOU'D BE ANGRY THAT I MADE YOU MY SHINSHI.
REALLY?
BUT I'M GLAD.
I'M RELIEVED...
...THAT YOU'RE NOT ANGRY AT ALL–
BE...
...ANGRY?
MY BLOOD IS BOILING!
ME!
Mikage-san's Tomoe-kun does such a good job.
EVEN THE KAMI SAY THAT ABOUT TOMOE-SAMA THE SHINSHI!
I AM SO HUMILIATED THAT I HAVE TO SERVE AN INCOMPETENT GIRL LIKE YOU!

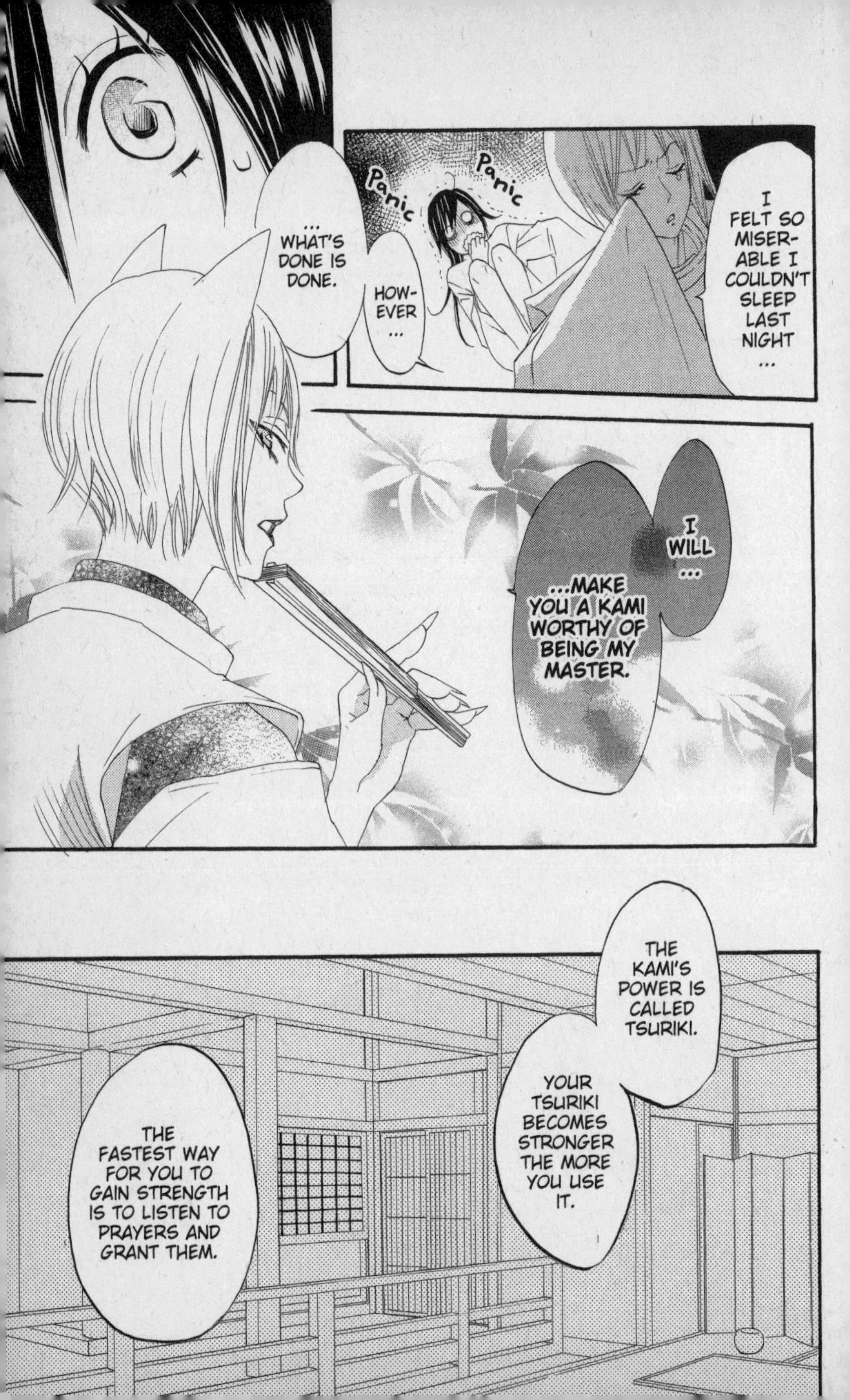
I FELT SO MISERABLE I COULDN'T SLEEP LAST NIGHT...
Panic
Panic
...WHAT'S DONE IS DONE.
HOWEVER...
I WILL...
...MAKE YOU A KAMI WORTHY OF BEING MY MASTER.
THE KAMI'S POWER IS CALLED TSURIKI.
YOUR TSURIKI BECOMES STRONGER THE MORE YOU USE IT.
THE FASTEST WAY FOR YOU TO GAIN STRENGTH IS TO LISTEN TO PRAYERS AND GRANT THEM.

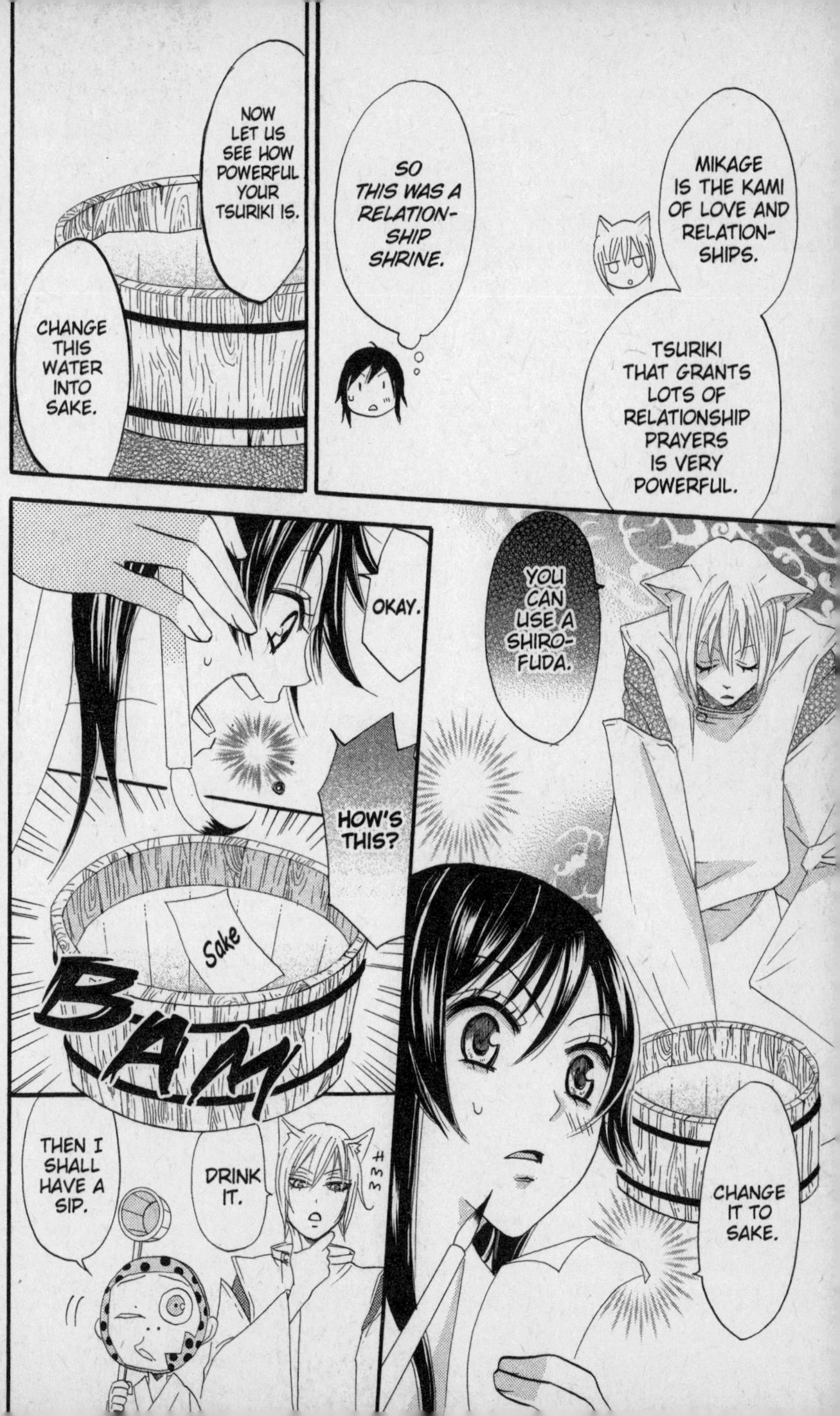
MIKAGE IS THE KAMI OF LOVE AND RELATION-SHIPS.
TSURIKI THAT GRANTS LOTS OF RELATIONSHIP PRAYERS IS VERY POWERFUL.
SO THIS WAS A RELATION-SHIP SHRINE.
NOW LET US SEE HOW POWERFUL YOUR TSURIKI IS.
CHANGE THIS WATER INTO SAKE.
YOU CAN USE A SHIRO-FUDA.
CHANGE IT TO SAKE.
OKAY.
HOW'S THIS?
Sake
BAM
DRINK IT.
THEN I SHALL HAVE A SIP.

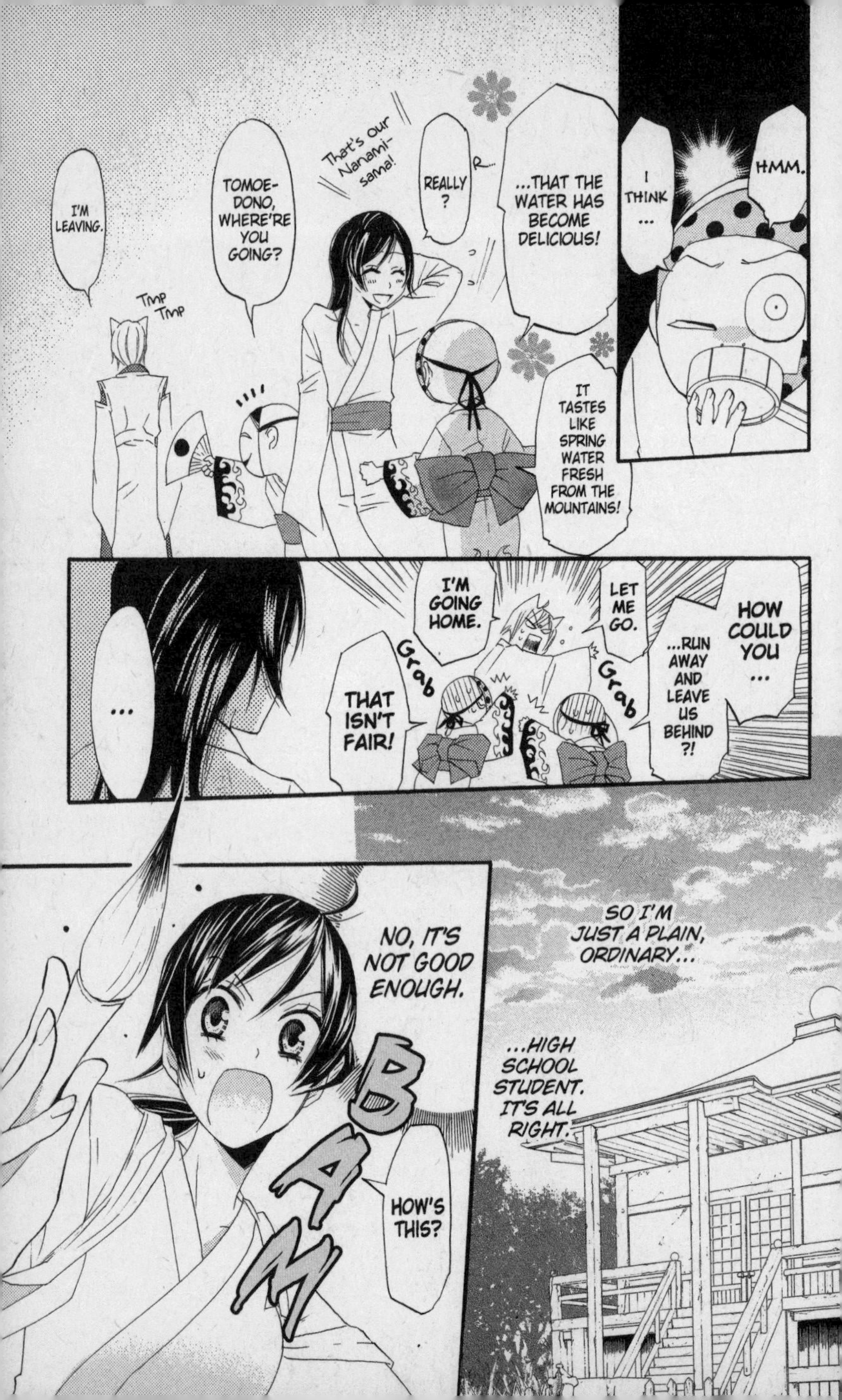
HMM.
I THINK...
...THAT THE WATER HAS BECOME DELICIOUS!
IT TASTES LIKE SPRING WATER FRESH FROM THE MOUNTAINS!
R...
REALLY?
That's our Nanami-sama!
TOMOE-DONO, WHERE'RE YOU GOING?
Tmp Tmp
I'M LEAVING.
HOW COULD YOU...
...RUN AWAY AND LEAVE US BEHIND?!
LET ME GO.
Grab
I'M GOING HOME.
Grab
THAT ISN'T FAIR!
...
SO I'M JUST A PLAIN, ORDINARY...
...HIGH SCHOOL STUDENT. IT'S ALL RIGHT.
NO, IT'S NOT GOOD ENOUGH.
BAM
HOW'S THIS?

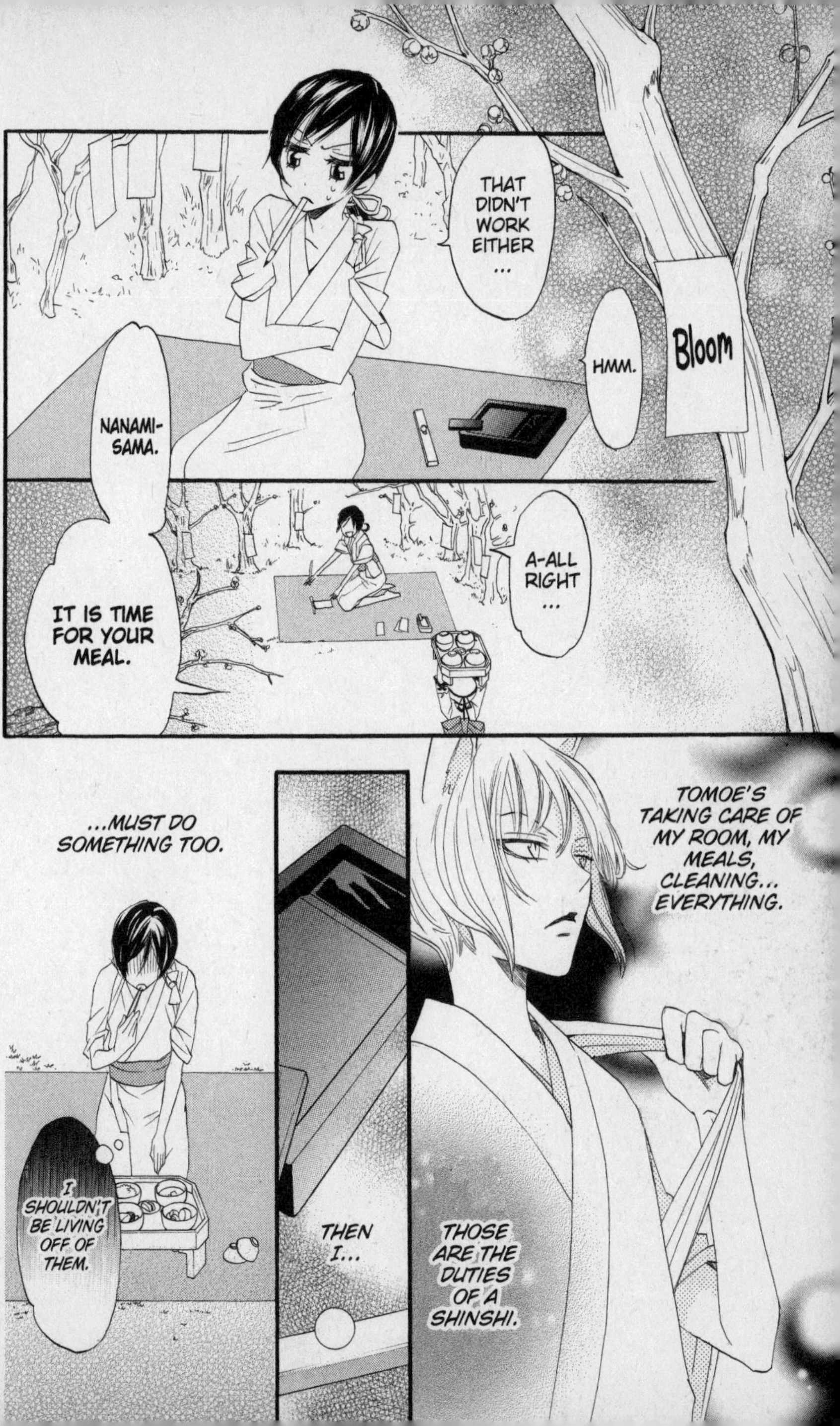
Bloom
THAT DIDN'T WORK EITHER...
HMM.
NANAMI-SAMA.
IT IS TIME FOR YOUR MEAL.
A-ALL RIGHT...
TOMOE'S TAKING CARE OF MY ROOM, MY MEALS, CLEANING... EVERYTHING.
THOSE ARE THE DUTIES OF A SHINSHI.
THEN I...
...MUST DO SOMETHING TOO.
I SHOULDN'T BE LIVING OFF OF THEM.

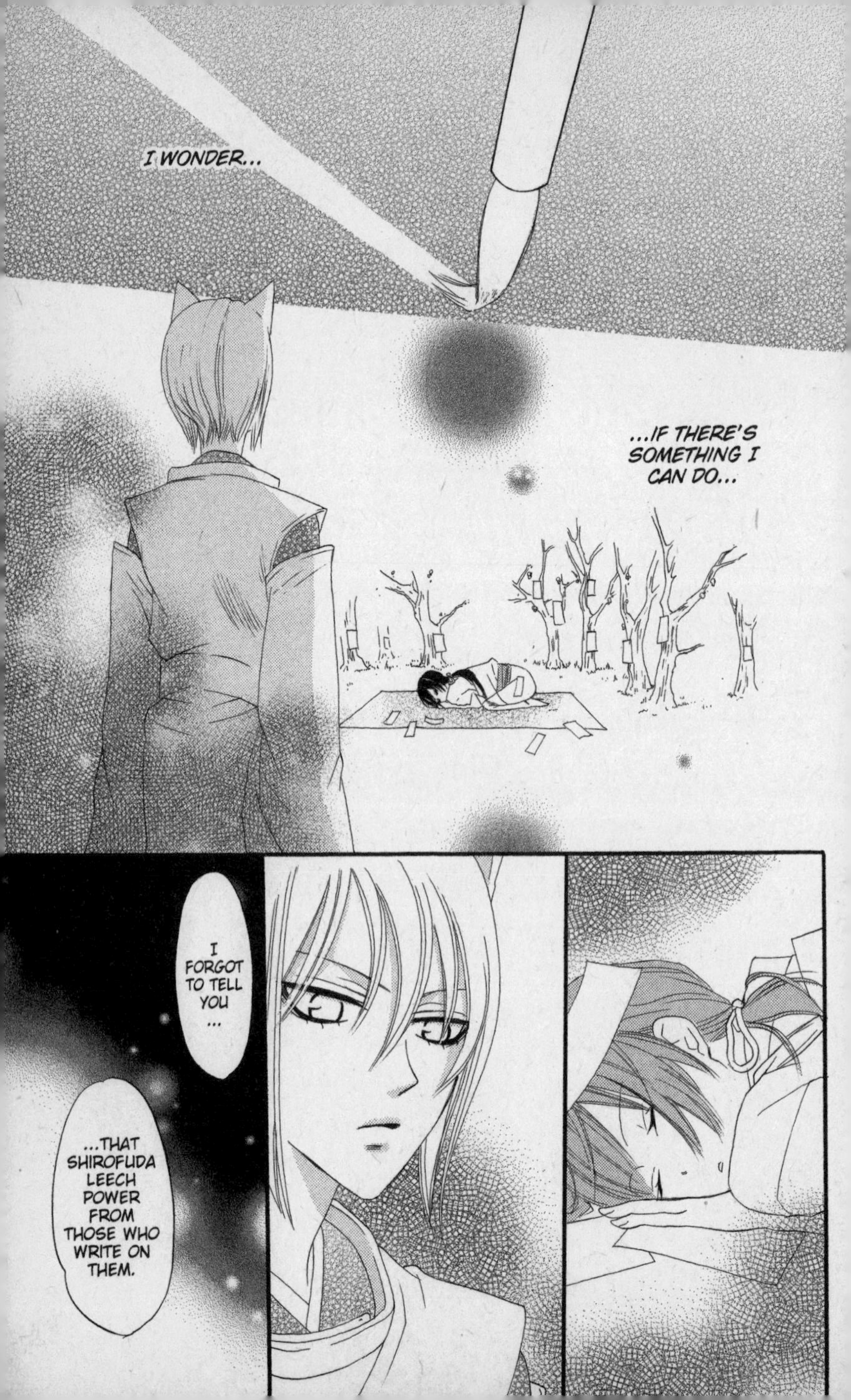
I WONDER...
...IF THERE'S SOMETHING I CAN DO...
I FORGOT TO TELL YOU ...
...THAT SHIROFUDA LEECH POWER FROM THOSE WHO WRITE ON THEM.

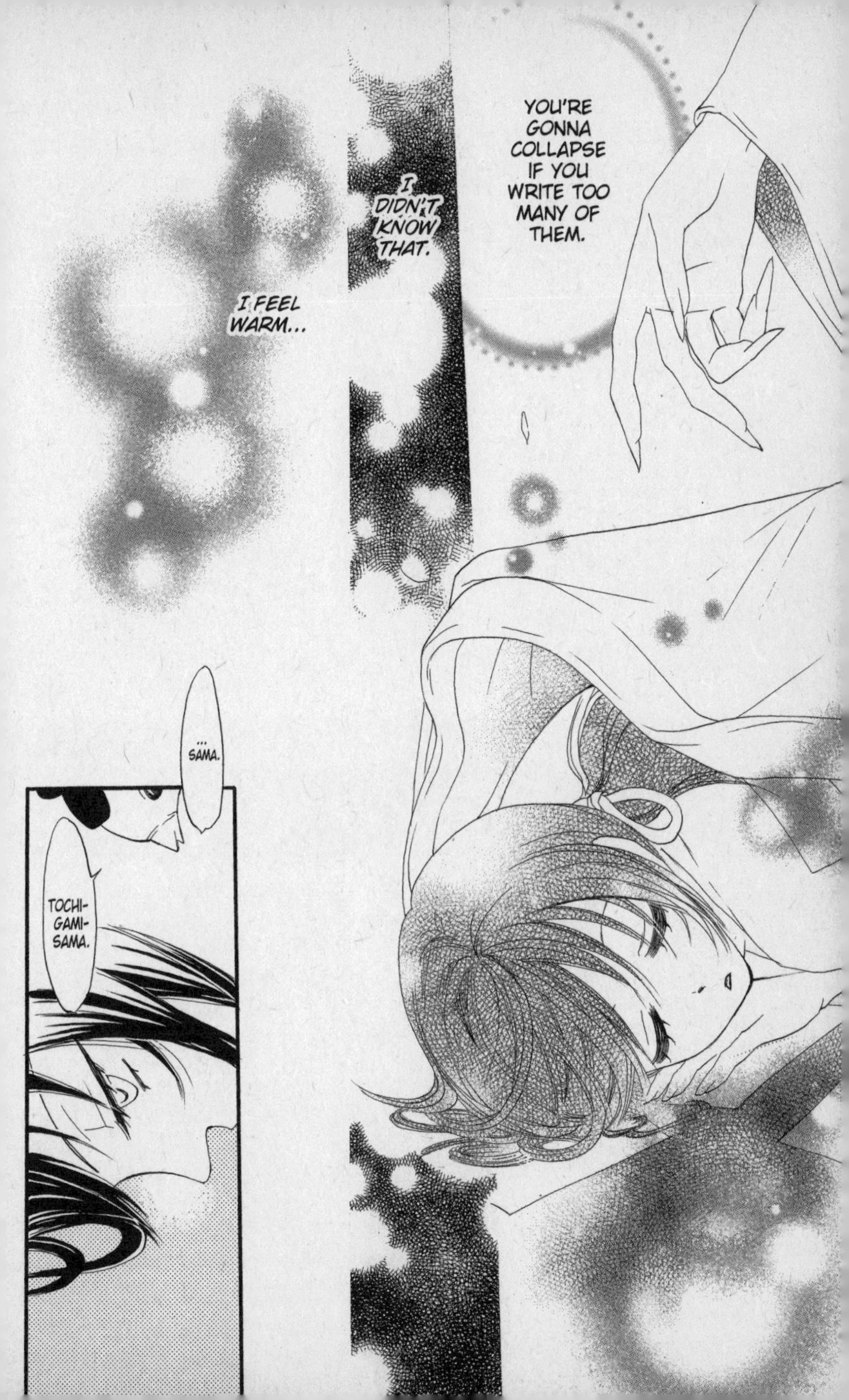
YOU'RE GONNA COLLAPSE IF YOU WRITE TOO MANY OF THEM.
I DIDN'T KNOW THAT.
I FEEL WARM...
...SAMA.
TOCHI-GAMI-SAMA.

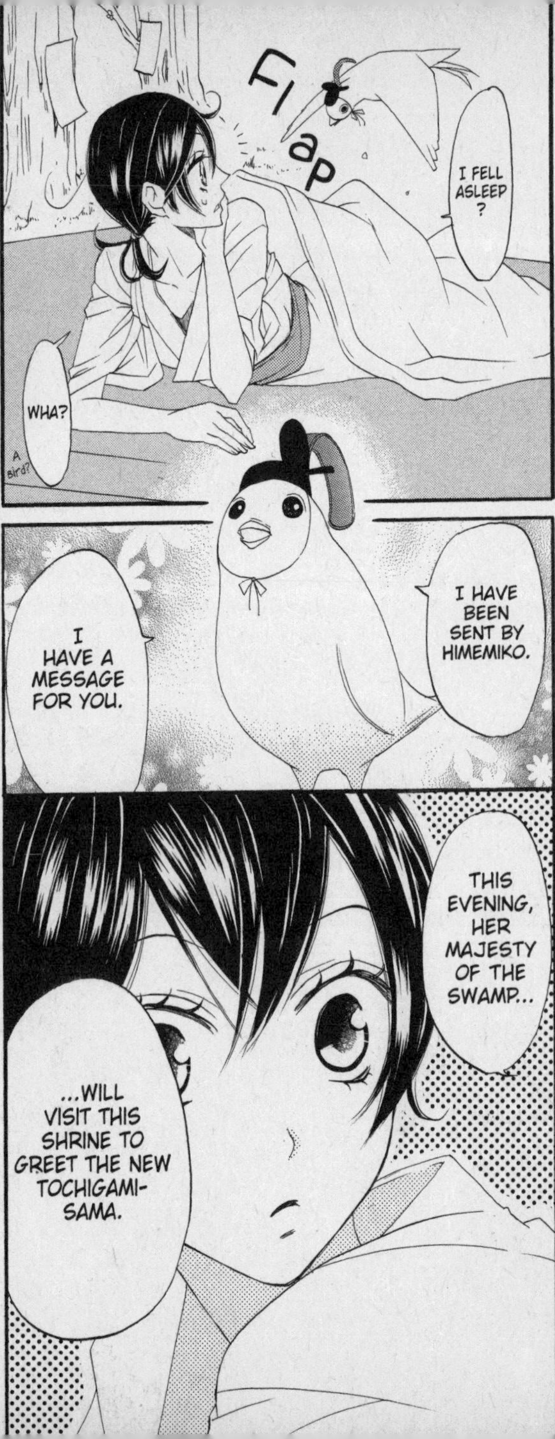
Flap
I FELL ASLEEP ?
WHA?
A bird?
I HAVE BEEN SENT BY HIMEMIKO.
I HAVE A MESSAGE FOR YOU.
THIS EVENING, HER MAJESTY OF THE SWAMP...
...WILL VISIT THIS SHRINE TO GREET THE NEW TOCHIGAMI-SAMA.

The other day I went to Hokkaido for the first time.

The green leaves were amazingly yellowish green, and I felt like I was in a foreign country.

I was only able to stay for half a day, but I was able to eat crabs, which I wanted to do, so I was very happy!

I bought lots of Shiroi Koibito. I'd only eaten it twice before, but the packaging had changed, and I was impressed.

I hope I can spend some time sight-seeing next time.

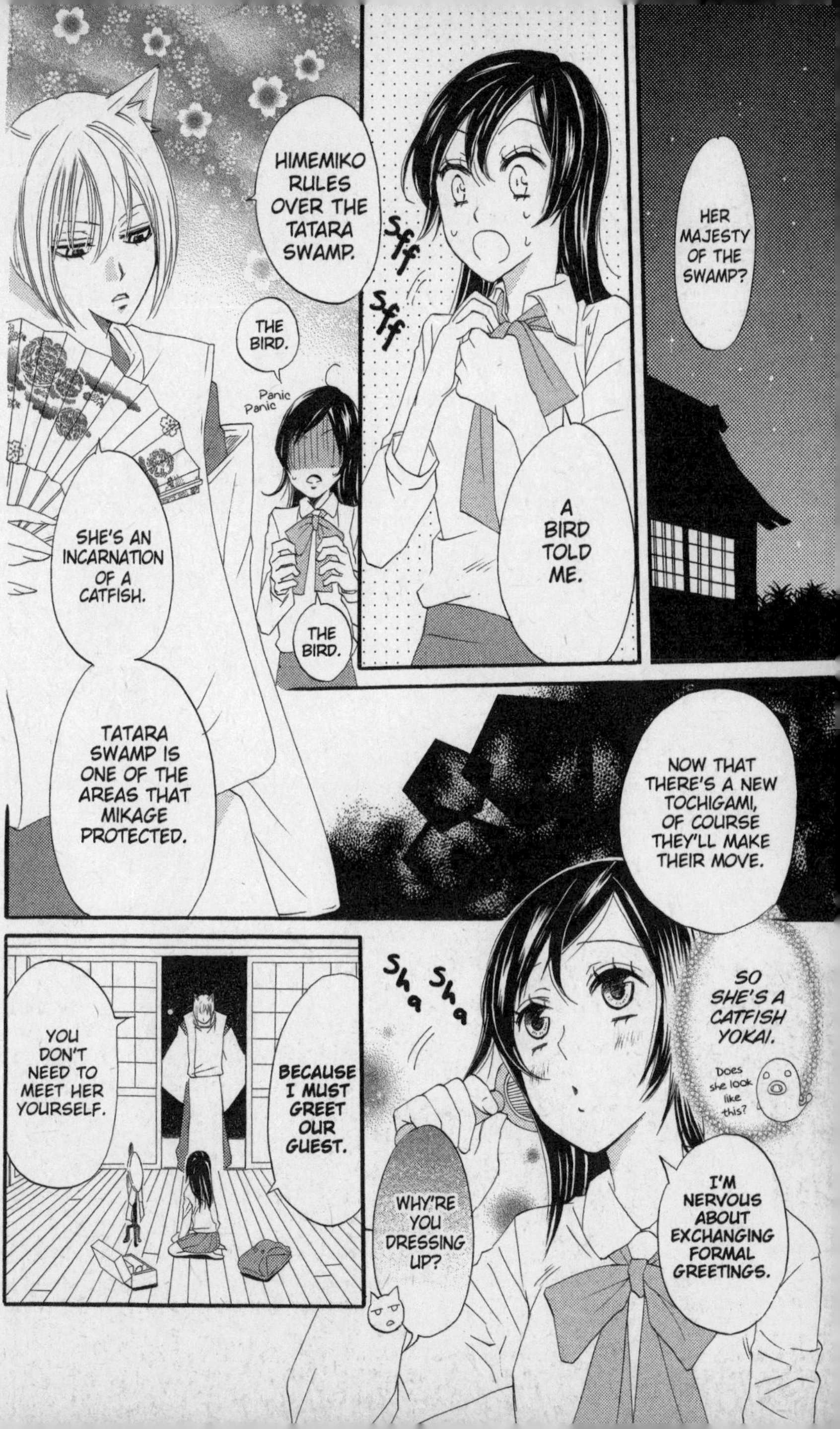
HER MAJESTY OF THE SWAMP?
Sff
Sff
A BIRD TOLD ME.
HIMEMIKO RULES OVER THE TATARA SWAMP.
THE BIRD.
Panic Panic
THE BIRD.
SHE'S AN INCARNATION OF A CATFISH.
TATARA SWAMP IS ONE OF THE AREAS THAT MIKAGE PROTECTED.
NOW THAT THERE'S A NEW TOCHIGAMI, OF COURSE THEY'LL MAKE THEIR MOVE.
SO SHE'S A CATFISH YOKAI.
Does she look like this?
Sha Sha
WHY'RE YOU DRESSING UP?
I'M NERVOUS ABOUT EXCHANGING FORMAL GREETINGS.
BECAUSE I MUST GREET OUR GUEST.
YOU DON'T NEED TO MEET HER YOURSELF.

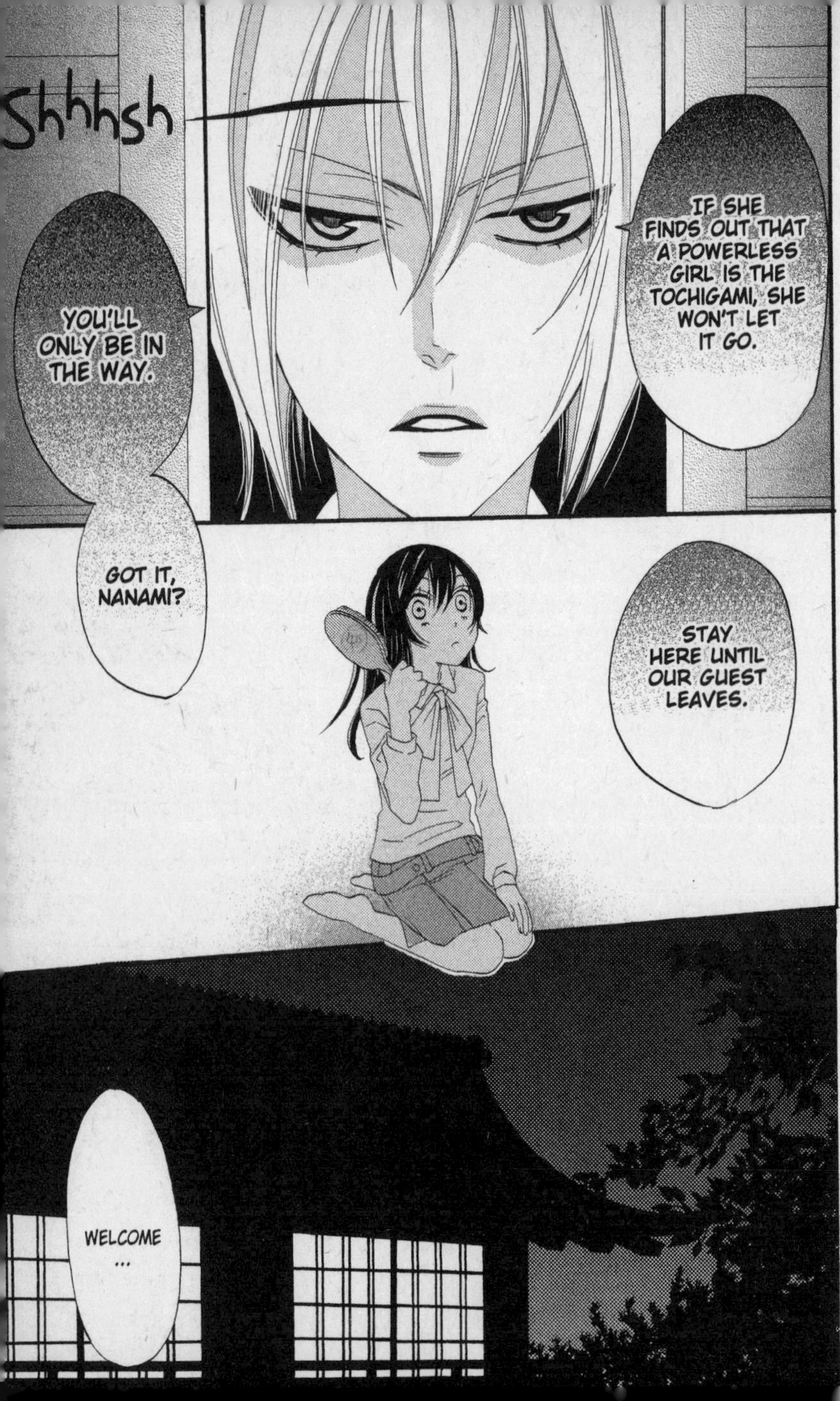
IF SHE FINDS OUT THAT A POWERLESS GIRL IS THE TOCHIGAMI, SHE WON'T LET IT GO.
Shhhsh
YOU'LL ONLY BE IN THE WAY.
STAY HERE UNTIL OUR GUEST LEAVES.
GOT IT, NANAMI?
WELCOME ...

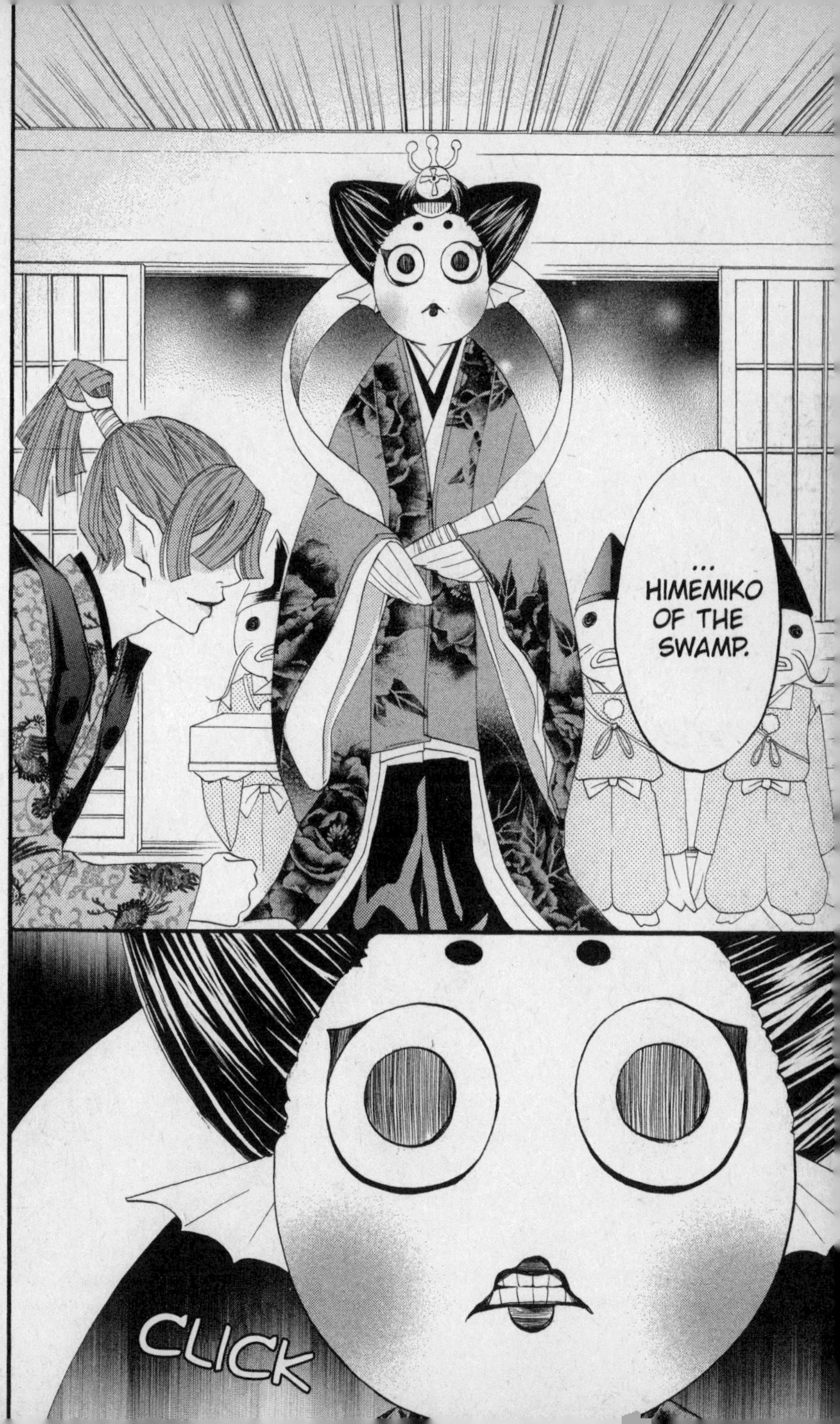
...
HIMEMIKO
OF THE
SWAMP.
CLICK

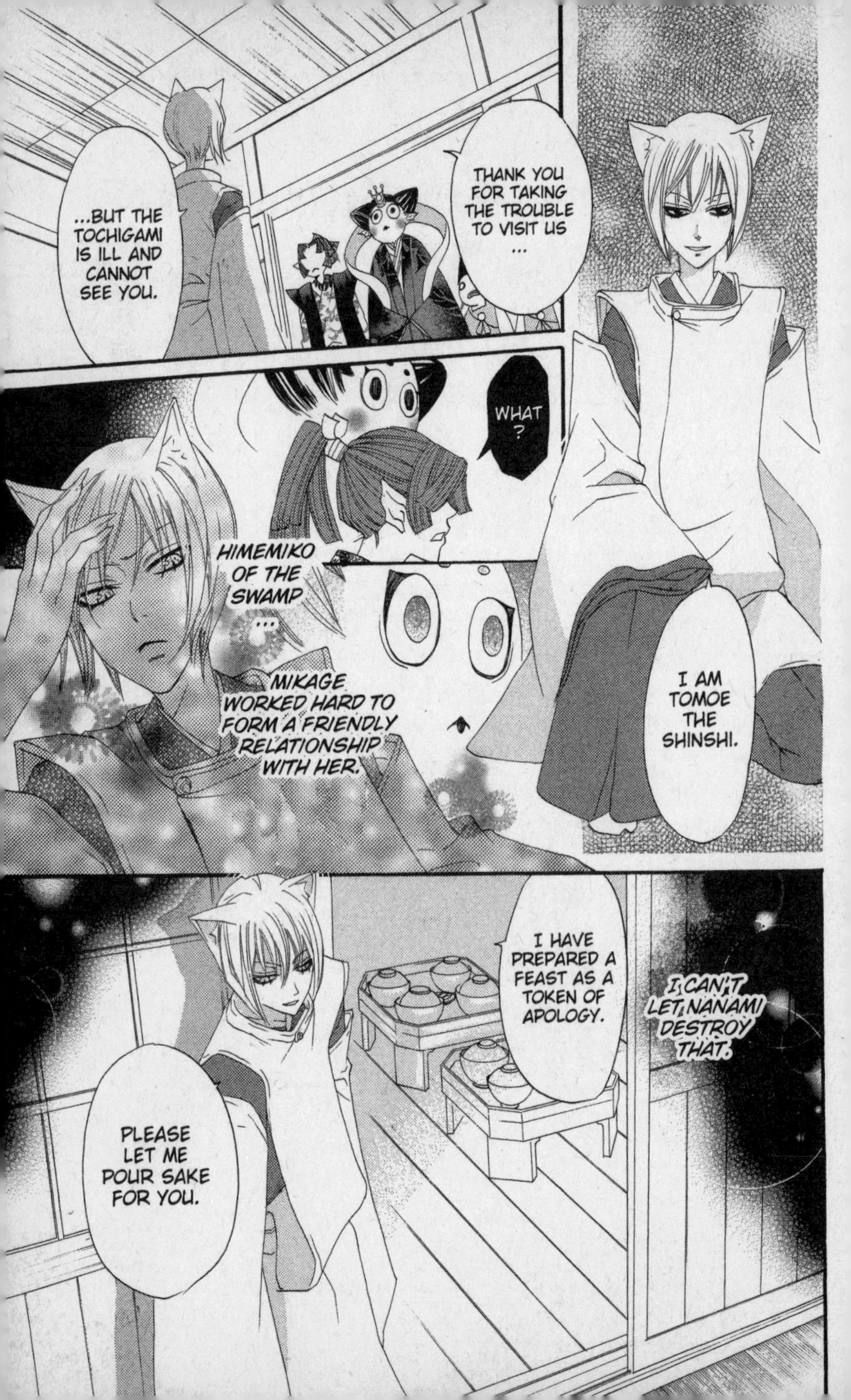
I AM TOMOE THE SHINSHI.
THANK YOU FOR TAKING THE TROUBLE TO VISIT US ...
...BUT THE TOCHIGAMI IS ILL AND CANNOT SEE YOU.
WHAT?
HIMEMIKO OF THE SWAMP ...
MIKAGE WORKED HARD TO FORM A FRIENDLY RELATIONSHIP WITH HER.
I CAN'T LET NANAMI DESTROY THAT.
I HAVE PREPARED A FEAST AS A TOKEN OF APOLOGY.
PLEASE LET ME POUR SAKE FOR YOU.

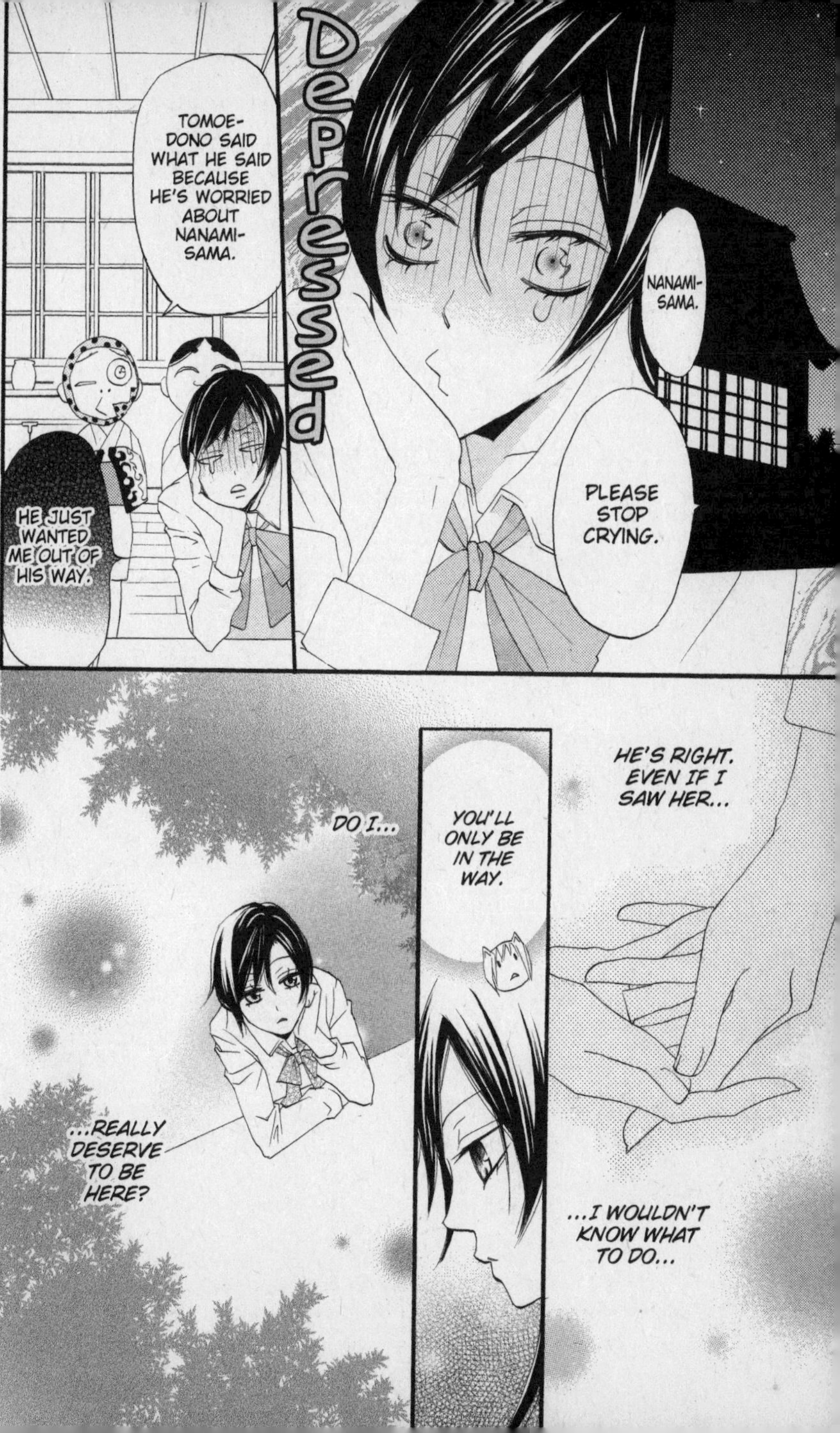
NANAMI-SAMA.
PLEASE STOP CRYING.
Depressed
TOMOE-DONO SAID WHAT HE SAID BECAUSE HE'S WORRIED ABOUT NANAMI-SAMA.
HE JUST WANTED ME OUT OF HIS WAY.
HE'S RIGHT. EVEN IF I SAW HER...
...I WOULDN'T KNOW WHAT TO DO...
YOU'LL ONLY BE IN THE WAY.
DO I...
...REALLY DESERVE TO BE HERE?

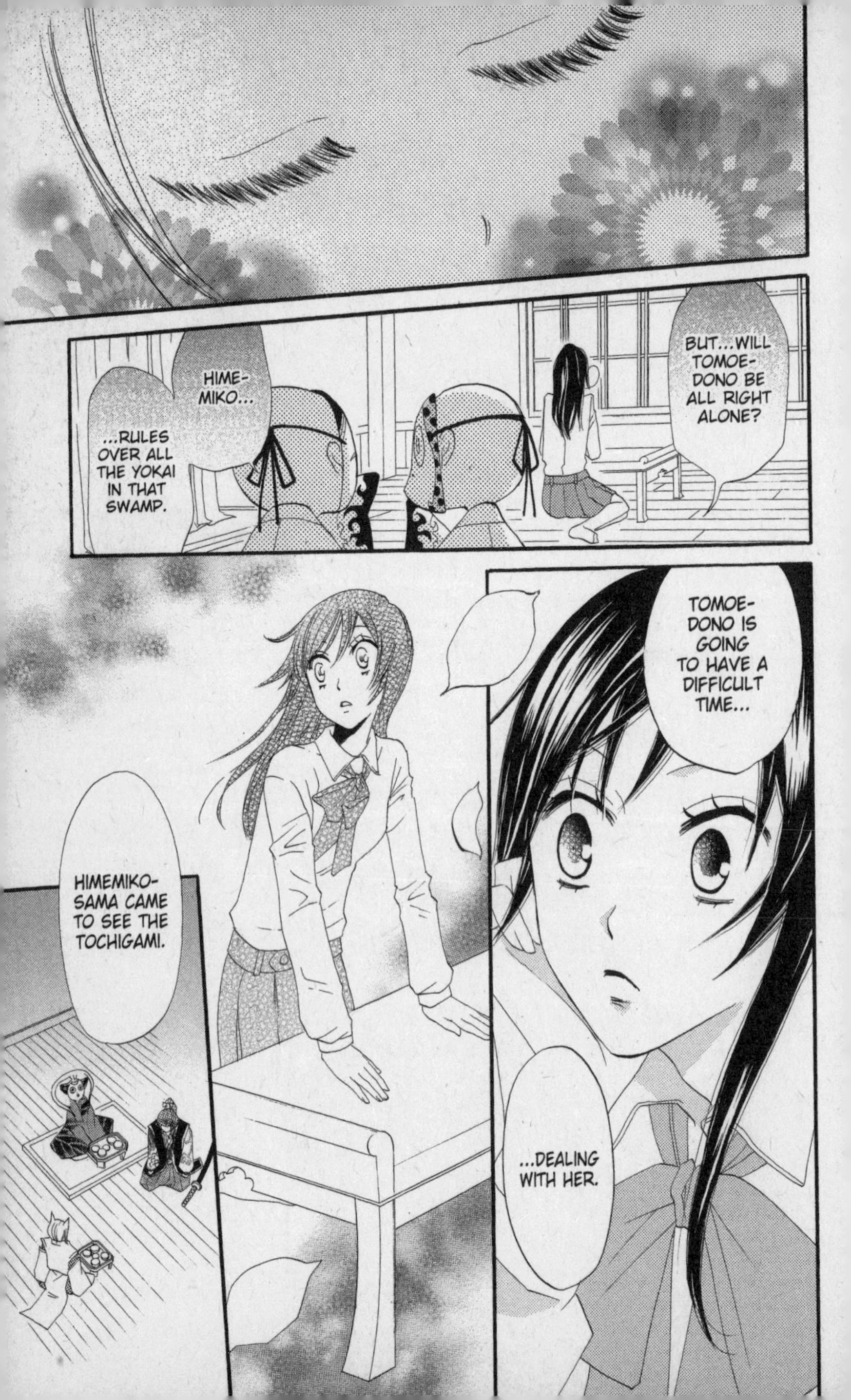
BUT...WILL TOMOE-DONO BE ALL RIGHT ALONE?
HIME-MIKO...
...RULES OVER ALL THE YOKAI IN THAT SWAMP.
TOMOE-DONO IS GOING TO HAVE A DIFFICULT TIME...
...DEALING WITH HER.
HIMEMIKO-SAMA CAME TO SEE THE TOCHIGAMI.

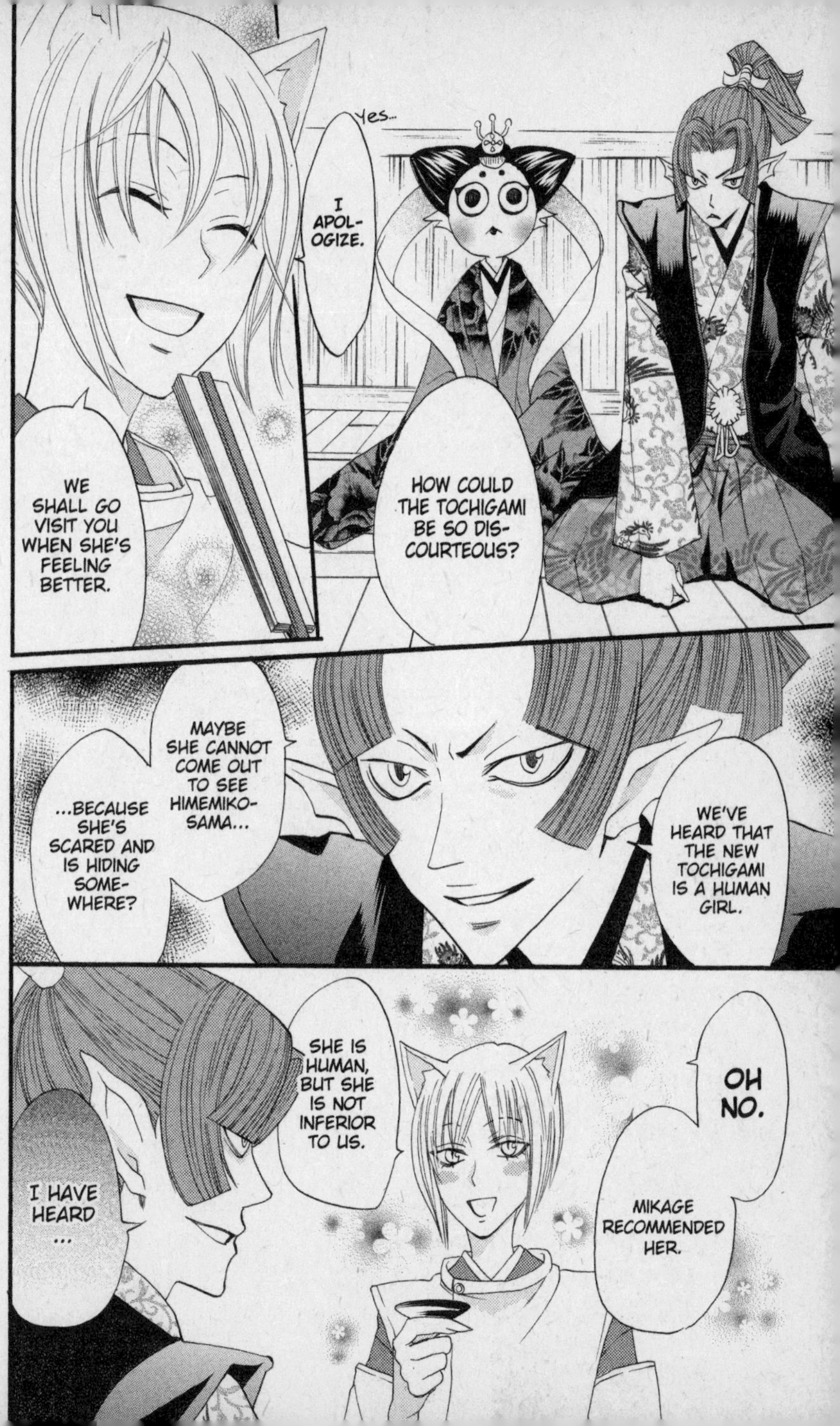
HOW COULD THE TOCHIGAMI BE SO DIS- COURTEOUS?
Yes...
I APOL- OGIZE.
WE SHALL GO VISIT YOU WHEN SHE'S FEELING BETTER.
WE'VE HEARD THAT THE NEW TOCHIGAMI IS A HUMAN GIRL.
MAYBE SHE CANNOT COME OUT TO SEE HIMEMIKO- SAMA...
...BECAUSE SHE'S SCARED AND IS HIDING SOME- WHERE?
OH NO.
MIKAGE RECOMMENDED HER.
SHE IS HUMAN, BUT SHE IS NOT INFERIOR TO US.
I HAVE HEARD ...

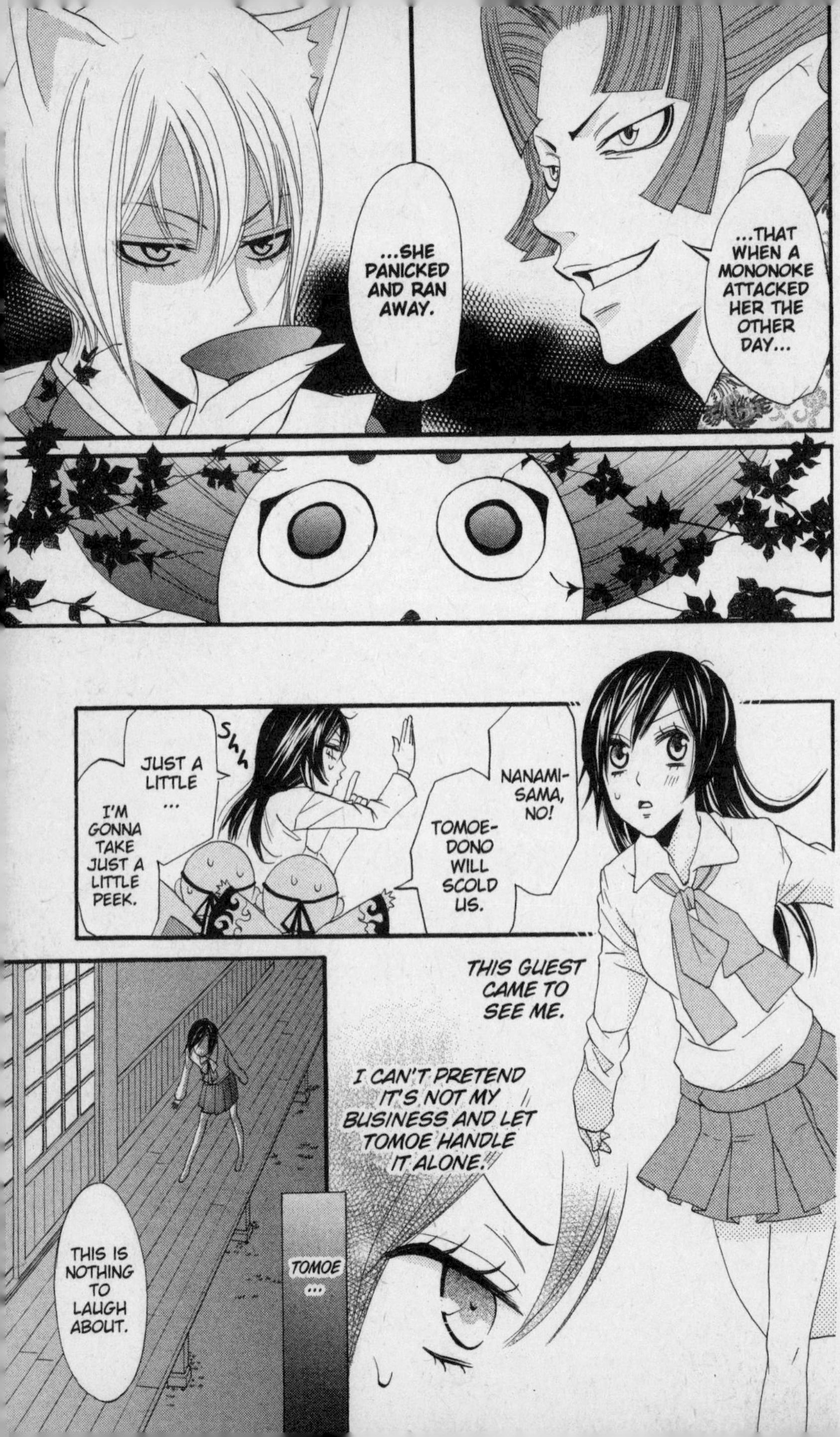
...THAT WHEN A MONONOKE ATTACKED HER THE OTHER DAY...
...SHE PANICKED AND RAN AWAY.
THIS GUEST CAME TO SEE ME.
I CAN'T PRETEND IT'S NOT MY BUSINESS AND LET TOMOE HANDLE IT ALONE.
NANAMI-SAMA, NO!
TOMOE-DONO WILL SCOLD US.
Shh
JUST A LITTLE ...
I'M GONNA TAKE JUST A LITTLE PEEK.
TOMOE ...
THIS IS NOTHING TO LAUGH ABOUT.

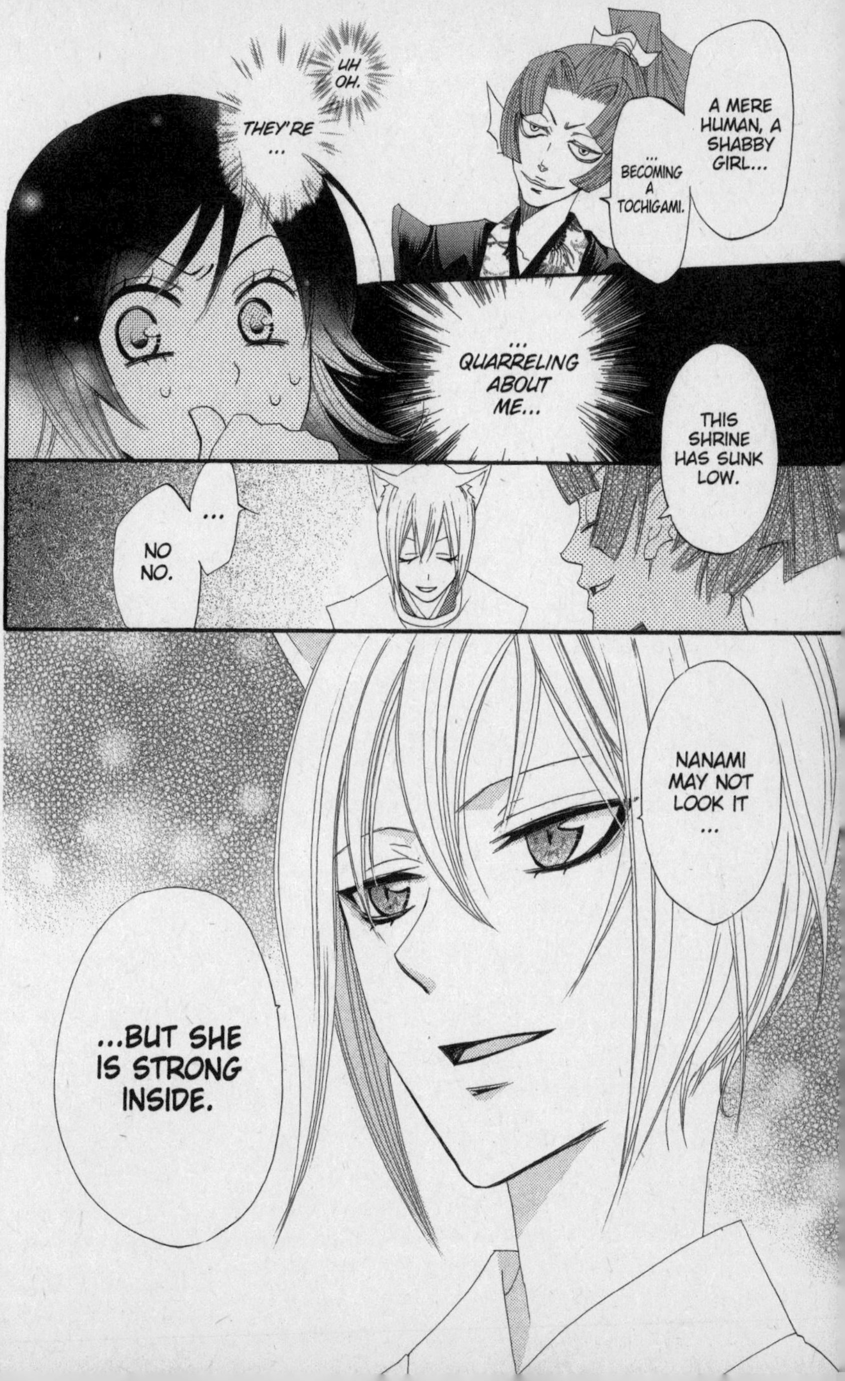
A MERE HUMAN, A SHABBY GIRL...
...BECOMING A TOCHIGAMI.
UH OH.
THEY'RE ...
...QUARRELING ABOUT ME...
THIS SHRINE HAS SUNK LOW.
... NO NO.
NANAMI MAY NOT LOOK IT ...
...BUT SHE IS STRONG INSIDE.

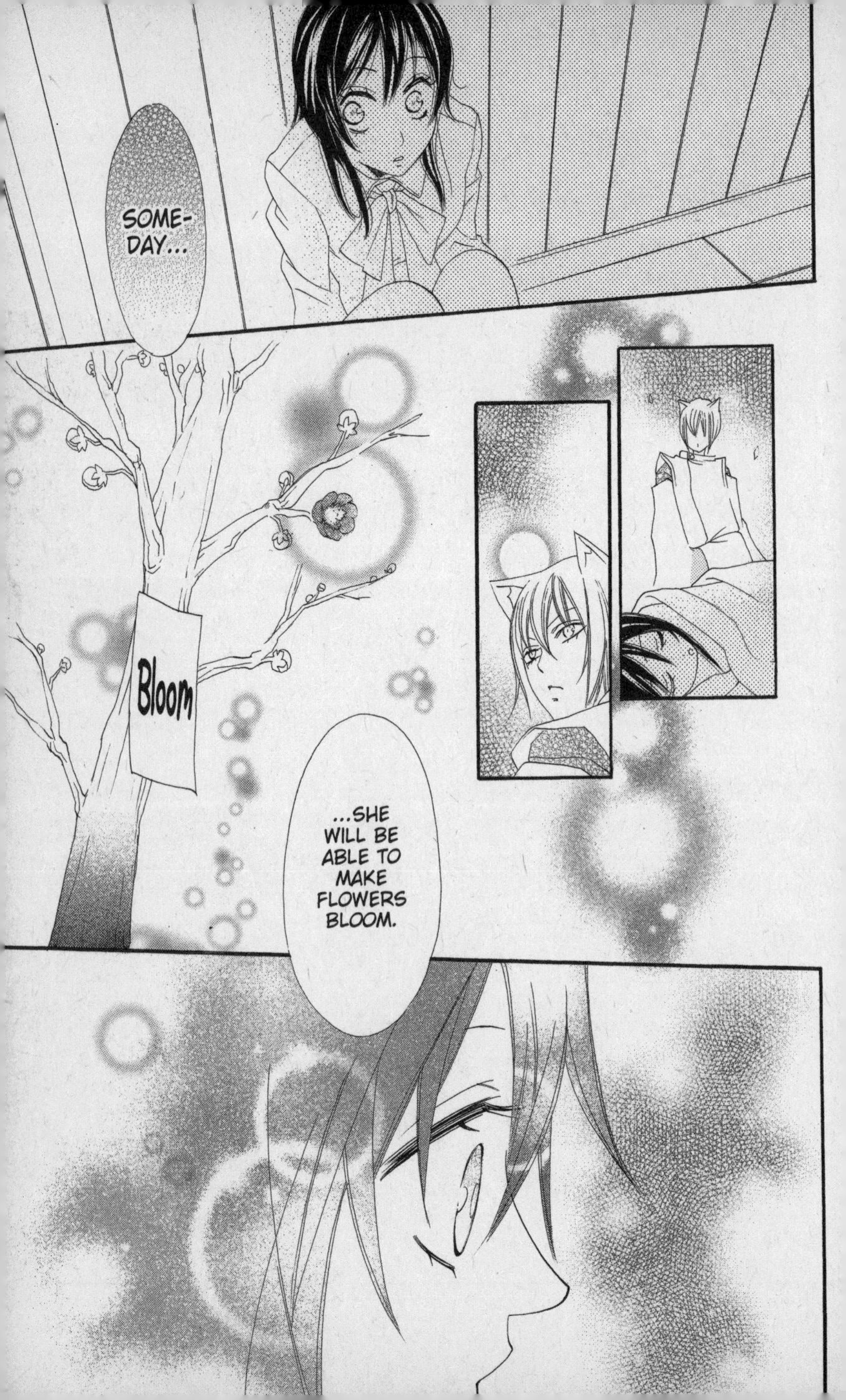

SOME-DAY...
Bloom
...SHE WILL BE ABLE TO MAKE FLOWERS BLOOM.

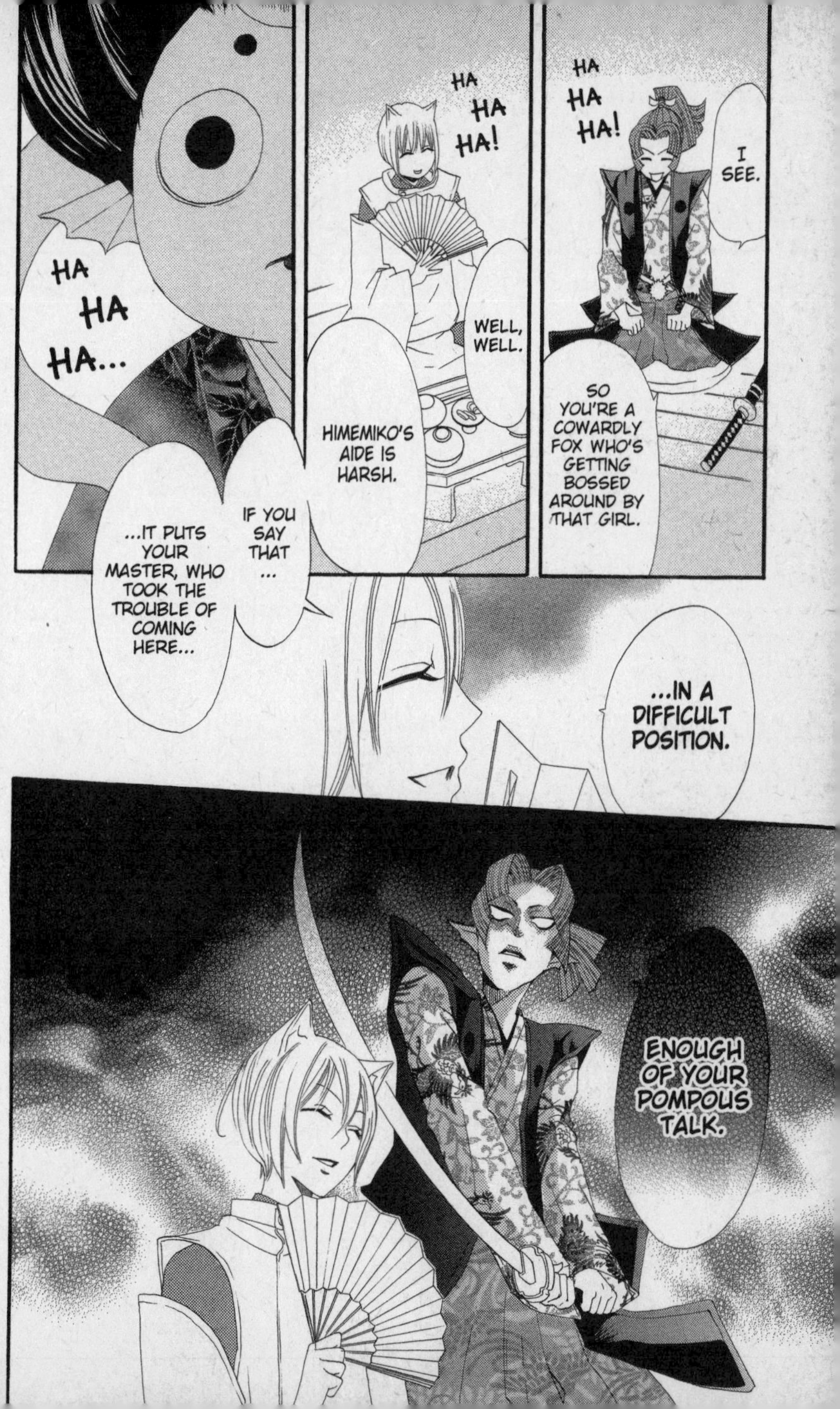
HA HA HA!
I SEE.
SO YOU'RE A COWARDLY FOX WHO'S GETTING BOSSED AROUND BY THAT GIRL.
HA HA HA!
WELL, WELL.
HIMEMIKO'S AIDE IS HARSH.
HA HA HA...
IF YOU SAY THAT ...
...IT PUTS YOUR MASTER, WHO TOOK THE TROUBLE OF COMING HERE...
...IN A DIFFICULT POSITION.
ENOUGH OF YOUR POMPOUS TALK.

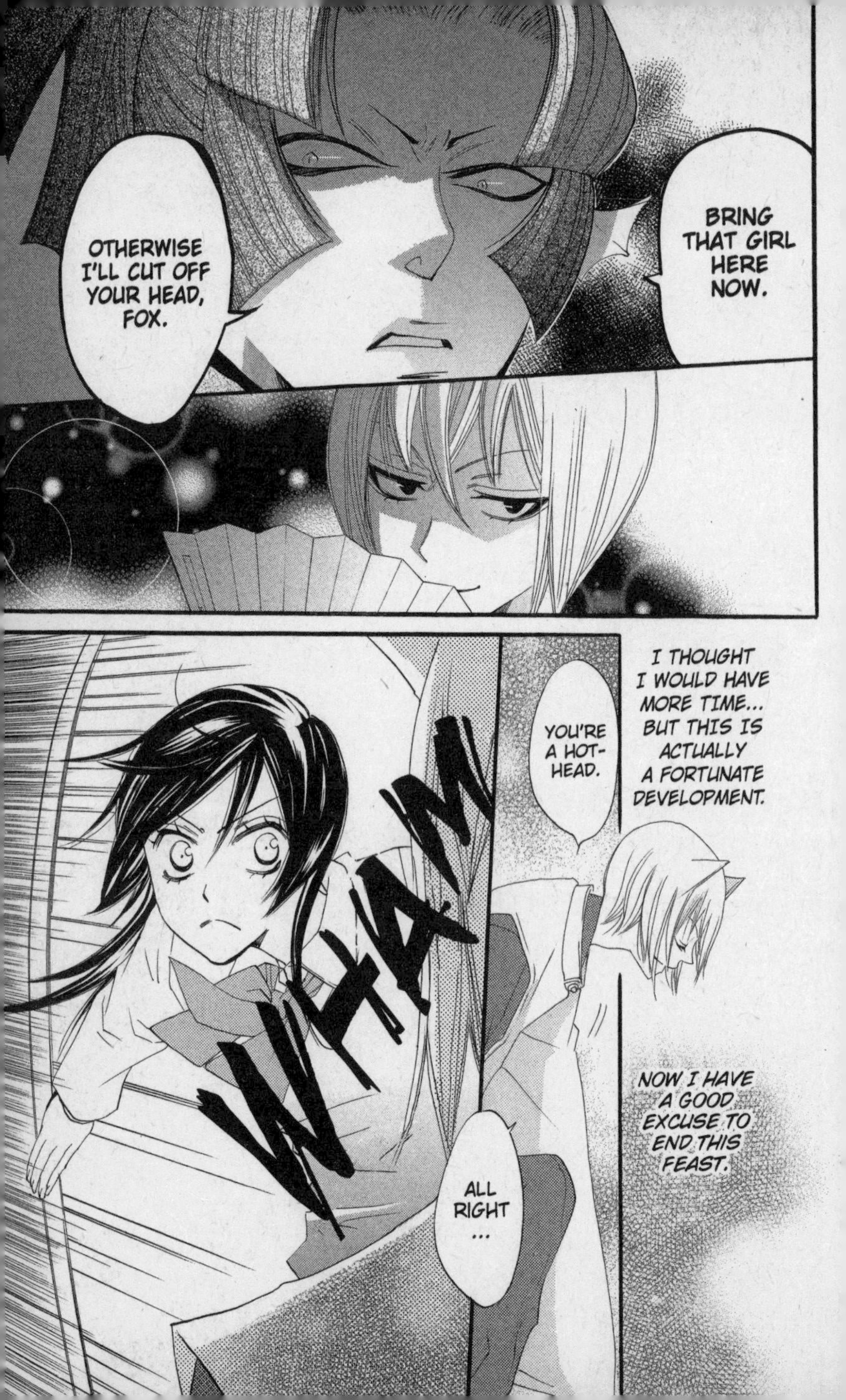
BRING THAT GIRL HERE NOW.
OTHERWISE I'LL CUT OFF YOUR HEAD, FOX.
I THOUGHT I WOULD HAVE MORE TIME... BUT THIS IS ACTUALLY A FORTUNATE DEVELOPMENT.
YOU'RE A HOT-HEAD.
WHAM
NOW I HAVE A GOOD EXCUSE TO END THIS FEAST.
ALL RIGHT ...

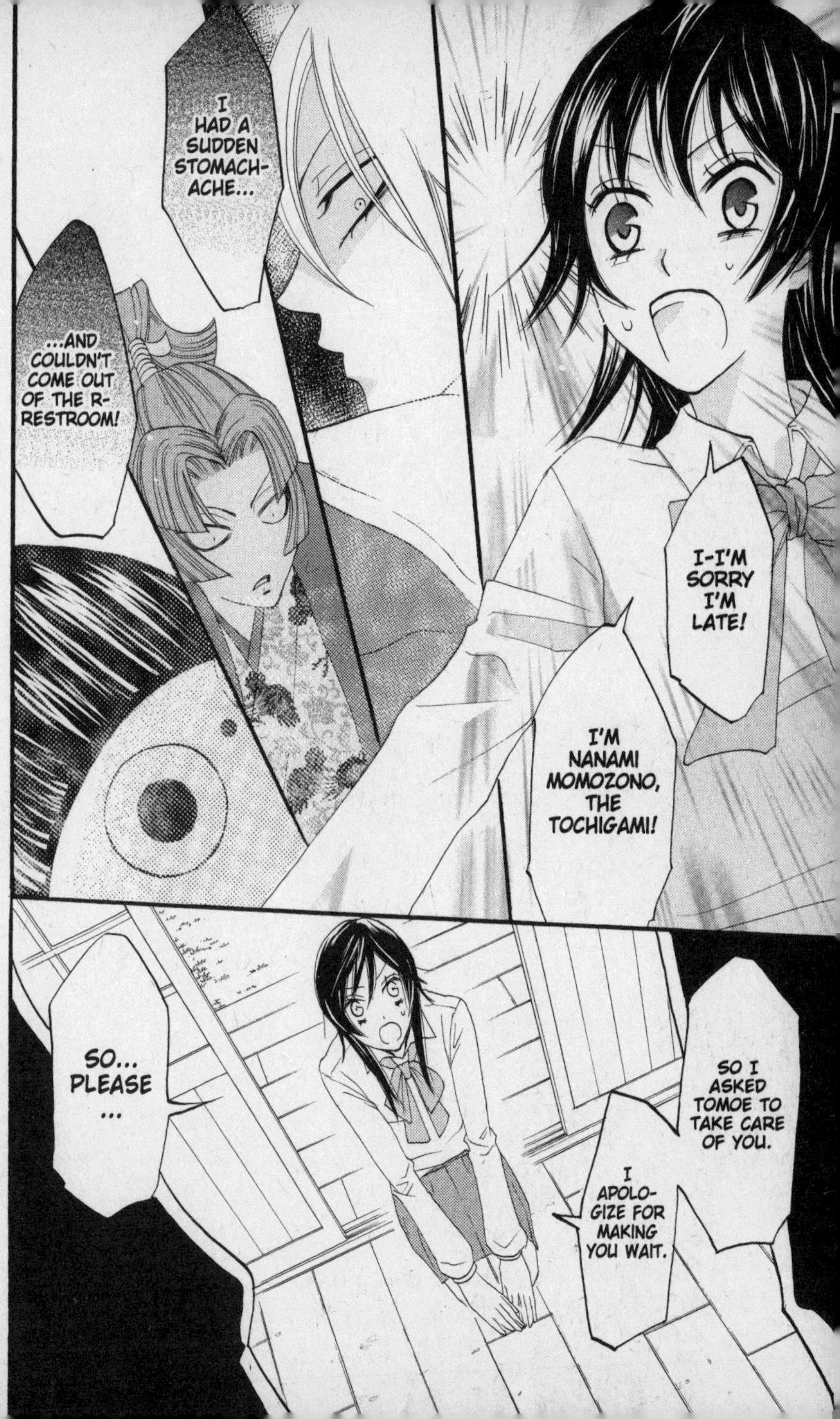
I-I'M SORRY I'M LATE!
I'M NANAMI MOMOZONO, THE TOCHIGAMI!
I HAD A SUDDEN STOMACH-ACHE...
...AND COULDN'T COME OUT OF THE R-RESTROOM!
SO I ASKED TOMOE TO TAKE CARE OF YOU.
I APOLOGIZE FOR MAKING YOU WAIT.
SO... PLEASE ...

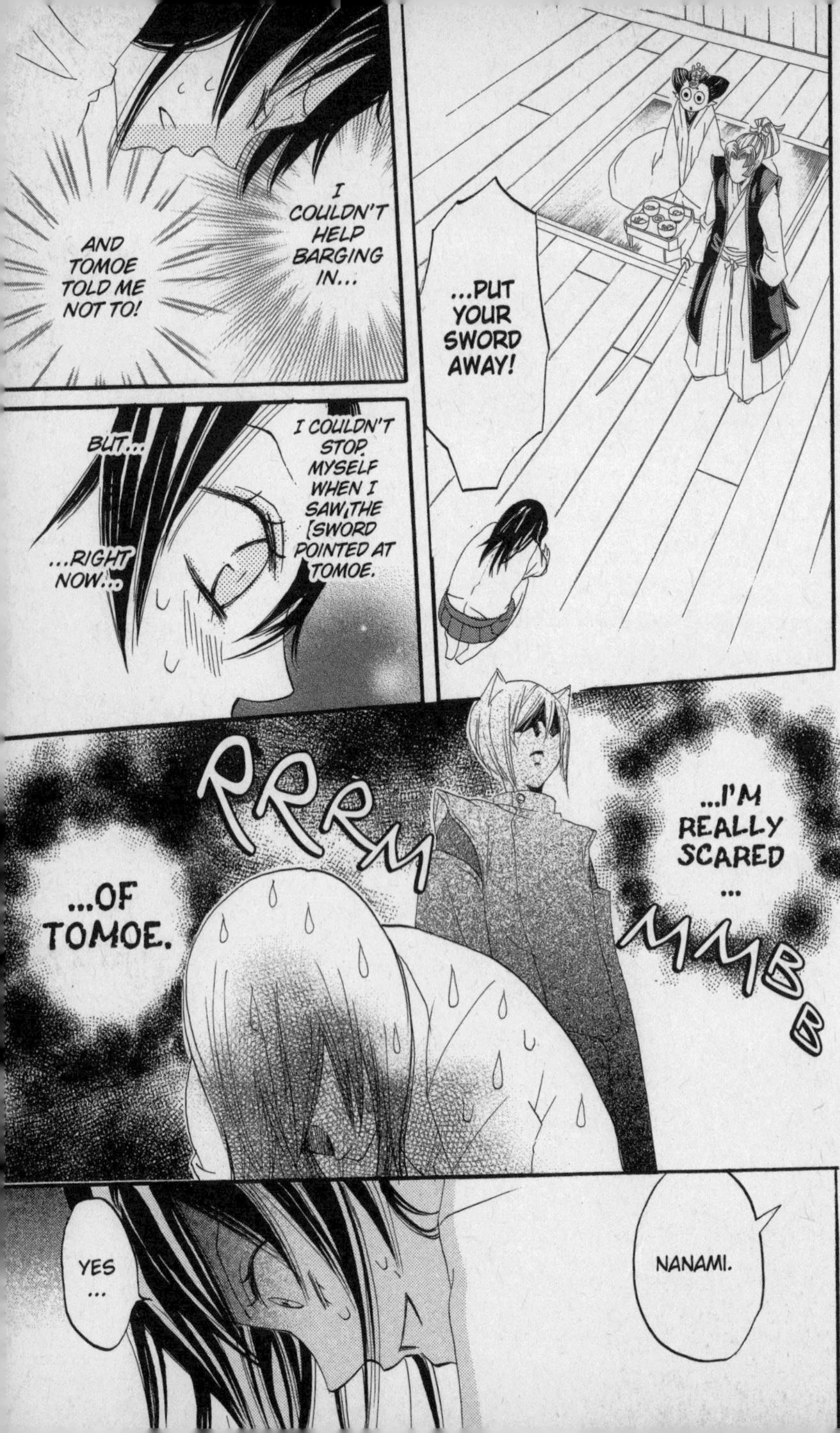
...PUT YOUR SWORD AWAY!
I COULDN'T HELP BARGING IN...
AND TOMOE TOLD ME NOT TO!
I COULDN'T STOP MYSELF WHEN I SAW THE SWORD POINTED AT TOMOE.
BUT...
...RIGHT NOW...
...I'M REALLY SCARED ...
RRRM
MMBB
...OF TOMOE.
NANAMI.
YES ...

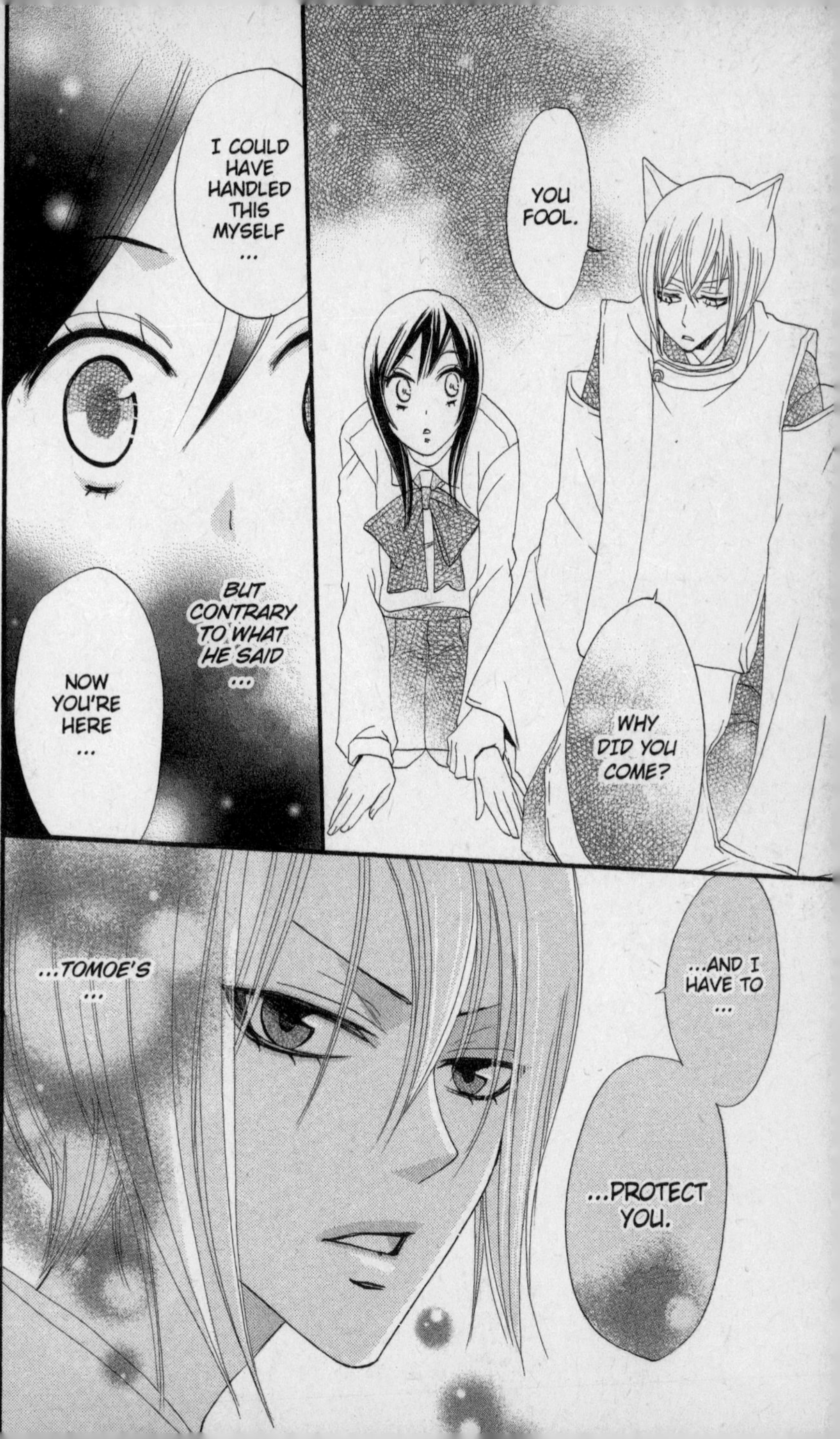
YOU FOOL.
WHY DID YOU COME?
I COULD HAVE HANDLED THIS MYSELF ...
BUT CONTRARY TO WHAT HE SAID ...
NOW YOU'RE HERE ...
...AND I HAVE TO ...
...PROTECT YOU.
...TOMOE'S ...

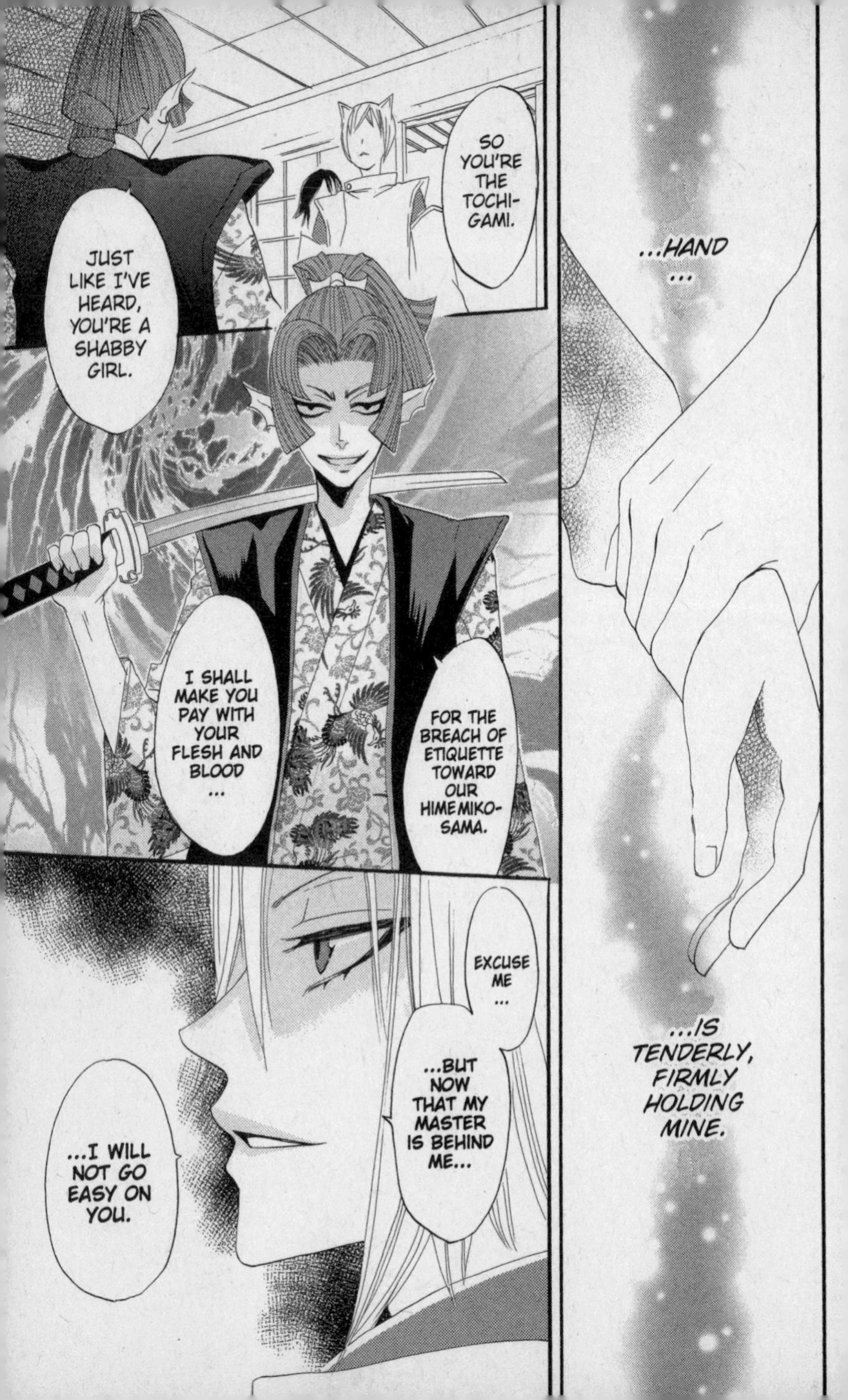
...HAND ...
...IS TENDERLY, FIRMLY HOLDING MINE.
SO YOU'RE THE TOCHI-GAMI.
JUST LIKE I'VE HEARD, YOU'RE A SHABBY GIRL.
FOR THE BREACH OF ETIQUETTE TOWARD OUR HIMEMIKO-SAMA.
I SHALL MAKE YOU PAY WITH YOUR FLESH AND BLOOD ...
EXCUSE ME ...
...BUT NOW THAT MY MASTER IS BEHIND ME...
...I WILL NOT GO EASY ON YOU.

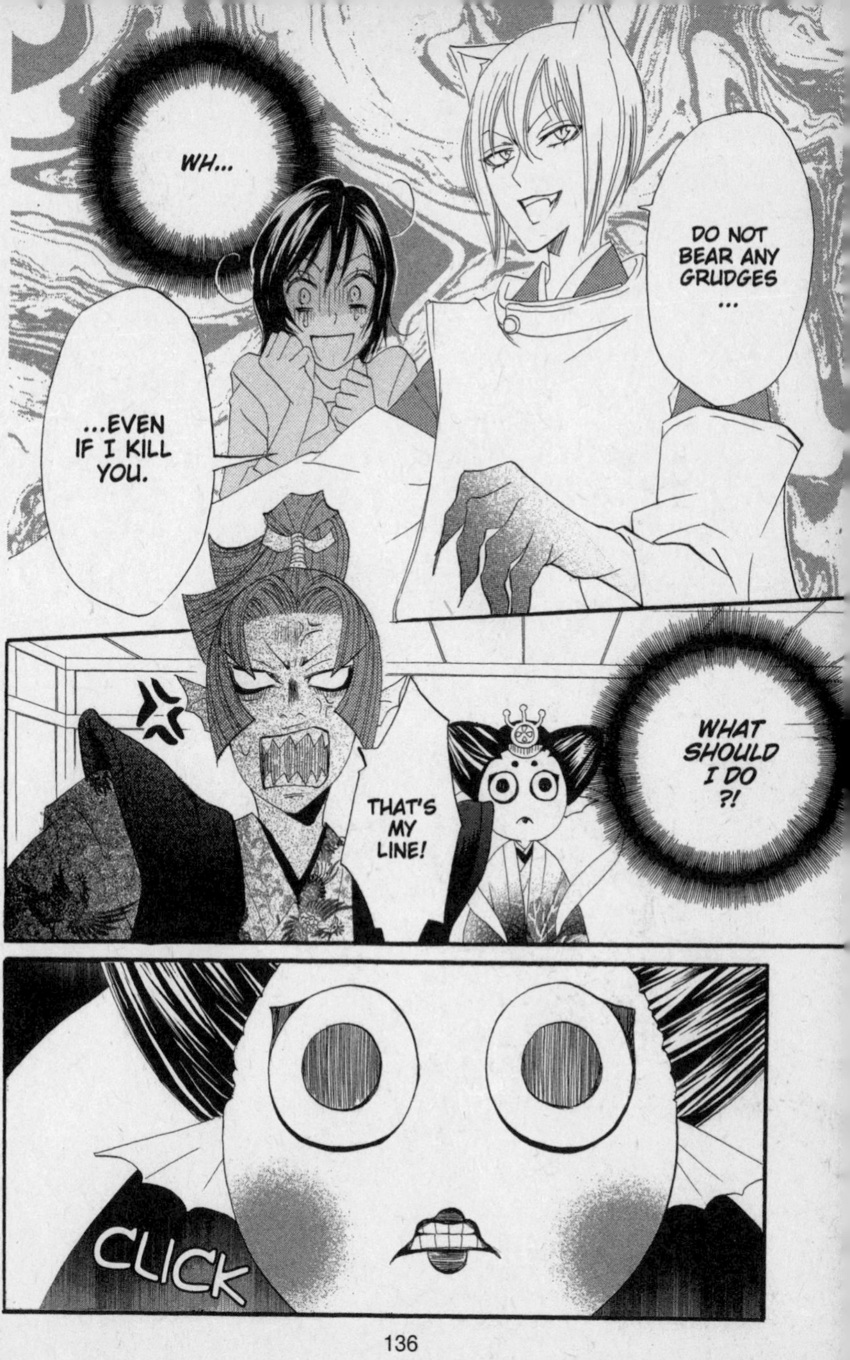
DO NOT BEAR ANY GRUDGES ...
...EVEN IF I KILL YOU.
WH...
WHAT SHOULD I DO ?!
THAT'S MY LINE!
CLICK

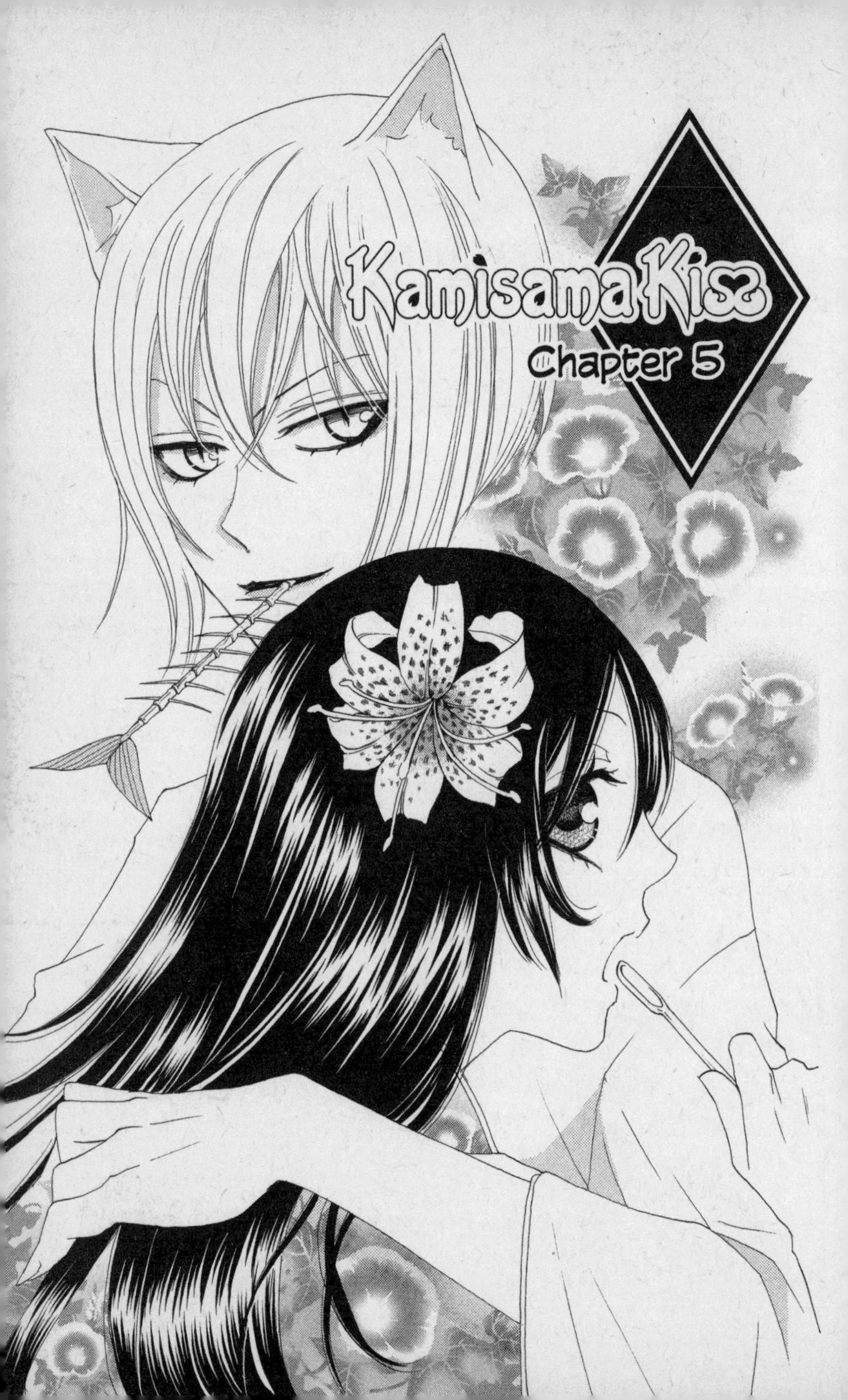
Kamisama Kiss
Chapter 5

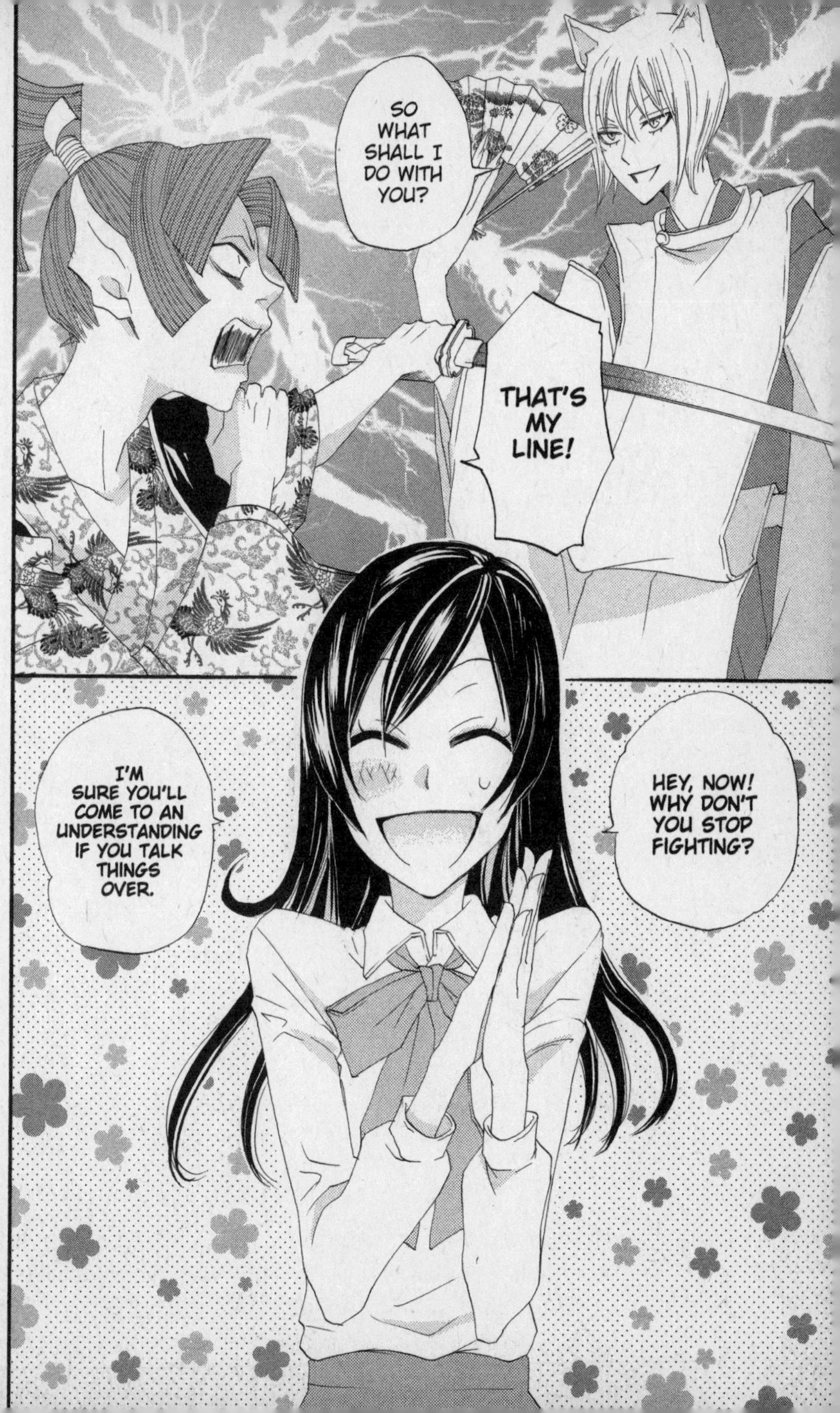
SO WHAT SHALL I DO WITH YOU?
THAT'S MY LINE!
HEY, NOW! WHY DON'T YOU STOP FIGHTING?
I'M SURE YOU'LL COME TO AN UNDERSTANDING IF YOU TALK THINGS OVER.

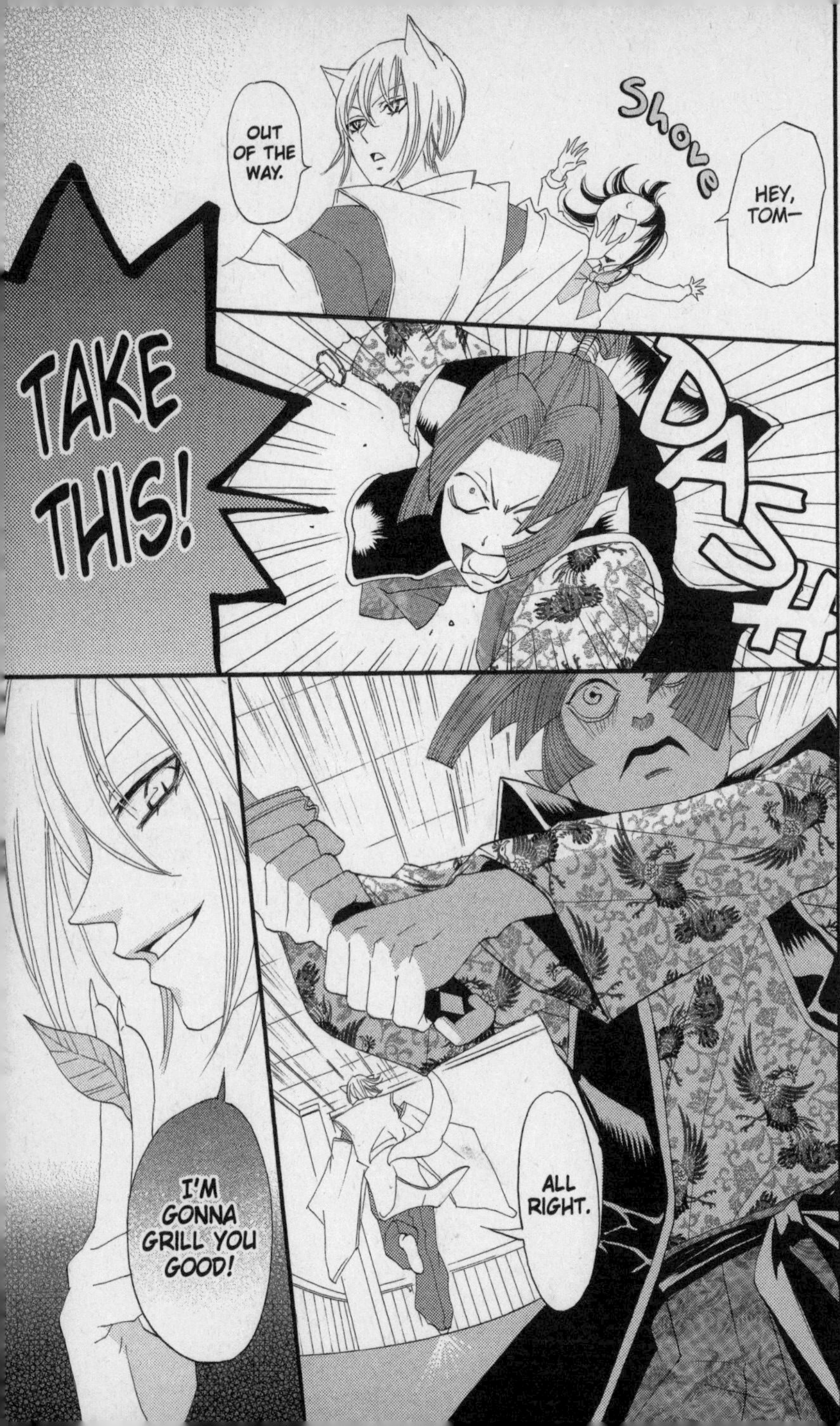
HEY, TOM—
Shove
OUT OF THE WAY.
DASH
TAKE THIS!
ALL RIGHT.
I'M GONNA GRILL YOU GOOD!

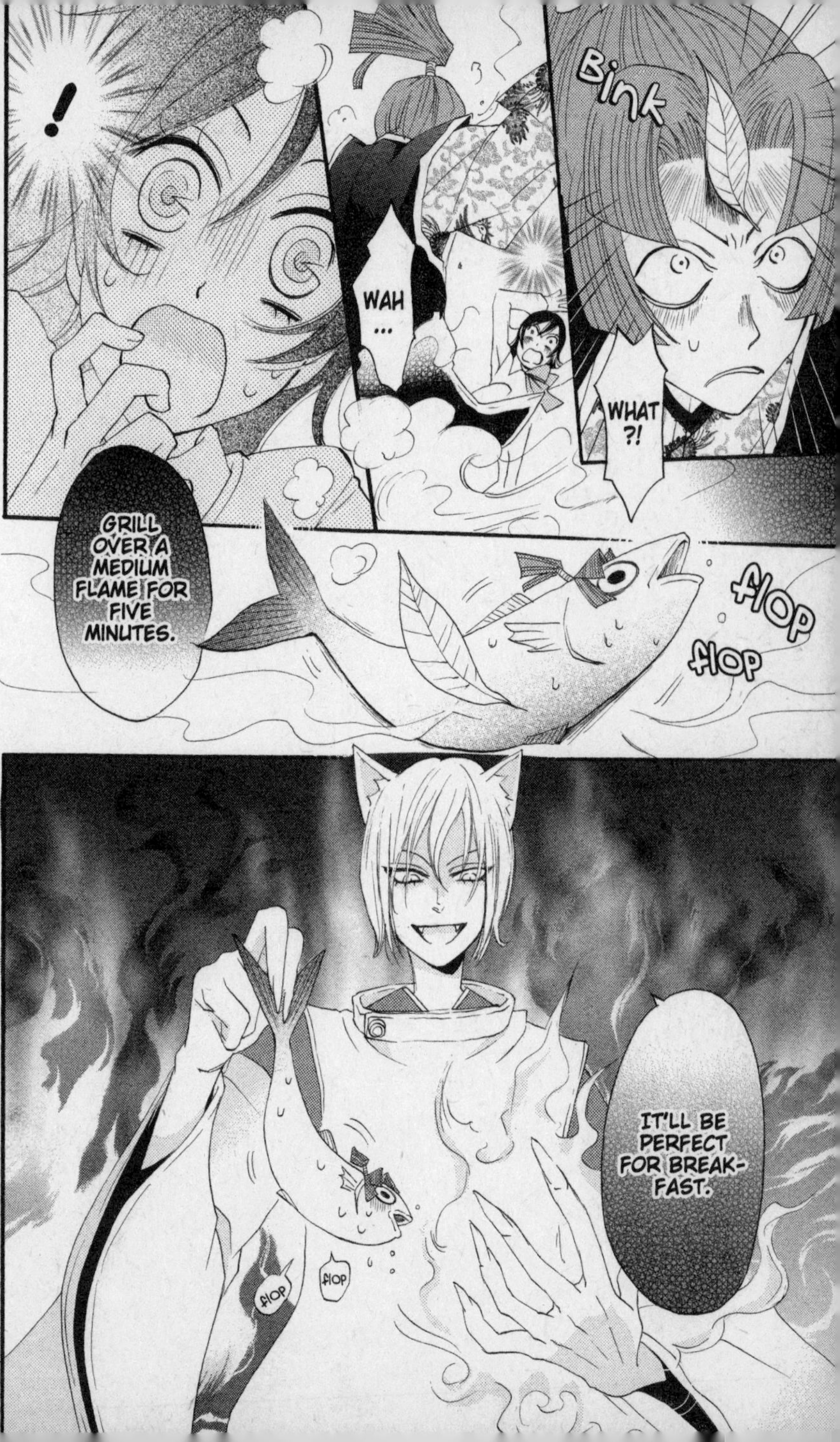
Bink
WHAT ?!
WAH ...
!
flop
flop
GRILL OVER A MEDIUM FLAME FOR FIVE MINUTES.
IT'LL BE PERFECT FOR BREAK-FAST.
flop
flop

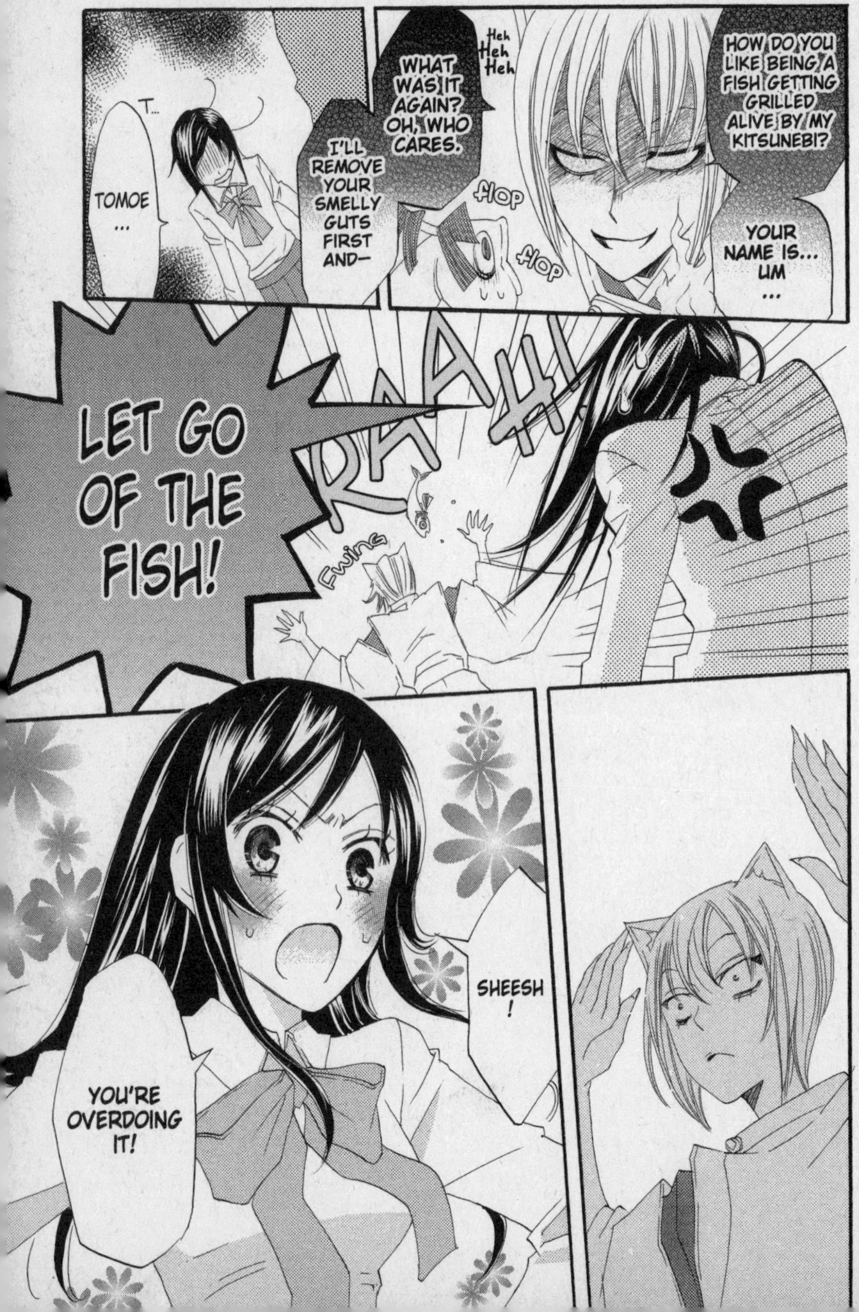
HOW DO YOU LIKE BEING A FISH GETTING GRILLED ALIVE BY MY KITSUNEBI?
YOUR NAME IS... UM ...
Heh Heh Heh
WHAT WAS IT AGAIN? OH, WHO CARES.
I'LL REMOVE YOUR SMELLY GUTS FIRST AND—
flop
flop
T...
TOMOE ...
RAAH!
LET GO OF THE FISH!
Fwing
SHEESH!
YOU'RE OVERDOING IT!

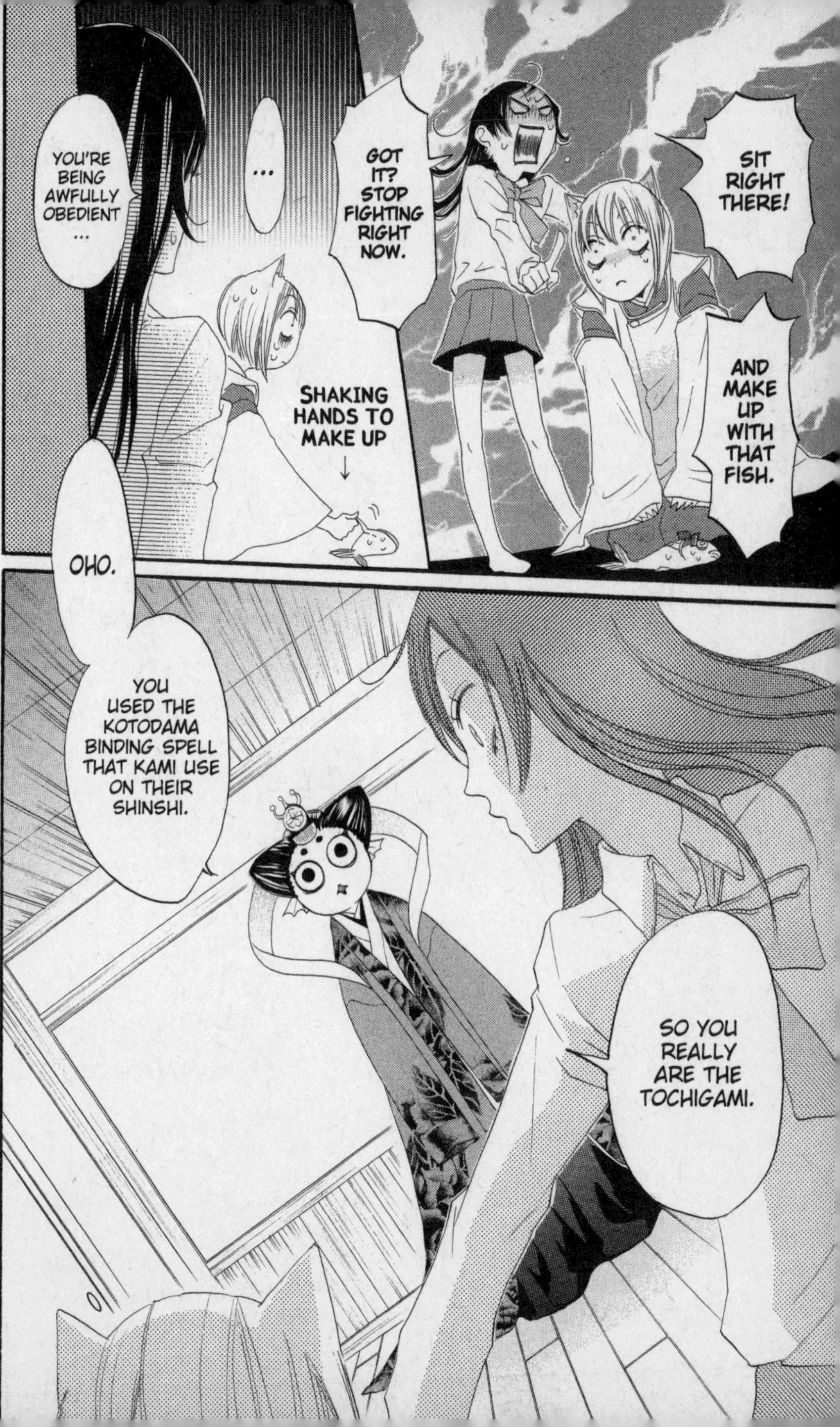

SIT RIGHT THERE!
AND MAKE UP WITH THAT FISH.
GOT IT? STOP FIGHTING RIGHT NOW.
SHAKING HANDS TO MAKE UP ↓
...
YOU'RE BEING AWFULLY OBEDIENT ...
OHO.
YOU USED THE KOTODAMA BINDING SPELL THAT KAMI USE ON THEIR SHINSHI.
SO YOU REALLY ARE THE TOCHIGAMI.

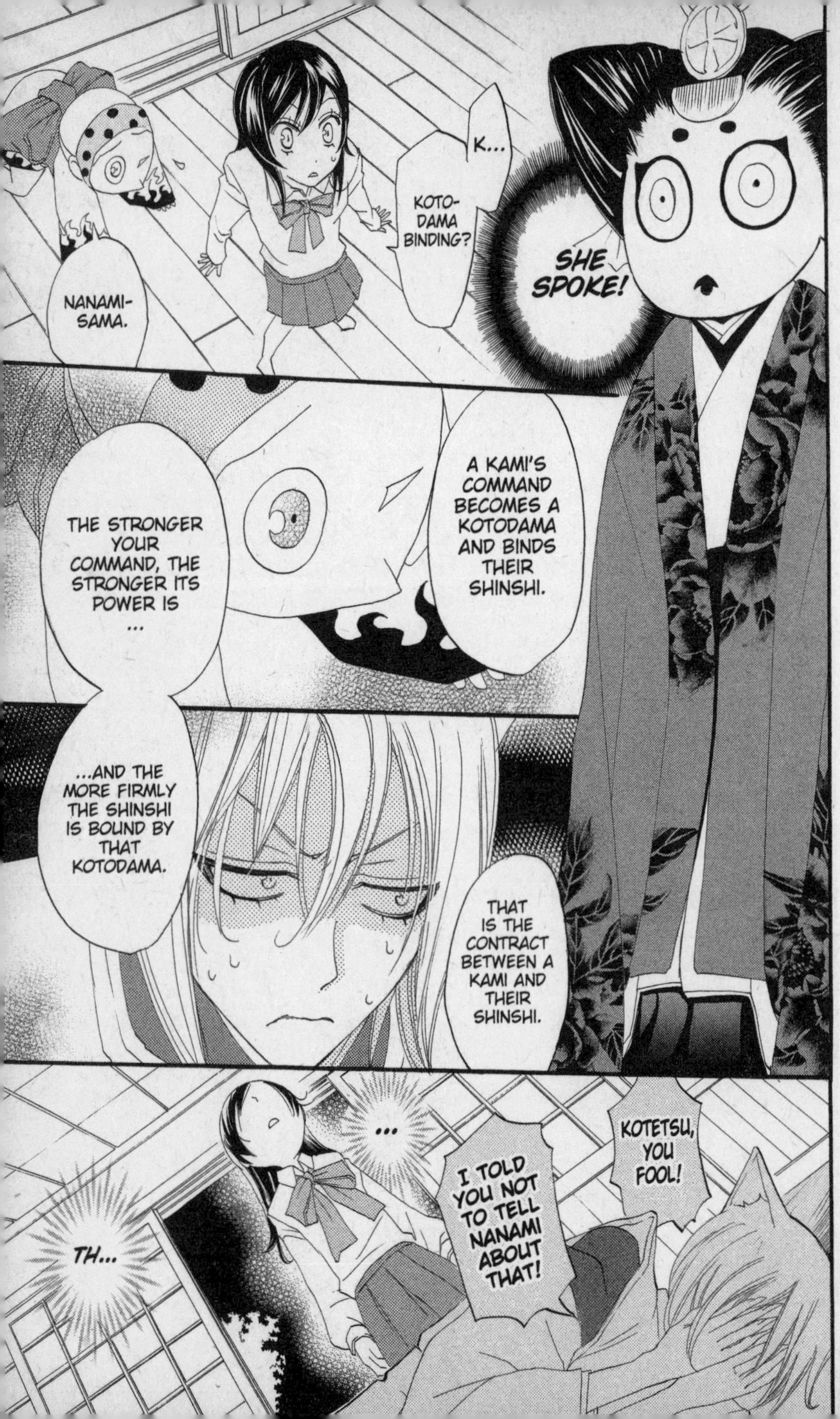
SHE SPOKE!
K...
KOTO-DAMA BINDING?
NANAMI-SAMA.
A KAMI'S COMMAND BECOMES A KOTODAMA AND BINDS THEIR SHINSHI.
THE STRONGER YOUR COMMAND, THE STRONGER ITS POWER IS ...
...AND THE MORE FIRMLY THE SHINSHI IS BOUND BY THAT KOTODAMA.
THAT IS THE CONTRACT BETWEEN A KAMI AND THEIR SHINSHI.
KOTETSU, YOU FOOL!
I TOLD YOU NOT TO TELL NANAMI ABOUT THAT!
...
TH...

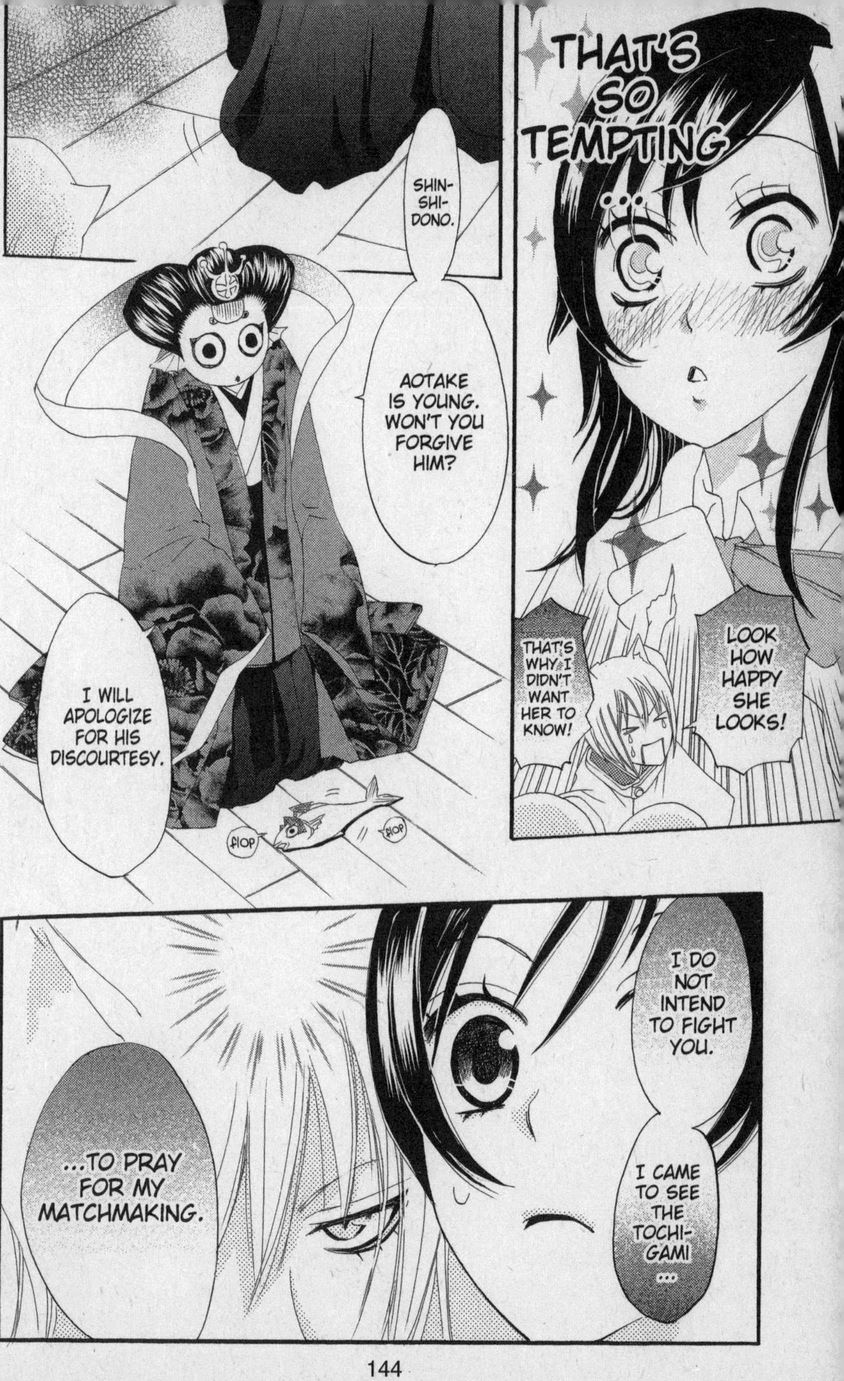
THAT'S SO TEMPTING ...
LOOK HOW HAPPY SHE LOOKS!
THAT'S WHY I DIDN'T WANT HER TO KNOW!
SHIN-SHI-DONO.
AOTAKE IS YOUNG. WON'T YOU FORGIVE HIM?
I WILL APOLOGIZE FOR HIS DISCOURTESY.
FLOP
FLOP
I DO NOT INTEND TO FIGHT YOU.
I CAME TO SEE THE TOCHI-GAMI ...
...TO PRAY FOR MY MATCHMAKING.

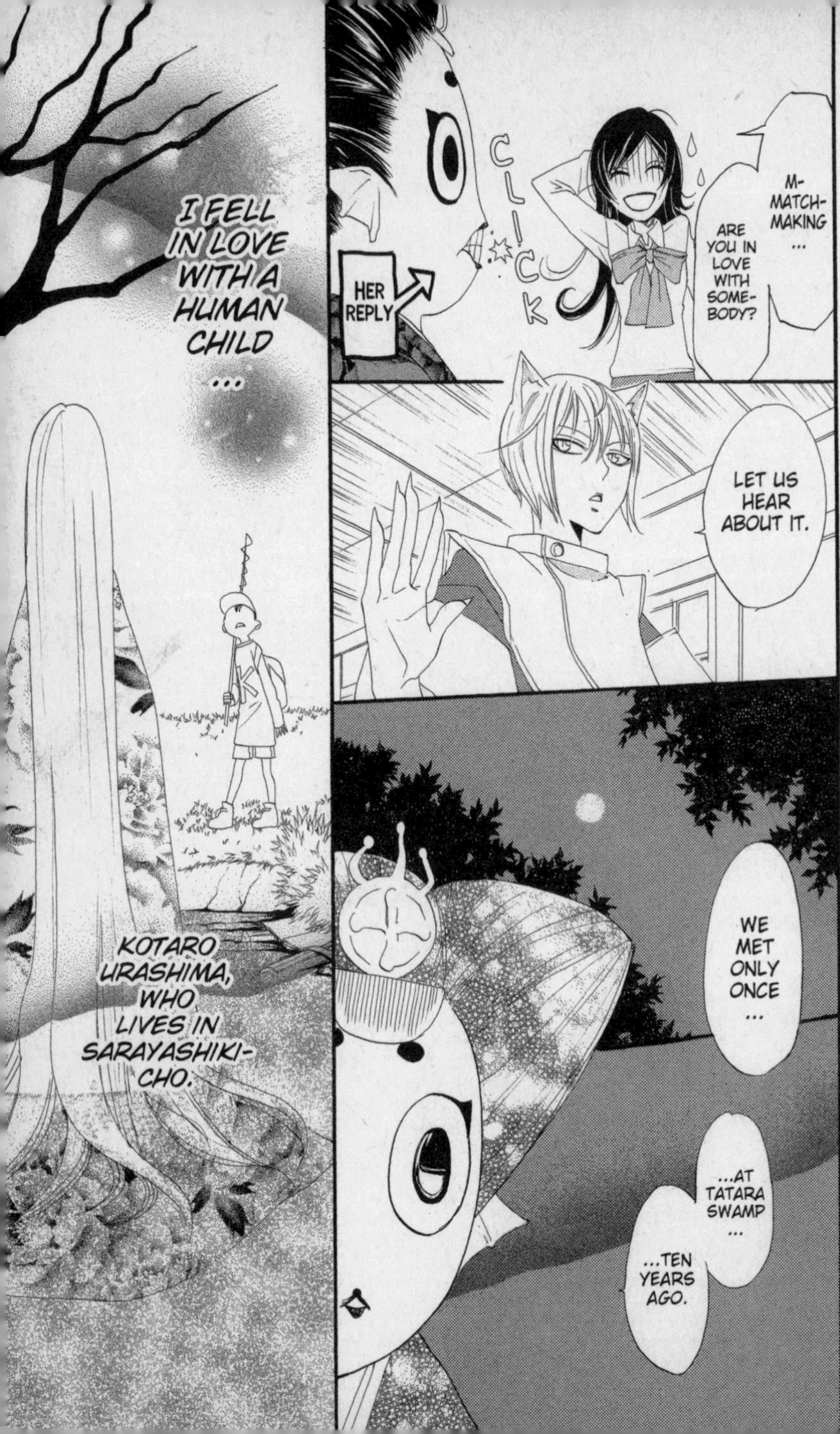
M-MATCH-MAKING...
ARE YOU IN LOVE WITH SOME-BODY?
CLICK
HER REPLY
LET US HEAR ABOUT IT.
WE MET ONLY ONCE...
...AT TATARA SWAMP...
...TEN YEARS AGO.
I FELL IN LOVE WITH A HUMAN CHILD...
KOTARO URASHIMA, WHO LIVES IN SARAYASHIKI-CHO.

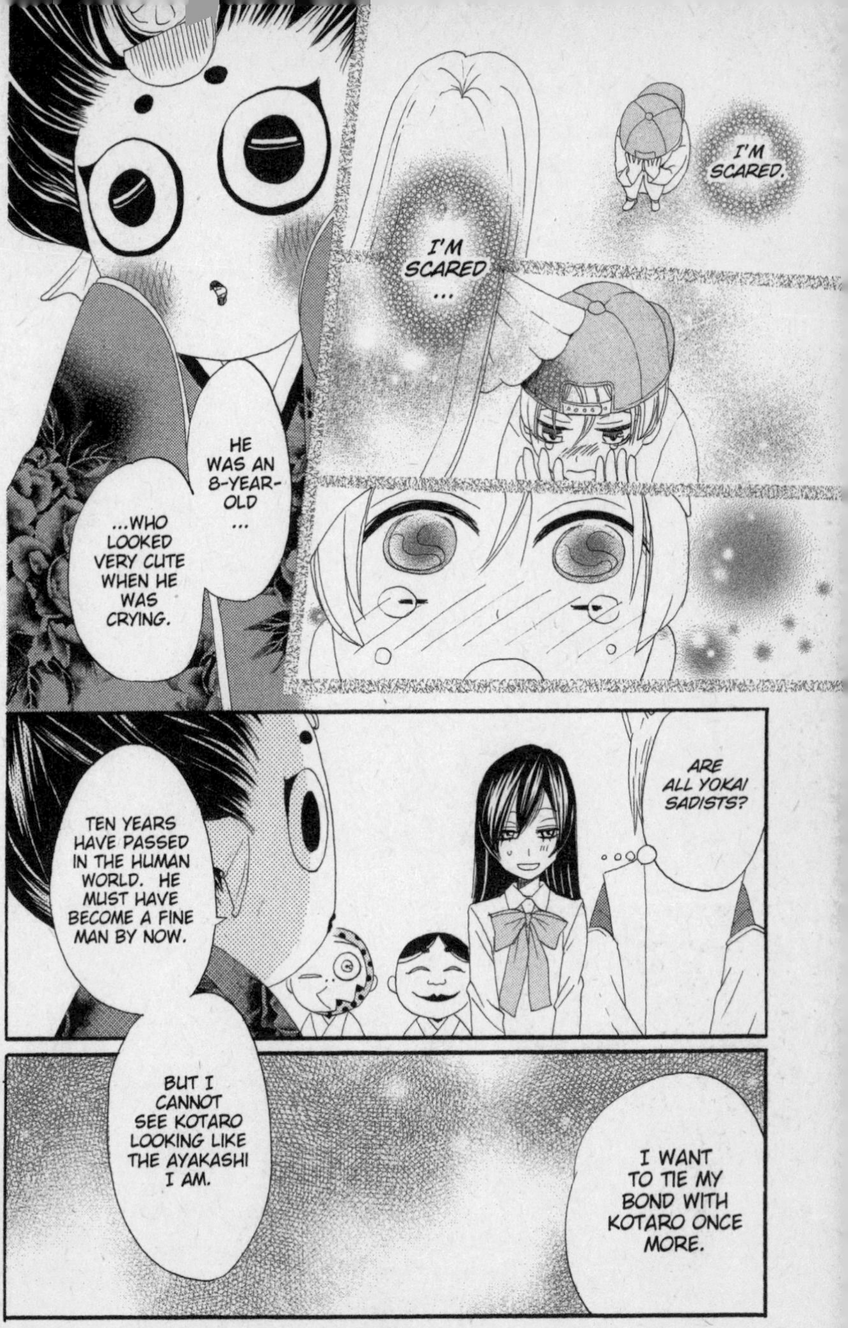
I'M SCARED.
I'M SCARED ...
HE WAS AN 8-YEAR-OLD ...
...WHO LOOKED VERY CUTE WHEN HE WAS CRYING.
ARE ALL YOKAI SADISTS?
TEN YEARS HAVE PASSED IN THE HUMAN WORLD. HE MUST HAVE BECOME A FINE MAN BY NOW.
I WANT TO TIE MY BOND WITH KOTARO ONCE MORE.
BUT I CANNOT SEE KOTARO LOOKING LIKE THE AYAKASHI I AM.

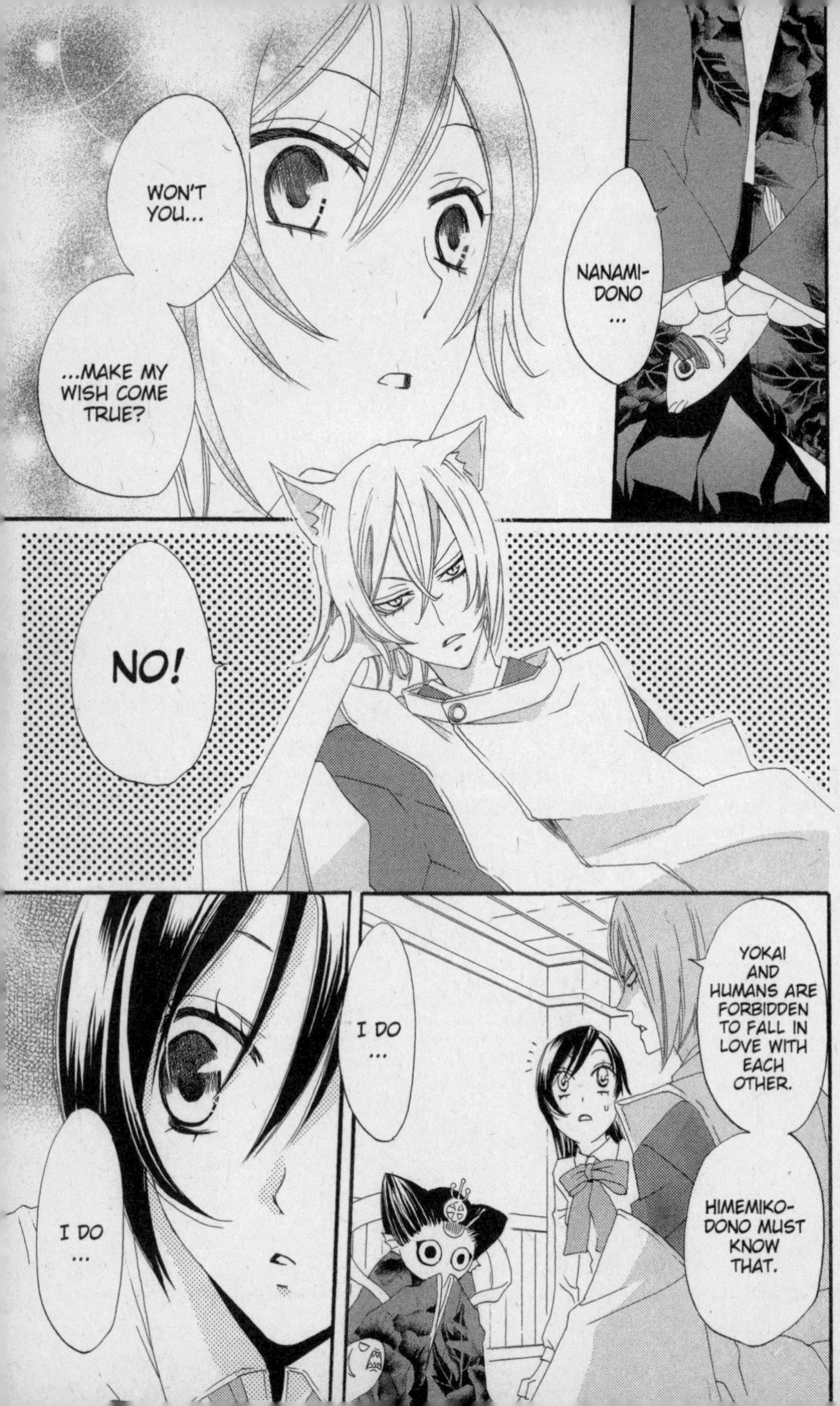
NANAMI-DONO ...
WON'T YOU...
...MAKE MY WISH COME TRUE?
NO!
YOKAI AND HUMANS ARE FORBIDDEN TO FALL IN LOVE WITH EACH OTHER.
HIMEMIKO-DONO MUST KNOW THAT.
I DO ...
I DO ...

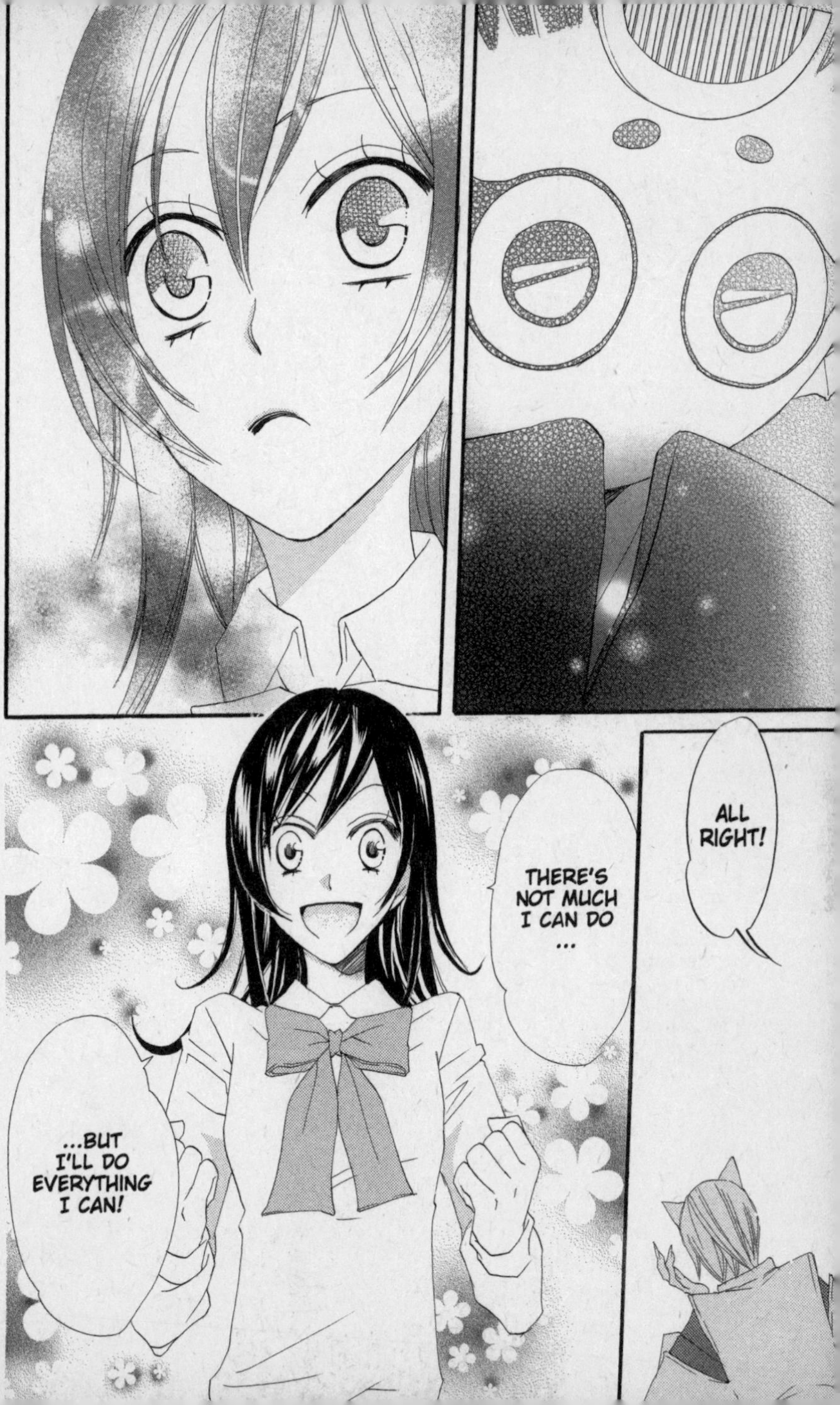
ALL RIGHT!
THERE'S NOT MUCH I CAN DO ...
...BUT I'LL DO EVERYTHING I CAN!

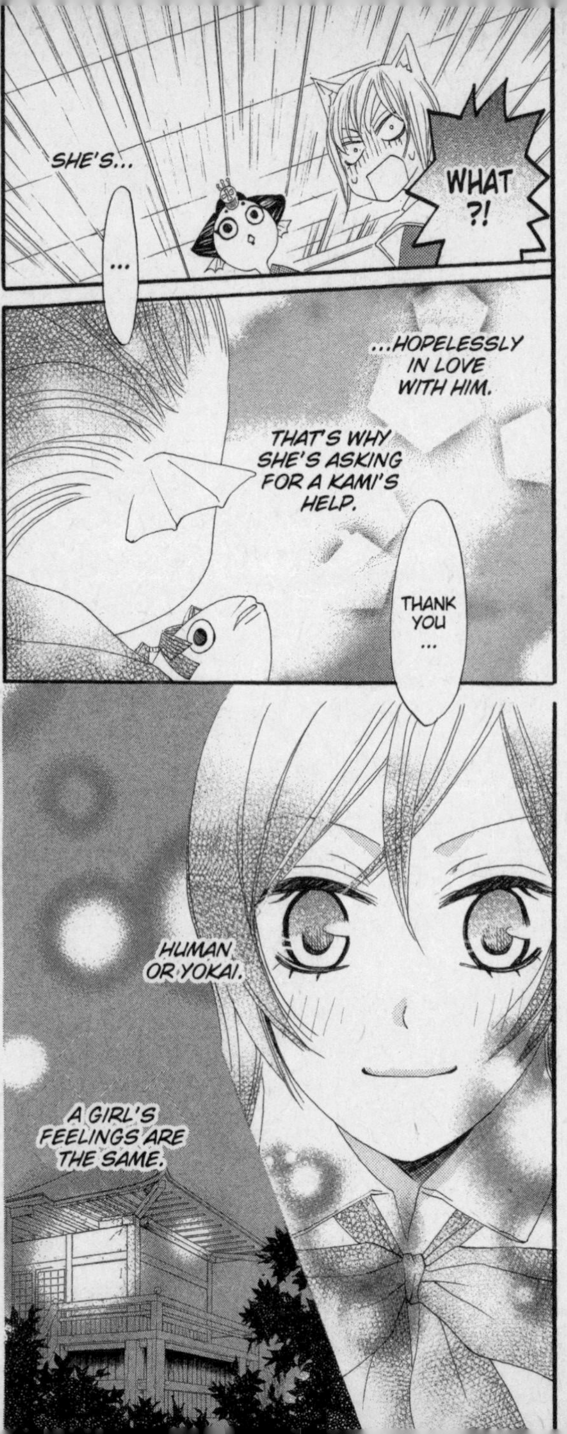
WHAT ?!
SHE'S...
...
...HOPELESSLY IN LOVE WITH HIM.
THAT'S WHY SHE'S ASKING FOR A KAMI'S HELP.
THANK YOU ...
HUMAN OR YOKAI.
A GIRL'S FEELINGS ARE THE SAME.

I'd only played Dragon Quest up to 6, but I borrowed 8 the other day, so I played it a little! (I haven't finished the game).

Dragon Quest..!

Uses polygons now...!!

The monsters that roll and die are 3-D and are awfully cute. I like the striped cat. I felt like playing Dragon Quest 3 on the Famicom again. I wish they'd release it for PS2.

I'm looking forward to the new Biohazard game too. On PS2, please. Because that's all I have...

Oh, I have a Wii too.

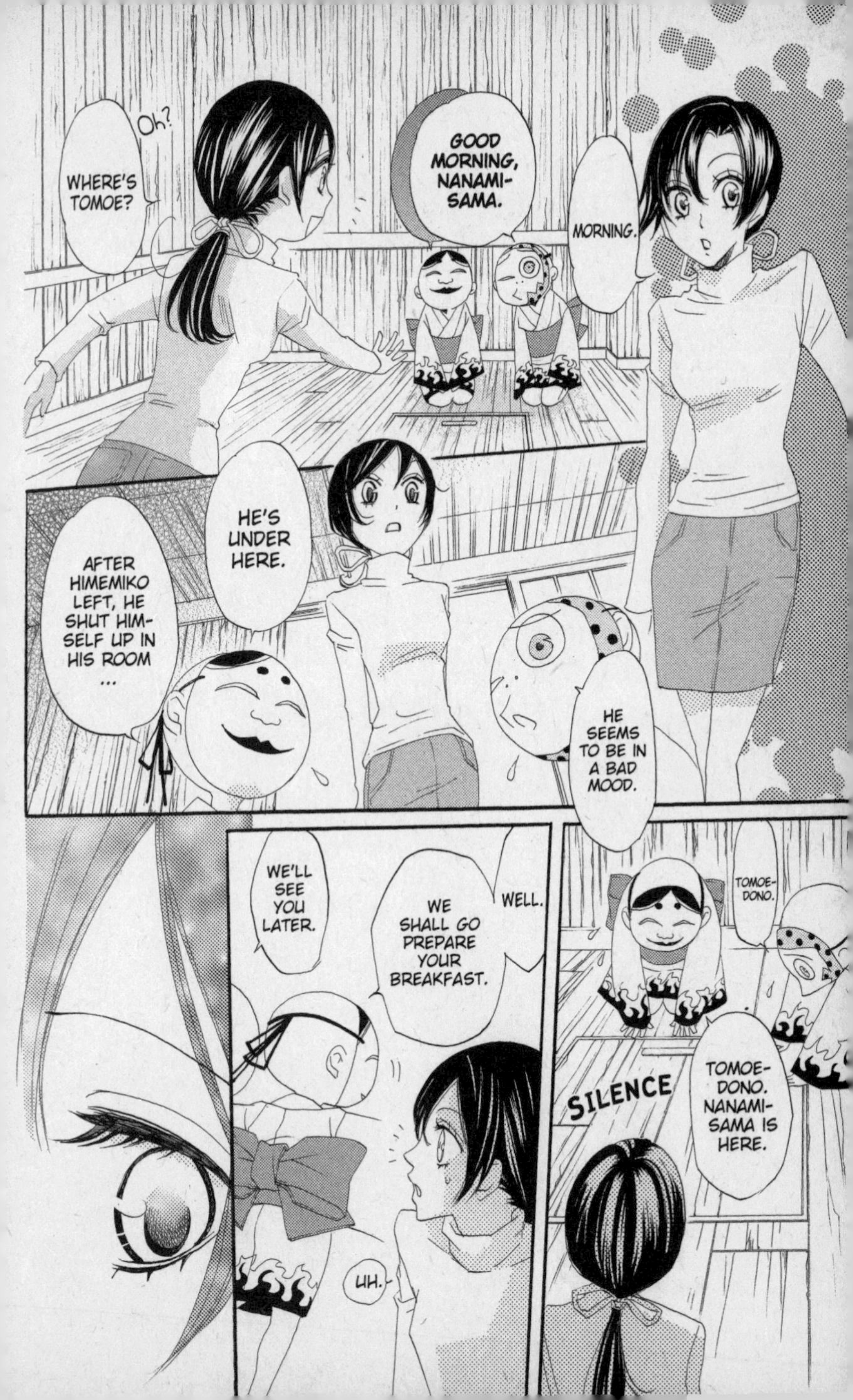
GOOD MORNING, NANAMI-SAMA.
MORNING.
Oh?
WHERE'S TOMOE?
HE'S UNDER HERE.
AFTER HIMEMIKO LEFT, HE SHUT HIMSELF UP IN HIS ROOM ...
HE SEEMS TO BE IN A BAD MOOD.
TOMOE-DONO.
TOMOE-DONO. NANAMI-SAMA IS HERE.
SILENCE
WELL.
WE SHALL GO PREPARE YOUR BREAKFAST.
WE'LL SEE YOU LATER.
UH.

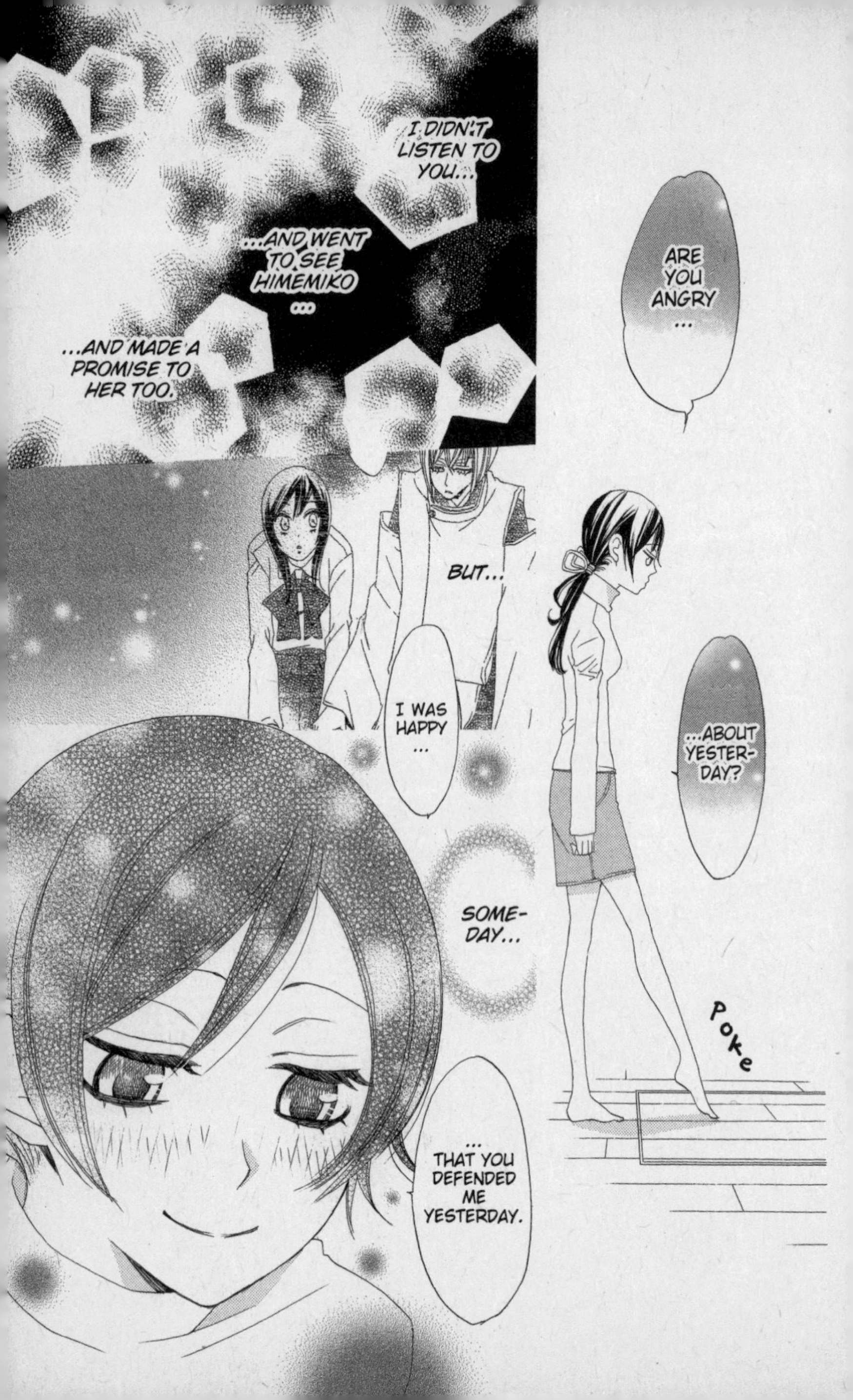

ARE YOU ANGRY...
...ABOUT YESTERDAY?
Poke
I DIDN'T LISTEN TO YOU...
...AND WENT TO SEE HIMEMIKO...
...AND MADE A PROMISE TO HER TOO.
BUT...
I WAS HAPPY...
SOMEDAY...
...THAT YOU DEFENDED ME YESTERDAY.

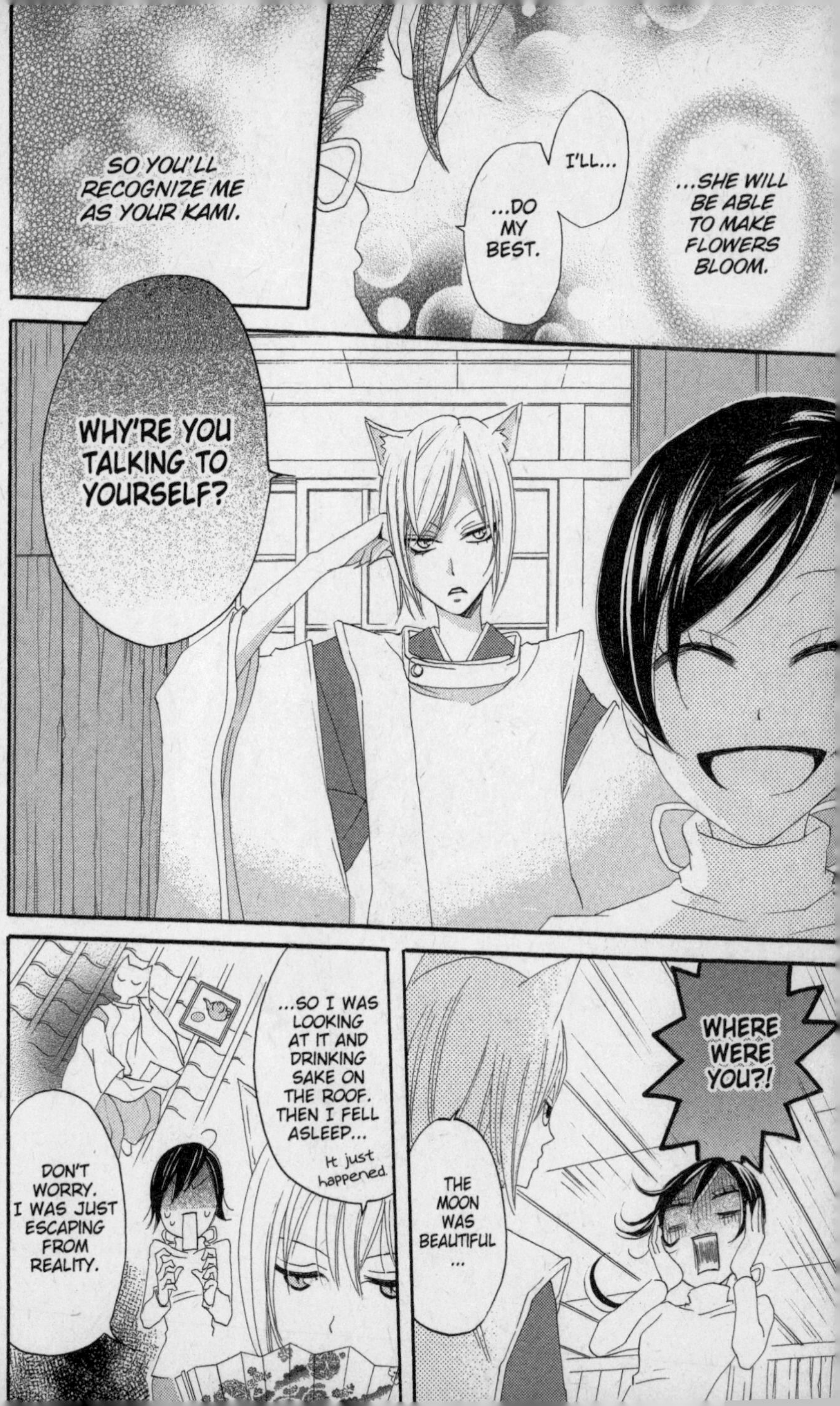
...SHE WILL BE ABLE TO MAKE FLOWERS BLOOM.
I'LL...
...DO MY BEST.
SO YOU'LL RECOGNIZE ME AS YOUR KAMI.
WHY'RE YOU TALKING TO YOURSELF?
WHERE WERE YOU?!
THE MOON WAS BEAUTIFUL...
...SO I WAS LOOKING AT IT AND DRINKING SAKE ON THE ROOF. THEN I FELL ASLEEP...
It just happened.
DON'T WORRY. I WAS JUST ESCAPING FROM REALITY.

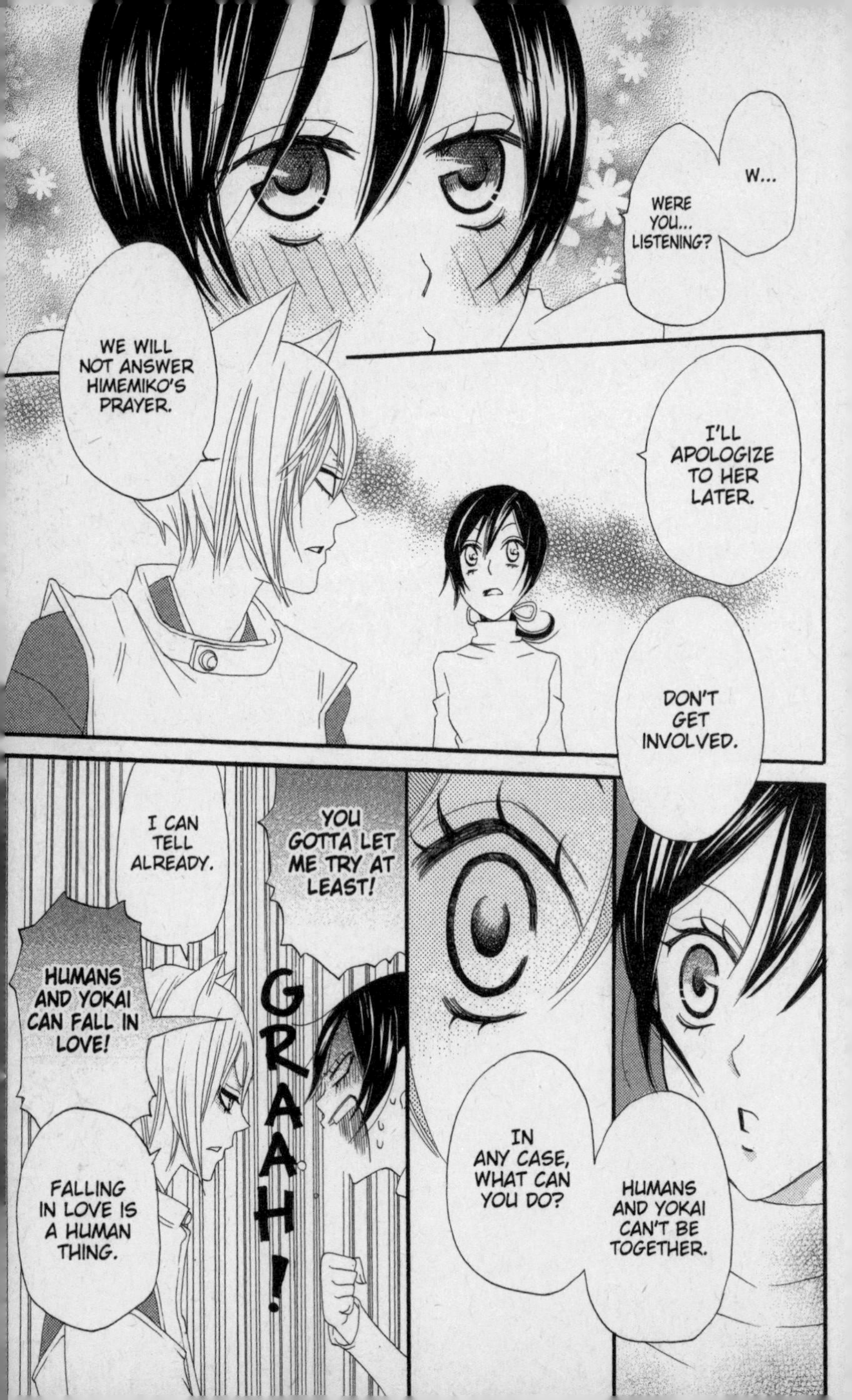
W...
WERE YOU... LISTENING?
WE WILL NOT ANSWER HIMEMIKO'S PRAYER.
I'LL APOLOGIZE TO HER LATER.
DON'T GET INVOLVED.
HUMANS AND YOKAI CAN'T BE TOGETHER.
IN ANY CASE, WHAT CAN YOU DO?
YOU GOTTA LET ME TRY AT LEAST!
GRAAH!
I CAN TELL ALREADY.
HUMANS AND YOKAI CAN FALL IN LOVE!
FALLING IN LOVE IS A HUMAN THING.

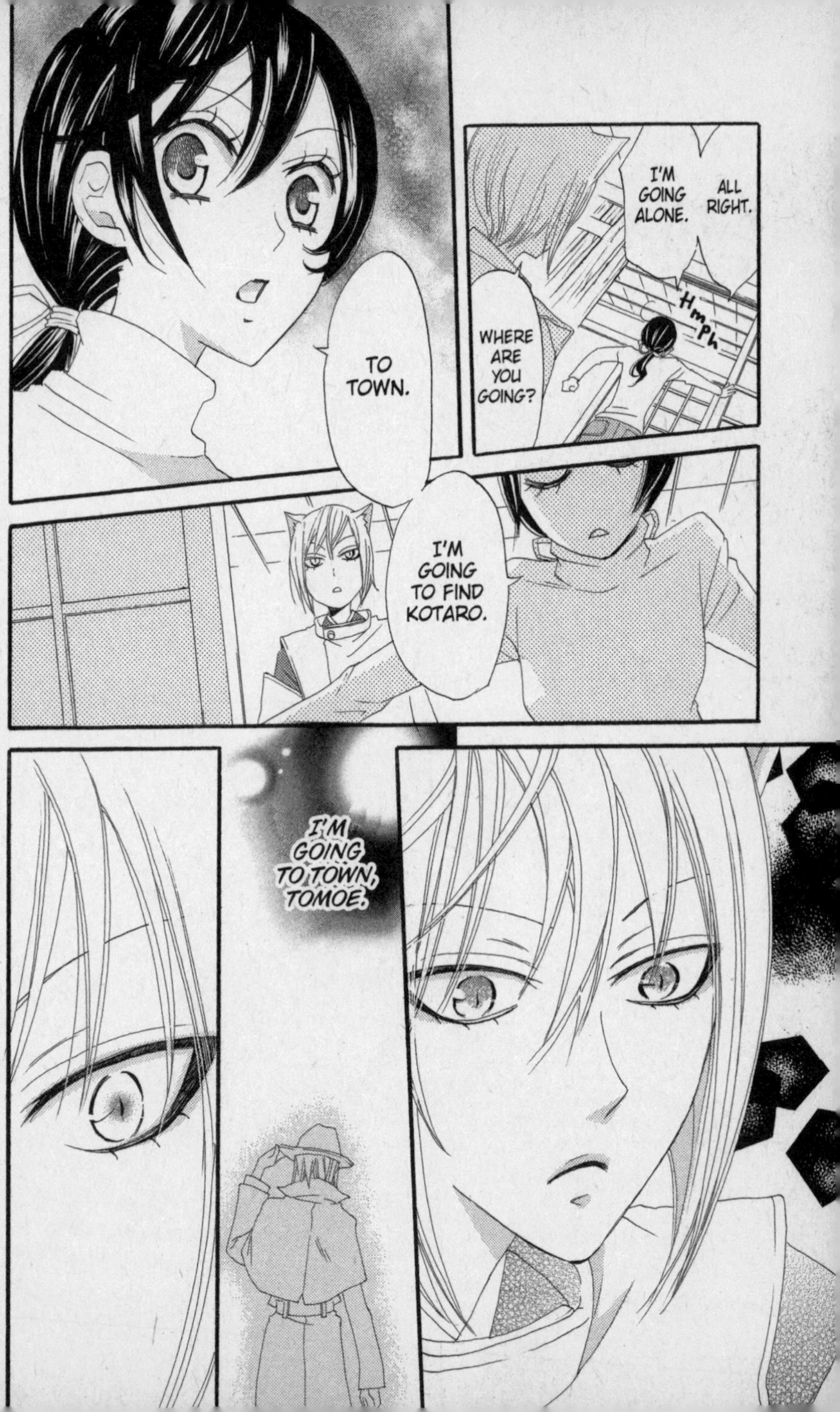
ALL RIGHT.
I'M GOING ALONE.
Hmph
WHERE ARE YOU GOING?
TO TOWN.
I'M GOING TO FIND KOTARO.
I'M GOING TO TOWN, TOMOE.

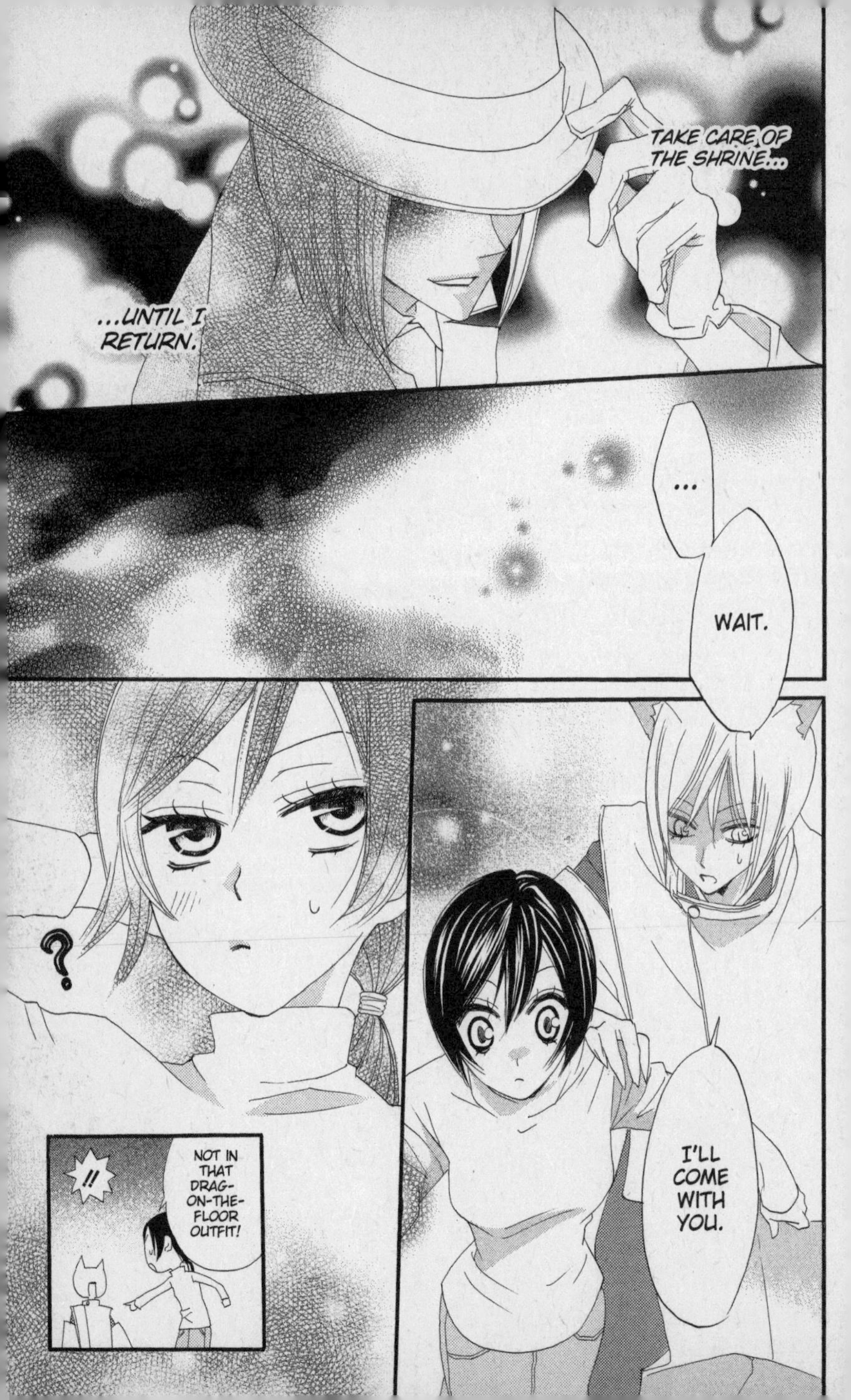
TAKE CARE OF THE SHRINE...
...UNTIL I RETURN.
...
WAIT.
I'LL COME WITH YOU.
?
!!
NOT IN THAT DRAG-ON-THE-FLOOR OUTFIT!

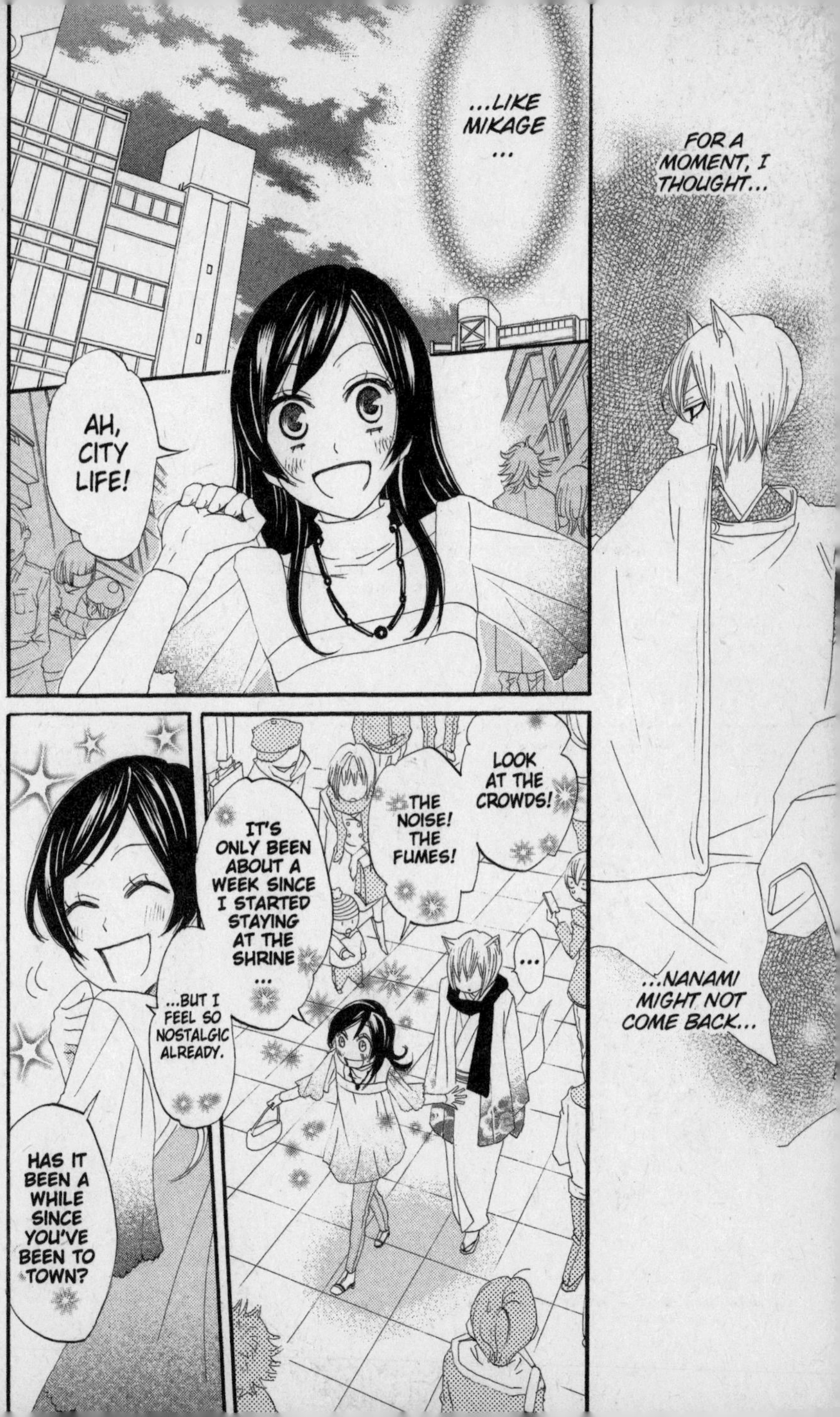
FOR A MOMENT, I THOUGHT...
...NANAMI MIGHT NOT COME BACK...
...LIKE MIKAGE ...
AH, CITY LIFE!
LOOK AT THE CROWDS!
THE NOISE! THE FUMES!
IT'S ONLY BEEN ABOUT A WEEK SINCE I STARTED STAYING AT THE SHRINE ...
...
...BUT I FEEL SO NOSTALGIC ALREADY.
HAS IT BEEN A WHILE SINCE YOU'VE BEEN TO TOWN?

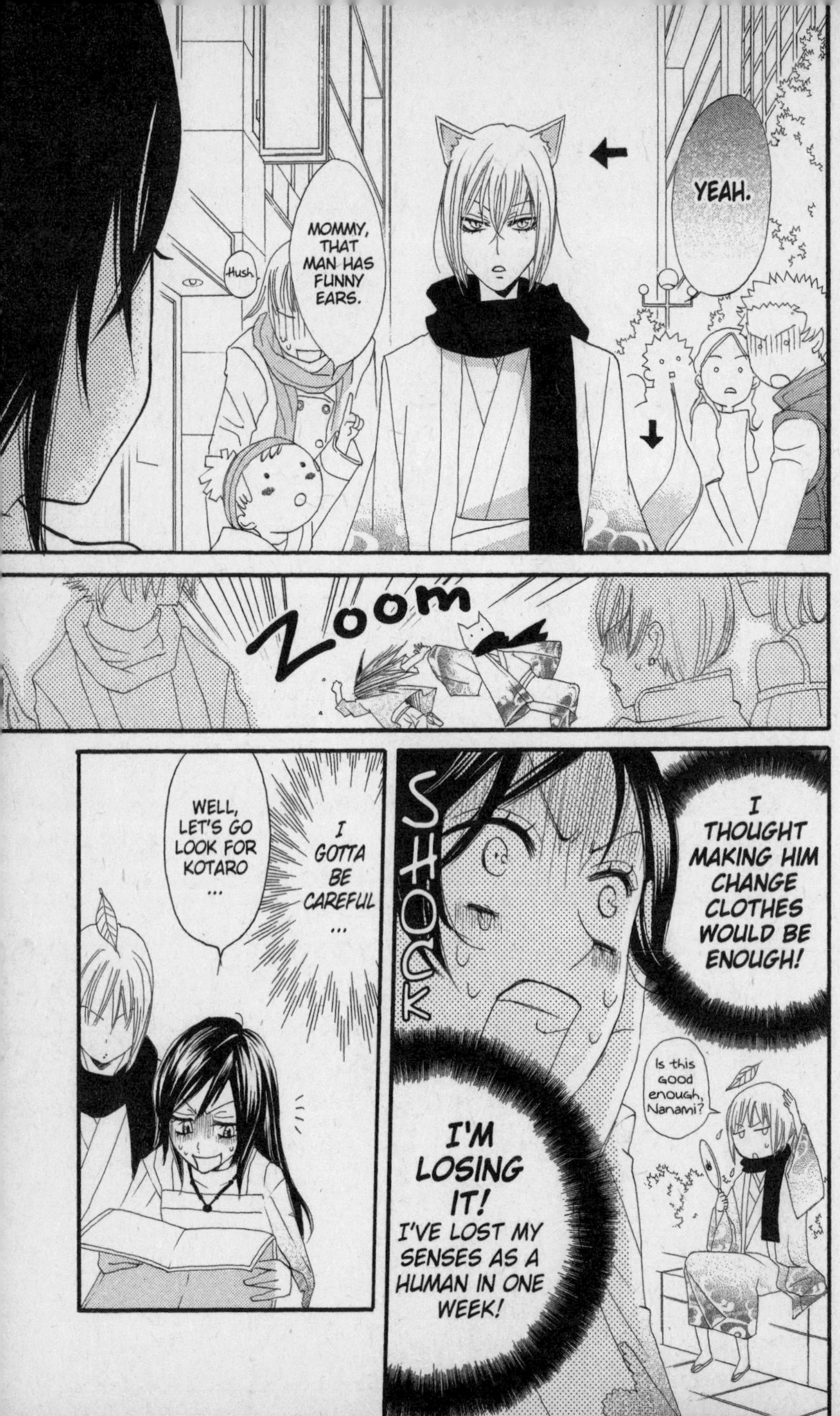
YEAH.
MOMMY, THAT MAN HAS FUNNY EARS.
Hush.
Zoom
I THOUGHT MAKING HIM CHANGE CLOTHES WOULD BE ENOUGH!
SHOCK
Is this good enough, Nanami?
I'M LOSING IT! I'VE LOST MY SENSES AS A HUMAN IN ONE WEEK!
I GOTTA BE CAREFUL ...
WELL, LET'S GO LOOK FOR KOTARO ...

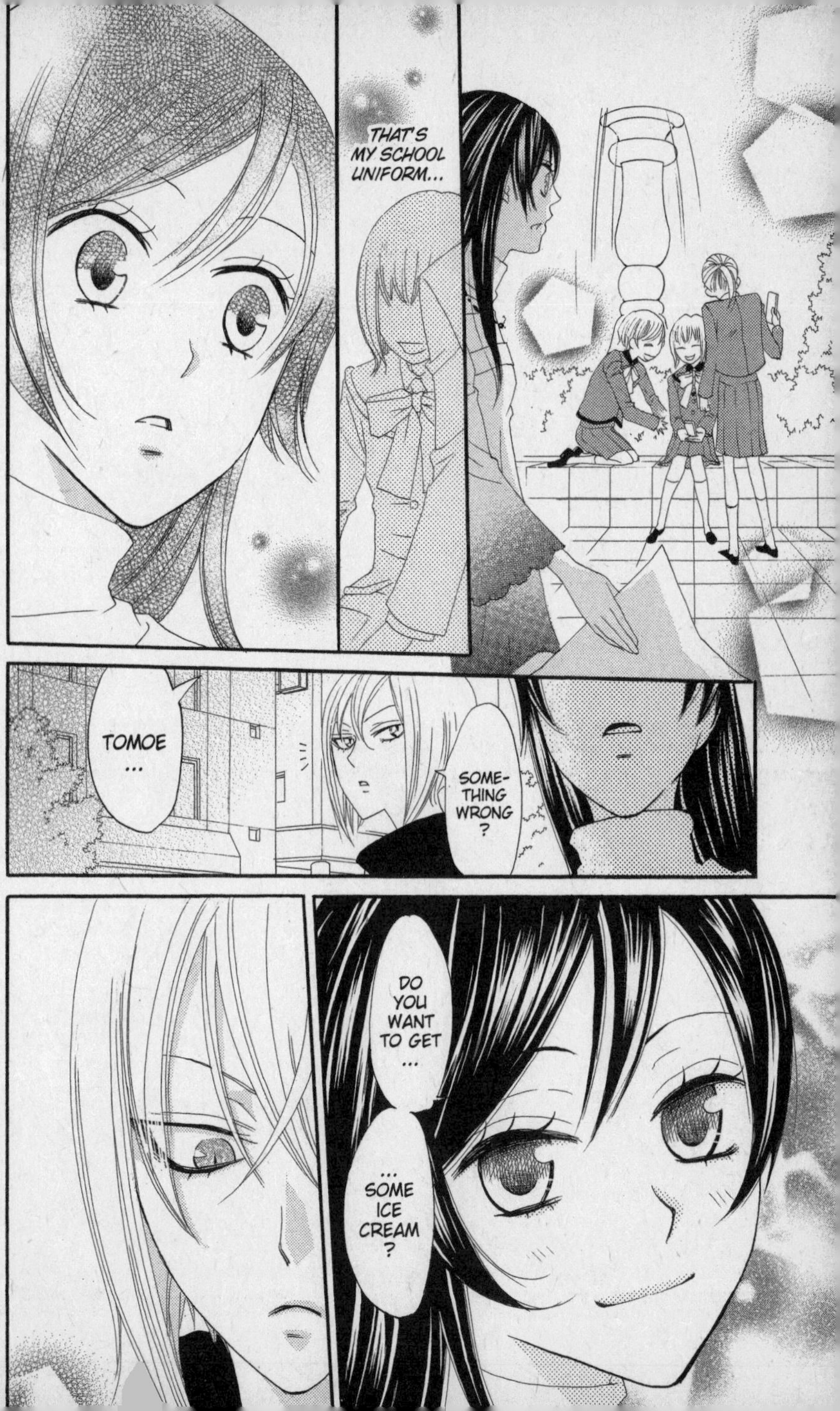
THAT'S MY SCHOOL UNIFORM...
SOME-THING WRONG?
TOMOE...
DO YOU WANT TO GET...
...SOME ICE CREAM?

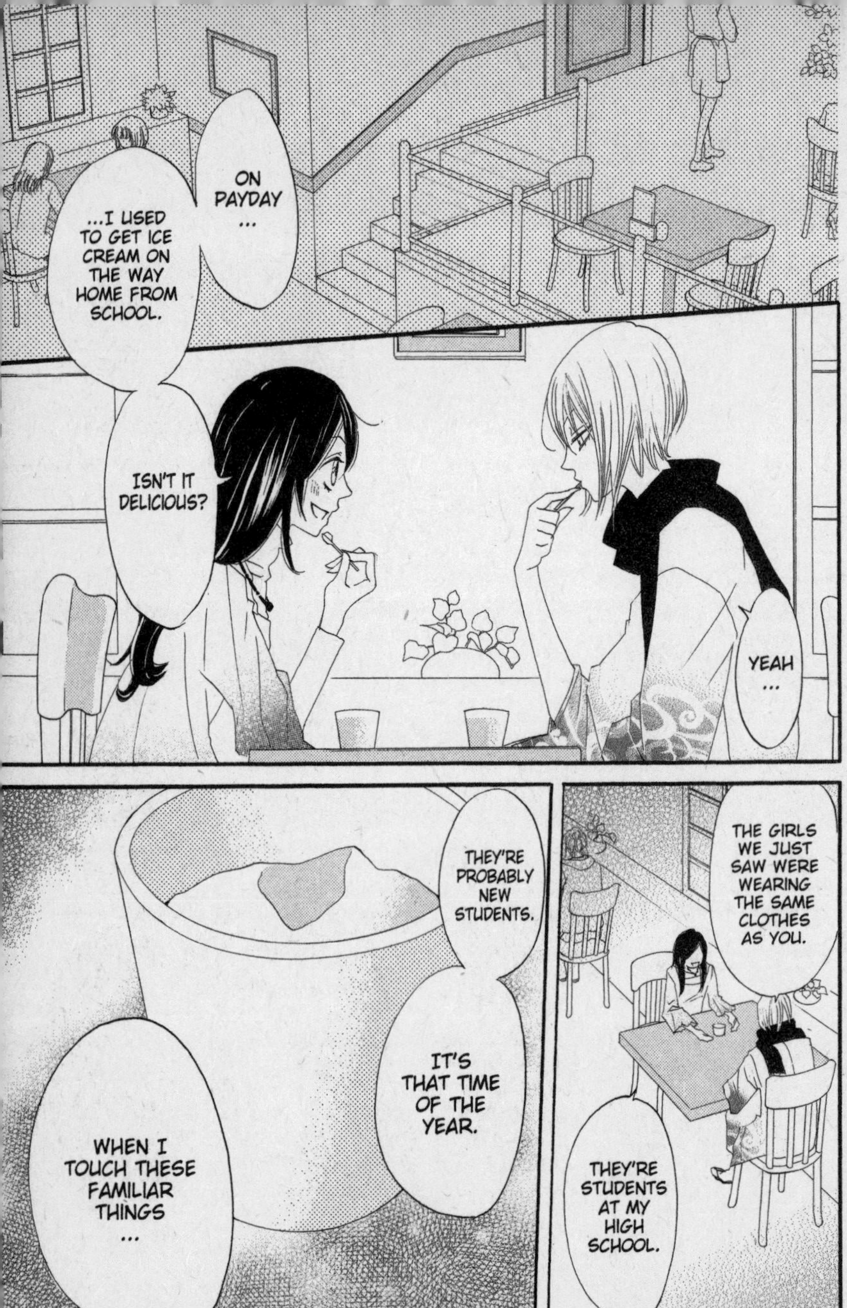

ON PAYDAY ...
...I USED TO GET ICE CREAM ON THE WAY HOME FROM SCHOOL.
ISN'T IT DELICIOUS?
YEAH ...
THE GIRLS WE JUST SAW WERE WEARING THE SAME CLOTHES AS YOU.
THEY'RE STUDENTS AT MY HIGH SCHOOL.
THEY'RE PROBABLY NEW STUDENTS.
IT'S THAT TIME OF THE YEAR.
WHEN I TOUCH THESE FAMILIAR THINGS ...

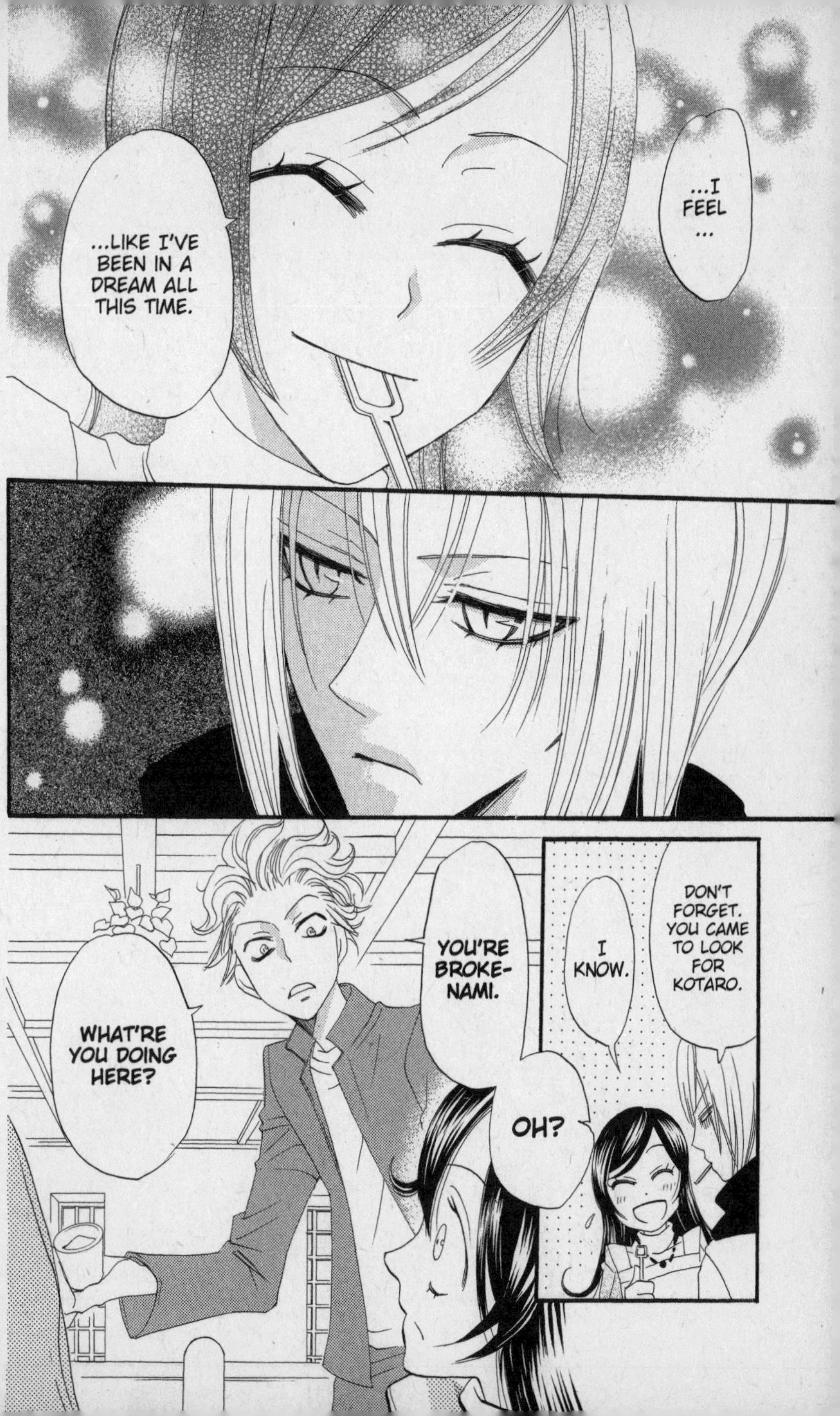
...I FEEL...
...LIKE I'VE BEEN IN A DREAM ALL THIS TIME.
DON'T FORGET. YOU CAME TO LOOK FOR KOTARO.
I KNOW.
YOU'RE BROKE-NAMI.
OH?
WHAT'RE YOU DOING HERE?

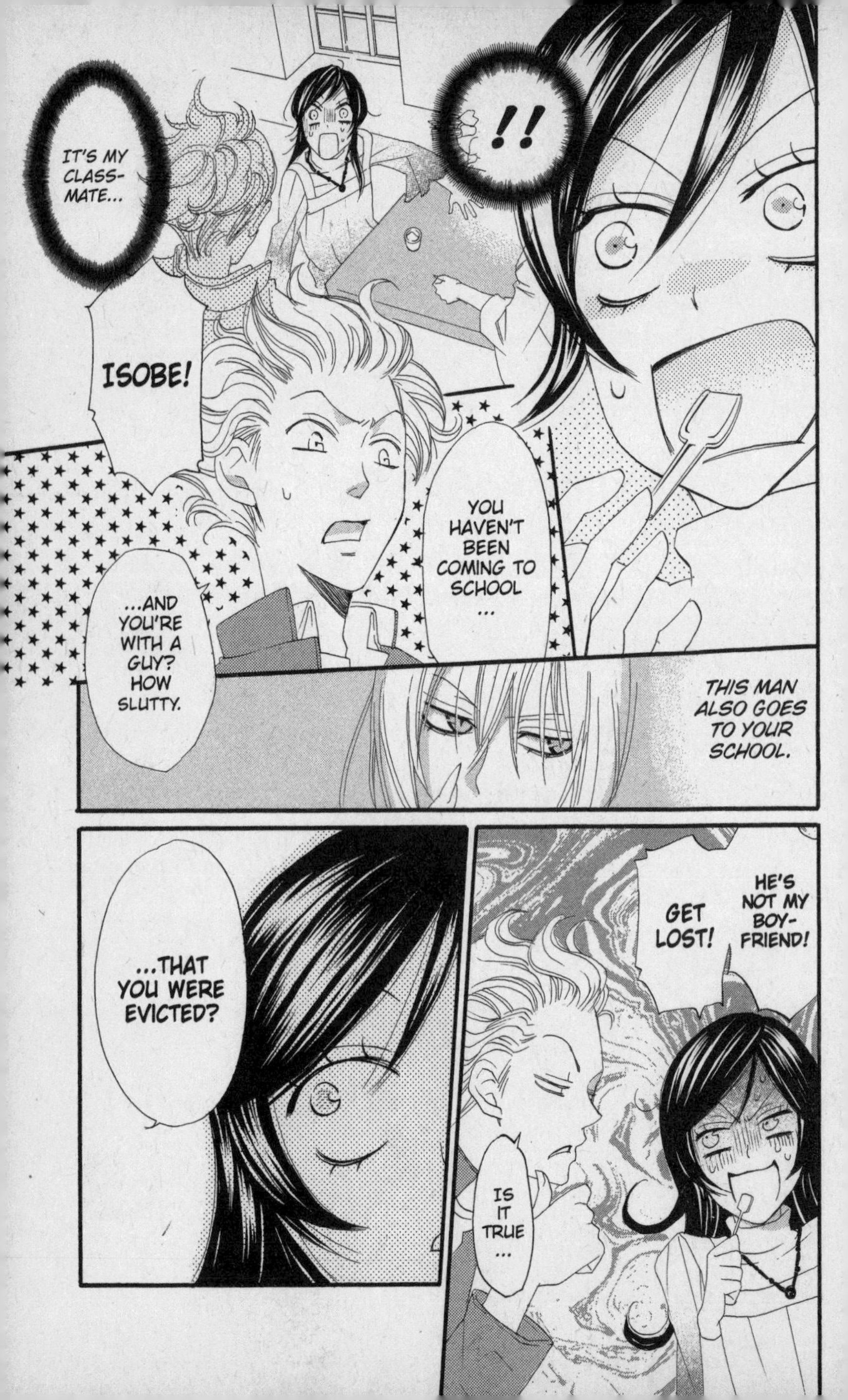
!!
IT'S MY CLASSMATE...
ISOBE!
YOU HAVEN'T BEEN COMING TO SCHOOL...
...AND YOU'RE WITH A GUY? HOW SLUTTY.
THIS MAN ALSO GOES TO YOUR SCHOOL.
HE'S NOT MY BOY-FRIEND!
GET LOST!
IS IT TRUE...
...THAT YOU WERE EVICTED?

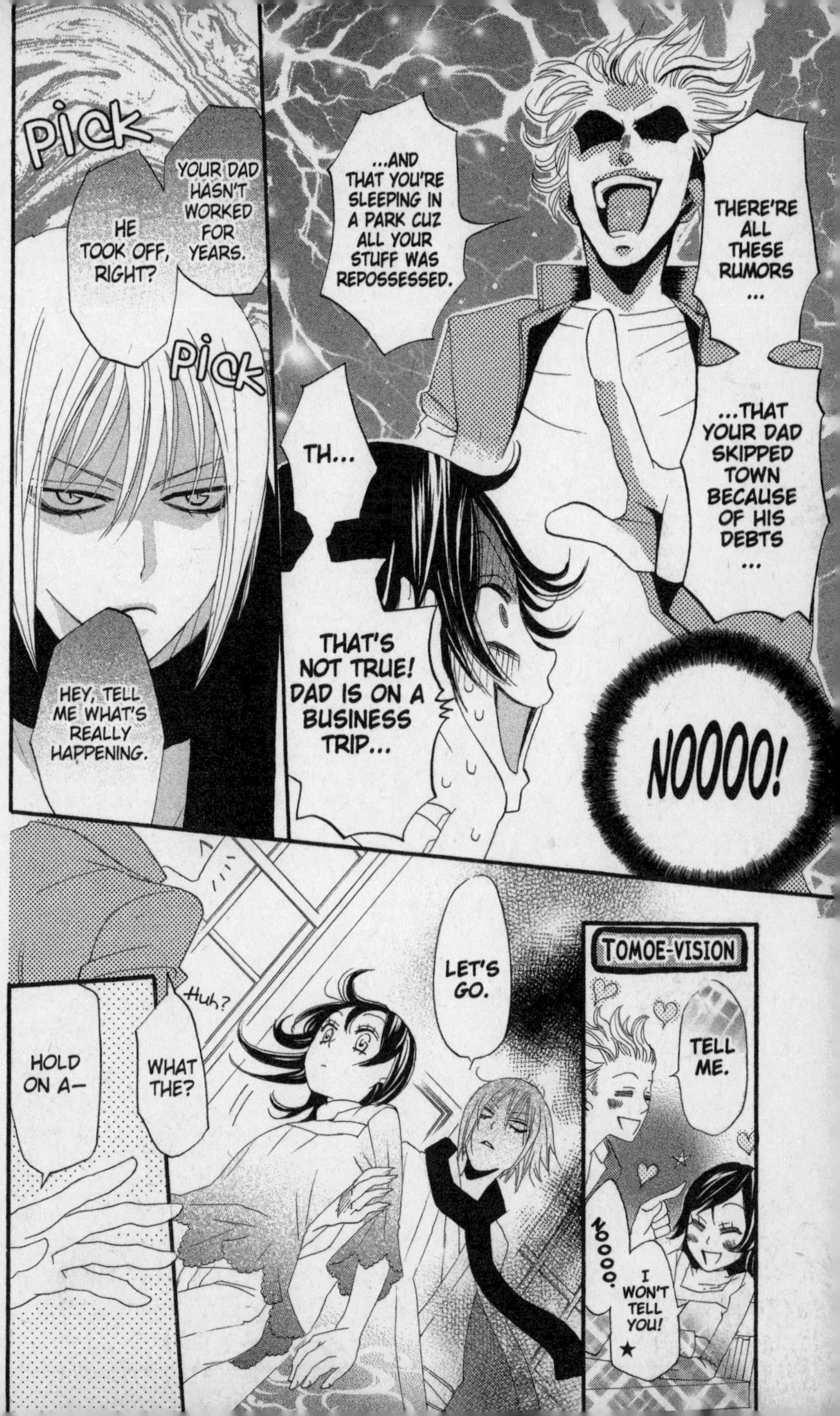
THERE'RE ALL THESE RUMORS...
...THAT YOUR DAD SKIPPED TOWN BECAUSE OF HIS DEBTS...
...AND THAT YOU'RE SLEEPING IN A PARK CUZ ALL YOUR STUFF WAS REPOSSESSED.
TH...
THAT'S NOT TRUE! DAD IS ON A BUSINESS TRIP...
NOOOO!
PICK
YOUR DAD HASN'T WORKED FOR YEARS.
HE TOOK OFF, RIGHT?
PICK
HEY, TELL ME WHAT'S REALLY HAPPENING.
TOMOE-VISION
TELL ME.
NOOOO.
I WON'T TELL YOU! ★
LET'S GO.
Huh?
WHAT THE?
HOLD ON A—

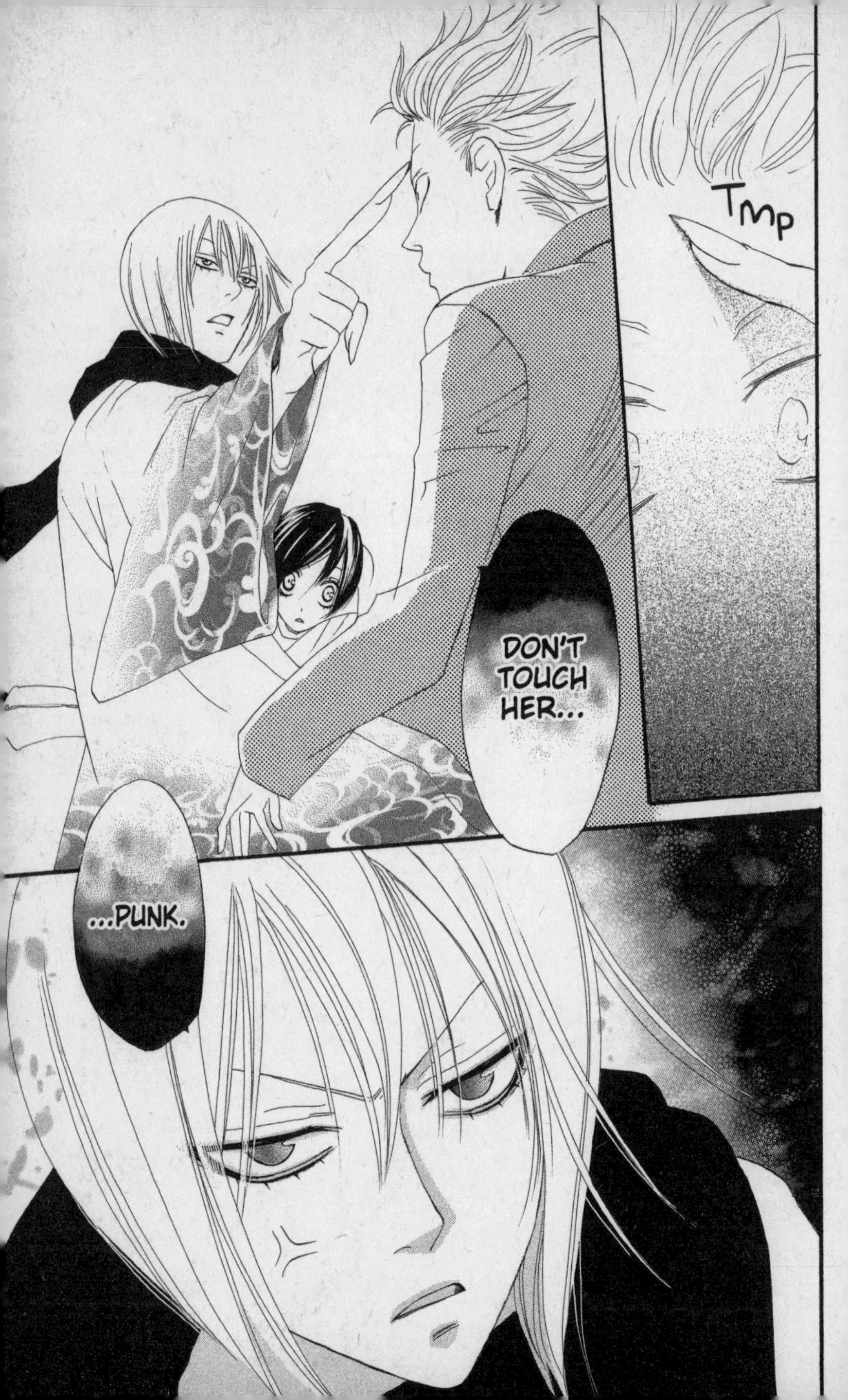
TMP
DON'T TOUCH HER...
...PUNK.

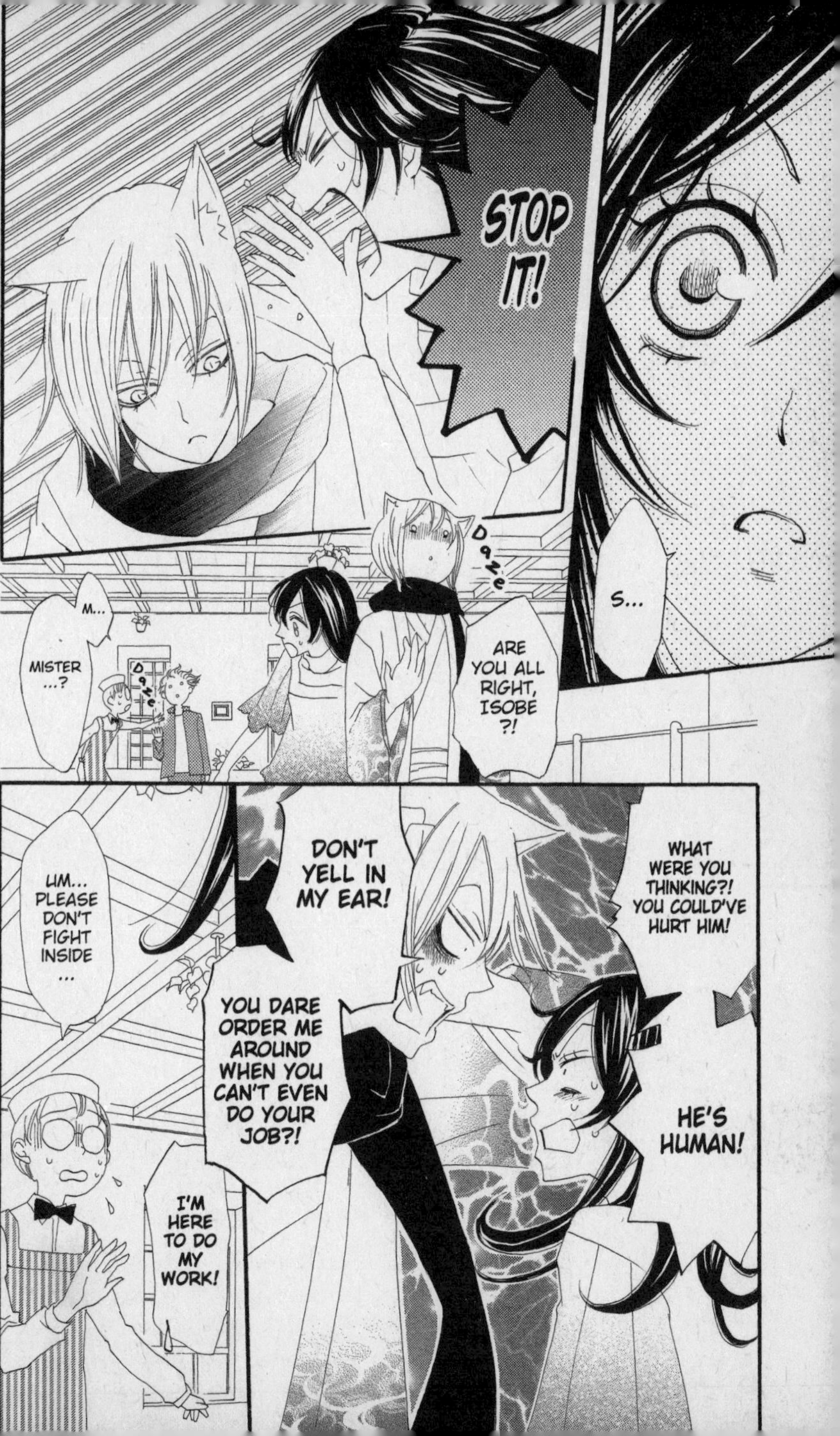

S...
STOP IT!
ARE YOU ALL RIGHT, ISOBE?!
Daze
M...
MISTER ...?
Daze
WHAT WERE YOU THINKING?! YOU COULD'VE HURT HIM!
HE'S HUMAN!
DON'T YELL IN MY EAR!
YOU DARE ORDER ME AROUND WHEN YOU CAN'T EVEN DO YOUR JOB?!
I'M HERE TO DO MY WORK!
UM... PLEASE DON'T FIGHT INSIDE ...

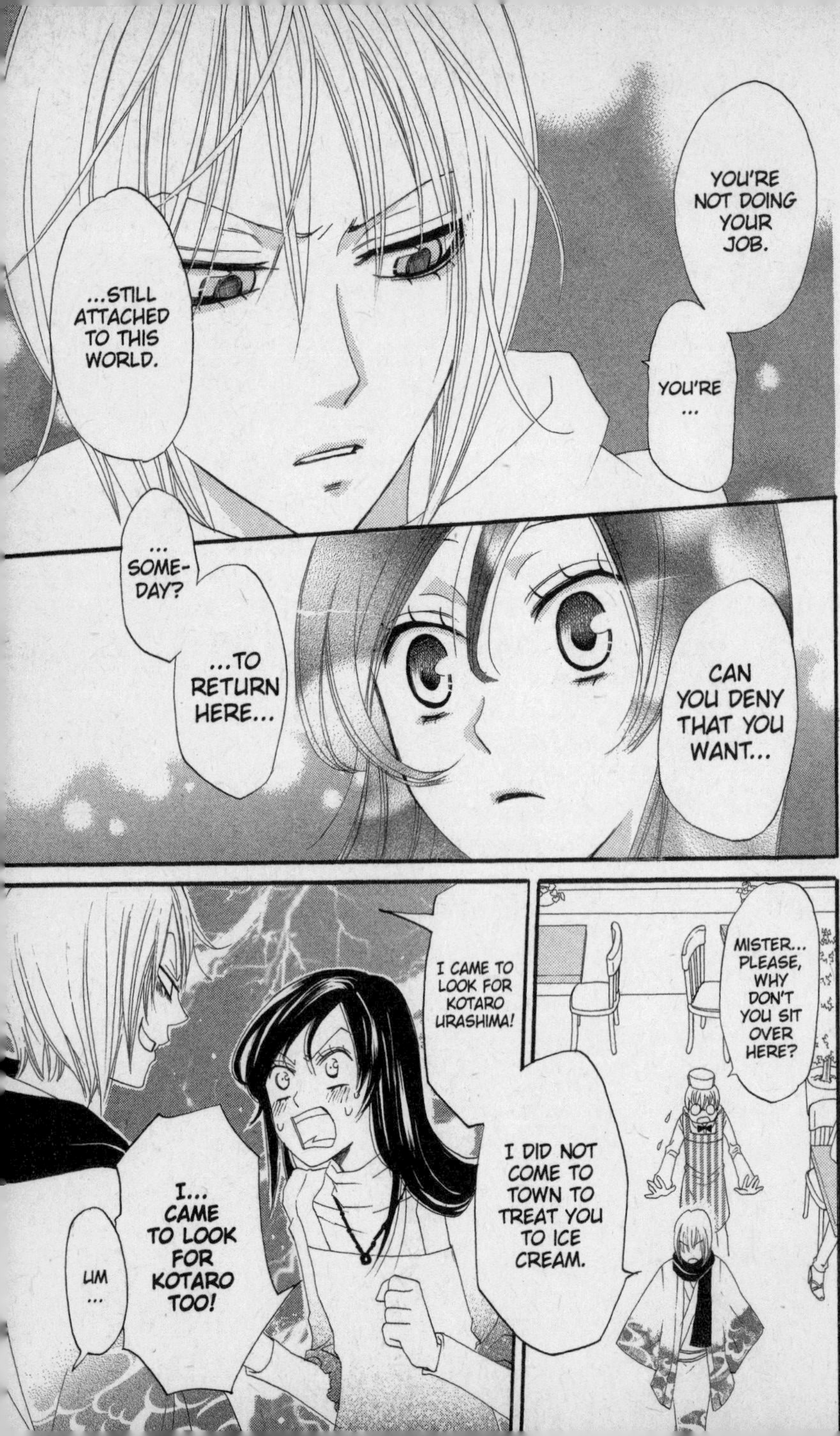
YOU'RE NOT DOING YOUR JOB.
YOU'RE ...
...STILL ATTACHED TO THIS WORLD.
CAN YOU DENY THAT YOU WANT...
...TO RETURN HERE...
... SOME-DAY?
MISTER... PLEASE, WHY DON'T YOU SIT OVER HERE?
I CAME TO LOOK FOR KOTARO URASHIMA!
I DID NOT COME TO TOWN TO TREAT YOU TO ICE CREAM.
I... CAME TO LOOK FOR KOTARO TOO!
UM ...

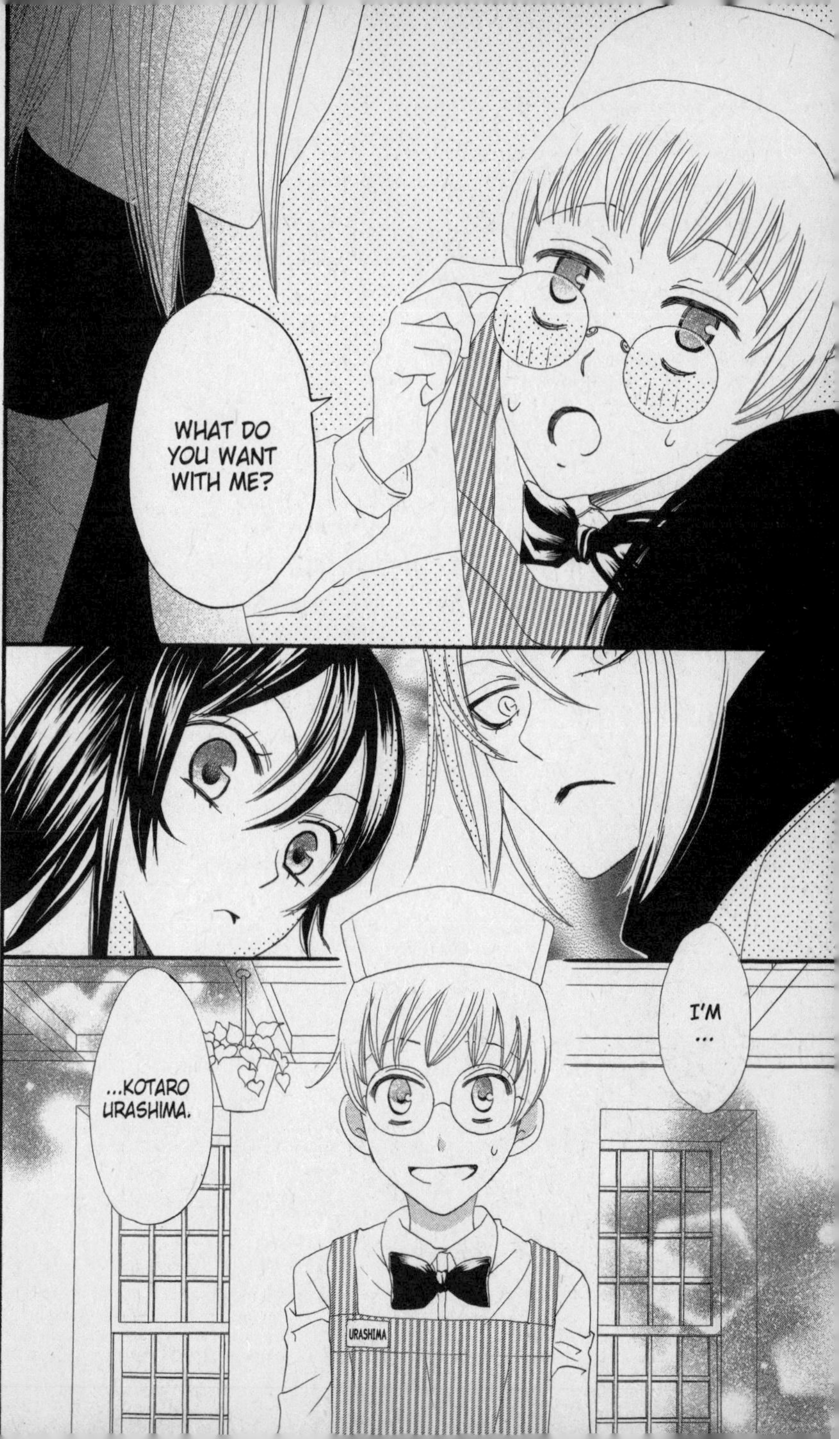
WHAT DO YOU WANT WITH ME?
I'M ...
...KOTARO URASHIMA.
URASHIMA

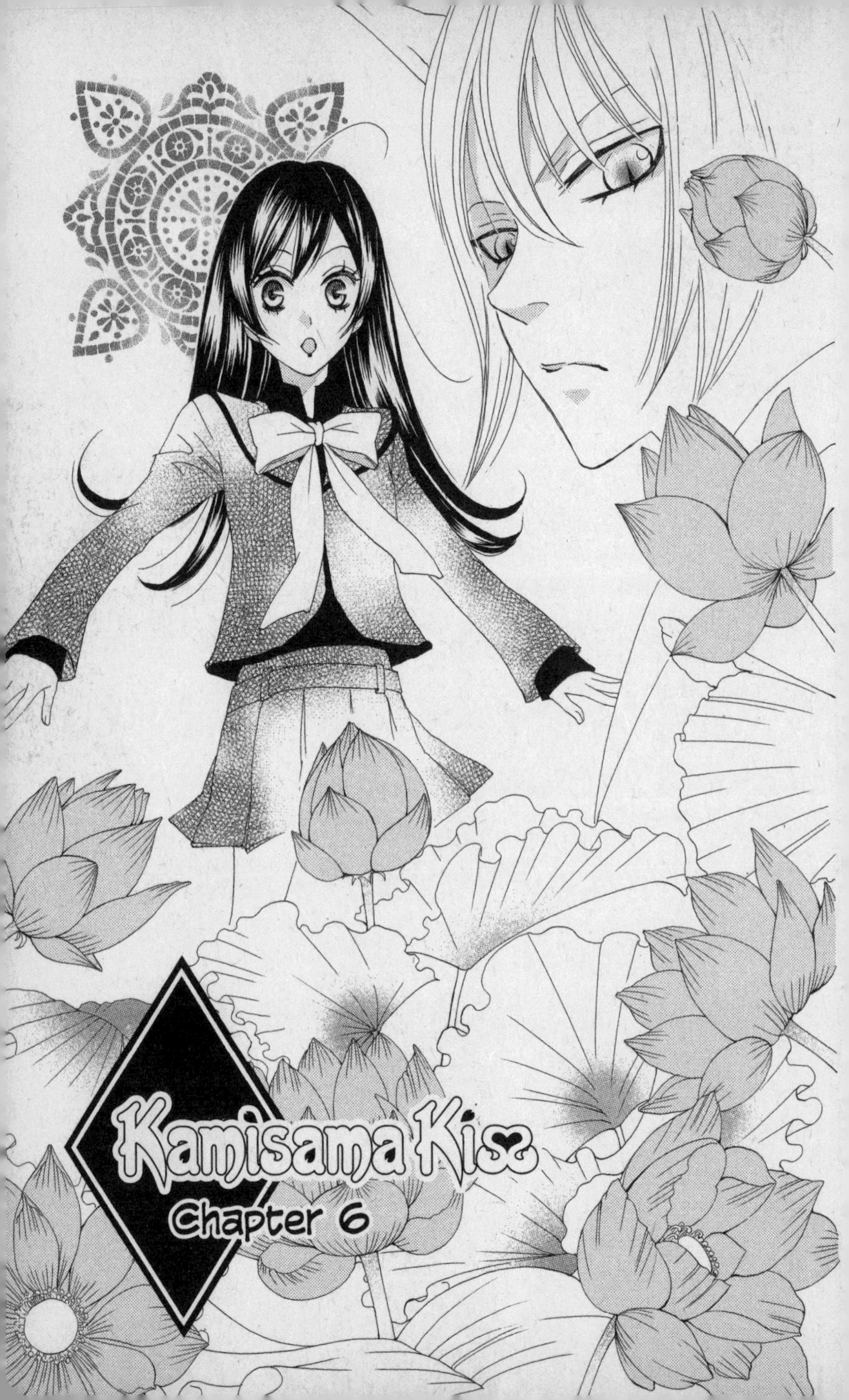
Kamisama Kiss
Chapter 6

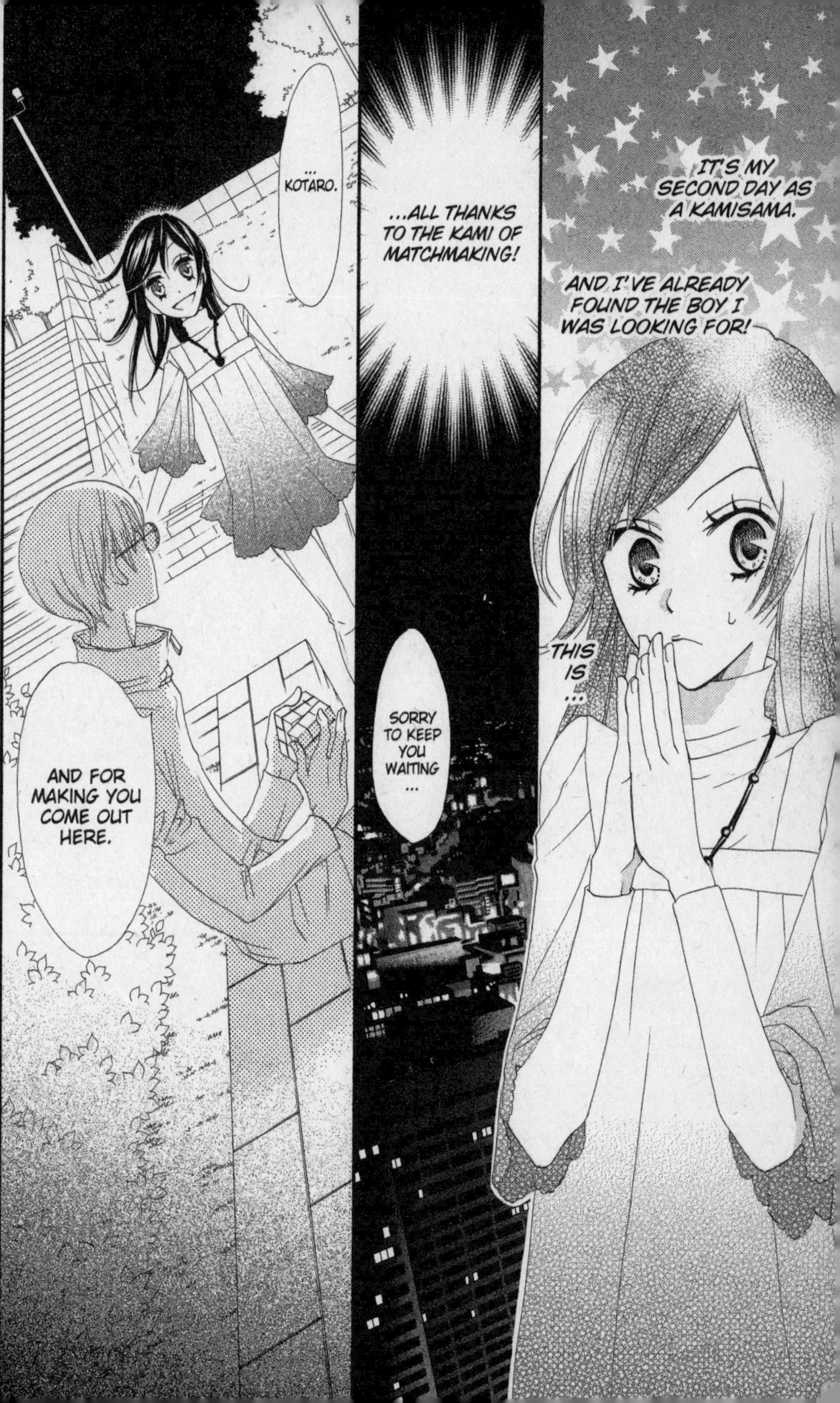
IT'S MY SECOND DAY AS A KAMISAMA.
AND I'VE ALREADY FOUND THE BOY I WAS LOOKING FOR!
THIS IS ...
...ALL THANKS TO THE KAMI OF MATCHMAKING!
SORRY TO KEEP YOU WAITING ...
... KOTARO.
AND FOR MAKING YOU COME OUT HERE.

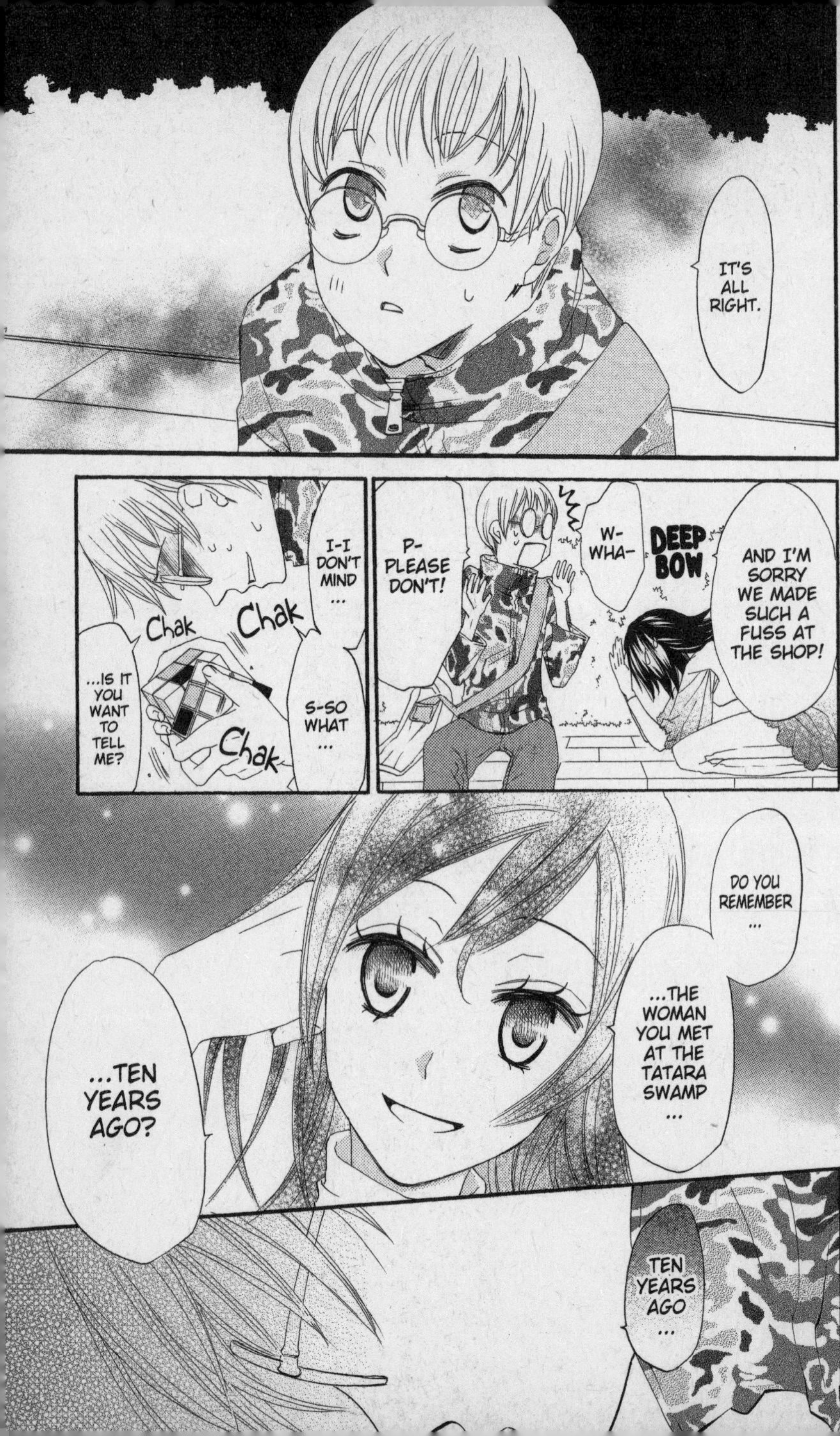
IT'S ALL RIGHT.
AND I'M SORRY WE MADE SUCH A FUSS AT THE SHOP!
DEEP BOW
W-WHA-
P-PLEASE DON'T!
I-I DON'T MIND ...
S-SO WHAT ...
Chak
Chak
Chak
...IS IT YOU WANT TO TELL ME?
DO YOU REMEMBER ...
...THE WOMAN YOU MET AT THE TATARA SWAMP ...
...TEN YEARS AGO?
TEN YEARS AGO ...

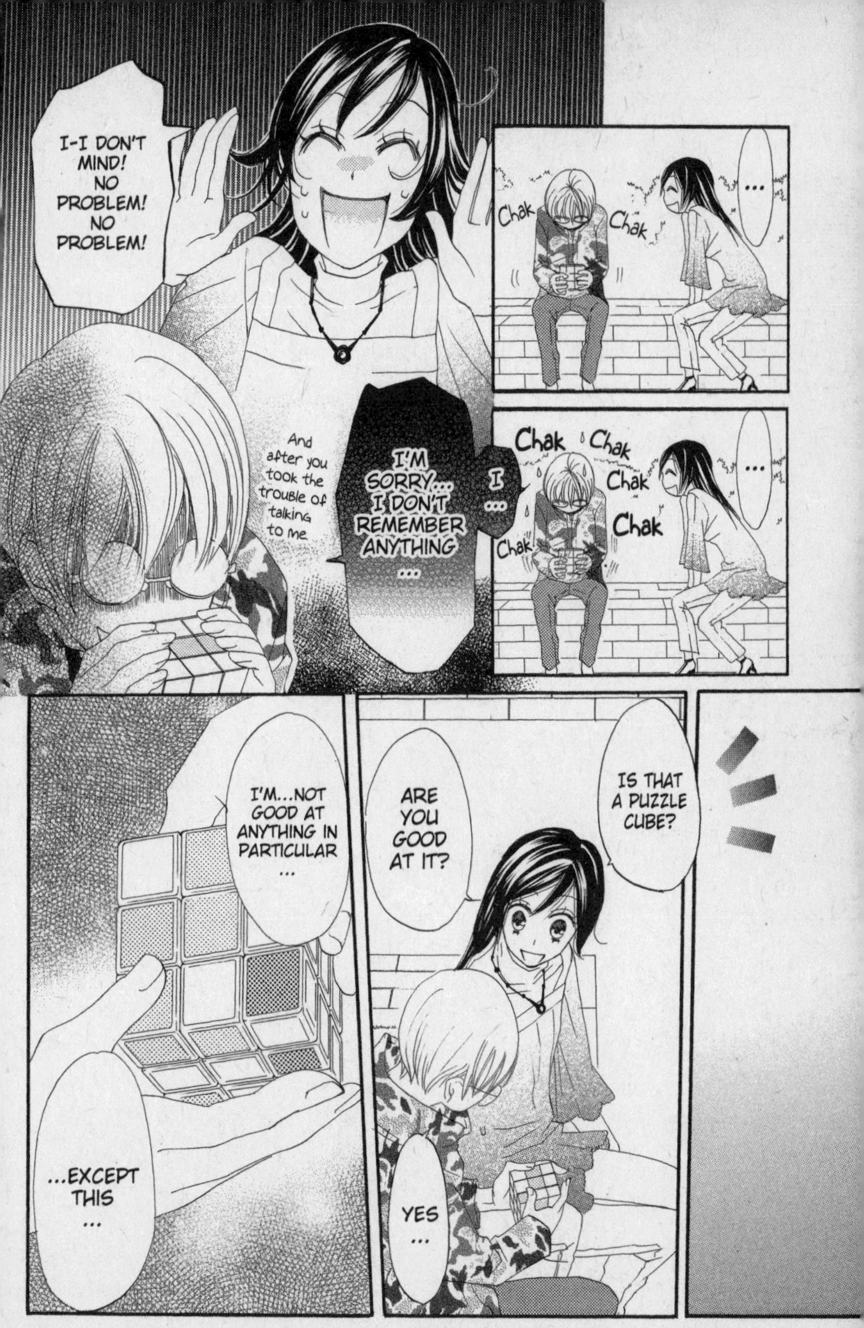
...
Chak
Chak
...
Chak
Chak
Chak
Chak
Chak
I ...
I'M SORRY... I DON'T REMEMBER ANYTHING ...
And after you took the trouble of talking to me
I-I DON'T MIND! NO PROBLEM! NO PROBLEM!
IS THAT A PUZZLE CUBE?
ARE YOU GOOD AT IT?
YES ...
I'M...NOT GOOD AT ANYTHING IN PARTICULAR ...
...EXCEPT THIS ...

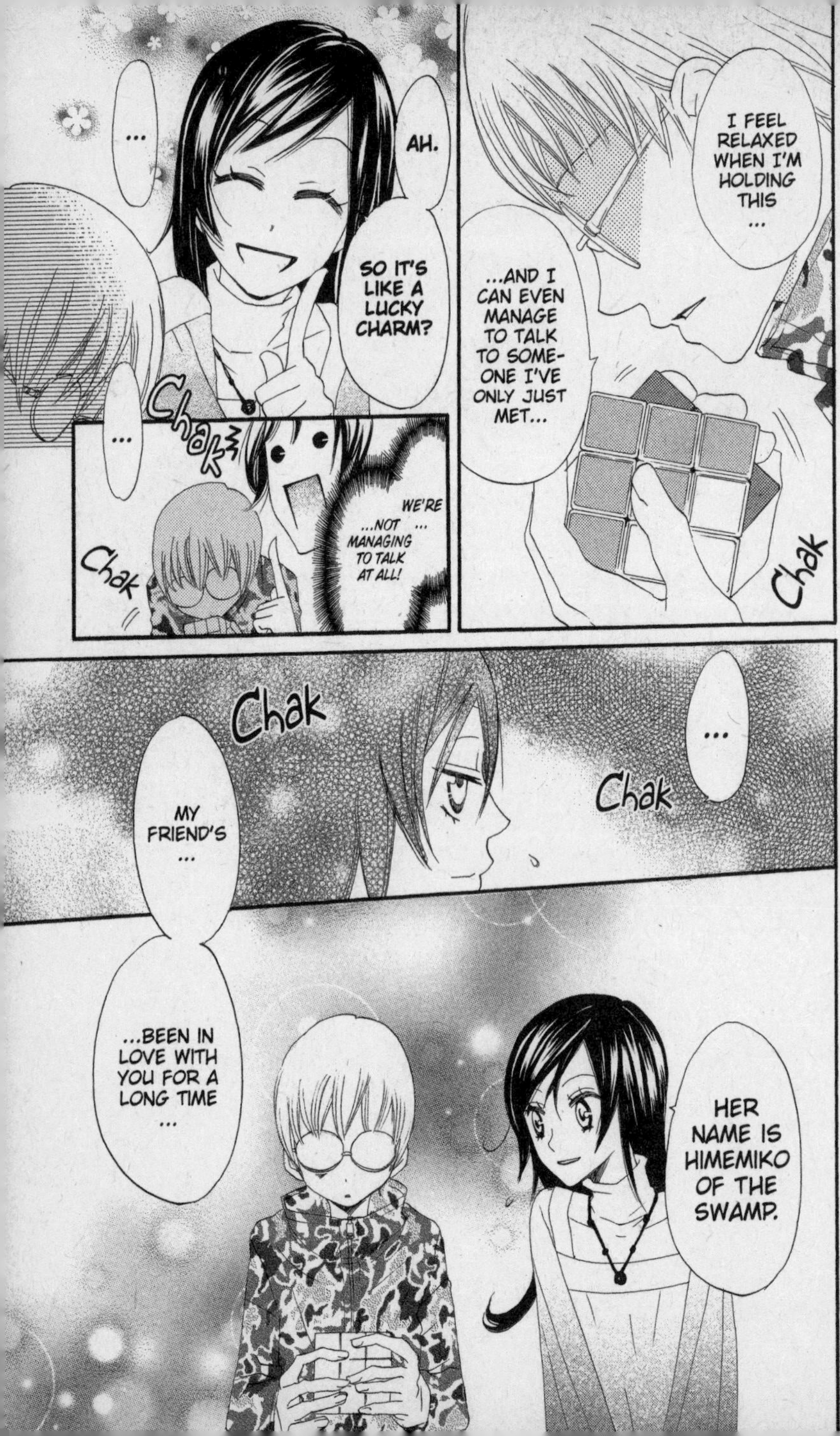
I FEEL RELAXED WHEN I'M HOLDING THIS ...
...AND I CAN EVEN MANAGE TO TALK TO SOME-ONE I'VE ONLY JUST MET...
Chak
AH.
SO IT'S LIKE A LUCKY CHARM?
...
...
Chak
WE'RE ... ...NOT MANAGING TO TALK AT ALL!
Chak
...
Chak
Chak
MY FRIEND'S ...
...BEEN IN LOVE WITH YOU FOR A LONG TIME ...
HER NAME IS HIMEMIKO OF THE SWAMP.

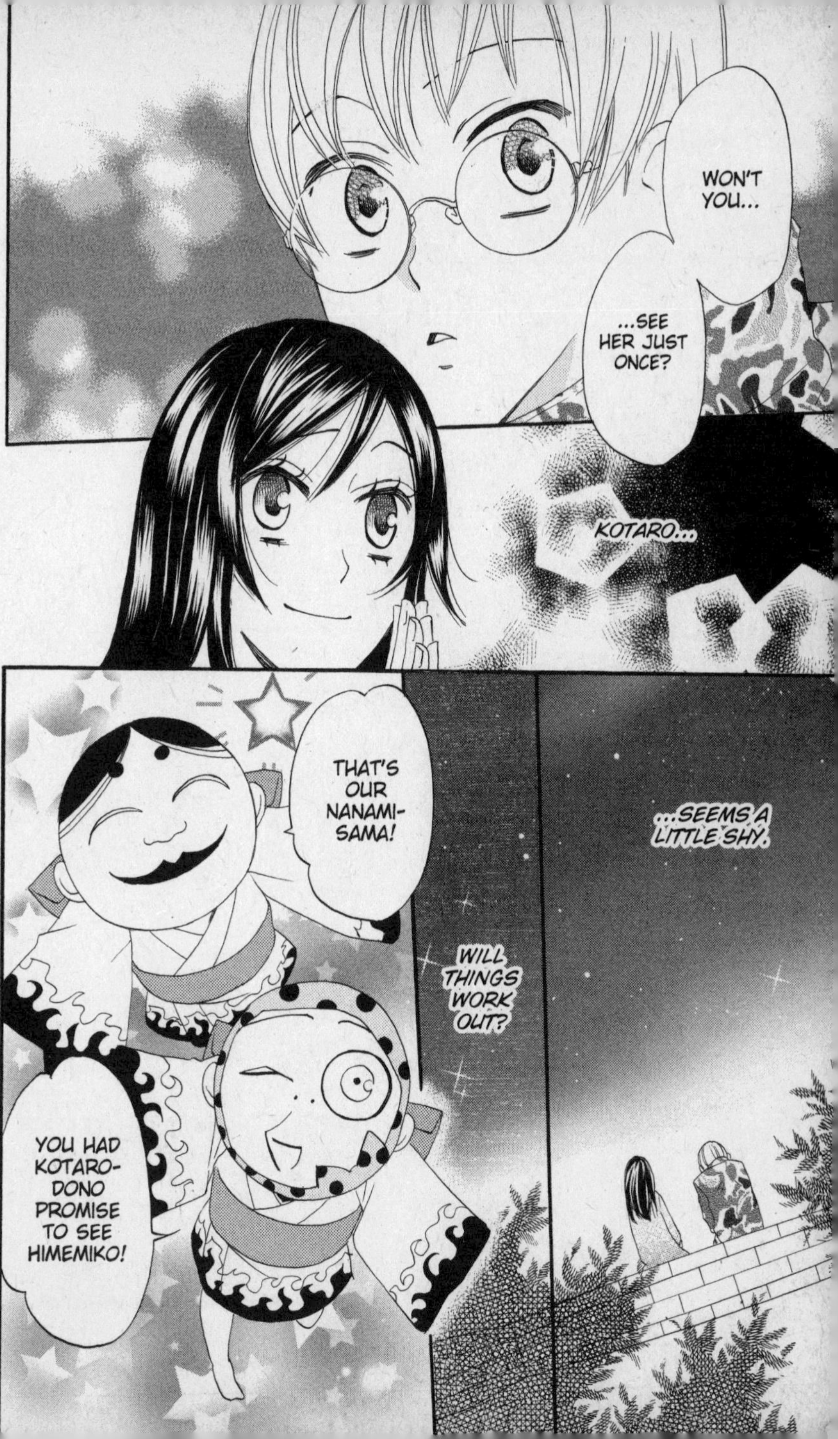
WON'T YOU...
...SEE HER JUST ONCE?
KOTARO...
...SEEMS A LITTLE SHY.
WILL THINGS WORK OUT?
THAT'S OUR NANAMI-SAMA!
YOU HAD KOTARO-DONO PROMISE TO SEE HIMEMIKO!

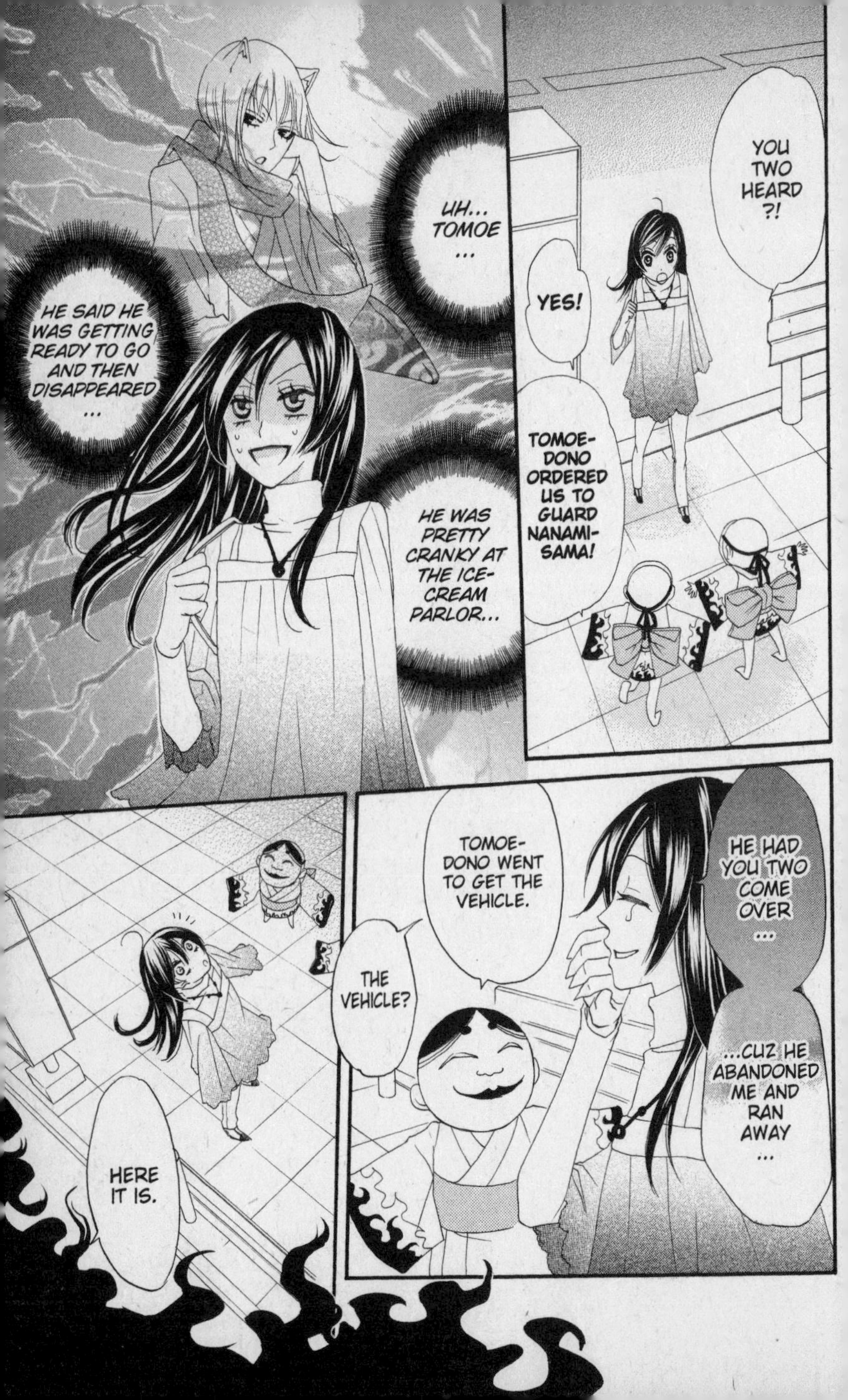
YOU TWO HEARD ?!
YES!
TOMOE-DONO ORDERED US TO GUARD NANAMI-SAMA!
UH... TOMOE ...
HE SAID HE WAS GETTING READY TO GO AND THEN DISAPPEARED ...
HE WAS PRETTY CRANKY AT THE ICE-CREAM PARLOR...
HE HAD YOU TWO COME OVER ...
...CUZ HE ABANDONED ME AND RAN AWAY ...
TOMOE-DONO WENT TO GET THE VEHICLE.
THE VEHICLE?
HERE IT IS.

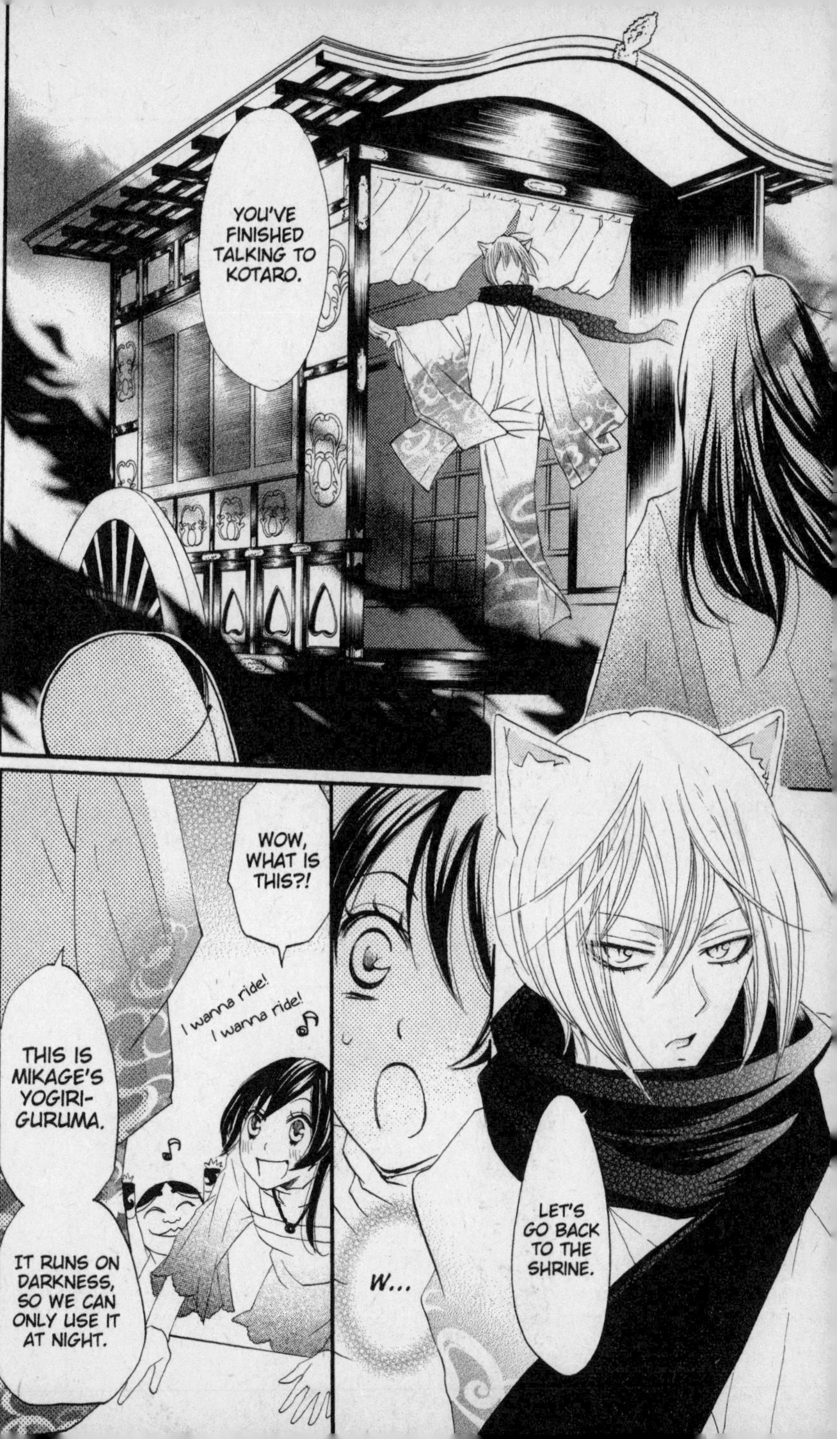
YOU'VE FINISHED TALKING TO KOTARO.
LET'S GO BACK TO THE SHRINE.
W...
WOW, WHAT IS THIS?!
I wanna ride! I wanna ride!
THIS IS MIKAGE'S YOGIRI-GURUMA.
IT RUNS ON DARKNESS, SO WE CAN ONLY USE IT AT NIGHT.

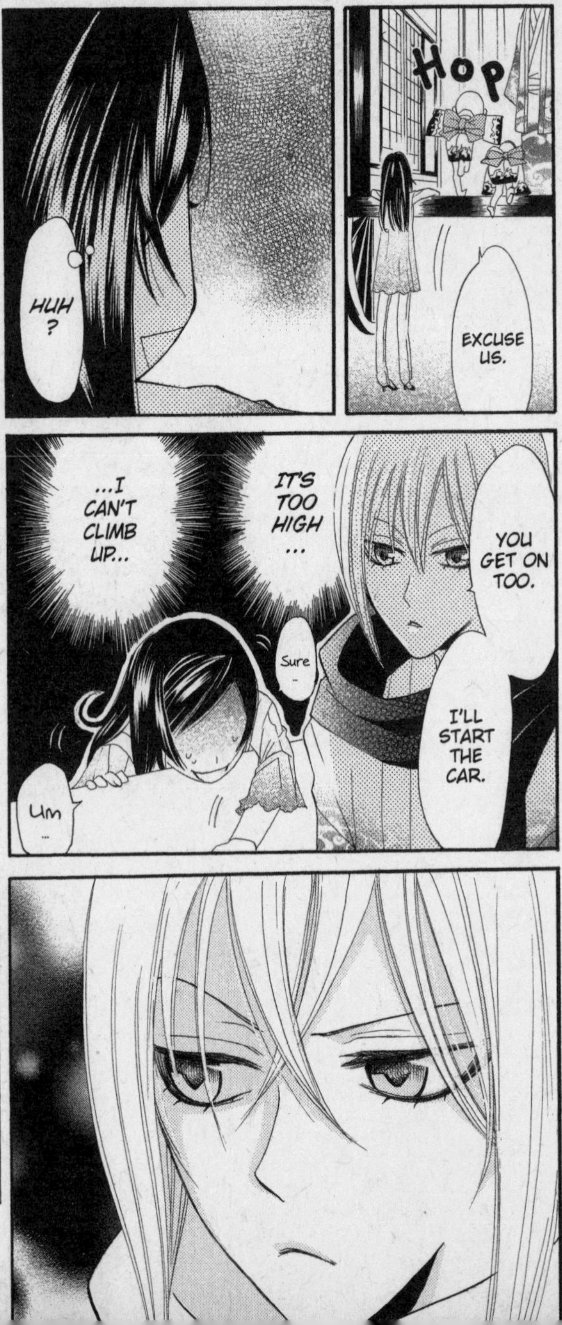
HOP
EXCUSE US.
HUH?
YOU GET ON TOO.
I'LL START THE CAR.
IT'S TOO HIGH...
...I CAN'T CLIMB UP...
Sure...
Um...

Thank you for reading this far! This is the last sidebar.

If you have any comments, I'd be happy if you send letters to the following address:

Julietta Suzuki
c/o Shojo Beat
VIZ Media, LLC
P.O. Box 77010
San Francisco, CA 94107

Well then! I pray that we'll be able to meet again in volume 2!

-Julietta Suzuki

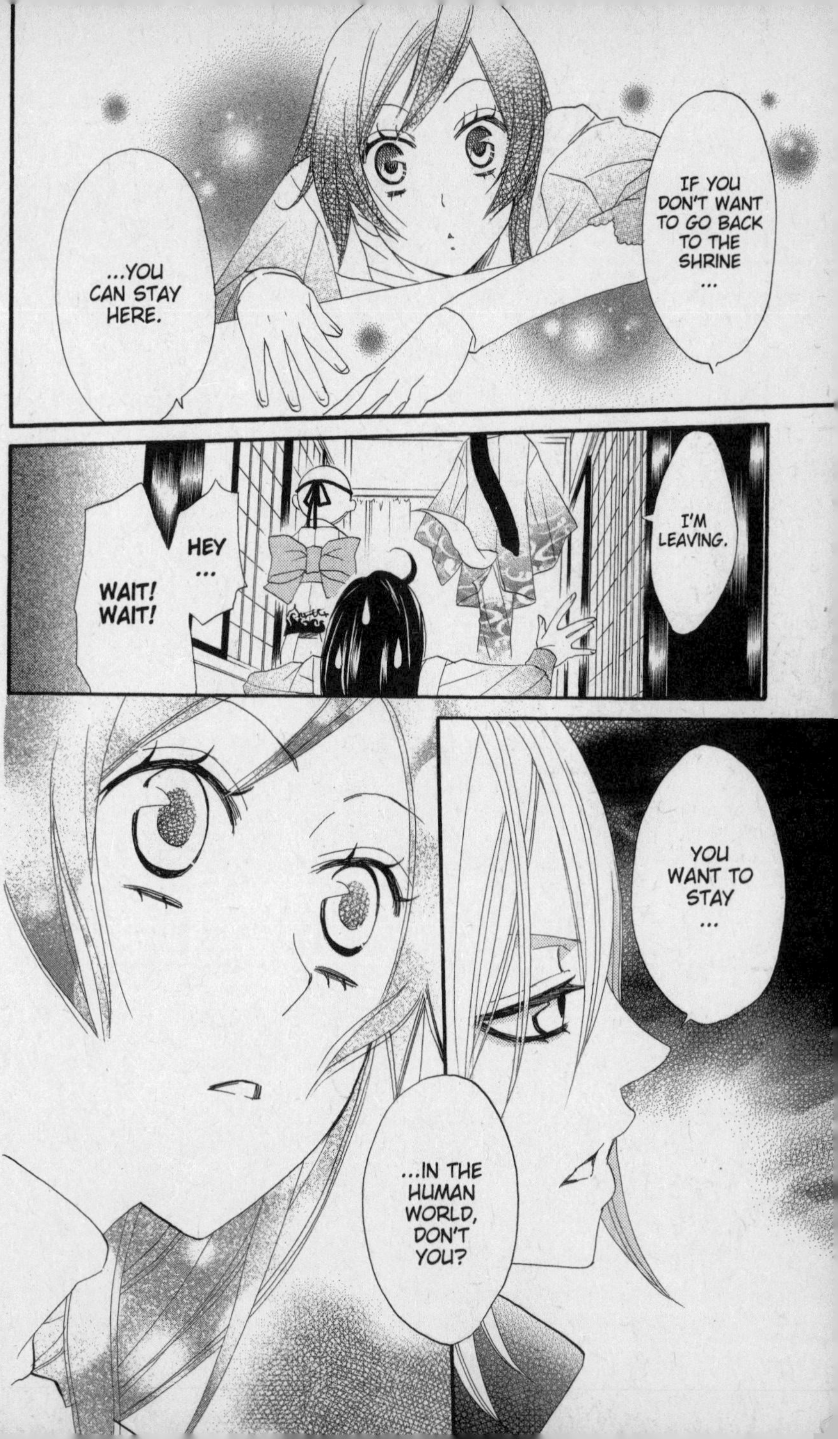
IF YOU DON'T WANT TO GO BACK TO THE SHRINE ...
...YOU CAN STAY HERE.
I'M LEAVING.
HEY ...
WAIT! WAIT!
YOU WANT TO STAY ...
...IN THE HUMAN WORLD, DON'T YOU?

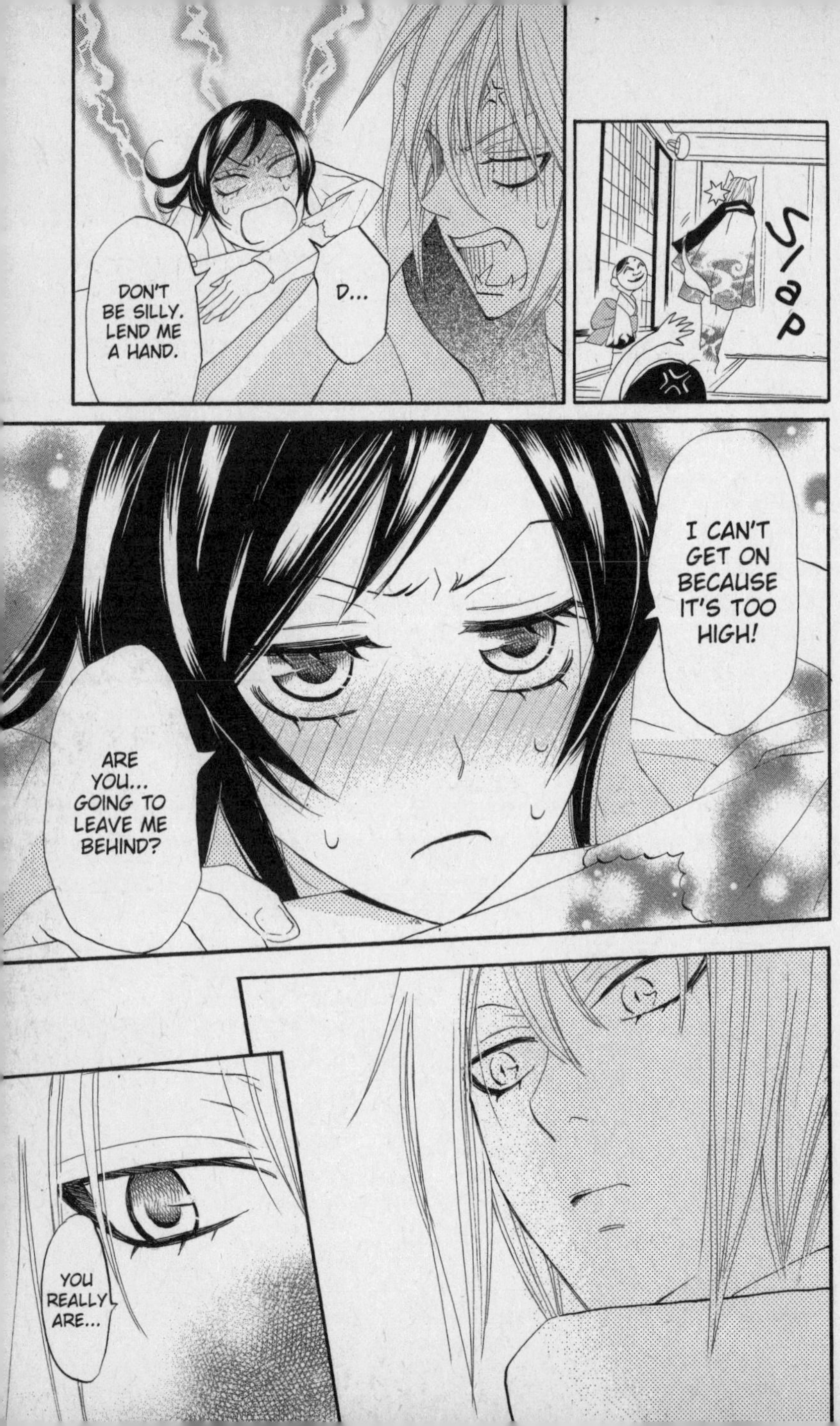
Slap
D...
DON'T BE SILLY. LEND ME A HAND.
I CAN'T GET ON BECAUSE IT'S TOO HIGH!
ARE YOU... GOING TO LEAVE ME BEHIND?
YOU REALLY ARE...

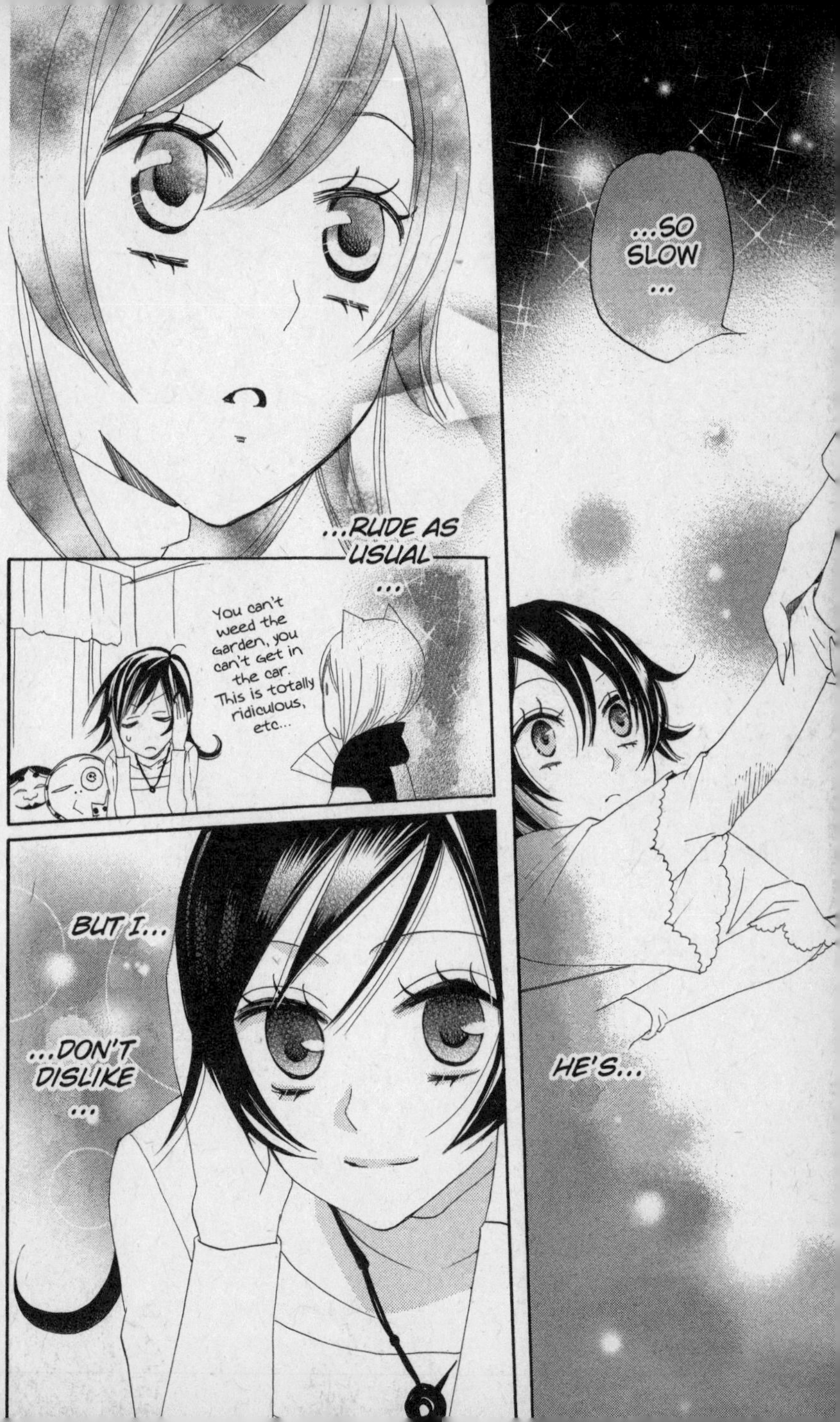
...SO SLOW ...
HE'S...
...RUDE AS USUAL ...
You can't weed the garden, you can't get in the car. This is totally ridiculous, etc...
BUT I...
...DON'T DISLIKE ...

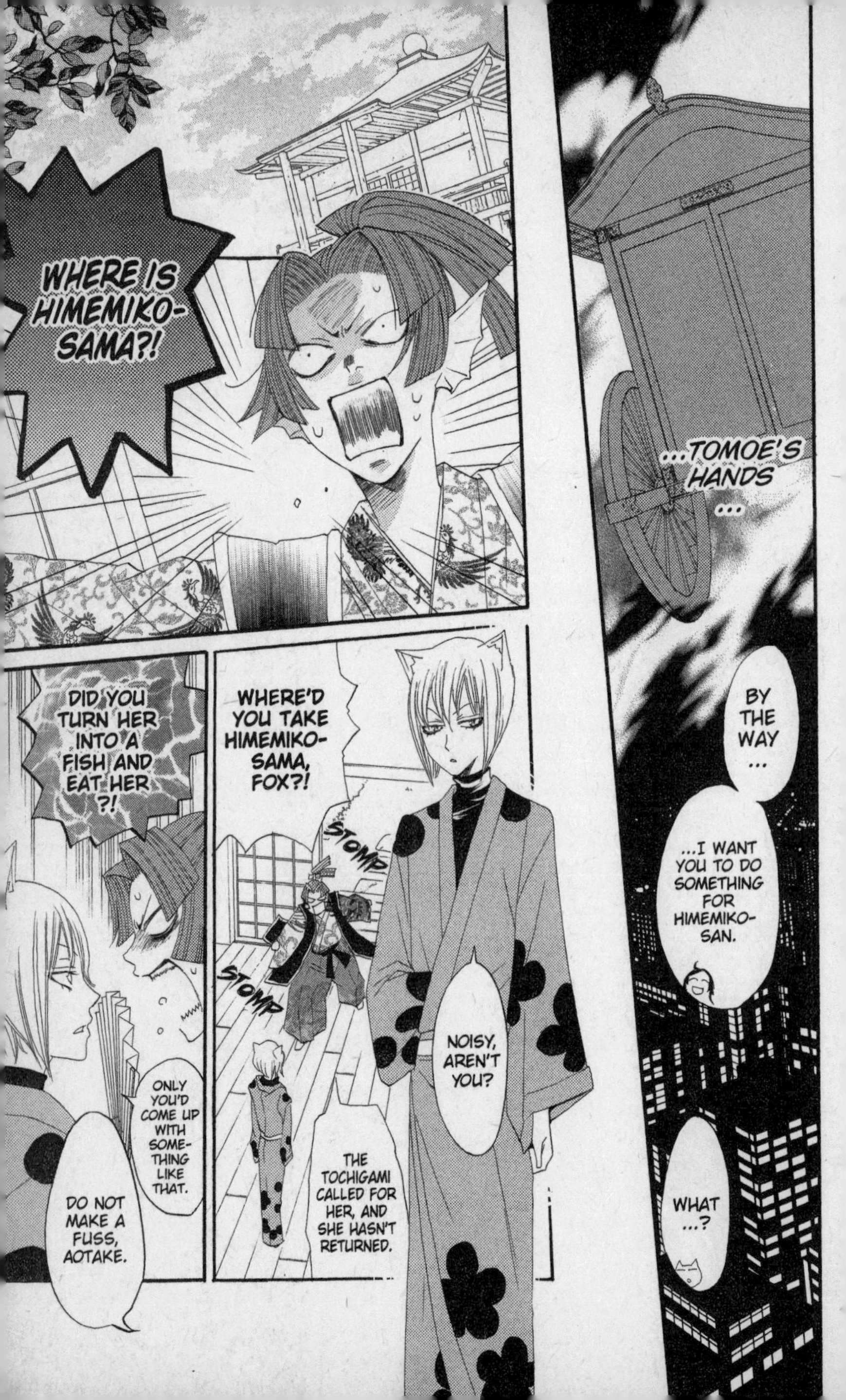
...TOMOE'S HANDS ...
BY THE WAY ...
...I WANT YOU TO DO SOMETHING FOR HIMEMIKO-SAN.
WHAT ...?
WHERE IS HIMEMIKO-SAMA?!
WHERE'D YOU TAKE HIMEMIKO-SAMA, FOX?!
STOMP
STOMP
NOISY, AREN'T YOU?
THE TOCHIGAMI CALLED FOR HER, AND SHE HASN'T RETURNED.
DID YOU TURN HER INTO A FISH AND EAT HER ?!
ONLY YOU'D COME UP WITH SOMETHING LIKE THAT.
DO NOT MAKE A FUSS, AOTAKE.

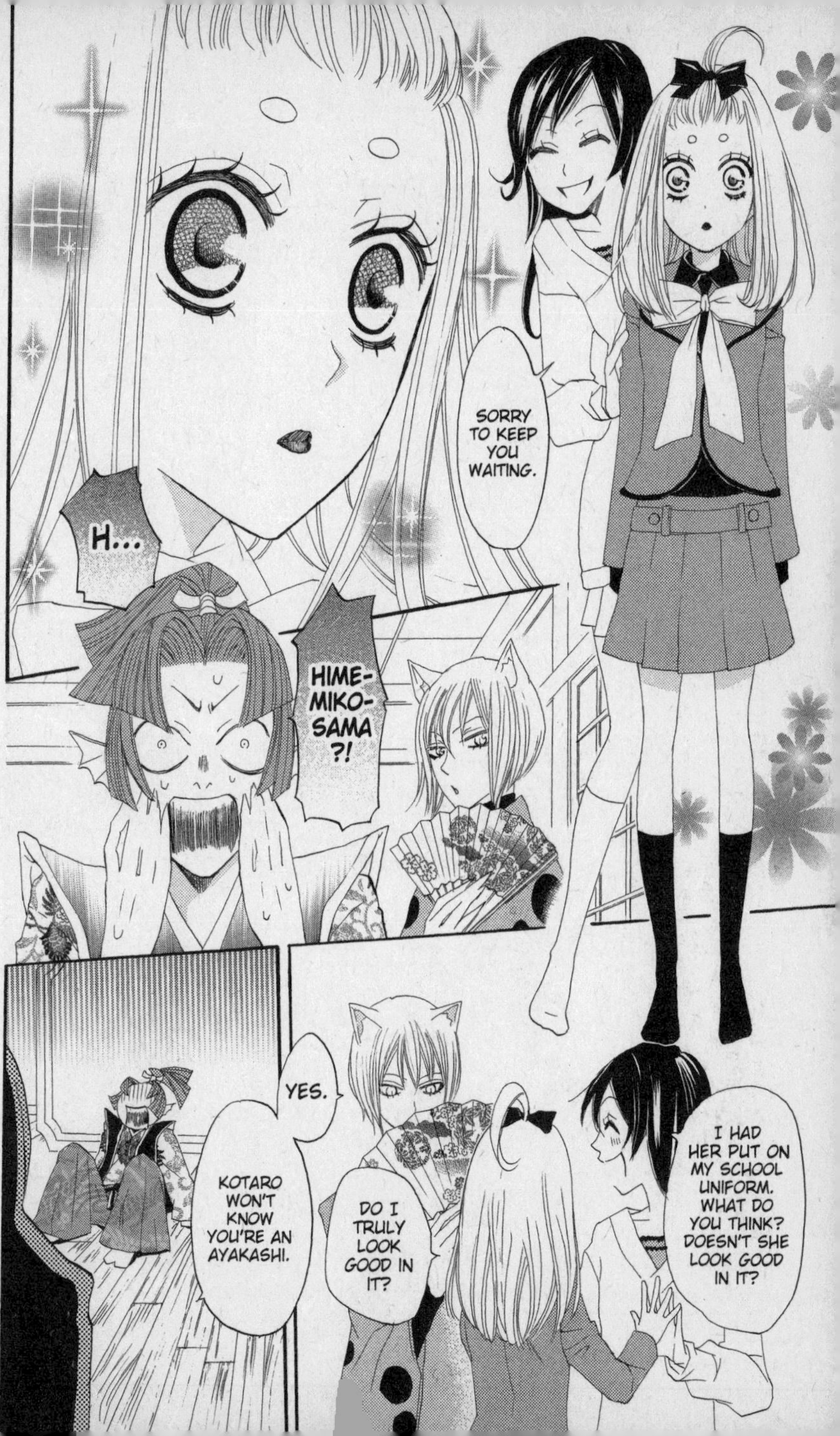
SORRY TO KEEP YOU WAITING.
H...
HIME-MIKO-SAMA?!
I HAD HER PUT ON MY SCHOOL UNIFORM. WHAT DO YOU THINK? DOESN'T SHE LOOK GOOD IN IT?
DO I TRULY LOOK GOOD IN IT?
YES.
KOTARO WON'T KNOW YOU'RE AN AYAKASHI.

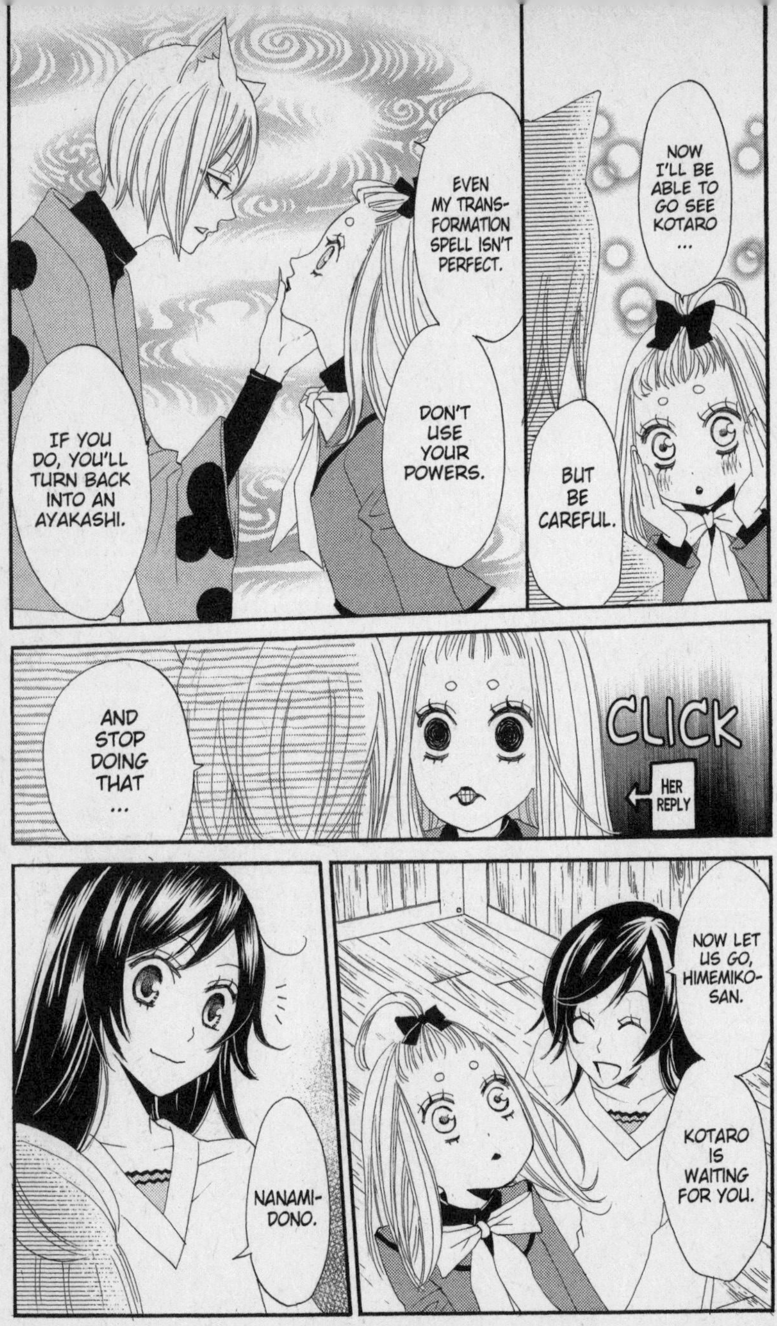
NOW I'LL BE ABLE TO GO SEE KOTARO ...
BUT BE CAREFUL.
EVEN MY TRANS-FORMATION SPELL ISN'T PERFECT.
DON'T USE YOUR POWERS.
IF YOU DO, YOU'LL TURN BACK INTO AN AYAKASHI.
CLICK
HER REPLY
AND STOP DOING THAT ...
NOW LET US GO, HIMEMIKO-SAN.
KOTARO IS WAITING FOR YOU.
NANAMI-DONO.

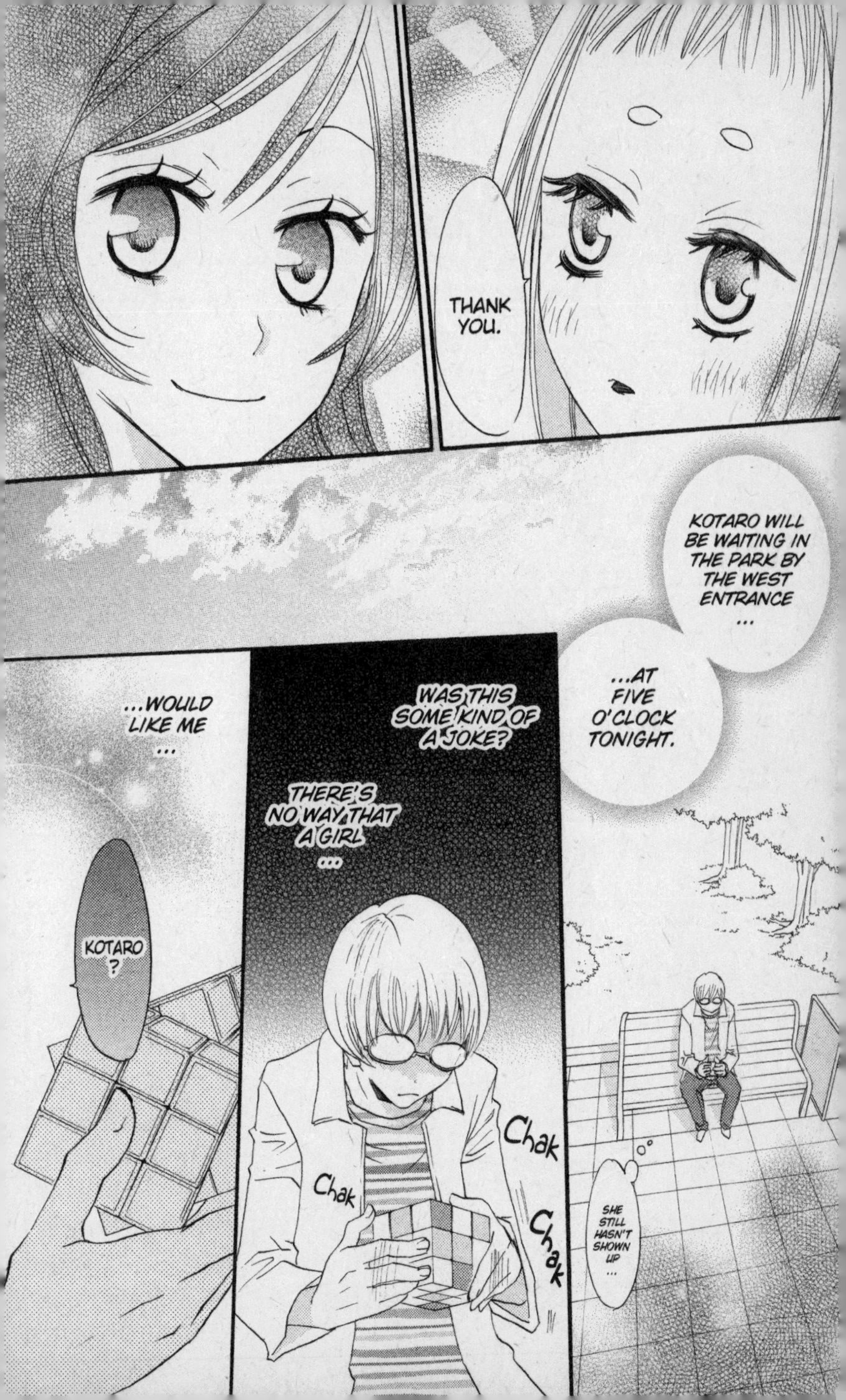
THANK YOU.
KOTARO WILL BE WAITING IN THE PARK BY THE WEST ENTRANCE ...
...AT FIVE O'CLOCK TONIGHT.
SHE STILL HASN'T SHOWN UP ...
WAS THIS SOME KIND OF A JOKE?
THERE'S NO WAY THAT A GIRL ...
Chak
Chak
Chak
...WOULD LIKE ME ...
KOTARO ?

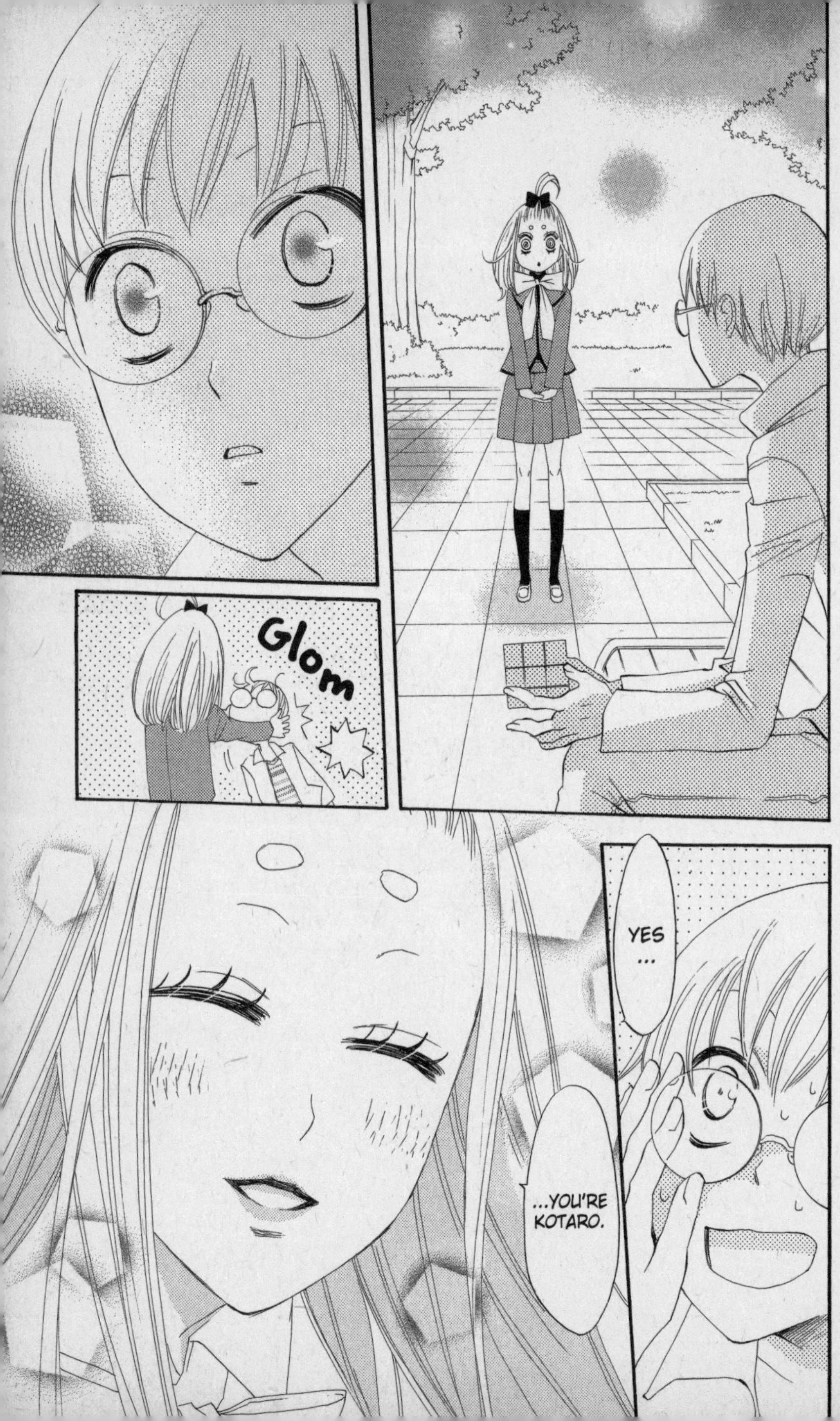
Glom
YES ...
...YOU'RE KOTARO.

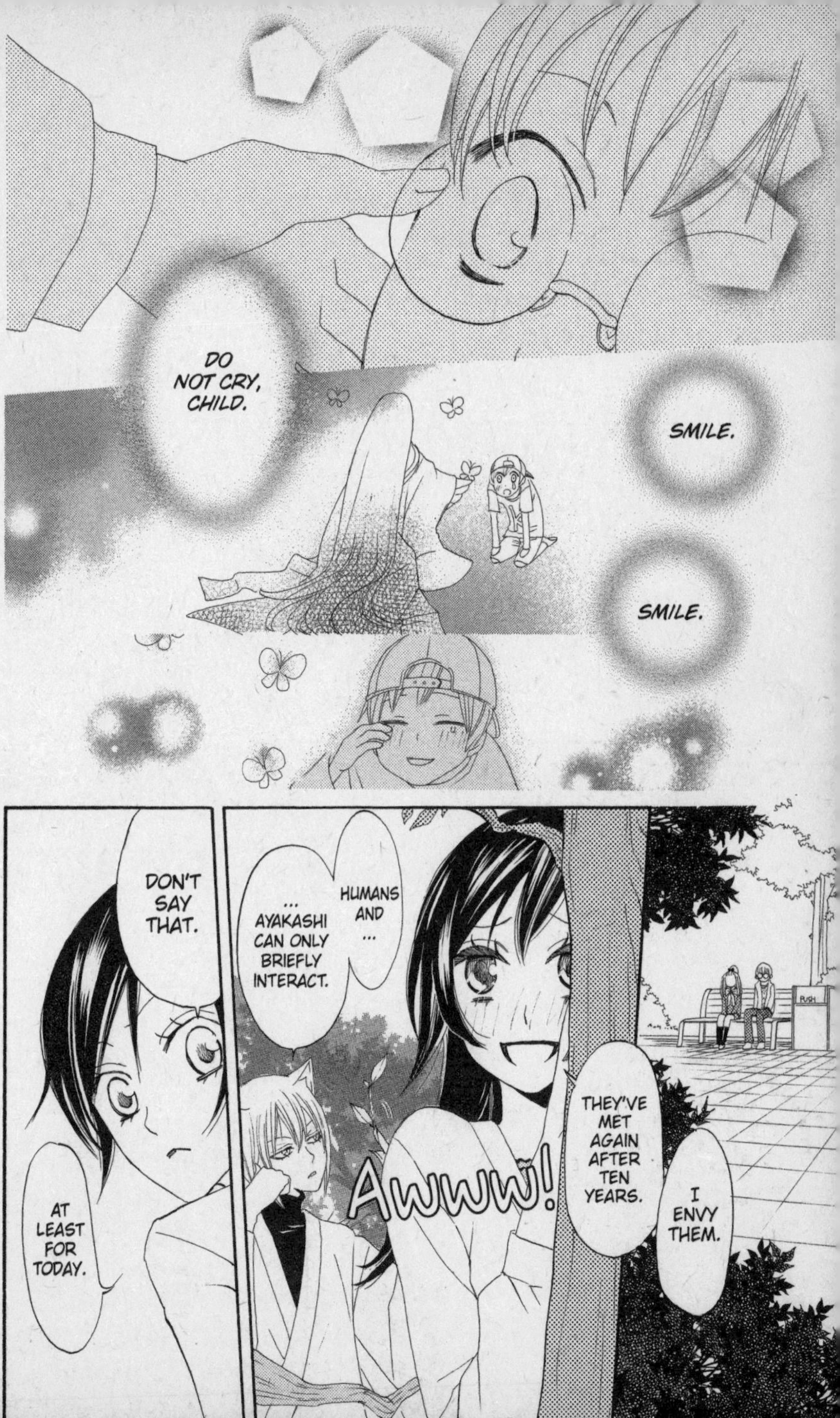
DO NOT CRY, CHILD.
SMILE.
SMILE.
THEY'VE MET AGAIN AFTER TEN YEARS.
I ENVY THEM.
Awww!
HUMANS AND ...
... AYAKASHI CAN ONLY BRIEFLY INTERACT.
DON'T SAY THAT.
AT LEAST FOR TODAY.

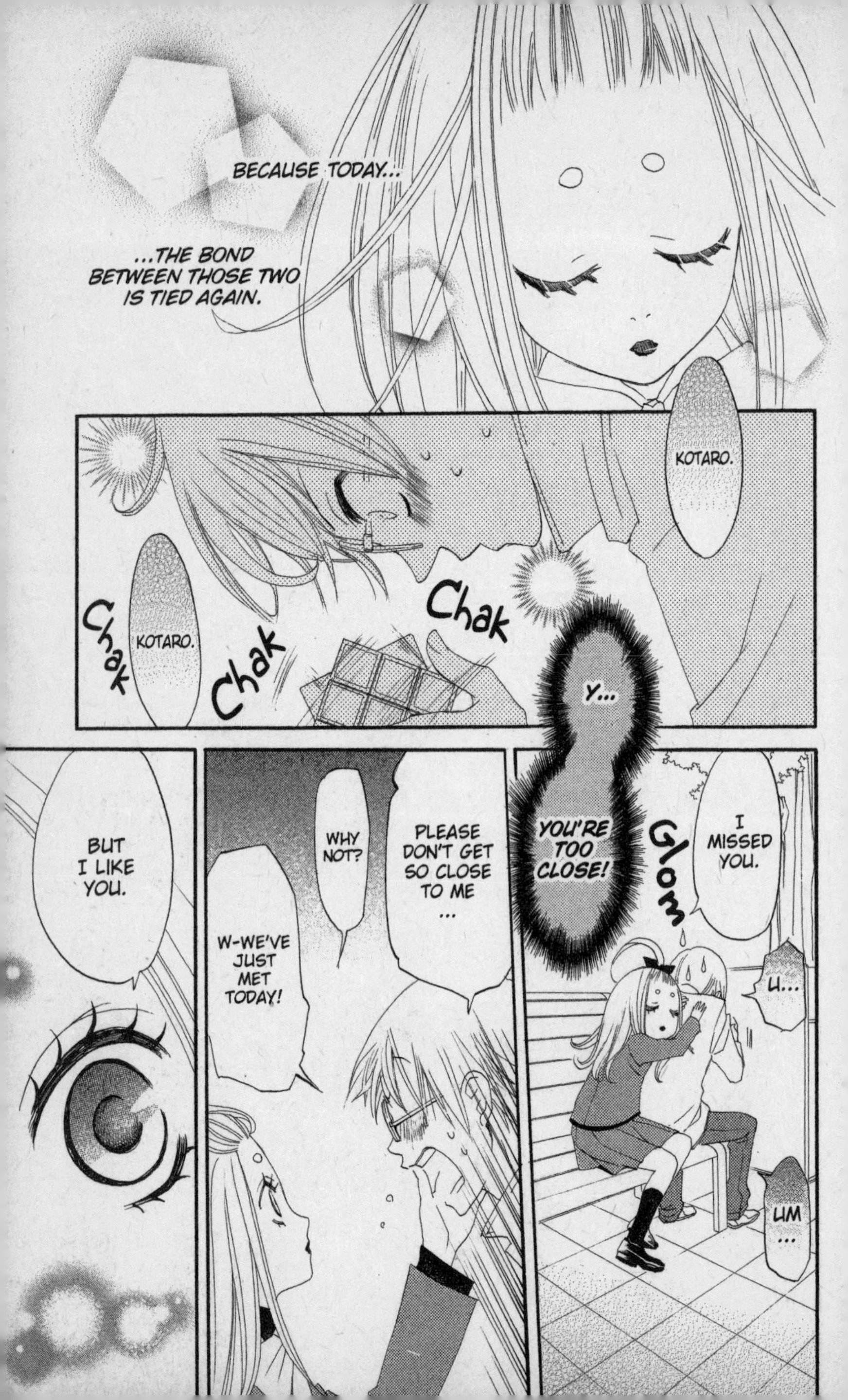
BECAUSE TODAY...
...THE BOND BETWEEN THOSE TWO IS TIED AGAIN.
KOTARO.
Chak
KOTARO.
Chak
Chak
Y...
I MISSED YOU.
Glom
YOU'RE TOO CLOSE!
U...
UM ...
PLEASE DON'T GET SO CLOSE TO ME ...
WHY NOT?
W-WE'VE JUST MET TODAY!
BUT I LIKE YOU.

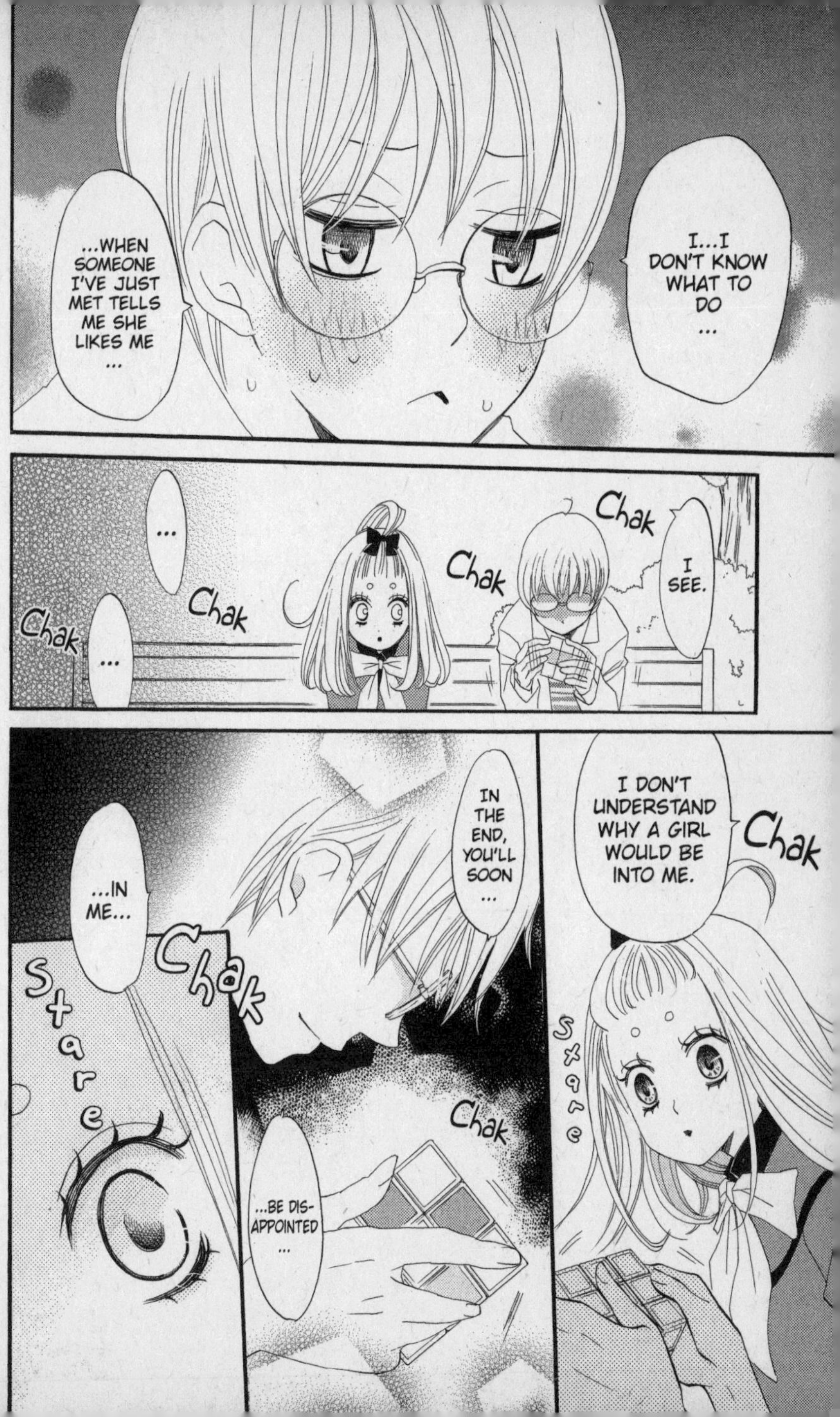
I...I DON'T KNOW WHAT TO DO ...
...WHEN SOMEONE I'VE JUST MET TELLS ME SHE LIKES ME ...
Chak
I SEE.
Chak
...
Chak
Chak
...
I DON'T UNDERSTAND WHY A GIRL WOULD BE INTO ME.
Chak
Stare
IN THE END, YOU'LL SOON ...
...IN ME...
Chak
Chak
...BE DIS-APPOINTED ...
Stare

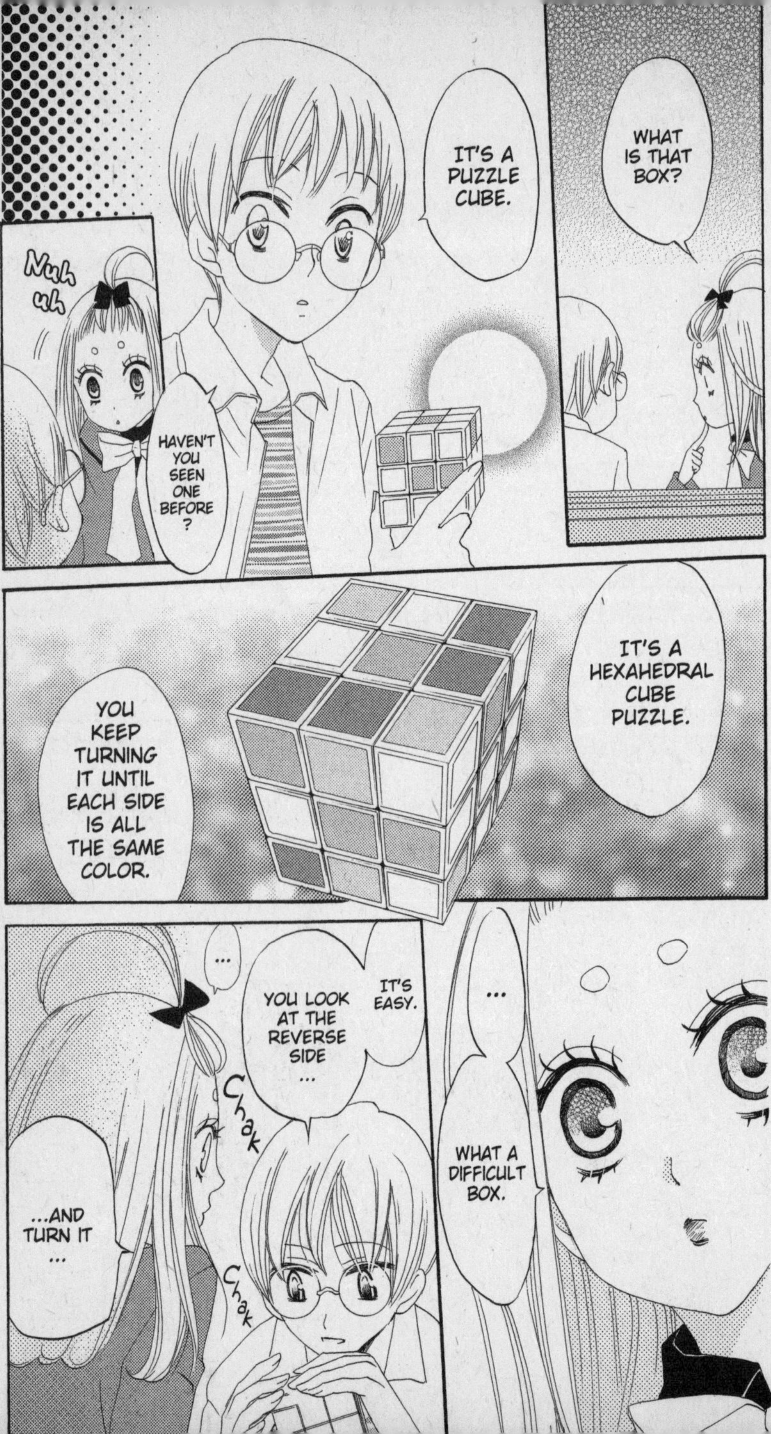
WHAT IS THAT BOX?
IT'S A PUZZLE CUBE.
HAVEN'T YOU SEEN ONE BEFORE?
Nuh uh
IT'S A HEXAHEDRAL CUBE PUZZLE.
YOU KEEP TURNING IT UNTIL EACH SIDE IS ALL THE SAME COLOR.
...
WHAT A DIFFICULT BOX.
IT'S EASY.
YOU LOOK AT THE REVERSE SIDE ...
...
Chak
...AND TURN IT ...
Chak

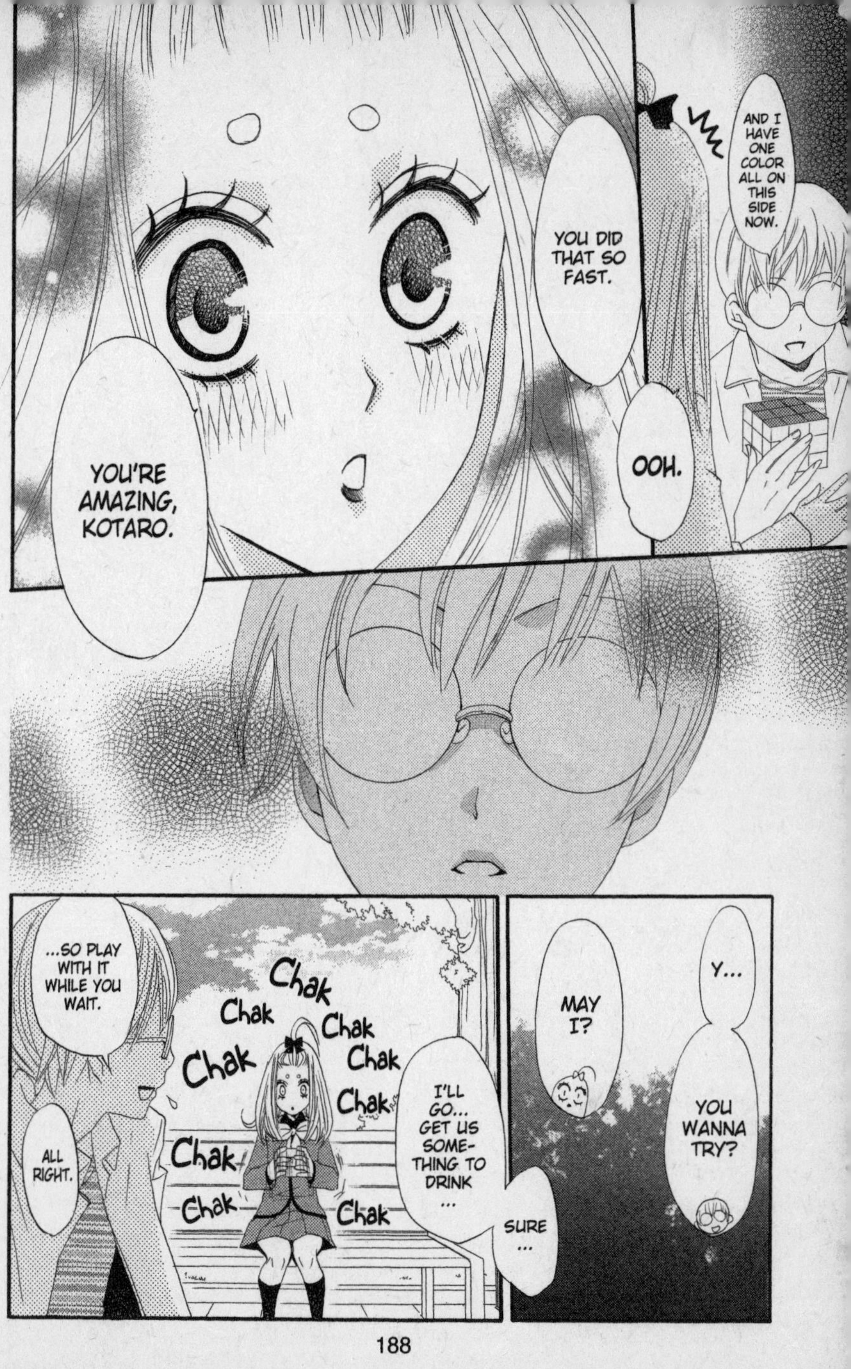
AND I HAVE ONE COLOR ALL ON THIS SIDE NOW.
OOH.
YOU DID THAT SO FAST.
YOU'RE AMAZING, KOTARO.
Y...
YOU WANNA TRY?
MAY I?
I'LL GO... GET US SOME-THING TO DRINK ...
SURE ...
Chak
Chak
Chak
Chak
Chak
Chak
Chak
Chak
Chak
...SO PLAY WITH IT WHILE YOU WAIT.
ALL RIGHT.

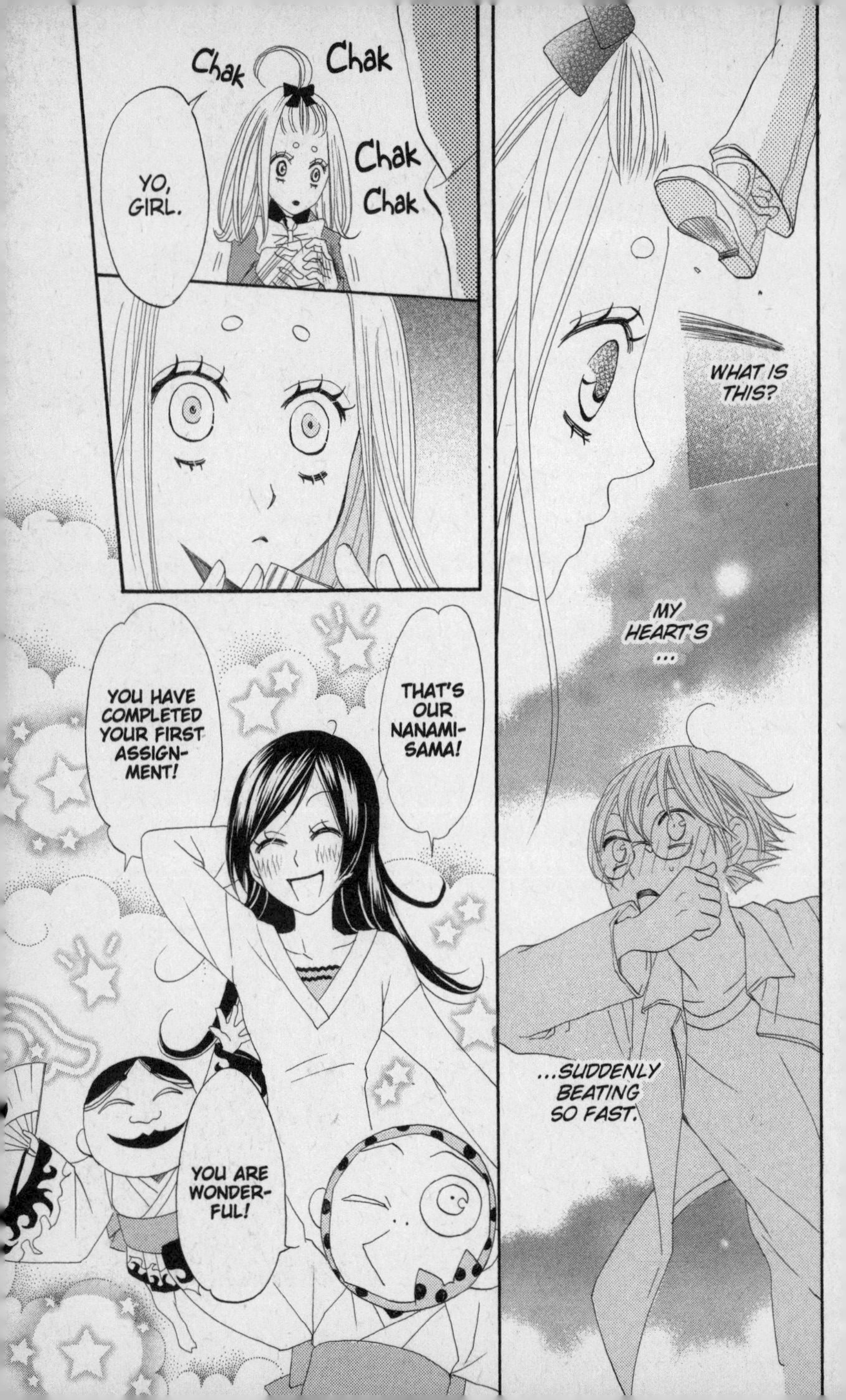
WHAT IS THIS?
MY HEART'S ...
...SUDDENLY BEATING SO FAST.
Chak
Chak
Chak
Chak
YO, GIRL.
THAT'S OUR NANAMI-SAMA!
YOU HAVE COMPLETED YOUR FIRST ASSIGNMENT!
YOU ARE WONDERFUL!

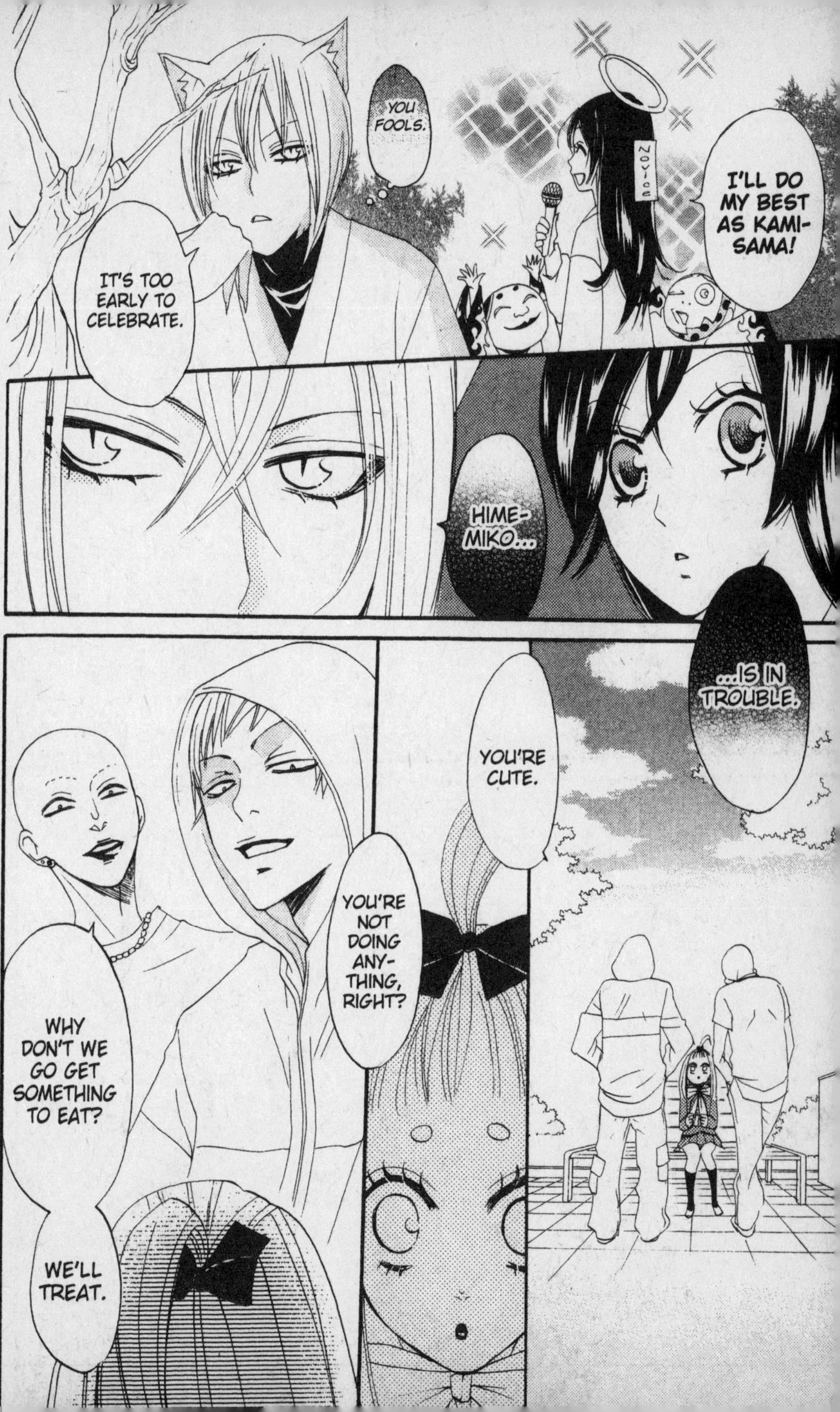

I'LL DO MY BEST AS KAMI-SAMA!
NOVICE
YOU FOOLS.
IT'S TOO EARLY TO CELEBRATE.
HIME-MIKO...
...IS IN TROUBLE.
YOU'RE CUTE.
YOU'RE NOT DOING ANYTHING, RIGHT?
WHY DON'T WE GO GET SOMETHING TO EAT?
WE'LL TREAT.

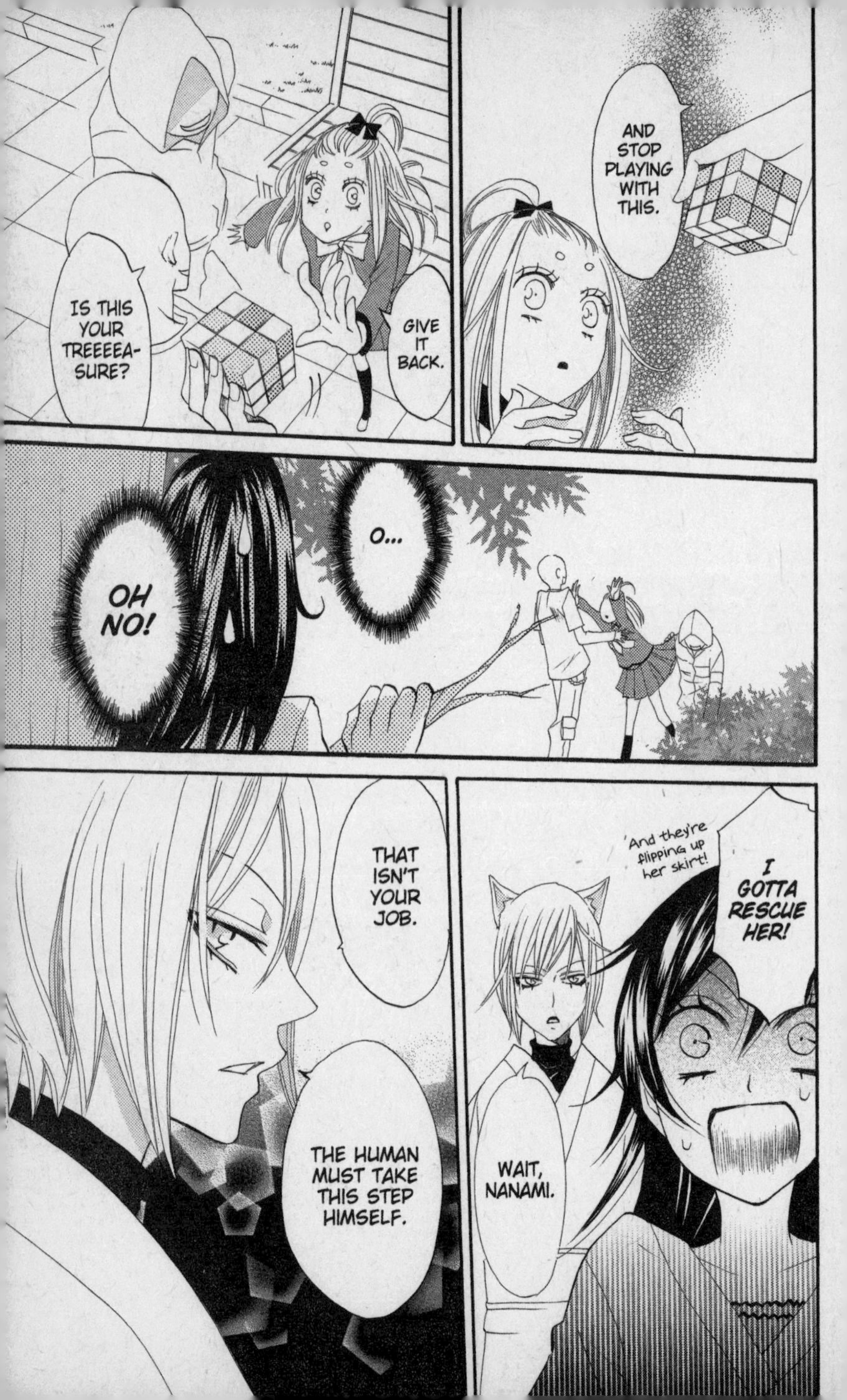
AND STOP PLAYING WITH THIS.
GIVE IT BACK.
IS THIS YOUR TREEEEA-SURE?
O...
OH NO!
And they're flipping up her skirt!
I GOTTA RESCUE HER!
WAIT, NANAMI.
THAT ISN'T YOUR JOB.
THE HUMAN MUST TAKE THIS STEP HIMSELF.

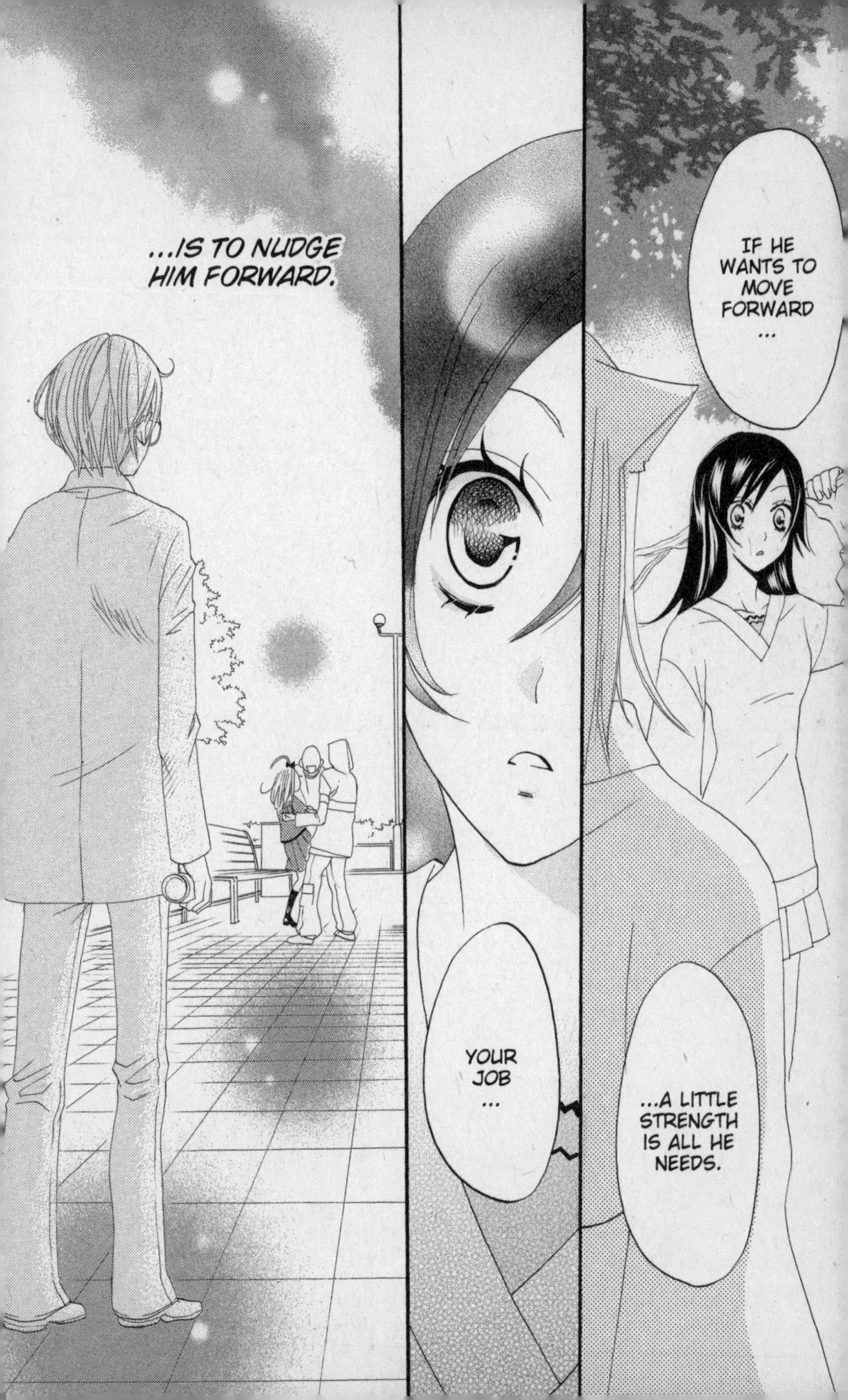
IF HE WANTS TO MOVE FORWARD ...
...A LITTLE STRENGTH IS ALL HE NEEDS.
YOUR JOB ...
...IS TO NUDGE HIM FORWARD.

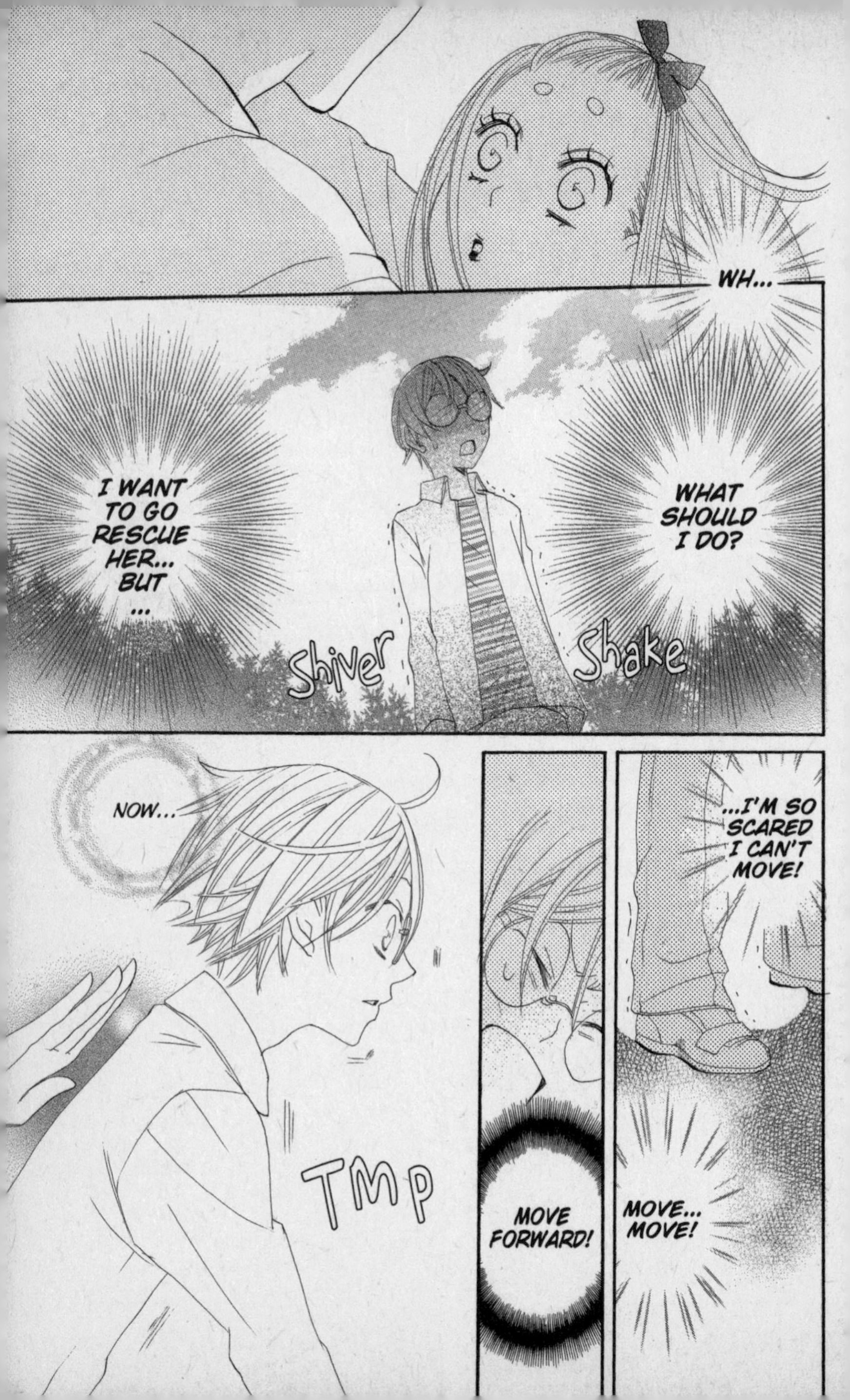
WH...
WHAT SHOULD I DO?
I WANT TO GO RESCUE HER... BUT ...
Shake
Shiver
...I'M SO SCARED I CAN'T MOVE!
MOVE... MOVE!
MOVE FORWARD!
NOW...
TMP

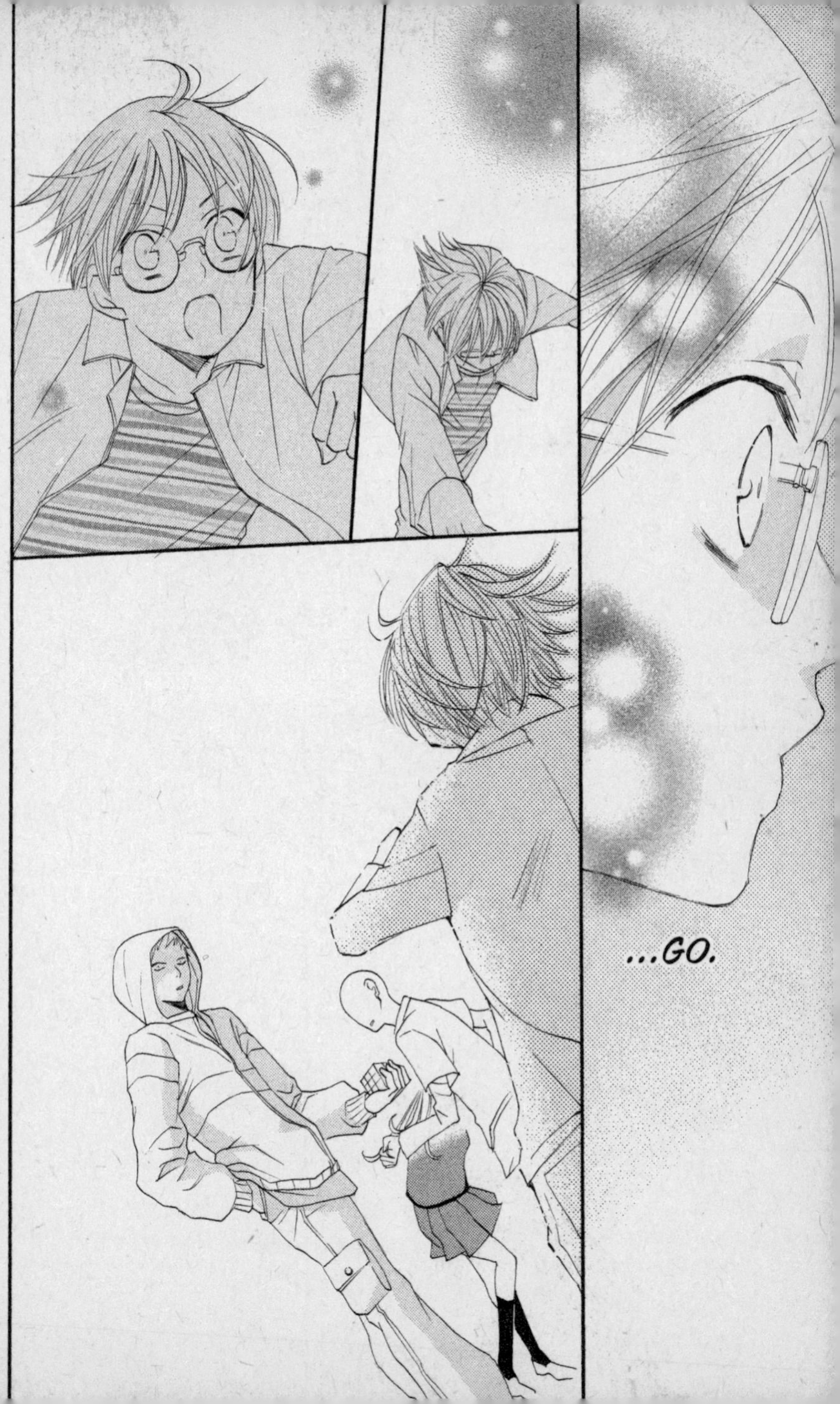
...GO.

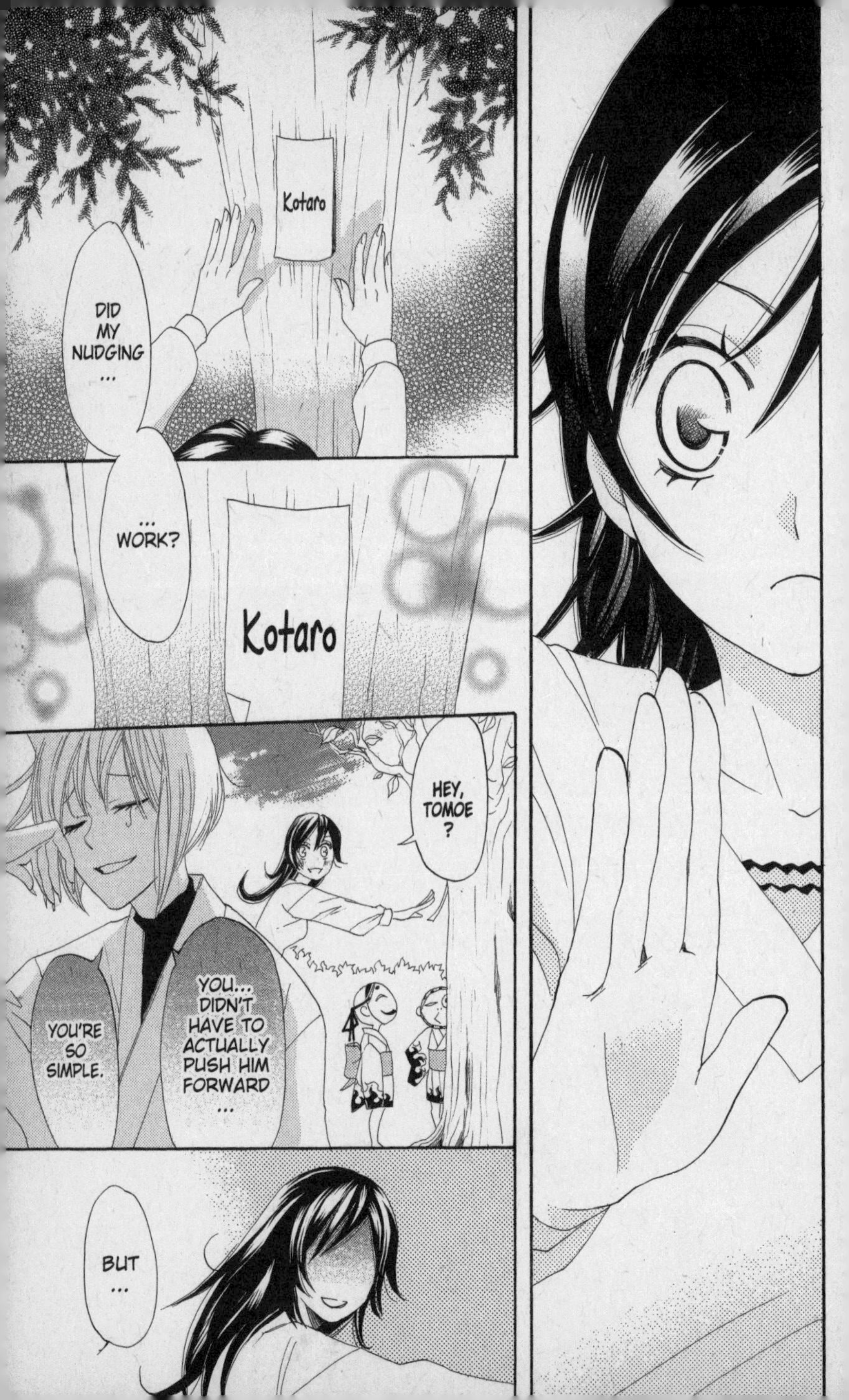
Kotaro
DID MY NUDGING ...
... WORK?
Kotaro
HEY, TOMOE ?
YOU... DIDN'T HAVE TO ACTUALLY PUSH HIM FORWARD ...
YOU'RE SO SIMPLE.
BUT ...

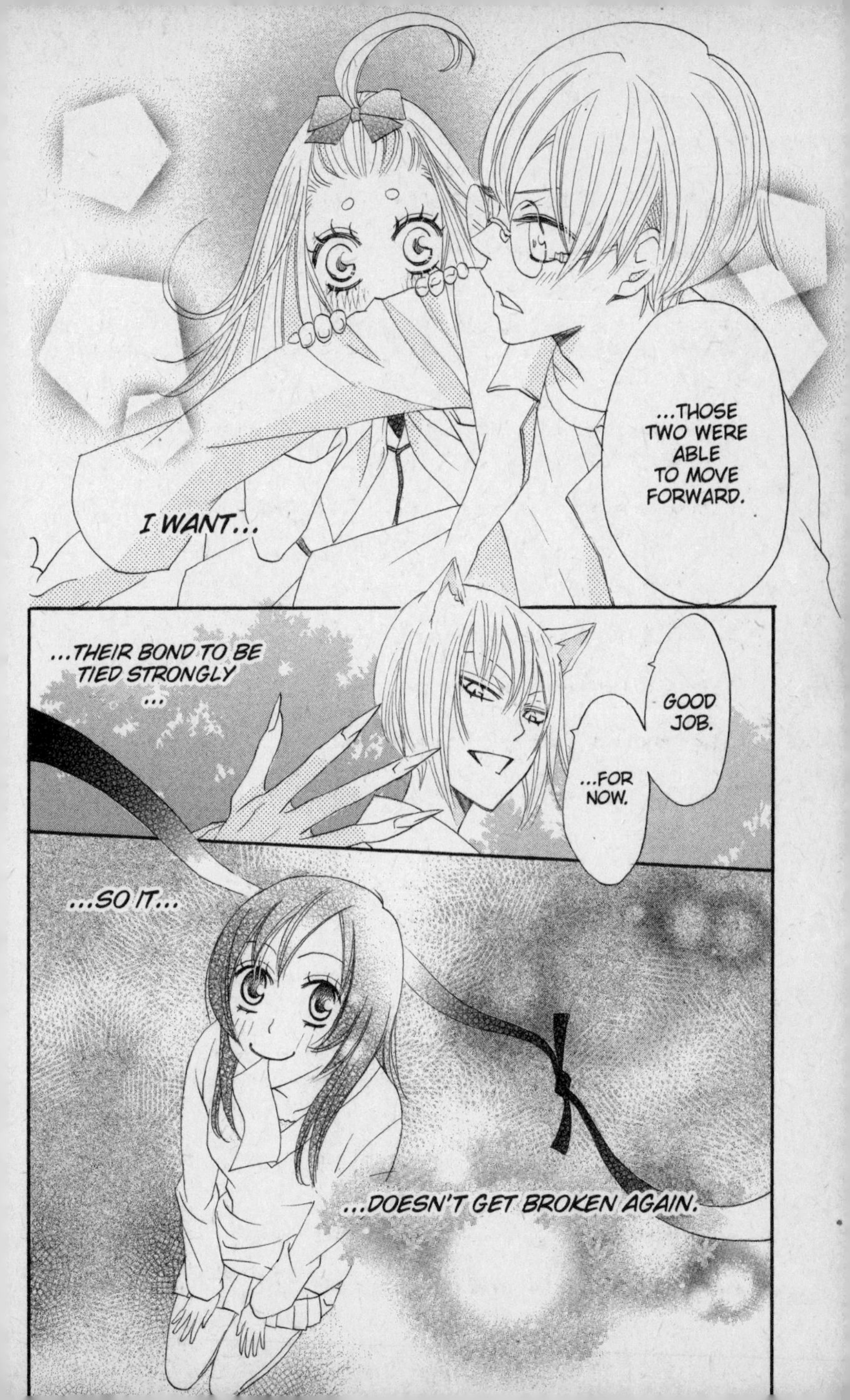
...THOSE TWO WERE ABLE TO MOVE FORWARD.
I WANT...
GOOD JOB.
...FOR NOW.
...THEIR BOND TO BE TIED STRONGLY ...
...SO IT...
...DOESN'T GET BROKEN AGAIN.

The Otherworld

Kami are Shinto deities or spirits. The word can be used for a range of creatures, from nature spirits to strong and dangerous gods.

Kitsunebi literally means "foxfire" and are the flames controlled by fox spirits.

Komainu are a pair of guardian statues placed at the gate of a shrine, usually carved of stone. Depending on the shrine, they can be lions, foxes or dogs.

Mononoke is the overall term for Japanese supernatural creatures and encompasses ghosts, spirits and demons.

Shinshi are birds, beasts, insects or fish that have a special relationship with a kami.

Tochigami (or *jinushigami*) are deities of a specific area of land.

Onibaba is literally an "old woman ogre."

Onibi-warashi are like will-o'-the-wisps.

Yogiri-guruma is literally "night fog carriage."

Yokai are demons, monsters or goblins.

Honorifics

-danna means "master" but is more like "sir" or "mister."

-dono roughly means "my lord," although not in the aristocratic sense.

-himemiko is a title that means "Imperial princess," although a Japanese princess is not the same as a Western one and isn't necessarily the daughter of a king.

-kun is used by persons of superior rank to their juniors. It can sometimes have a familiar connotation.

-sama is used with people of much higher rank.

-san is a standard honorific similar to Mr., Mrs., Miss or Ms.

Notes

Page 11, sidebar: Paper fortunes
Omikuji are slips of paper with fortunes written on them and can be found at many shrines and temples.

Page 47, panel 1: *Sasamochi*
Mochi (sticky rice cakes) wrapped in *sasa* (bamboo leaves).

Page 63, panel 1: Inari Shrine
Inari, or Inari-no-kami, is one of the most popular deities in Japan. Foxes are the typical guardians at Inari shrines.

Page 77, panel 5: *Ofuda*
A strip of paper or small wooden tablet that acts as a spell.

Page 114, panel 1: Shrine for relationships
A shrine's type is decided by which kami is enshrined. Shrines can also be multi-purpose, so a shrine can be for love and relationships, safe births and warding off evil.

Page 142, panel 3: *Kotodama*
Literally "word spirit," the spiritual power believed to dwell in words. In Shinto, the words you speak are believed to affect reality.

Page 187, panel 3: Himemiko's nod
In Japanese, negative questions like this are answered differently than in English. She nods because she means "Yes, I haven't."

Julietta Suzuki's debut manga *Hoshi ni Naru Hi* (The Day One Becomes a Star) appeared in the 2004 *Hana to Yume Plus*. Her other books include *Akuma to Dolce* (The Devil and Sweets) and *Karakuri Odette*. Born in December in Fukuoka Prefecture, she enjoys having movies play in the background while she works on her manga.

KA

Shojo Beat Edition

STORY AND ART BY
Julietta Suzuki

English Translation & Adaptation / Tomo Kimura
Touch-up Art & Lettering / Joanna Estep
Cover Design / Hidemi Dunn
Interior Design / Yukiko Whitley
Editor / Pancha Diaz

Printed in Canada

Published by VIZ Media, LLC
P.O. Box 77010
San Francisco, CA 94107

10 9 8 7 6 5
First printing, December 2010
Fifth printing, June 2015

www.viz.com
www.shojobeat.com

RATED T FOR TEEN

PARENTAL ADVISORY
KAMISAMA KISS is rated T for Teen and is recommended for ages 13 and up. This volume contains fantasy violence.
ratings.viz.com

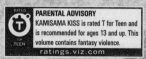